The Atrocity of Education

THE ATROCITY OF EDUCATION

ARTHUR PEARL
University of Oregon

ST. LOUIS, MISSOURI / NEW CRITICS PRESS, INC. / 1972

Published simultaneously in Canada by Clarke, Irwin & Company
Limited, Toronto and Vancouver

Library of Congress Catalog Card Number: 73–146987
SBN 0–87853–001–0

Grateful acknowledgment is made to the following for permission to use
copyright material:

Delacorte Press for excerpts from *Teaching as a Subversive Activity* by
Neil Postman and Charles Weingartner. Copyright © 1969 by Neil Postman
and Charles Weingartner. Reprinted by permission of the publisher, Delacorte
Press.

Harper & Row for excerpts from *The Disadvantaged: Challenge to
Education* by Mario D. Fantini and Gerald Weinstein. Copyright © 1968
by Mario D. Fantini and Gerald Weinstein. Reprinted by permission of
Harper & Row, Publishers, Inc.

Alfred A. Knopf, Inc., for the poem "Motto" from *The Panther and
the Lash* by Langston Hughes. Copyright © 1967 by Langston Hughes.
Reprinted by permission of Harold Ober Associates, Inc.

The World Publishing Company for excerpts from *What They Are
Doing to Your Children* by Max Rafferty. An NAL book. Copyright © 1964
by Max Rafferty. Reprinted by permission of The World Publishing
Company.

This book is dedicated, as inadequate appreciation, to those many, many students who have, through the years, added so much to my continuing education.

And also, to those valiant elementary and secondary school teachers who stand in there—against politicians, bullies and administration brutes—to keep education alive.

Contents

Contents

The Atrocity of Education

A Sorry State of Affairs

[In which I explain that the mess in education is attributable to a failure to identify goals that are relevant to the last third of the 20th century. I insist that the way out must start with defining deferrable and soluble goals; and continue with specifying procedures to implement these goals. In this first chapter I introduce the goals and set the stage for the book.]

The machinery of our secondary education is rigid where it should be yielding and lax where it should be rigid.

—Alfred North Whitehead

The American is subjected, from cradle to grave, to an intense drive to organize and Americanize him.

—Jean-Paul Sartre

Training is everything. The peach was once a bitter almond; cauliflower is nothing but cabbage with a college education.

—Mark Twain

I suffer much from being misunderstood. But I'd suffer much more if I was understood.

—Clarence Darrow

This has been a vintage year for critics of public schools. Nearly everybody has gotten in his licks. The left, the right, and all shades in between have "socked it" to "education." And while this has been great fun and even financially profitable for some and, undeniably, enormously politically profitable for others—nothing much has happened as a consequence. The educational system is the old system yet—and at best a few more people have become upset.

The reasons for failure of the agitation to produce results are both complicated and simple. Reduced to essentials, the critics are as irrelevant as the education they criticize. They do not define or defend education as it *should be*. Therefore they offer no stable bench marks against which education can be meaningfully evaluated.

This book begins where the others leave off. It starts by answering these *basic* questions. What is the educational enterprise all about? What is it trying to accomplish? What are the goals of a good educational system?

The primary goal of education in a technologically advanced free society is to enable every citizen to exercise autonomy in an interdependent world. The purpose of an adequate education is to enable a person to exercise choice. There are at least four areas of life in which education must take on the responsibility for increasing the options for individuals. These are:

1) The considered choice of life career. Everyone, regardless of background or circumstance, should have the opportunity to compete equally for desirable employment.

2) The ability to exercise intelligent choice in democratic decision-making.

3) The acumen to make intelligent choice in cultural matters. Everyone must not only be able to exercise choice in enjoyment of general culture but must also be able to appreciate the contributions of the variety of cultures and subcultures that make up a pluralistic society.

4) The ability to develop oneself and live harmoniously with one's neighbors. Everyone must be provided with the "know how" to choose, among the myriad of social roles available to him, those personality characteristics which provide him the greatest gratifications. He must also develop those skills and sensitivities that will keep him from impinging on the growth and enjoyment of others in a world where man is thrust in ever-more-crowded and complicated relations with his neighbors.

This book, in its essence, is an elaboration of these four goals of education. Herein the reader will find a justification for each goal and descriptions of good and bad educational practices in relationship to these goals. But before we come to that, observe the sorry condition that sloth has brought about.

Education and Alienation

An aimless education *must* lead to alienation of students. Critics of education have waxed endlessly if not eloquently about alienation, and yet they have failed to identify its cause. Alienation occurs at two distinct levels. At one level we find the poor and the minorities—they are alienated because school plays a significant role in denying them equal opportunity for a decent job, political power, cultural identity, and personal gratification. How this is done is dwelt on in this volume at length. The victims of such alien- ation sometimes are driven by their frustrations to violence or abusive use of drugs.

A second, very different, level of alienation can be attributed to education. The alienation stems from the lack of relationship be- tween schooling and nature. Educational activities as currently im- plemented are ecologically indefensible. Students are taught in- credible absurdities about work, politics, cultural activities, and interpersonal relationships. They are discouraged when they raise ecologically relevant issues. Students are not encouraged to crit- ically examine the structure of employment. They are not led to question the legitimacy of work efforts which deplete the earth of its scarce resources without improving the quality of life. Students are not stimulated to invent new criteria for assessing work ac- tivities nor are they intellectually prepared to suggest new kinds of work to replace activities that are destructive.

A similar lack of connection exists between education for citizenship and the "real world." In school the relationship between such vague concepts as "rights" and the everyday struggle for sur- vival are obfuscated, not clarified. The exercising of power for en- vironmental preservation and the impact that different actions have on population, pollution, and consumption of resources are *not* examined in school. The relation between political activity and war, poverty, and racism—and the connection that this trio of horsemen has to mankind's immediate and ultimate survival—is, when touched upon in school, only likely to lead to the further confusing of an already confused student.

Cultural education consistent with survival requires a general and universal appreciation of aesthetics, a passion for scholarship, and an empathy for persons different from oneself. None of this happens. As will be shown, the student is instead encouraged in his isolation and ethnocentrism; he is denied a historical perspective; he is crippled in his ability to use language; he is foiled in his tenta- tive attempts to analyze and conceptualize a life style for man that would be consistent with nature, and he is forbidden to experiment with ways of relating to other humans which violate, even innocuously, cherished shibboleths.

The alienated of the second level are not discernable by their deviance. No. They are complacent. They are only too willing to do what they are told. They may be so totally alienated that they no longer are capable of recognizing the very real danger of impending ecological disaster. Here we find the students of Dr. Pangloss, bursting with eagerness to echo his statement that "Here at last is the best of all possible worlds." They believe, because as good students they are taught to believe, that the threat of population growth is vastly exaggerated, that business and government are doing what is sufficient to curb pollution (and that it is only right that the cost of such curbing be borne by the consumer), and they believe that there *will* be oil, iron, rubber, space, water, and air *somewhere* after we have exhausted all that we now have.

The extent of our alienation from ecological reality stands bold-face in the travesty of Earth Day—April 22, 1970. On that day we, as an educated nation, were to commit ourselves to our survival. On that day we would set a new course and reorient our life enterprises to compatibility with nature. On that day we would ask our best minds to come forth and help us zero in on strategies to overcome our threatened extinction.

We had all the help imaginable. The media leaped in; our elected officials gave their solemn bipartisan pledges. Scientists, cheek to jowl, with aggregate statistics and pie charts, laid it all out there for everybody to see. And yet nothing of significance happened. Every action hostile to nature goes on just as if Earth Day had never happened.

Earth Day was a fraud because nowhere was there a careful and detailed analysis of the relationship between a stable human society and the distribution of wealth and power. Earth Day was a fraud because nowhere was there a proposed plan to adequately finance an effective antipollution campaign. Earth Day was a fraud because nowhere was the relationship between war, poverty and racism, and ecological imbalance spelled out. Instead of signaling a redirection of man's destiny, Earth Day was reduced to a one-day, nationwide antilitter campaign (and look around you to see just how effectively that trivial goal was achieved).

Much of this book is devoted to the second level of alienation and the kinds of activities that schools must get with if there are to be many more earth days—days on earth.

Two Illusions of Progress:
The Efficient School and the Open School

Critics of education *do* prepare remedies. These solutions almost inevitably fall into one of two camps. There are the advocates of efficiency and there are the proponents of humanity. Among the former group are those who favor improving basic skills through principles of engineering. They are product-oriented. Define the outcome, analyze it for its elements, train the teachers to be precise and hold them accountable for the end result. Throughout this book we encounter in various guises the educational engineer who would have us upgrade education by doing what we are doing now— only better. He is, at this writing, the darling of the funding agencies. He is not treated with high regard here. This type of innovator tells you *how* to do things, but he doesn't question whether they should be done at all. He is very much caught up in measurement (a very worthy concern), but because he has no ultimate educational goals, he always ends up with an answer, and insists that someone make up a question to go with it. For example, he knows how to design an "achievement" test and train people to score highly on it. He is engaged in the exciting (?) pastime of taking persons suffering from the first type of alienation and making them victims of the second type. And my Mother asks yet again, "From this nonsense he makes a living?"

In the other camp are those who react violently to the rigidity and inherent totalitarianism of the first group. They are less concerned with *what* children learn and more occupied by how children *feel* about their school experience. The humanists are concerned with the dignity of the student. They tend to be Rousseau-esque in their philosophy and believe that intellectuality will out if not blunted by insensitivity and brutality. The advocate of the open school operates with the notion that children know best what is good for them. In this book the open school is roughed up quite a bit and charged with short-changing youth in their efforts to attain self-reliance in a world which does, and will continue to, structure work and political, cultural, and social relationships.

The failure to define a set of educational goals for a world fit for human beings leads to many calamitous symptoms. The symptoms themselves unremedied, in turn generate new problems. Education becomes caught up in the vortex of all this. Illustrative of the inability of education to play a useful role in a serious social problem is the hodgepodge of efforts surrounding the issue of "white racism."

Education and "White Racism"

Lacking a guiding star, the wayward course of education has contributed heavily to the major social problems of our time. Not the least of the problems for which education must bear important responsibility is white racism. White racism here is defined as those structures and attitudes of our society that have "locked" certain minority groups into positions of inequity and robbed them of dignity. As used here it extends beyond a matter of skin color and includes also biases based on economic and ethnic considerations. Our educational leaders cry, "Not fair!" when so accused. It is their opinion that they cannot be held accountable because others in the society establish the norms which dictate educational policy. They argue that major business concerns, mass media, urban and suburban developers are the major culprits and that educational policy can only follow where the more powerful lead. In one superficial sense, at the level of immediate decision-making involving school board action or bond elections, this argument has some credibility (although, even here, action taken which reinforces social inequity and bigotry is often more the consequence of weak educational leadership than it is the result of overwhelming, overt racist influences). But more basically, education must take the responsibility for the "racists" and the unconcerned among us. It cannot be denied that the powerful leaders of industry, government, commerce, and communication received their education in this country, as did the persons who accept them as leaders. We continue to refuse to accept what parsimony surely implies, that we educate people to be "white racists," and while we do a poor job of education in other areas, we do an excellent job here. Even when we try to do something positive about this disturbing problem, its pervasiveness gets in the way. The "Kerner Report" is a case in point.

The "Kerner Report"—Good Intentions and Latent Racism

In March of 1968, back in those days before "benign neglect" was national policy, a Report of the National Advisory Commission on Civil Disorders was made available to the public. The report had blockbusting impact. Authored by a group of moderates, it nonetheless told it "how it is," asserting that "White racism is essentially responsible for the explosive mixture which has been accumulating in our cities since the end of World War II." [1]

The Commission recommended a variety of actions to right the injustices that "white racial attitudes" had wrought. The areas the Commission selected as crucial targets for remediation were employment, education, welfare, and housing. While all the areas have some relevance to this book, for the present the recommendations dealing with educational change will be given concentrated attention.

The report did not water down its attack on education. The Commission identified the difficulties the poor, in general, and the black, in particular, encounter in public schools. Specifically, the Commission cited the following as key factors leading to educational failure of disadvantaged youth:

1) Increased racial and social class isolation in the schools.

2) Less experienced and less qualified teachers.

3) Overcrowded classrooms.

4) Dilapidated and poorly equipped classrooms.

5) Curriculum and materials which are alien to the life of the student.

6) Disproportionately small share of the tax dollar.

7) Increased estrangements between the school and the community.

8) An environment which is antagonistic to education.

The Commission enunciated strategies to right the educational wrongs they defined. Included in a broad-gauge attack was a smorgasbord of remedies.

The Commission wanted an end to "de facto" segregation. They believed that integration could be accomplished through technical assistance to school districts; through providing bonuses to de-

---

[1] *The New York Times* (eds.), *Report of the National Advisory Commission on Civil Disorders,* E. P. Dutton, New York, 1968, p. 203.

segregating schools; through the development of "magnet" schools which could, because of their outstanding offerings, attract white middle-class students; and through the establishment of "educational parks" which, by their location, could insure multiracial and multiclass associations.[2]

The Commission recommended that ghetto schools offer "quality education," and suggested a number of prescriptions to achieve it. Talented persons could be attracted to the ghettos to teach through the expansion of the Teacher Corps. Prospective teachers and teachers currently assigned to ghetto schools could be made more effective if they received specialized training in the problems of the slum resident. The slum school could offer an education of enhanced quality if it would remain open the year-round and provide imaginative and innovative programs. To offset the accumulated deprivation of slum living there should be marked expansion of early childhood education modeled after the "proven success of Head Start." There could be improved educational practice in the schools if teachers received incentive pay, classroom size was reduced, there was recognition of the history and culture of the disadvantaged youth, residents were involved as teacher aides and tutors, and students were enrolled in intensive programs to improve verbal skills.[3]

To improve school and community relations the Commission recommended decentralization of control over educational policy, education programs designed to serve the needs of all residents in the community, employment of local residents to serve as teacher aides and tutors, and regularly scheduled reports to the community on student progress.[4]

The Commission also directed its attention to Higher Education. Here its concern was for creating new opportunities for the disadvantaged. Included in a variety of proposals was an expanded "Upward Bound" program to prepare the disadvantaged for college, the removal of financial barriers to college education, and an increase in vocational education offerings to the disadvantaged.[5]

The Kerner Report was widely acclaimed. In the Introduction Tom Wicker commented:

---

[2] *Ibid.*, pp. 440–442.
[3] *Ibid.*, pp. 444–450.
[4] *Ibid.*, pp. 450–452.
[5] *Ibid.*, pp. 452–454.

Reading it is an ugly experience but one that brings, finally, something like the relief of beginning. What had to be said has been said at last, and by representatives of that white, moderate, responsible America that, alone, needed to say it.[6]

The report was, however, not universally well received. It was attacked as overly negative and unrealistically expensive. However, neither the critics nor the supporters got to the heart of the matter, and that is that *the Kerner Report is irrelevant!* If it were adopted *in toto*, it wouldn't make a whit of difference, because, stripped to its essentials, the Report of the National Advisory Commission on Civil Disorders is a racist document. It is racist because, in the absence of precisely defined goals, it reduces to an advocacy of continued current policy. Very simply, the Commission concludes that all that is really needed in the Great Society is a greater amount of the Great Society. And therein lies the report's weaknesses and its fallacy.

Sprinkled throughout the Commission's recommendations are proposals that could, if put into effect, only reinforce class, race, and ethnic inequality. Examine two programs that the Commission commends: Head Start and Upward Bound. There is the call for expansion of Head Start to build upon its "proven success." And who could possibly quarrel with an expansion of a proven good thing, except that Head Start has *never* been *proved* a success. In fact, there is no universally accepted standard against which Head Start can even be assessed. But even more important than a statement of the alleged quality of Head Start is an appreciation of its undergirding premises. Head Start justifies its existence on the postulated inadequacies of the upbringing of poor children. It is assumed that poor children are doomed even before they start school because of the accumulated deprivations of their preschool experiences. It is argued that they fail in school because they have been denied the benefits that the children of advantaged parents receive.

Note how little we have learned in the past four centuries. See how eager we are to assume another "white man's burden" and impose our ideas with missionary zeal on some luckless poverty-stricken people. With an arrogance almost impossible to describe

---

[6] *Ibid.,* p. xi.

we jump to the conclusion that lack of initial success in school is the consequence of inadequate preparation. Nowhere is the suggestion that the school, riddled as it is with racist teachers and racist structures, must be adjusted to meet the students' needs.

It is curious that a report which points the finger to white racism doesn't logically conclude that relief must come with the extirpation of white racists from positions of authority in education and the reformation of the structures of the society which buttress social inequality.

Look, now, to the persons who really benefit from Head Start. Those who reap the most in wages from a Head Start program are those who are not poor. Head Start has opened up opportunities for the middle class. The teacher in charge is the only member of the staff who receives a halfway decent salary. She invariably is a person possessing the necessary credentials. She is frequently a well-situated member of the Establishment. Her values, her language, and her perceptions have been conditioned by her life experiences. She may even be an out-and-out racist, but frequently she is a well-intentioned liberal who, because of the nature of her training and upbringing, judges the poor as inferior merely because they are different.

Head Start follows the Commission's recommendations that local residents be hired as aides and tutors. But the wages they receive are hardly sufficient to allow an escape from poverty. Although there are rare exceptions, the aide usually cannot move upward. If there is any career ladder at all, it is extremely truncated. Only in the most unusual situations is it possible for the aide to graduate to upper-echelon positions in Head Start or in other educational institutions. Training, an essential part of the upgrading process, is, when offered to the aide, almost always a traditional education. This education (as will be explained at length later) is saturated with race, class, and ethnic bias.

There is a game that low-income blacks play. It is called "the dozens." The dozens is a form of verbal assault in which the competitor attempts to score by insulting the opponent's mother. Head Start is a sophisticated form of the dozens. It institutionalizes the attack. In a variety of subtle or not so subtle ways the poor child is informed upon entrance into the program that he has a "lousy mother." He is hardly in the position to respond to such an assault. In point of fact Head Start reflects all the inequity that the poor have had to face in their negotiations with the Establishment.

The key to early childhood education is schools which are free of social prejudice. The basic values, the kinds of language that are accepted, the opportunity to process grievances are the crucial factors in such a school. But even more important is the substantive nature of the school—the materials that are to be taught, the persons who are to do the teaching, and the evaluation of effective scholarship. Unless clearly specified the school will perforce become afflicted with the paramount social prejudices of the society. Because those who lead Head Start, like the Commission, talk very little or are silent on these matters, Head Start, as currently constituted, cannot be even a part of the solution.

At the other end of the educational spectrum the Commission recommends expansion of Upward Bound programs to enable many more disadvantaged persons to get through college. At first glance this proposal makes eminent good sense. Ours *is* a credential society. To exercise occupational choice persons *must* successfully negotiate many, many years of formal education. Entry positions in the largest and most prestigious enterprises call for at least a college degree. Any effort to facilitate the poor person's attainment of a college education would appear to have unchallenged worth. But, lamentably, that just isn't the case. Upward Bound, like Head Start, is undermined by faulty assumptions and blatant prejudices. In a typical Upward Bound program, disadvantaged youth are brought to a college campus for a summer between their junior and senior years in high school. They receive follow-up support back at their high schools during their senior year and return for another summer prior to their entrance into college. At the college campus the students receive some academic stimulation, some individual tutoring, and some remedial work. These services are continued in the final high-school year and culminate during the second summer's experience at college. The Upward Bound program is designed for that very small fraction of disadvantaged youth who have been identified as academically able and who have "underachieved" in high school. The call for Upward Bound can be understood only as a candid admission that traditional educational establishments and approaches have failed. And yet Upward Bound rewards and gives power to those established institutions—the very same colleges who trained the teachers and administrators who so ingloriously flopped in the first place. Upward Bound failed because it recapitulated the evils that have befallen the disadvantaged throughout their school career.

The Upward Bound student encounters white racism on the campus. The teachers in the Upward Bound program reflect the biases of the institution. The college and university, even more than the elementary and secondary school, are disproportionately staffed by white and middle-class persons. The cultural deprivation thesis is quite popular on the campus (and seemingly is accepted un-critically by members of the Advisory Commission on Civil Dis-orders as well), and persons working in an Upward Bound program are receptive to such thinking (forgetting that whenever another's culture is viewed as inferior, it necessarily implies that one's own is superior; and that is the stuff from which white racism is made). And in those rare Upward Bound programs that are free of mani-fest bias and in which blame of failure to educate is laid to the public school, there is also a problem. The program emphasis is upon remedy making up for the failures of the prior schooling. And while there is no frontal attack upon the student or his family, the effect is the same. The program does not draw upon the individual and cultural strengths of the student because the staff member, limited by experience, wouldn't recognize these strengths if he en-countered them. Upward Bound programs suffer because staff members can only do "their thing," and their thing is not only in-appropriate but is also saturated with class, race, and ethnic bias.

There are all kinds of inducements and corruptions in Upward Bound programs. The programs are funded annually, and the pri-mary criterion used for evaluation is an ability to play the "num-bers game." If the institution can keep its students without an out-break or publicized trouble it has done a good job, and can expect to be funded once more. To insure that students remain, scholar-ship and intellectual content very often are watered down, and the program degenerates into "fun and games." As further insurance, institutions work hard to recruit persons who might do very well without additional help.

Upward Bound programs are "spoiled image programs." [7] The student is made to feel that he is a charity case; other students are quick to remind him of his low status. Certain individuals in the administration and faculty feel free to extend gratuitous insults.

There is great concern and debate in the high councils of the university as to whether inclusion of a handful of disadvantaged

---

[7] See Erving Goffman, *Stigma*, Prentice-Hall, Englewood Cliffs, N.J., 1963.

youth will or will not undermine the hard-won "standards" of that institution. Over and over again the Upward Bound student is reminded that he is a parasite, with his maw in the public trough, by persons who receive their salaries from public monies or whose education is financed by public support.

The Upward Bound program is often a cruel delusion. There is no commitment of the institutions to the student. The university or college does not even promise to admit the Upward Bounder to its entering class, and many of those who are admitted are not destined to stay long. In most instances the Upward Bound participant is "dumped" into the university. The university offers no special program to its common, everyday enrollee, so in the name of fair play and other things holy the Upward Bound student receives equal treatment. More than one-third of the regular admissions fail to complete the first year in the university. It is no wonder that at least that high a percentage of the Upward Bound students come a cropper of the university deselection process. For a great many disadvantaged youth, Upward Bound is a glimmer of hope—that straw for which a dying man grasps. But it turns quickly into a nightmare, another illusive reward that one chases and never catches.

The university or college is a hostile place for anybody who is different. But the disadvantaged youth in a college setting is, to paraphrase A. E. Housman, a stranger and afraid in a place he never made. Everything about the college smacks of race or ethnic or class prejudice. The admissions policy is racist. Persons are admitted who resemble those who are already there (white and at least middle income). The dorms are racist—the behavior of only certain subgroups and cultures is found to be acceptable. The dorm counselor, typically a nice, compliant white, middle-class student, perceives his job to be to help shape up or ship out those who are different. The food served at the dorms or in the student union reflects only the dominant culture. There is no "soul" food, nor is "soul" reflected in any other aspect of dorm living. Blacks, Mexicans, Indians, and poor whites suffer in the dorms. They are subjected to insults which the dorm counselor ignores (if he isn't the instigator of them). Petitions are sometimes circulated in the dorms requesting that the university stop bringing undesirables to the campus. Even if not personally abused, the poor and the minority youth find the university a lonely place. They aren't invited to much that is going on, and, even if invited, they lack the wherewithal to feel comfortable.

The financial assistance program is racist. Persons in charge of the program distinguish between the deserving and the undeserving, and the deserving are invariably persons who resemble those who disperse the money. The financial assistance program is rotten at its core. It simply doesn't supply *enough money for the poor!* Financial assistance is sufficient for those who have some resources but not enough to easily manage college. There isn't any consideration in financial assistance for the student who may not even have enough money to buy clothes or meet a special contingency. Not only is the disadvantaged student expected to skimp along with support less than necessary to survive, but he's expected to do this while thrust into proximity with persons of means who own automobiles and expensive clothes and who talk about exciting things happening at wondrous places.

But worse than all of the above is the racist nature of the academic fare. The classes are taught in a racist language. The history is an apology of injustices perpetrated on blacks, Mexicans, Indians, and poor whites. The Social Sciences are thinly veiled rationalizations to justify current injustices. The professional school generates an ideology which militates against underclass students. (This aspect will be discussed at length later.) The university maintains itself as a place of the racists, by the racists, and for the racists. Whenever challenged on the possibility of maintaining racist tradition and curriculum, the university usually investigates itself and declares itself to be pure.

Universities demand exorbitant dues from their disadvantaged enrollees. The university insists that the disadvantaged students conform to its rules and mores. The disadvantaged student must make all of the "changes," but first-class membership is not even conferred on the disadvantaged student who does all that is asked of him. He is not a full-fledged member of the club. He does not get the same rewards even if he is submissive and obsequious. If finally convinced that inequity exists, university officialdom requests patience, arguing that all possible progress is being made at deliberate speed. But there is no evidence of progress, and it is so easy to tell someone else that, in deference to reality, he must accept unequal treatment, while the person counseling patient humility piously benefits from the inequality.

Upward Bound inevitably becomes a "safe" program. Neither the university nor the federal government is willing to sponsor

programs that encourage militancy. In crystal-clear tones those
paternal figures sing out that Alma Mater doesn't allow militants to
play in here. And when the response to such challenge is, "We
don't care what you Mothers allow, we're going to be militant anyhow," the program is the recipient of all the fury a university is
capable of mustering. Because the programs are safe and because
the institution is determined to create an illusion of doing a good
job, it is difficult to assess how bad a job the university actually is
doing. A cautious conclusion is expressed by John Egerton,[8] after
an intensive survey of university activities for the disadvantaged:
"Most of the nation's colleges and universities have not yet decided
whether they have the responsibility, the resources, the skills or the
desire to serve them."

All the criticism of the Kerner Commission's recommendations have been predicated on the assumption that higher education
is a good thing. And here the Commission may have engaged in
some bad timing. They are recommending that universities and colleges open their doors to the disadvantaged at the very moment
many of the advantaged have had it with the university. Students
have become vociferous in their criticism of college programs. They
are unhappy about their impotence in matters that affect their
lives. They do not like the dreariness of the classroom or the irrelevance of the material taught. And though the majority of students are not in sympathy with hard-core radicals who resist and
riot, their quarrel is with the methods, not the cause. Recruiting
disadvantaged students to the campus may make for less change
than the members who comprise the Commission on Civil Disorders think. Probably disadvantaged students are merely exchang-
ing the settings in which they will experience second-class citizenship.
Many observers have commented on the student in the university. Donald McCulloch describes the interpersonal arrangements in the university as unilateral relationships, with the student
low man in the pecking order. "In the typical unilateral relationship the dominant member does not simply believe that he knows
more than the other, he believes that he knows better." [9] Now that is

---

[8] John Egerton, "High Risk," *Southern Educational Report,* Mar. 1968,
p. 14.
[9] Donald J. McCulloch, "The Community of the University" in *The
University Game,* Adelman and Lee (eds.), Anansi Press, Toronto, 1968,
p. 27.

exactly what is told to poor youth in the ghetto. Therefore, if he is
allowed on campus, he will join only the most under of the under
classes. As McCulloch observed: "It may seem a very long leap
from the situation of the Negro, the Indian and the chronically
poor to the situation in our universities but the differences in material circumstances must not be allowed to obscure the essential
similarities." [10] The students have learned, like all other disadvantaged, that . . . "their thoughts, their imaginings, their feelings,
their concerns are of secondary or no importance as compared to
that of the teachers." [11] And woe be to that poor black student
who insists on his rights. He'll learn very quickly what happens to
an ingrate who fails to appreciate all that has been done for him.

Upward Bound is similar to Head Start in one very critical
aspect—"It's the rich what gets the gravy, and the poor what gets
the blame." Decent paying jobs in the program go to the college
faculty or to high-school teachers or to graduate students who form
the staff. Even those most hostile to the program benefit from the
distribution of money that universities receive in overhead expenses.

Having directed an Upward Bound program, I also recommend that these programs be expanded but for very different reasons than those advanced by the Kerner Commission. It is the
university which needs the poor, rather than the reverse. An Upward
Bound program can force the campus into some considerations of
reality. Those mythologies passing for social science theory which
now go unchallenged can be opened up for disputation and debate.
In the process, life can be breathed into a moribund institution,
and intellectual leadership can supplant the disgraceful condition
that now exists. An Upward Bound program may provide a base
for developing meaningful teacher-training programs to replace
those shabby facsimiles of preparation currently in effect. An Upward Bound program may generate dialogue between black and
white, rich and poor. An Upward Bound student population can
confront those who are now in power (or who are soon to assume
power) on their racism.

The Commission on Civil Disorders is unable to extricate itself
from its provincialism. It bases its solution on the extension of current services. The major problem, as perceived by the Commission,
is inadequacy of the poor as a consequence of policies of segrega-

---

[10] *Ibid.,* p. 32.
[11] *Ibid.*

tion and prejudice. This misses the target completely. It is not the poor who need to do the changing. The inadequacies are in the institutions. It's the college that must be altered to fit the needs of the people. It is not only the disadvantaged who receive shabby treatment in higher education; everyone else shares the raw deal. But because the Commission on Civil Disorders lacks a clear picture of good education it is hardly in the position to make intelligent recommendations. For want of precise goals the Commission is unable to come up with a coherent plan of attack. The recommendations, like all eclectic approaches, are a hodgepodge of nonrelated, even contradictory, proposals. Amitai Etzioni had this to say: The Kerner Commission managed to come up with a report in which "The road to hell of conservative status quo is paved with heavenly liberal rhetoric." [12]

Because the Commission cannot clearly conceive specific outcomes it is inevitable that they end up steering a course between the extremes of right-wing desire to crush conspiracies and left-wing agitation for control of local institutions. In final analysis the conclusion of the Commission report may prove not only to be too little but may have come too late. The call for integration without guarantee of equal treatment may lack credibility to people betrayed too often by authorities who purport to have their interest at heart.

Since the Kerner Commission came and went without making a dent, other commissions have strutted and fretted their hours on stage, only to signify nothing. These other commissions, which delved into such things as crime in the streets and college disruption, shared with the Kerner Commission an inability to relate their findings to the goals of education. As a consequence of this failing, the *only* accomplishment of those investigations is a public (stirred up by a Vice President who has a mouth which is disconnected from central nervous system control) that would prefer to be silent about matters they think they cannot solve.

Does It Really Matter Who Mismanages the School?

The Kerner Commission rejects the notion of black control of black intercity schools as a retreat from "direct confrontations with

---

[12] *Amitai Etzioni,* "Making Riots Mandatory," *Psychiatry and Social Science Review,* Vol. II, No. 5, May 1968, p. 3.

American society on the issue of integration" and as "an accommodation to white racism." [13] Others, however, view transfer of
control of education as the basic solution for its ills. The reasoning isn't too hard to grasp. A growing number of black people believe that white-run education is now, has always been—and they
have no reason to doubt—will always be racist. They desire that
black communities be given the responsibility for education of
black youth. The Commission on Civil Disorders makes slight mention of this in its grab bag of proposals by recommending ". . . centralized control over educational standards and the raising of
revenue while decentralizing control over other aspects of educational policy." [14] But for many critics of the system, more drastic
measures seem necessary. They argue that only with black control
can there be black dignity:

> It is no longer reasonable to expect that black people will continue
> to accept oppressive colonization by the white majority; nor that
> black people will submit to a genocidal system that deprives white
> as well as black of certain potentialities for human development.
>   Black people in American cities are in the process of develop-
> ing the power to assume control of these public and private institu-
> tions in our community. The single institution which carries the
> heaviest responsibility for dispensing or promulgating those values
> which identify a group's consciousness of itself is the education
> system.[15]

Advocates of community control see in such proposals, as
those of the Kerner Commission, a diluting of power. To them
this is merely an artifice to keep control in the hands of the oppressive majority. The Kerner Commission, in asking for centralized
control over educational standards, opts for development of educational subsystems in the inner city. This is flatly rejected by a growing number of black educators:

> Black people will not be satisfied with the compromise which sub-
> systems represent. We will do whatever is necessary to gain control
> of our schools. We view movements toward incorporation of the
> concept of community control into school systems whose basic

---

[13] *Report of National Advisory Commission on Civil Disorders*, p. 235.
[14] *Ibid.*, p. 451.
[15] Position statement of the Five-State Organizing Committee for Community Control addressed to the Harvard Conference on Education Subsystems by a caucus group, Jan. 25, 1968, *Phi Delta Kappan*, Vol. XLIX,
Apr. 1968, No. 8, p. 450.

control remains with the white establishment as destructive to the movement for self determination among black people.[16]

Implicit on all the arguments for black control is the conviction that control over policy influences educational programs, and the belief that American education suffers because those who control it are bad people. This, however, is not my view. The people who run education are not bad; they are merely fools. They do not do what they do primarily because of malice, but rather because of ignorance. Again, the absence of clearly defined goals leads to all manner of corruption. It is perfectly possible that an exchange of whites for blacks in board control would be a difference that makes no difference. The classroom experience would still be just as dreary. Black youth would be just as bored by classes in black history as white students are bored with classes in white history. Classroom activities could prove to be just as irrelevant and the teachers as poorly qualified as they are now. The board as the body which determines school policy may in itself be an antiquated notion that gets in the way of quality education.

That the school must be responsible to the community is an incontestable notion. Any other school is perforce a totalitarian intrusion. But local control over policy, while necessary, is not sufficient to insure quality education. There must be enunciation of the ends that are desired and the means to be used to obtain those ends. Any assumption that transfer of control will magically produce the strategies and tactics necessary for a good society flies in the face of history.

Education and the Essences of Modern American Life

To be relatively autonomous a person must have the knowledge, the skill, and the experience to cope with his environment. Clearly, education must contend with technological change, the media of communication, complex social organization, and the changing ecology of human life. These concerns crop up in various guises throughout this book and are only lightly treated now as part of the panorama of introduction.

1. Technological Advancement. Sophisticated technology intrudes into every aspect of modern life, markedly altering employ-

---

[16] *Ibid.,* p. 450.

ment, leisure, and even influencing child-rearing and religious worship. While the school has been slightly influenced by technology, "computer assisted instruction" is a much exaggerated term for the actual programs which have been developed. There is little in the school program or in teacher education that prepares staff to utilize technology effectively. As a consequence, the school and, later, the graduate from the school become the prisoners of the machine. Rather than forcing the machine to serve man's need, we restrict man to the computer's limitations.

2. *Mass Media.* Neither the school nor the family has a monopoly on educating youth. Television, motion pictures, and the recording industry are also in the game. The mass media disseminate data, influence language, affect behavior, and establish social values. This simple truth doesn't get through to the advocates of the 3 r's. They just don't understand that a deadly grating classroom offers no competition to the Grateful Dead. Many parents have difficulty getting this message. And often they blame the school for the radical notions and the radical behavior of their once well-behaved children. It is precisely because of mass media that modern youth have become the most learned and sophisticated generation to come down the pike, and they got that way despite, rather than because of, formal educational establishments. To be relevant, schools must swing! Classrooms must tie in to that emerging youth culture that is reflected in the mass media. The bridge that will interest youth in art, music, history, and literature is the tentative searching efforts of youth. The class may retain a relevance only when it is placed in contrast with the works of a John Lennon, a Bob Dylan, or a James Brown. A curious phenomenon has developed as the world evolves and it becomes more impossible for us parents to control the world of our children, no matter how desperately we try.

3. *Complicated Social Organization.* No individual or local community can claim self-sufficiency. Each of us relies on complicated organization to survive. No individual even controls the air he breathes or the water he drinks. Complicated social control is required to determine whether water will or will not contain fluorides. Individuals depend upon sophisticated structures for food. Huge bureaucracies control the production, marketing, stor-

ing, and transporting of foodstuffs. These bureaucracies tend to overwhelm and depersonalize all the individuals involved. But meanwhile, back in the ranch-style schoolhouse, a make-believe primitive social organization prevails. Students compete individually in meaningless tasks. It is no wonder that so many find it impossible to fit into the outside world. Relevant education is education that simulates outside-of-school realities and generates social relationships in the school which resemble the interdependence of modern day life.

4. Population Explosion and Exploding Populations. An already crowded world will nearly double in population before the next century. This gruesome fact places new challenges on vital life stuffs, production, and distribution; and if this prospect is not sufficiently disquieting, most of the world's population will be in constant turmoil. The future can be seen only through a glass darkly, but some inevitabilities appear in bold-face—the poor will not be content with their poverty, the nonwhite will resist white domination, the advancement to technological sophistication by economically underdeveloped nations will not be smooth or tranquil, and national aspirations overlaid by internationalism will threaten the existence of mankind. These truths place unique challenges upon the leadership role of the United States in the years ahead. We must look for that leadership among those who are now our students. The schooling they receive will determine the course of history. Relevant education, thus, is simply a life-or-death proposition.

Education and the Problems of Bureaucracy,
Segregation, Nonredemptiveness,
Loss of Privacy, and Uselessness of Person

The Kerner Commission's biggest shortcoming was that it focused on the symptom and ignored the underlying cause of social problems. Racism, while contributing and extending America's difficulties, is a resultant condition of more pervasive social malaise. We are hamstrung because we haven't developed the techniques and the organization to match our mountainous problems. As a consequence we have developed systems to maintain an operation which limps along, but in such a manner that a rising number of casualties is one of the results.

To deal with complicated social interaction (without developed appropriate leadership) bureaucracies have been formed; their principal characteristic is intransigence. They are inflexible and mechanical. Bureaucratic intransigence allows the human to abdicate responsibility—and this is essential because humans have not been prepared for such awesome responsibilities. In place of human leadership a manual of operation is generated which forces conformity upon the humans in the system. Decision-making is automatic. Rules and regulations are slavishly followed. The justification of a program becomes distorted, in a manner reminiscent of Big Brother's domination in Orwell's *1984*: "War becomes peace, slavery becomes freedom, and ignorance becomes strength." The hallmark of a good bureaucratic system is efficiency, and efficiency is determined by conformity.

In actual practice the most active supporters of bureaucracy are those who pride themselves on being the conservatives. They are dedicated to an economy which can be attained through a reduction in unnecessary government spending. But they inevitably end up opting for big government because, in the final analysis, they see things in simple blacks and whites. To illustrate, their simplest solution to deviant behavior is to declare such behavior illegal. The argument goes thusly: Permissiveness encourages delinquency, whereas severe and certain punishment deters delinquency. Therefore a publicly supported police power would solve the problem of crime through severe and certain punishment. This is an eloquently simple approach. There's just one problem. It doesn't work! Deviant behavior has never been deterred by the passage of proscriptive laws. In most instances, the deviant is immune or oblivious to law. But increasing the police force does add to the size of government. The consequences of police action—the courts, the probation officers, the correctional systems, the parole bureau—enlarges the bureaucratic structure. This inevitable consequence never seems, even fleetingly, to occupy the thoughts of the advocates of increasing police power.

The devastating effects of bureaucratic intransigence are felt everywhere. Discretion gives way to ritual, justice to consistency, passion to ruthlessness, and wisdom to habit. Red tape gums up the works at every level. Procedures take precedence over social imperatives. It is no overstatement that necessary changes in a higher education program may take half a decade before finally being approved by a faculty curriculum committee. Commissions authorized to make systems of operation more efficient always lead to procedures that are even more cumbersome than those they replaced.

Parkinson's Law [17] and *The Peter Principle* (of incompetence) [18] contribute heavily to bureaucratic intransigence. Bureaucratic organizations function like cancer. They grow without reason and metastasize in every possible direction. As the span of control gets larger, the necessity to limit independent decision-making is the inevitable result. Bureaucratic organization generates that set of conditions which prizes innocuous behavior in the lower stations to such an extent that this alone becomes the primary criterion for promotion to higher levels. The persons who have offended no one are more likely to be promoted than one whose activities for progress ruffled a feather or two. Thus it is possible for people to be continually promoted on the basis of minimal competence until such time as they prove themselves inadequate, and once at a certain level, because of the typical lethargic nature of the bureaucratic processes, there they will remain until death or retirement. Bureaucratic process inhibits initiative. All the actors function as if they were suspended in Jello. Bureaucratic organization inhibits creativity and undermines the individual. Political ideology has little to do with the matter. Hard-core, conservative Republicans are as bureaucratic in their management of private business as are unreconstructed New Deal Democrats in the administration of a public agency. The problem is less one of ideology and more one of paucity of talent and leadership.

The system is most bureaucratic in the realm of work. The credential society has imposed a ritualistic complex which both locks in and locks out the individual. The worker is selected, advanced, and transferred on impersonal criteria. [19] Because of the crucial nature of work, the development of a credential society has its impact on all other systems. The school is no longer a sanctuary.

---

[17] C. Northcote Parkinson, *Parkinson's Law,* Houghton Mifflin Co., Boston, 1957.
[18] Laurence Peter and Raymond Hull, *The Peter Principle,* or *Why Things Always Go Wrong,* W. Morrow, New York, 1969.
[19] *See New Careers for the Poor,* Pearl, Riessman, *op. cit.,* and Pearl, "One Solution to Poverty," in *Social Policies for America in the 70's: Nine Divergent Views,* Robert Theobald, ed., Doubleday, Garden City, N.Y., 1968.

It is not a place where you go to learn; it is a place where you pre-pare to earn. Any behavior that jeopardizes a standing in the school can also jeopardize future earning power. The reinforcement this gives to the bureaucracy is awesome and thus becomes an over-whelming influence on the dehumanization and depersonalization of man.

Segregation

Ours is an extremely segregated society and, because of all the influences mentioned earlier and because of bureaucratic in-transigence, it is becoming increasingly segregated. Segregation distorts every aspect of American life. By feeding xenophobic re-sponses our society devotes a considerable amount of its energies to paranoid ruminations and to the development of exclusionary systems. The worst thing about segregation is that it inhibits growth. As man is restricted in his contact so is he restricted in his stimu-lation. Segregation reduces breadth of language, magnifies unessen-tial differences, and blunts the sensitivities to essential differences. Segregation is directly influenced by the credential society. A sys-tem that establishes prerequisites of years of formal training for entrance into the growth industries perforce excludes from partici-pation all those never deemed eligible for higher education. Once individuals are denied admission to lucrative and prestigious employ-ment, they are thereby denied admission to areas of residence which depend upon income, to social activities which depend upon con-tacts developed on the job, to intellectual stimulation which comes from dialogue with persons from diverse walks of life. But even more important, those it locks in are also handicapped. They, too, are denied intellectual stimulation that comes from wisdom not obtained within school walls and they are denied introduction to the essence of life which accompanies the day-to-day struggle for existence.

Uselessness of Person

To some extent all individuals in a society which is com-plexly organized and diffuse in its delegation of responsibilities feel a sense of helplessness and uselessness, conditions which are markedly influenced by bureaucratic intransigence and segregation.

Uselessness of person is particularly burdensome for youth, who, within the framework of a credential society, are reduced to a passive, dependent state for more than two decades. This is all the more galling, since youth are continually chided that they are not contributing, while at the same time they are denied an opportunity to do anything constructive. It should be evident that it is impossible for a person to be psychologically healthy, to have a positive self-image of himself, if he serves no useful function in society. The feeling of uselessness often prevails throughout one's life. It is difficult for a person to obtain a sense of personal importance in organizations where rules and regulations determine behavior. If systems are developed which deny individuals any responsibility for important decision-making, the result must be disastrous to the individual. Apathy must supplant commitment, dedication give way to disinterest, and hopelessness replace hope. Laurence Peter depicts it vividly:

> Dorothea D. Ditto had been an extremely conforming student in college. Her assignments were either reasonable facsimiles of textbook or journal excerpts, or transcriptions of the professor's lectures. She always did exactly as she was told—no more, no less. She was essentially neutral in the learning process—adsorbent rather than absorbent. She was considered a competent student, and graduated with honors from the teachers training college.
>
> When she became a teacher, she taught precisely as she herself had been taught. She followed exactly the textbook, the curriculum guide and the bell schedule.
>
> Her work goes fairly well, except when no rule or precedent is available. When a water pipe burst recently and flooded the classroom, Miss Ditto kept on teaching until the principal appeared and rescued the class.
>
> Although she never breaks a rule or disobeys an order, she is often in difficulty when problem-solving situations arise. She has reached her "level of incompetence" as a classroom teacher, and will therefore remain in that position throughout her career.
>
> Mr. N. I. Skigh was an inspiring and popular science teacher. His lessons and lab periods were exciting. His students spent many extra hours in the laboratory and kept it in order. Skigh was not a proficient record keeper, but this weakness was more than counterbalanced by his success as a teacher. Skigh was regarded as competent; therefore he was eligible for and in due time received a promotion.
>
> In his present job as head of the science department, Skigh has to order supplies and keep extensive records. His incompetence is now evident. For three years running, he has ordered Bunsen

Burners but no tubing for connecting them. As the old tubing deteriorates, fewer and fewer burners are operable, although new ones accumulate on the storeroom shelves.

Skigh is not considered for further promotion. His ultimate position is one for which he is incompetent. He has reached his level.[20]

The End of Privacy

Interdependence, technology, and complicated social organization have eroded personal privacy. In a relatively simplistic society there was a certain protection of self resulting from remoteness and inefficiency. In a complicated society the various agents of that society pry into every aspect of personal life. What a person earns and how he earns it must be reported to the government. In applying for a job the applicant must reveal whether or not he has ever been convicted of a crime. Friends and relatives are questioned before credit is established or insurance sold. Electronic devices monitor private conservations and even eavesdrop into the intimacies of the bedroom. In the school, personal privacy is not respected. Under the guise of counseling, a student is persuaded to discuss matters of utmost sensitivity. Under the guise of therapy, children are persuaded to become finks against their parents. This practice continues and even proliferates, although there's not a smidgen of evidence to suggest that a child is actually assisted by these investigating processes.

The invasion of privacy is doubly handicapping. There is a nonredemptive quality to it. Once labeled—forever labeled! Once identified as a disturbed child, it is virtually impossible for the student to escape the classification. All behavior is interpreted in the context of a prior history. In the school setting, this history can be examined by any "privileged communicant," e.g., teacher, counselor, or psychologist.

What happens as a consequence of such examination is often horrendous. The following is not an untypical occurrence.

A young lady from a poor background is offered an opportunity to attend a university. She is recruited into an unusual Upward Bound program which offers its precollege preparation to persons with very unfortunate backgrounds. The sole parent of this girl was virtually incapacitated by fits of despondency. On

---

[20] Laurence Peter, *op. cit.*

numerous occasions the girl had attempted to escape unhappiness by running away. As a consequence of such "incorrigibility" she was ultimately committed to a mental hospital for "treatment." She was released from the hospital to enter the scholastic program.

From the moment of entrance she participated eagerly in the program. Despite a prevailing atmosphere of racial conflict on the campus that unnerved even those entrusted to exercise professional leadership, the girl maintained her "cool." She not only maintained her equilibrium, she prospered.

In the fall she entered the university and made a good start. Shortly before the end of the first quarter her grandmother, the most stable member of the family, died. The girl got drunk in public and was apprehended by the police. The matter was referred to the university health service, and, with a week to go before the end of the quarter, the psychiatrist ordered her to be expelled *immediately* from school for the protection of herself and the school.

Reflect on that. The girl's behavior, while not to be recommended, was not particularly heinous. If everyone who got drunk at the university was asked to leave there would be very few people left—including the faculty. The act itself did not prompt the psychiatrist to his decision; it was her "reputation."

Responses to Bureaucratic Intransigence, Segregation, and Uselessness of the Individual

There is lawfulness in a society which reduces the individual to a cog in a machine. Individuality is processed out, and in its place is symptomatology of a variety of predictable types. The most prevalent and probably the most pernicious is the conformist response. Here we find the beaten-down people. They are certain that City Hall cannot be fought. They are horrified at the prospect of rocking the boat. They are not only leery of any change but tend to suspect anyone advocating change as being a subsidized conspirator. In a society undergoing rapid change, a system that generates a suspicion of change is sowing the seeds of its own destruction.

Another response to a society in which one feels overwhelmed is flight. There is a drive to want out, to escape, to reject the society, and to refuse to participate. What makes this response dysfunctional is that it can't happen. And while there is undeniable charm in Timothy Leary's slogan: "Turn on, tune in and drop out," there is also a glaring flaw in it. Those who dominate the society will not allow it. They will insist upon everyone participating in wars. They will insist upon submission to laws. And they will even invade the home base of those who want no part of the society and regulate behaviors. This is the supreme irony. The more the individual chooses not to participate, the more strength he gives to those in power to "mess him over."

Yet another response to an overwhelming structure is direct effort to introduce change. The introduction of change takes many forms, from modest efforts to repair to calls for total upheaval. Campaigns that are doomed from the start because of a lack of constituency have a pathological influence on further efforts. The changes which society desperately needs never happen because those who desire the change become fatalistic. They believe that the cause is hopeless. They refuse to analyze the appropriateness of their tactics or strategy. Most individual efforts or even small-group efforts directed against the system are doomed to such failure. In almost every instance those who "attack" the system lack the essential prerequisites for victory: the analytical and conceptual skills to assess the situation. As a consequence they make the error of overgeneralization and tend to perceive a monolith in organizations that are ridden by factions of every stripe and aspiration. One of the other skills generally lacking in those who attack the system is the ability to enlist allies. The essence of a modern structure is its size and complex organization. These attributes serve as forces of inertia against change. The Establishment can either ride out the attack and deplete the resources of the attackers or it can slowly restore itself to its original shape after the impact of the attack is over. Thus it is imperative that if people are to change a given system, they have the competence both to persist and to enlist others to their cause. And because the organizations they confront are more difficult to engage than anything ever previously developed, their talent and their skill must be proportionately greater than the leaders of social movements in the past.

Differential Impact of Bureaucratic Intransigence, Segregation, and Uselessness

In a complex society not all members of that society are equally affected or afflicted. Even the most inefficient and corrupt of societies distributes benefits to some of its constituent members.

Thus while all of us, to some extent, become impatient with bureaucracy and are victimized by segregation and feel queasy about our lack of usefulness, these conditions are much more intense for the poor person. The disadvantaged are more put upon by bureaucracy because they have no resources to use for escape. They are much more restricted by the segregative systems of our society. They are denied access to decent living areas, are denied options and choices of school, and, in a variety of unsubtle ways, are informed of their uselessness. Not only are they victimized by these institutional inflictions but they lack the resources for personal renewal. Even more tragic is that those agencies in the society which have ostensibly been created for the specific purpose of facilitating mental health are riddled by the same oppressive conditions.[21] In actual practice these agencies not only do not produce their desired ends but actually contribute to the further destruction of the individual. Mental health services for the disadvantaged are bureaucratically organized. Because of the strictures of economy, humans are processed into more and more tight-fitting schedules rather than treated according to their individual needs.

There is a segregation process built into the best mental-health programs. The labeling of a person as disturbed carries with it segregation. And when the treatment, because of the demands of economy, is offered in an institution there is further segregation. Once stigmatized, the treated person is mired deeper into a segregation process which takes on the capacity to sustain itself. In time, the treatment becomes a "way of life" and the patient is comfortable only with others of similar disability. The more his contact is restricted to those similar to himself, the less he is able to sustain contact outside this milieu. The process distorts relationships in the broader areas of commerce, entertainment, education, etc. And that impact must be a further distortion of sense of self.[22]

Mental health interventions tend to reinforce the feeling of uselessness. As Peter Blau argues,[23] there is an exchange relationship

---

[21] For example, see: Riessman, Cohen and Pearl, *Mental Health for the Poor,* Free Press, New York, 1964.

[22] For further elaboration of this concept see Erving Goffman, *Stigma,* Prentice Hall, Englewood Cliffs, N.J., 1963.

[23] Peter Blau, *Exchange and Power in Social Life,* John Wiley, New York, 1964.

between therapist and patient (counselor and student, etc.); for the helper to sustain his sense of usefulness, the helpless has to remain helpless. The creation of a spoiled image misshapes all mental health processes at the present time, but this is particularly true with the treatment offered low-income patients.[24] The same argument can be made for the inappropriateness of organization of correctional services. These, too, victimize the poor, segregate them into a criminal way of life with the attendant destruction of persons and expense to the society.

Bureaucratic Intransigence, Segregation, and Uselessness in the Schools

Nowhere is bureaucracy more repressive than in the schools. Administration of personnel is depersonalized ritual. Management of students tends to take on the same coloration. The curriculum is prepackaged and, in California, the State Printing Office delivers the approved textbooks. School boards and parent groups serve to discourage initiative. By and large, teachers accept this bureaucratic organization of schools. Time after time they wail their impotence to produce necessary change. The lessons of bureaucracy are well taught. For a dozen years, students are indoctrinated to participate in a system characterized by its inflexibility. Throughout this period of time I have observed teachers who clearly communicate that "one cannot successfully or legitimately fight City Hall." Thus, the teachers become a strong influence in the dehumanization and depersonalization of man.

What *must* be communicated in classrooms from preschool to graduate school is the message that *every human* must be prepared to change society or be enslaved by it.

Nature, Extent, and Strategy of Change in Education

This is a book that calls for enormous change in education. Almost everything now done in the name of education is challenged. There are at least three forms that change can take. These

---

[24] See for example, Redlich and Hollingshead, *Social Class and Mental Illness,* John Wiley, New York, 1958.

are repair, revolution, and reform.[25] Repair suggests that the basic system is sound but that certain processes need fixing. It is my position that education is beyond repair. Minor alterations will not get us out of the mess. Merely altering the curriculum, or patching on some in-service training, or introducing more media into the proceedings, or combining the teachers into teams, or studying the interactions between teacher and student simply will not do it. The concerns of our society are so great, and the school fails to meet these concerns at so many different points, that repair is out of the question.

At the other extreme is revolution. By revolution I mean a complete overthrow of the system. When such a revolution occurs there is a total exchange of power. It is the view of some that education needs this kind of a revolution. I do not (at least at the time of this writing) believe that there is any potential for revolution. Those in control of the system, while beset by problems beyond their competence, have sufficient strengths to maintain their power. Arranged against them is a relatively small minority with diverse complaints not even joined by common ideology. Revolution occurs when the Establishment is weak and without popular support and the opposition, while often few in numbers, can resonate with the concerns of the majority. There is not even at this time a rallying slogan to mobilize support. Nothing comparable to "Peace, Bread and Land" or "No Taxation Without Representation" is forthcoming from those opposed to current educational practice. Revolution is always a measure of last resort. The wrench of revolution is inevitably accompanied by pain and the inefficiency of dislocation, and once something as drastic as a revolution gains momentum its ultimate consequences are unpredictable and often out of keeping with the original precipitating concerns. In fact, the major social revolutions of the twentieth century have not come to grips with twentieth century problems. The injustices and the inhumanities associated with bureaucratic intransigence are as much in evidence in the new regimes as they were present in the structures that were overthrown. The alienation of youth and prejudices against minorities appear to be immune to revolution—at least as currently conceived.

---

[25] I am indebted to Hobert Burns for this formulation.

But perhaps even more important is the recognition that revolution isn't necessary. Not all those in power positions need to be overthrown. There are, sprinkled here and there, persons in authority dedicated to radical change. Moreover, education has fallen far behind the technology and communication processes of the broader society. To bring education into line with the other enterprises of the society would strain the concept of revolution beyond utility.

What is needed is sweeping reform—extending to every aspect of education. The power system that controls policy must be altered to include those now unrepresented or underrepresented. The curriculum must be changed so that socially relevant matters are included. The teaching force must be drawn from all strata of the population. The style of presentation and media used in the classroom must be updated to conform to modern technology. The narrow provincialism of current school concerns must be supplanted by national and international outlooks. The distinction between reform and revolution is important. With the former it is possible to analyze the current scene and build upon defensible activities. With the former, power is viewed as a means to achieve an improved educational program rather than as an end in itself.

A Beachhead Strategy for Educational Reform

There is too much to do in education, and too few forces available to get the job done, to realistically introduce change everywhere at once, and educational leadership certainly cannot be accused of racing headlong in all directions to meet the challenge of our time. To the contrary, leadership can, with impunity, be charged with snail-pacing every which way, and, through the combination of timidity and mindlessness, some trivia is generated. Programmed learning is one such minor development—and not only does this inconsequential innovation fail to improve the situation, it inevitably only makes matters a little worse. However, as if proclamation will make all things right, such nonsense is blissfully fanfared as a major breakthrough. More literally than figuratively, little children are offered as sacrifice by educational leaders to maintain a system that has long outlived its usefulness. To reform education, beachheads must be established.

A beachhead must be a school program with clearly identified objectives which are relevant to the basic issues of our time. A set of procedures must be outlined which are specifically linked to the desired outcomes. Careful evaluation and continuous debugging must accompany every activity. The beachhead, in effect, is the educational program described in this book transformed into an operating model.

The beachhead must be established in a favorable environment. It will be tough enough, in the most receptive situation, to generate an educational program with all of the reforms indicated here. It would be madness to attempt it in an atmosphere of antagonism. For an environment to be receptive there must be:

1) Administrative support.

2) Community understanding.

3) A teaching staff with more than a modicum of knowledge and the willingness to reflect critically on current performance.

4) Creative leadership to ramrod, cajole, elucidate, empathize, and inspire whenever each of the above is the appropriate thing to do.

There are places in this country where all the conditions for a *beachhead* exist, and such places must be viewed as the proving grounds for real educational change. But the beachhead must be more than mere demonstration—more than a program that lives its hour and then is heard of no more. The beachhead must also generate a program for expansion. The gains must be transferred to other settings and tested for applicability there. One major problem for educational innovators is that they are often more interested in the experimental test than they are in wholesale application. They lose interest once they demonstrate that their idea *can* work, forgetting that it is relatively simple to generate a laboratory situation and, in the artificial setting, obtain *almost* any effect the experimenter desires. Unfortunately, however, trying to introduce those kinds of changes into existing bureaucratic structures is a much different proposition.

The beachhead must become the training center for new educational leadership. Once armed with expertise, these leaders must be entrusted to establish new beachheads, and those they train must be given similar responsibility. By such a strategy both leadership and reform can grow quite rapidly because of the pyramiding effect. The beachhead can be used for development of curriculum and for identification of potential danger points, both of which will be invaluable for those who press ahead.

Each individual can establish a personal beachhead. Teachers, administrators, parents, etc., all have some latitude for action. Too often individuals use as a defense for no action at all their inability to do everything they desire. Any activity that moves toward achieving one of the four major goals of education is necessary and important. However, it is never sufficient to stop at that level. An introduction of change within the classroom can be the wedge that is used to bring about more wide-sweeping changes. Other teachers can be encouraged to analyze their efforts. The greatest obstacle to educational change is the defeatist attitude of so many in the system. Teachers and administrators, like so many others, are victims of a society that overwhelms, depersonalizes, and renders useless. A beachhead established by a single person can set into motion a chain reaction that can alter this state of hopelessness. And all of us are in a position to do something and then map out a strategy to extend the influence of our efforts.

The beachhead makes possible efficient use of scarce government and private foundation funds. Currently these funds are frittered away on projects that, even if they proved to be successful, couldn't conceivably make an iota of difference to education. Those who control the funds must be convinced that bold approaches are urgently needed. If the entire structure is on fire a pencil-thin stream of water on some shrub in the garden—which is what support for educational change actually amounts to—is more ludicrous than pathetic. This book attempts to point the way for effective expenditure of funds. But we have dallied long enough.

CHAPTER II

The Goal of Career Choice

[In this chapter I describe public education's failure to give many students much choice in earning a living. I establish the case that education must take on markedly more responsibility for work preparation now than was the case ever before in history. I stress the importance of keeping *all* students eligible for college and the procedures which are necessary to accomplish this goal. I call for radical change in the content, structure, and nature of instruction about the work.]

I like work. It fascinates me. I can sit and look at it for hours.
—Jerome K. Jerome

It is the first of all problems for a man to find out what kind of work he is to do in this universe.
—Thomas Carlyle

Work consists of whatever a body is obliged to do, and play consists of whatever a body is not obliged to do.
—Mark Twain

If you treat an individual as he is, he will stay as he is, but if you treat him as if he were what he ought to be and should be, he will become what he ought to be and could be.
—Goethe

Mental health is the capacity to work and to love.
—Sigmund Freud

Freedom becomes a mockery unless one has many alternatives for life's work. Without choice of career, a person cannot determine where he is to live, how he is to enjoy his leisure time, or what will be the education of his children. In short, without choice of career, all those things that make life worth living are negatively affected.

Education must take into consideration the changes that have occurred in the last few decades in the world of work. Today, everything that goes on in the school, from reading instruction in the first grade to science instruction in the twelfth, affects choice of life careers. It wasn't always thus. Half a century ago education wasn't necessarily crucial to occupational choice. Henry Ford did not have a high-school education; he lacked substantial capital, but he succeeded. A major factor in his success was that his competitors, Chevrolet and the rest, had no more. But now education must take into account: (a) the declining demand for unskilled labor in the country; (b) the change in organization of work from relatively simplistic family-centered operations into depersonalized bureaucratic structures; (c) the continued and continuing urbanization of America, and (d) the demand by employers for successful completion of many years of formal education before one is eligible for entry into even the lowest rungs of employment.

The largest and fastest growing industries of the country—the health, education and welfare establishments—require at least four years of education beyond high school before one is permitted entry into all but a few menial, dead-end positions. We live in a *credential society*. For occupational choice one has to go through twelve years of irrelevance, to be eligible for four years of irrelevance, to be eligible for several more years of irrelevance in order to get in the front door. Lacking a credential, one must have effective sponsorship. But effective sponsorship is hard to come by. Barry Goldwater, for example, was able to derive the benefits of effective sponsorship. Although he couldn't get through one year of college in two tries, his family found something for him to do around the store. However, very few people from even moderately affluent backgrounds—and certainly none from disadvantaged backgrounds—have fathers who own businesses. Therefore, to provide the essentials for occupational choice, it is incumbent upon the educational system to offer credentials, if not in inverse proportion to the income and occupation of the students' parents, at least unrelated to such factors. The reverse is now the case.

An assessment of educational offerings leads to the conclusion that the unassailable evidence of the existence of a credential society is blissfully ignored. To the contrary, in the interest of efficiency the vast majority of disadvantaged youngsters are discouraged or actually prevented from seeking a college education. As long as formal education is a requirement for entrance into most prestigious, secure, and highly paid positions in our society, it is necessary for the school to keep each one of its students alive academically. The only other choice is to give every poor child a rich father.

If every child is to have a wide range of career choice the school must keep everyone eligible for the credential society and provide knowledge in depth about the work world.

Both of these aims require specific facilitating processes. If career choice is to become a reality the school must initiate a total strategy; there must be continuity of effort from preschool through graduation. The effort must be developmental and consistent with the current state of knowledge about maturational processes. (Although here, too, one must not allow some tentative conclusions about maturity to be used to further insult the intelligence of youth.) How well are schools doing in the matter of facilitating career choice? To answer this question one need only heed Al Smith's advice and "Look at the record."

Keeping Everyone Eligible for the Credential Society—A Critique

Here the schools fail miserably, although, with some distortion of fairness, they cannot be faulted, since those who control schools have never taken seriously the notion that they must educate everyone equally. In fact, rather than making everyone eligible for the credential society they have the opposite intention. They view "deluding" certain youngsters into thinking that they may possibly have the cerebral power to ultimately become a doctor or even a teacher as both inefficient and cruel. Thus they search for those who have the "horsepower" for the credential society. This search starts early.

From the first day a child begins school a sorting process begins. The school begins to direct children to different stations of life. When my youngest child entered the third grade my wife was informed by the teacher that he was college material. That meant, of course, that other parents were delighted to discover that their children were welfare or warehouse material. This process goes on without even pause for reflection. Once having assigned a child an educational ceiling, the school sets into motion the machinery to insure that the initial classification does, indeed, become the terminal state.

The classification and sorting system affects all segments of the population, but not equally. There is some redress for those with means. Parents with money or education have some power to select schools or influence decision-making within the school. The poor are most sorely treated. There is now abundant evidence that the educational establishment considers disadvantaged children to be educationally backward upon entrance into the school system. Rather than rectifying that situation, the school reinforces the condition. The school expects less from poor children, offers less, and is satisfied with less. More than any other group the school assigns these children to less challenging educational tasks. Some are sorted into "bluebirds," others to "canaries," and still others to "robins." And the problem is, "Once a bluebird, always a bluebird." Children are grouped with others of alleged similar ability, and thus they continue to fall farther behind in academic performance. By the fourth grade it is possible to accurately predict their educational future.

Christina Tree had this to say about the student who is assigned to low-ability groups in New York City:

> Chances are he is a Negro or Puerto Rican boy, and, more important, that he comes from a poor family. Chances are he had changed elementary school more than once. To teachers and peers, his place in a slow class indicated that little was expected of him. To his future employer this general diploma will signify the same.[1]

How assignment to a reading group in first grade affects one's life-work history is really not difficult to fathom. It is the old "loss of a kingdom for want of a horse" problem. If one is not taught adequately to read, write, or engage in simple mathematical computations, one cannot successfully negotiate an elementary school. If one fails in elementary school, it becomes literally impossible to succeed in high school. And if one fails in high school, one is precluded from entrance into college; and if one does not get a college degree, one does not have the credential necessary for entrance into the growth industries of our country.

Here we must pause and look at this business of assessing intelligence. At the present time we have no valid way of making such a determination for any group. Nor is it likely that we will

---

[1] Christina Tree. "Grouping Pupils in New York City," *The Urban Review*, Vol. 3, No. 1, Sept. 1968, p. 9.

ever have a valid means of testing intelligence. We certainly have no valid means of comparing ability of different races, social classes, or ethnic groups. On the face of it, intelligence is much too complex a matter to be reduced to some simple 2- or 3-digit code obtained from responses to a relatively restricted universe of inquiry, and yet that is precisely what we do. With scarcely any examination of the underlying assumptions governing the determination of intelligence, various testing devices are treated as gospel, and from such flimsy stuff a child's life may be ruined. I am hardly suggesting that all people have identical capabilities, although this possibility should not be dismissed. Boyer and Walsh make a strong point in arguing that until we have evidence to the contrary "We should base our policy in the most generous and promising assumptions about human nature rather than the most niggardly and pessimistic." [2]

Many observers have noted, and some have even supplied evidence, that teacher expectations influence classroom performance: "When teachers and principals have a low opinion of the children's learning ability the children seldom exceed those expectations." [3]

Because of the relationship between schooling and opportunities for life work the possible influence of a "self-fulfilling prophecy" on educational success must be examined in some depth. Rosenthal and Jacobson have compiled a comprehensive summary of investigations of this phenomenon.[4] Citing a variety of sources they develop a convincing argument that, indeed, behavior of organisms is markedly influenced by expectation of persons in authority. To culminate this effort they report the findings of a study they conducted which was to be a critical test of the nature and extent of influence that teacher expectations have on student performance.

The Rosenthal and Jacobson experiment consisted of (a) administering a group test purporting to measure intelligence to students entering 1st through 6th grade in an elementary school; (b) informing teachers that the test was capable of identifying students with the potential to spurt ahead; (c) leaking to the teachers a list of names of a randomly selected group (the experimental group)

[2] William H. Boyer and Paul Walsh, "Are Children Born Unequal?" in *Saturday Review of Literature*, Oct. 1968, p. 78.

[3] *Youth in the Ghetto*, Harlem Youth Opportunities Unlimited, Inc. (HARYOU) 1964, p. 203.

[4] Robert Rosenthal and Lenore Jacobson, *Pygmalion in the Classroom*, Holt, Rinehart and Winston, New York, 1968.

with ostensible "spurting potential"; (d) comparing achievement in IQ change reading ability and assessed social adjustment of the experimental and control groups (those not identified as "spurters").

Rosenthal and Jacobson's results tend to support the contention that teacher expectations influence student performance, but not very convincingly. They found this phenomenon in grades 1 and 2 but not in grades 5 and 6. They also did not find the same results in different schools. They comment, parenthetically, that their results are not universal, and thus they tend to dilute the importance of expectation in classroom behavior.

It is amazing they got any results at all! For whatever their study was, it was NOT a study of impact of teacher expectation on student performance. In fact, they have no data to even suggest that teachers "heard" what was told them about the student's spurting potential. To the contrary, evidence is offered that teachers were not even tuned in to the experiment:

> While all teachers recalled glancing at their lists, most felt they paid little or no attention to them. Many teachers threw their lists away after glancing at them.
>
> . . . eighteen names were recalled as having been on the original list when, in fact, they had been control group children.[5]

The experiment was badly conceived in many ways. It was modeled after a rat study in which some experimenters were informed that the rat subjects were from a "bright" strain, and other experimenters were informed that identical rats were from a "stupid," strain, with the result that the "bright" rats learned the problem better than the "stupid" rats.[6] But it is not likely that teachers look at students in the same way that researchers view rats. Teachers can draw upon a large conglomerate of clues for expectations. They may be influenced by race, income of parents, basal metabolic rate, language style, dress, sex, ethnic membership, performance of older siblings, peer alliances, facial expression, body odor, obedience to authority, concern for social amenities, apparent concern of parents for education, timbre of voice, height, weight, tempo of classroom activities, complexion, information obtained from colleagues, information obtained from classmates, test performance, ad infinitum. The rat researcher has no such rich res-

---

[5] *Ibid.*, pp. 154–155.
[6] *Ibid.*

ervoir of clues. Any little bit of information he garners is likely to
be pounced upon and used.

Teachers are involved with students in a manner much different than the relationship between the researcher and his rats.
There is also a difference in the reverse relationship—the student
views his teacher very differently (I can only suspect) than the rat
perceives his researcher. There are also important differences in arrangement of power. The rat researcher can, at the slightest whim,
exterminate a subject, while teachers do not have, as yet, such
authority. The rat researcher is committed to the rats' success
(negative findings are negatively received by journal editors). The
teacher, unfortunately, has no such commitment.

The study with human subjects lacked a vital component of
the rat study. On moral grounds no effort was made to produce
negative expectations of students in teachers. And while I am sympathetic to ethical considerations, I think this omission blew the entire experiment. *The problem that we confront is the influence of
negative expectations on students' performance.* We have good
reason to believe that negative attitudes are formed more readily
than positive attitudes and moreover, it appears that "latitudes of
rejection" influence more decisions and alliances than do "latitudes
of acceptance." [7]

Thus it would seem that Rosenthal and Jacobson threw away
the attempt to establish negative sets on ethical grounds and made
only a minimal—perhaps subliminal—effort to develop positive expectations. It is not surprising that the results were equivocal. If
Henry Higgins had done as little, Liza Doolittle would never have
deceived Zoltan Kaparthy.[8] But, in fact, *Pygmalion* is a poor reference for the study. In *Pygmalion* the student, through systematic
training, was able to affect the language and trappings of breeding
and culture. Henry Higgins not only had a conviction, he had a
plan of action. It is not demonstrated that the teachers in the Rosenthal and Jacobson study had either.

It is no mystery that 5th and 6th graders would respond dif-

---

[7] The terms "latitudes of rejection" and "latitudes of acceptance" are
borrowed from M. Sherif, C. Sherif, and R. Nebergoll, *Attitude and Attitude Change,* Saunders, Philadelphia, 1965. In this work the authors indicate
the extent to which negative outlooks predominate over positive attitudes
in interpersonal activity.

[8] Nepommuck was his name in the original George Bernard Shaw play.

ferently than 1st or 2nd graders in the study. The teachers of older students already had well-established expectations, and students had well-established self-images—they had long been identified by learning ability group, and their peers had boxed them into well-established roles. That a mere listing of identified "spurters" routinely transmitted to teachers would overcome all this doesn't seem very reasonable. Rosenthal and Jacobson mention this among half a dozen different possibilities:

> A second interpretation is that younger children within a given school have less well established reputations within the school. It then becomes more credible to a teacher to be told that a younger child will show intellectual growth.[9]

But because this interpretation is buried and not well developed, its importance is minimized and the reader is left with the conclusion that the "expectancy effect" is something enigmatical and yet easily produced. Peter and Carol Gumpert state that in the area of explaining how the relationship between teacher expectations and student performance works,

> Rosenthal and Jacobson are weakest in their analysis. Though they do speculate about some aspects of the problem, the heart of the matter remains untouched. In short, they have shown us that teachers' expectations of their students' performances have definite consequences for these (subsequent) performances. But they have not shown us how this process works.[10]

I believe that teachers' expectations have an enormous impact on student behavior. I believe that these influences are widespread and perhaps even universal. I believe that older children are as much influenced by the effect as younger children. I believe that race, ethnic, and social class biases contribute heavily to teacher expectations. I believe that factors which limit performance and thereby disqualify the student for the credential society are extremely powerful because they knit together so many influential persons in a student's life. Teachers influence students who, in turn, influence other students. Teachers influence other teachers. Teachers communicate to parents messages of no confidence in a child's ability, which influence relationships at home. Teachers strongly

---

[9] Rosenthal and Jacobson, *op. cit.*, p. 83.
[10] Peter and Carol Gumpert. "The Teacher was Pygmalion: Comments on the Psychology Expectation," *The Urban Review*, Vol. 3, No. 1, Sept. 1968, p. 21.

support ability grouping. In a nationwide survey, 58% of the teachers approved segregating students into *separate classes* according to ability as measured by IQ or achievement test scores.[11]

The less-than-equal education continues and proliferates in the high school. Here a variety of procedures are employed to sidetrack students from career choice. On the same invalid grounds as were used in grammar school, youth are assigned to different tracks. Those reputed to have the ability are placed in college preparatory or honors tracks, the others to noncollege preparatory tracks which, by definition, preclude the opportunity to obtain the visa into the world of work that comes with the college degree.

In the noncollege tracks there are, in disproportionately large numbers, the economically disadvantaged, the Indians, the Mexican-Americans, and the blacks. Of late, the legality of that system has been subjected to a challenge, and in Washington, D.C., the school system was forced to abolish its track program. Judge J. Skelly Wright, in decreeing that the school system be "permanently enjoined from operating the track system in the District of Columbia public schools," concluded: [12]

Education in the lower tracks is geared to . . . the "blue collar" student. Thus such children, so stigmatized by inappropriate aptitude testing procedures, are denied equal opportunity to obtain the white collar education available to the white and more affluent children.[13]

Programs offered under the aegis of Vocational education have certainly not augmented career choice. Vocational education is a misnomer. By and large those programs described as vocational programs are nonutilitarian and have become a dumping ground for youth not deemed to be college material. With almost a pathetic lack of vision, vocational education is geared and directed at the declining industries of this country. There is scarcely any need for a Stanley Steamer repairman now, and there is not likely to be the need for such a person in the future. Even in those rare instances where vocational education is preparing youth for viable job opportunity, there is a tendency to overlook the informal credentialing

---

[11] National Education Association Research Division, Teacher Opinion Poll, *NEA Journal*, 50:62, Apr. 1961.

[12] U.S. Court of Appeals, Judge J. Skelly Wright (Washington, D.C., school case), June 19, 1967.

[13] *Ibid.*

arrangement that has been negotiated between the union and the employer. The lack of reality orientation and the downgrading of vocational education in the high school is a serious condition and yet the malady, rather than a possible remedy to it, continues to be funded.

One of the most palpable absurdities of vocational education programs is the insensitivity to the racial biases that prevail among employers and unions. As previously emphasized, the great percentage of nonwhite minorities is not pointed to college, thus these groups are, by a process of exclusion, diverted to vocational education either within the public school or in such substitute programs as the Job Corps. But these industries have been traditionally hostile to nonwhites even in their periods of maximum growth. In 1897 Booker T. Washington, currently reviled for his lack of militancy, blistered the American Federation of Labor for its exclusion of Negroes from desirable crafts and trades, and got an angry denunciation by its leaders for his analysis.[14] W. E. B. Du Bois, who in other matters disagreed vehemently with Booker T. Washington, concurred with him on organized labor's treatment of the black workers,[15] and he, too, met with abrupt dismissal.

Black minorities were not the only minorities denied union membership. Chinese, Japanese, and Mexicans also were rejected, and the legacy of that policy lives with us today. Although the CIO emerged as a counterforce to the conservatism of the AFL, and although the rhetoric of this group trumpeted civil rights, and although the initial organizing drives in the 1940's in the South were based on racial equality, the thrust was short-lived. Racism has reappeared with the erosion of the vitality of the unions. The policy of racial exclusion may have given way grudgingly to more subtle devices, but the impact is clear, and now with the spirit and growth of organized labor on the wane there is great reluctance on the part of either membership or leadership to be venturesome. A basic conservatism views suspiciously any training vehicle over which there is no union control. Union members want to hold onto the declining new jobs for family and friends. AFL-CIO president George Meany finds it . . . "understandable that a man who has spent years learning a trade, who is proud of his skills, wants to pass it on to his son,

---

[14] AFL Convention, 1897, pp. 82–83.

[15] W. E. B. DuBois (ed.), *The Negro Artisan, A Social Study*, Atlanta U. Publication No. 7, 1902.

just as a merchant wants to pass on the business he had built to his son." [16] There is, from all reports, strong antiblack bias among white membership that is neither countered within or without the union. The barrier to equal opportunity to employment for those assigned to vocational education is real, and yet, for the most part, this aspect is swept under the rug when vocational programs are evaluated or planned.[17]

Vocational education fares no better with industry. Racial biases are as prevalent among businessmen as in any other segment of the society. And in addition, there is a growing cry from industry that training is best accomplished by the employer, particularly if tax funds are provided for this activity.

The lack of articulation between school vocational programs and the reality of the work world is an important obstacle for vocational education as currently constituted. But more important by far is the need for everyone to recognize that *even if vocational education could be made to work it shouldn't!* Underlying vocational education are differential stations in life. The school points the student to his appropriate place. Rather than enhancing choice, vocational education denies choice. The result is premature foreclosure on career. Certainly, students should be encouraged to develop skill in the use of power tools, or in motor repair, or in carpentry, or in typing. These offerings must be made available to *all* students. But their ultimate use is likely to be avocational rather than vocational. And this is a legitimate goal of education. (See Chapter VIII.) However, when occupation is the issue the overriding consideration must always be to keep the pathway leading to credentials open to all.

The nature of training and the link between training and employment resources is crucial if vocational education is to offer opportunity to youth. Training for skill is meaningful only if the employer recognizes that that skill has been engendered.

To optimize investment in vocational education, cooperative arrangements must be developed with prospective employers. Part

---

[16] *News from the AFL-CIO,* Aug. 1, 1962.

[17] Two contrasting views on attitudes and practice of contemporary labor toward the black worker can be found in *The Negro and the American Labor Movement,* Julius Jacobson (ed.) Anchor Books, Garden City, New York, 1968. In this work a critical view is presented by Herbert Hill. Gus Tyler's article is more sympathetic to organized labor.

of vocational education should be on-the-job training in which the student obtains high-school credits. Such a program has many potential benefits. The trainee, if he successfully completes the program, can be guaranteed a job, and the school system is spared the considerable expense of maintaining and continually updating a comprehensive skills center. Every secondary school should maintain a modest plant which should be manifestly prevocational or avocational in character. Here all students, regardless of their alleged ability or current aspirations, could develop much-needed typing skills or learn to manipulate power tools.

The partnership between the school and the community employment resource has the potential for ancillary gains to both parties. The community gains from more efficient absorption into employment, and the school derives not only expertise in training but also greater understanding of problems of educating modern youth.

Vocational education, however, cannot be obtained at the expense of general education. Clearly, only persons with sophistication beyond technological ability will have much opportunity for upward mobility. That portion of the education of the vocationally oriented student which occurs in the school must be as demanding, as exciting, and as real as the one offered to the college-bound youth. The youth who chooses to become an automobile mechanic must have the foundation and basic skills to allow him to become an engineer if, at some later date, he should aspire to such a goal.

The non-college-bound student will receive his fair share only if he is integrated into the same classes as the college-bound student. And while the bringing together of students with different aspirations and of alleged different abilities presents some challenge to the teachers, it is nonetheless a feasible arrangement. Dividing the students into separate classes does damage to both groups. It inevitably leads to a watering-down of the content to the non-college-bound and to a rarefied existence for the college-bound student which will restrict his ability to communicate to people of diverse backgrounds and blind his sensitivities to everyday realities. (A factor often alluded to when the college-situated are invidiously labled "eggheads.")

Vocational education at the secondary level must begin to emphasize human-service activities and prepare youth for entry positions into the rapidly expanding health, education, welfare, recreation, and conservation fields. To augment such a program, career ladders must be established which will allow talented and motivated persons to move from an entry position (attained at or even before high-school graduation) through intermediate steps (for example, community college) to ultimately attain a professional status. A carefully planned program of this kind could open up to the impoverished and to the minorities occupations where they are currently greatly underrepresented and could begin to reduce the segregation which is ripping our nation asunder. (More of this later when "New Careers" is discussed.)

Return again to the business of grouping students by alleged ability or aspiration. The culling and sorting of students by the schools has escalated sharply in recent years, because such efforts have been encouraged by support of federal funds. The Russians' space achievements energized the nation to ferret out its potential scientists, and this effort to segregate has been joined by federal support for aid to the handicapped and the disadvantaged.

The most handsomely funded government program, the Elementary and Secondary Education Act (which is designed to offer support for "educationally disadvantaged"), buttresses ability grouping. It is possible with federal money to divert students from mainstream education. Special classes are set up for the educationally disadvantaged but end up as a quarantining device rather than as a benefit. Creeping into the program is the theme that if the troublesome and the boneheaded are removed, the school can then get down to the business of educating the worthy.

Funds for the handicapped are also used to segregate youth from a path to a credential. Today there are over 30,000 teachers for retarded children working in special classes in the local public schools. The majority of the youth served in those classes are again the poor and the ethnic minority groups. Lloyd M. Dunn, the past president of the Council for Exceptional Children, reflects critically upon retirement from his post:

> In my best judgment, about 60 to 80 percent of the pupils taught by these teachers are children from low status backgrounds—including Afro-Americans, American Indians, Mexicans and Puerto Rican Americans; those from non-standard English speaking, broken, disorganized, and inadequate homes; and children from other non-middle class environments. This expensive proliferation of self-contained special schools and classes raises serious educational and civil rights issues which must be squarely faced. It is my

thesis that we must stop labeling these deprived children as mentally retarded. Furthermore, we must stop segregating them by placing them into our allegedly special programs.[18]

So be it for the conglomerate of activities and attitudes that shut students out from the credential society. The trick is to offer realistic alternatives.

Keeping Everyone Eligible for the Credential Society— Some Suggestions

Maintaining universal eligibility for the credential society is a many-faceted proposition, consisting of at least the following four components:

1) The replacement of ability-grouping with heterogeneous mixing;

2) The elimination of biased treatment of students through screening and training of teachers;

3) The utilization of technology;

4) The reduction of class load through the strategic use of nonprofessionals.

All of the above factors are necessary and, while not all could be accomplished immediately or with current resources, many changes could be started immediately. It is imperative that we begin.

Elimination of Ability-Grouping

Ability-grouping can be eliminated immediately, since it has served no useful educational purpose for ANY segment of the student population. And IF the poor and the nonwhite are ever to have career choice within the credential society, ability-grouping must go. There can be no equivocation—all ability-grouping at every grade level must be foresworn. There can be no game-playing. In New York City heterogeneous grouping is a term which is distorted to embrace strict ability-grouping:

In New York schools "heterogeneous" more often than not means *more precise* grouping by ability rather than the opposite. It is

---

[18] Lloyd M. Dunn, "Special Education for the Mildly Retarded—Is Much of It Justifiable?" *Exceptional Children*, Sept. 1968, p. 6.

confusing, ironic, but true that heterogeneous, which literally means a random mix, is the city's newest name for uniform ability grouping.

For subjects built around social considerations such as social studies and health education (and in some schools science) this class of students with differing abilities remain together; for skill subjects (such as math and reading) and "talent" subjects (music and art) the students are split up and placed with students of the same ability.[19]

The New York City system operates in complete contradiction to equality for the credential. The skill classes which are the most vital are those where sorting is used, and, if heterogeneity is to be begun piecemeal, it must begin with reading.

Complete heterogeneity in schools would be no panacea. A great many difficult situations can be anticipated. But with all the likely difficulties it would be an improvement over what we now have. When heterogeneous grouping is joined with better curriculum resources, improved and unbiased instruction, and reduced teacher-pupil ratios, the goal of keeping everyone eligible for the credential society will be within reach.

Even the severely retarded and the grossly handicapped should be included in the heterogeneous mixed classes. Some of these will prove to have capabilities no one ever suspected, and even those children who have been accurately assessed can benefit from the association with mainstream children. It is even more important that the allegedly normal and able children associate with those less fortunate than themselves because, through such associations, their understanding of man, his diversity, and his problems will be broadened. (More of this in Chapter 6.) The experience with deviant populations is also valuable preparation for those human-care services designed to help the handicapped and the infirm.

The Elimination of Biased Treatment of Students Through Screening and Training of Teachers

The teacher in the classroom exercises enormous control over a student's life. We, as a nation, have been rather cavalier with those whom we trust with such responsibility. Avowed drug-users or child-molesters are denied the privilege of teaching. In times of

---

[19] Christina Tree, *op. cit.,* p. 14.

political frenzy those accused of unorthodoxy are driven from the classroom. But all others are safe. Those who literally hate children can serve out a lifelong career without even a challenge. This is especially true when teachers are accused of racist attitudes. In fact there is no clearly defined set of principles upon which a case against even a self-proclaimed "racist" could be based, nor does there exist sufficient agreement on definition to initiate proceedings against anyone so accused. *The absence of guidelines reflects an absence of concern!* The educational establishment—shorthand for the teachers and their associations, the administrators, the school boards, the teacher-training institutions and the legislatures—does not view racism among the teaching force as a high priority issue. It is really the other way. The person who *does care* is likely to be in trouble; it is he who will be investigated as an agitator rather than the issue itself. In those rare instances when accusations of racism reach sufficient intensity to require formal proceedings, invariably the agency in question, after self-investigation, exonerates itself.

Should a child or parent approach a school administrator and complain that a teacher was prejudiced, the inevitable response would be, "Oh, no. I've known Mrs. Blank for years and she just isn't that way." And that would be the end of it.

But that cannot be the end of it. Racism is rampant among teachers. It takes two forms. There are many out-and-out bigots who are guided by a philosophy of overt racial superiority. These teachers just don't like Negroes and Mexicans, and they act as if their prejudices are a God-given right. They further suspect that any person not agreeing with their views is either perverted or unpatriotic or both. I have heard them at parties and in faculty lounges utter racial slurs, as coarse as any cracker's, only sometimes passing the remarks off as humor.

A liberal form of racism also prevails. These teachers treat minorities with a saccharine colonialism. They just are not going to wound the flawed egos of the poor savages by requiring effort beyond their limited capabilities. The liberal racists are horribly affronted when those held in their tender mercies first request and then demand their independence. Both forms of racism must be extirpated from the classroom.

The elimination of teacher bias begins with the assertion that such behavior is not tolerable. There has to be a clear, unmistakable ultimatum that *teacher tenure does not include the right to be a racist!* This principle *must* be unequivocally supported by teacher associations, administrators, and school boards. If a policy against teacher racism is to transcend mere rhetoric there must be:

a) A precise and well-advertised procedure for initiating grievances;

b) Ground rules for proceedings which have emerged as result of negotiations of school personnel and community;

c) A judicial procedure in which a system of due process is established that protects the accused from character-assassination while affording the aggrieved full opportunity for redress;

d) A precisely defined set of consequences for teachers who are proven to be racists, including expulsion from the profession for flagrant violators.

A policy which, if effected, could eliminate racists from teaching posts is not in itself sufficient. A system of training must be instituted. Racism is learned by teachers. What is learned can be unlearned. A program designed to eliminate racism among teachers can succeed if that program is both extensive and intensive.

To be liberated from racist attitudes the teacher must be confronted with every manifestation of the affliction. Teacher training (both pre-service and inservice) must include courses that deal directly with the history, culture, language, and style of minority groups. These concerns must be hard-hitting but also analytical. Prospective and experienced teachers must be brought into contact with minority groups. These engagements must be monitored, and all forms of racial insult must be forcefully brought to the attention of the current, or soon-to-be, teacher.

In a program sponsored by the National Defense Education Act for experienced teachers which I directed, four minority youths were hired to serve as instructors for teachers. The reversal of usual roles had a dramatic effect—both groups were in unique situations. For the first time poor black and Mexican youths had the opportunity to speak their minds and the authority to force the teacher to listen, and, conversely, for the first time teachers had to face their hostility and the underlying reasons for that hostility without the power to escape or forbid its expression. From all indices—reports of teachers and youths, other students and observers—there were significant changes in teacher attitudes and behavior. Similar strategies can be instituted in all teacher preparation programs and should be maintained throughout a teacher's career, because without continuity of effort these changes toward greater sensitivity are likely to be transient.

Teachers must also be trained to expect success from students. The training must be directed at the underlying conceptual support for negative expectations. The teacher must be continually challenged whenever he suggests that a student is intellectually inferior, that he is inadequately socialized, that he has been subjected to deprivations during critical early (preschool) learning periods, that he has been drawn from school concerns by "bad" companions, that he has deplorable study habits, etc. Instead of such explanations, which always relieve the teacher of responsibility, the teacher must be continually directed to look for causes of failure within the classroom. First and foremost the teacher must look to himself as the instrument of defeat. Through carefully structured simulation of classroom activity and through observations of classroom performance the teacher's "set" toward students can be changed.

If the Rosenthal and Jacobson study, discussed previously in this chapter, had really tried to test the impact of teacher expectation on student performance, the teachers involved should have been subjected to an intensive program of at least 8 to 10 weeks, to change their orientation toward students. The performance of the students instructed by these teachers should have been compared with the performance of a comparable group of students who had been carefully and precisely matched with the experimental group but who did not have teachers so trained.[20]

Many persons now teaching should never have been permitted to teach. They entered the field because there was no fair or logical way to keep them out. The major problem in establishing adequate screening devices is that not much information is available to a recruiter, and the little that is known about a prospective candidate isn't very relevant. There is a transcript which shows that the applicant survived an accedited institution for higher education and has taken the courses required for certification. The recruiter tries to deduce from an interview how a teacher might relate to a group of students and in some rare instances might even set up a situation

---

[20] To keep the influence of teacher variation under some control the teachers considered for the study should be sorted into matched pairs, and one of the pair drawn at random for intensive training, the unselected members to constitute the teachers of the control group.

where the candidate is expected to teach. But none of these is very satisfactory. Adequate screening can come into existence only if persons considering teaching are placed in meaningful teaching relationships with students very early in their undergraduate career. Only then is it possible for a student to "deselect" himself and decide that education isn't his forte before he has invested too much in the field and before other choices are foreclosed. Early involvements with students can bring to light negative expectations and other biases on which an adequate training program can "zero in" and begin to initiate change.

Even a near-perfect screening will not eliminate the problem of bias if the only group attracted to teaching are the middle income and, in disproportionate numbers, the white-skinned. The black, the Native American, the Mexican, and other Spanish-speaking and low-income persons will believe that the credential society is open to them only if they perceive their like (in numbers proportionate to their incidence in the population) in positions of authority in the largest and fastest growing of the credentialed industries—education.

Recruitment of large numbers of black, Puerto-Rican, Mexican, and other Spanish-speaking persons into teaching would not require a major departure from standard operating procedures if the suggestion of early involvement of students in teaching activities is heeded. Most universities have initiated programs to entice minority youth to the campus. Instead of allowing these students to flounder—which is the usual case—they should be sought out as candidates for teacher education. As freshmen they could be assigned to tutoring and other teaching activities for which they could be paid under the provisions of federally assisted work-study. As they advance in school they can be given more challenging assignments. (Another strategy for involving persons in teaching activity prior to college matriculation is presented later in the next chapter, when "New Careers" is discussed.) With this kind of subsidy, within four years a significant increase in the number of minority teachers could be obtained. The recently enacted Educational Professional Development Act (EPDA) could be used for staff to support such programs. This piece of legislation could be used to train and credential the large number of minority members currently functioning as paraprofessionals in schools. The EPDA could be used to train black, Puerto Rican, Asian, Native American, and Mexican teachers for administrative posts where their underrepresentation is even more marked than in teaching functions.

Heterogeneous grouping, coupled with more sensitive instruction, could do much to reduce the casualties of education, and, as a consequence, a far greater percentage of students could remain eligible for higher education. Certainly the degree of loss due to class and race bias could be greatly reduced. However, to accomplish the goal of keeping everyone eligible for credentials, much more must be done. Another important step would require modernization of the schooling process.

Utilization of Technology

Today's educational offerings differ but little from those of the days of the horse and buggy. The development of an electronic age impinges but slightly on the classroom. The inability of teachers to use modern technology effectively has grossly handicapped disengaged and economically disadvantaged students. Technology could be a valuable asset in maintaining truly heterogeneous groups. With such support it would be possible to individualize instruction while maintaining a grouping that cuts across all strata within the school.

Educational technology now makes possible, through the appropriate use of programmed instruction, computer-assisted instruction, "talking typewriters," videotapes, educational games, controlled readers, film strips, 8 mm projectors, etc., a program uniquely designed for each child's interests and development. That these innovations have been so badly used can be ascribed to the aimlessness of education and teacher innocence about modern technology. But there are exceptions.

Smethport, Pennsylvania—as unlikely a place as any could imagine—provides an example of what can be done. In this small, out-of-the-way rural community a traditional-appearing classroom within a traditional-appearing school has been metamorphosed into an electronic wonder world. This room has taken on the exotic quality of an igloo, although nothing more extraordinary was used to accomplish this feat than plain white sheeting. In one corner of the room is an impressive array of amplifiers, tape decks, slide and motion picture projectors, and a device that has the capability of transferring sound waves into electrical impulses. Behind the cotton sheeting is a bank of lights. Through activation of electronic equipment, tape recordings of children's voices or musical compositions are transformed into psychedelic light shows. The colors seen are a reflection of the auditory tones, and the intensity of light represents the intensity of the sound. Many educational functions are accomplished in this room. Reading—an essential requirement of the credential society—is taught here. And particularly assisted are those students with reading difficulties. Reading for these students in normal circumstances has become a drudgery, but in the new setting life is breathed into the experience. Moreover, the usefulness of reading can be explained more fully through the use of the apparatus. The initial stage of reading—decoding—requires the learner to associate sound with visual stimuli. If the student can see simultaneously what he hears, and can distinguish correct from incorrect responses, his proficiency is facilitated. While one student may be using the equipment for the purpose of improving his reading, yet another (or perhaps the same student) might be expanding his knowledge and whetting his interest in electronics. The cost of this innovative room is relatively modest, and administrators and teachers with imagination can at least duplicate, if not exceed, this kind of classroom—*if* they set their minds to it!

One need not go to special efforts to bring technology into the classroom. Much of the modern world is available to education if the educator would only deign to use it. This is especially true of television. While little of television programming has direct relevance to the world of work, much of television is applicable to the instruction of basic skills. Most three-year-olds have learned to "decode" because of television. If there are some readers who doubt this, take any three-year-old to a supermarket and try to buy "Wheaties" when that three-year-old wants "Cap'n Crunch." The three-year-old has learned to read because the person who taught him acted as if his job depended upon it. He expected success; he did not differentiate between levels of learners. He did not excessively restrict the behavior of his "student." He never insisted, "Before we do anything at all, the 'bluebirds' must turn to channel seven, the 'robins' to channel five, and the 'canaries' stay right here with me on channel three." Nor did he say, "I won't read this commercial until you are all sitting quietly in front of the TV set." Of course not! He did what he had to do. He said, "Kids, when you go to the store, make sure your mothers buy 'Cap'n Crunch,'" and showed the children the cereal box. And the children learned. It is only when youngsters come to school that they learn *not* to read! The teacher must appreciate the learning which the child brings to school and he must also utilize the learning which is concurrent with classroom activity.

Technology *can* offer valuable resources to education, *but only* if these innovations do not distort the educational offerings. At the present time most if not all of the value of technology is wasted because of the limited goals of the programs or the mechanistic approach to the learner. The machine is almost always used to inculcate a basic skill or transmit specific information—there is a a lack of flow or an intolerance for uniqueness of learning style, a fragmentation of effort or unconnection to work, politics, culture, or personal growth. The machine, at best, can only be an adjunct to the educational process. As presently used, the machine encourages passivity. There are even some who suggest that a machine might be devised that would obviate the need for a human teacher. No more ugly prospect could be envisioned, nor is any proposal more out of keeping with legitimate educational aims. Education in the future will require more, not less, human involvement. Work choices available to persons in the future will be predominantly in the area of human service, and these activities have already been too greatly depersonalized. Only with humans preparing humans for such service is there any hope of revitalization. Similarly the other goals of education—citizenship, culture-carrying and the ability to function with oneself and one's neighbors— also require more human beings in instructional roles. And even for the limited goal of maintaining student eligibility for the credential society, pupil-teacher ratios must be markedly reduced.

The Reduction of Class Load Through the Strategic Use of Nonprofessionals

A system based on one teacher for every 25 students cannot conceivably engage every student. With so many students a teacher is forced to "beam" his message to that segment of the student body that can resonate with him. There can be little accommodation for individual style, tempo, or background. All communication must be governed by the limitations imposed on the overloaded teacher. The arrangement of students that would allow for maximum communication would be groups of no more than ten pupils.

To accomplish this the numbers of persons in teaching roles would at least have to be doubled or perhaps tripled. I am not suggesting that there will be any gain by simply reducing class size and changing nothing else. Aimless education, irrelevant curriculum, and teachers with a hostile or ill-defined stance toward students are not changed by mere reduction in class size. However, if the goals of education are to be accomplished, reduction in pupil-teacher ratio is a necessary adjunct of the previously proposed changes in teacher-training and -screening.

Two major stumbling blocks stand in the way of achieving reduced classroom loads for teachers. One barrier is cost and the other is shortage of qualified personnel. Neither obstacle is insurmountable. Both are basically political problems. I will not attempt at this time to sketch a political strategy to overcome political resistance to reduced class size but will deal only with its feasibility.

The addition of 4 to 5 million more persons as teachers would cost the taxpayer 20 to 40 billions of dollars. In a nation fast nearing a trillion-dollar-a-year gross national product, a 40-billion-dollar item can be afforded. The issue is priority. The taxpayer must decide whether education is more important and vital to national interests and survival than is, for example, the burden of the military. The taxpayer must also decide whether tax rebates and write-offs to the wealthy take precedence over educational costs. The 40 billion extra dollars to reduce class size to less than half is precisely what Philip Stern claims is now given as tax support for the rich. He specifically wonders about this interesting anomaly: "Those who so vocally extol the virtues of budget balancing jealously safeguard each dollar of government outlays, but they are curiously silent about $40 billion the Congress is indirectly 'spending' through tax concessions." [21]

At the present time, in the scheme of priority, education is not valued highly. There are many explanations offered to explain this lack of public support. Educational leaders claim that there is a "taxpayer revolt," a right-wing conspiracy, a left-wing conspiracy and even a conspiracy of coalesced right- and left-wingers. What never seems to be seriously considered is that the taxpayer is objecting to paying top dollars for a shoddy product. Educational

---

[21] Philip Stern, *The Great Treasury Raid,* Random House, New York, 1962, p. 11.

spokesmen are not very good salesmen, but they may be better than the product they peddle. The political dilemma reduces to credibility. If reduction in pupil-teacher ratio is not to appear as merely another boondoggle of the educational establishment, then the use to which these additional teachers are to be put must be clearly enunciated. Accountability of educators must begin with specifying the goals that additional investment will attain. If the public can be persuaded that one ultimate result of reduced class size will be a more employable population, some political support will be engendered on humanitarian grounds, while others will concur on economic grounds.

Even if there was concensus that more millions of teachers were needed, this could not happen if only certified persons were considered for these roles. There just aren't enough certified teachers extant. The additional numbers must come from "lesser trained" groups and be distinguished from the credential teacher by such terms as paraprofessional or aide.

The call for millions of nonprofessionals in teaching roles needs to be reconciled with an earlier allegation that education is already saddled with too many persons not suited for teaching. There is really no contradiction between these two statements. The earlier reference was to persons whose hostility or racial biases corrupted the educational process. There is no evidence that credentials have much effect on these distortions. In fact it is possible that through intelligent use of nonprofessionals, the negative effect of bias and expectation of success could be markedly reduced. There is greater likelihood of drawing people with positive attitudes into teaching if the more than 80% of the population who lack college degrees could be considered for such posts. There is a much greater possibility of eliminating the unfit from teaching if the manpower shortage that that would cause could be alleviated through the use of nonprofessionals.

There are already many thousands of nonprofessionals in the schools, but they have limited utility and often serve only to make bad schools worse.

A policy and a program must be developed which transforms the nonprofessional from a supernumerary, who lends minimal support to indefensible educational practice, into an indispensable asset of a vital service. In the following chapter a philosophy and method of operation are described to revitalize not only education but all of human service. This program, "New Careers," would include persons with less than college education in multiple, meaningful roles in a wide range of different occupations and is viewed as necessary if the goal of unlimited occupational choice is to become a reality within the near future.

Providing Students With Knowledge About the Work World —A Critique and Some Suggestions

There is some strange notion, particularly prevalent in the elementary school, that children should be protected from the reality of the work world. And protected they are all the way through graduation. This is absurd! In a logical and developmental way, children should be provided relevant information about work almost from the moment they start to school. This is not likely to meet much resistance. Young children are eager to role-play adult activities. They play doctor and storekeeper with great relish, but these early efforts tend more to misinform and distort rather than develop a breadth of understanding because the effort is fragmented and is not used by the school to impart information or develop useful concepts. The storybooks that describe work functions are gross distortions. What is a child going to learn from froth like this:

> "Hello, Mr. Ringer," John called. "Hello, hello," called the driver. "Take care of my rig while I go in the house to get my coat.
>
> "Yes, if your dad and my boss say that it is O.K., we'd have a fine trip together." [22]

They certainly are not going to learn what a truckdriver's life is all about. They never will understand why most truckdrivers are not anxious to have children in the cab. They will not know anything about the teamsters' union and its complex dealings with the truckdriver. They will get no notion of the hazards of truck-driving and the prevalence of renal problems and back injuries among truckdrivers. They are not even going to get a flavor of job through the patois that always emerges from work activity. Apart from a word thrown in here and there to add color to the otherwise drab scene, Mr. Ringer the truckdriver sounds exactly like Dr. Robert-

---

[22] Josephine and Ernest Norling, *Pogo's Truck Ride,* Holt, New York, 1954.

son the M.D., Mr. Jackson the policeman, Mr. Emory the lawyer, or Mr. Fitch the grocer, and the other nonpersons children meet in their storybooks. Even when there is an effort to capture the essence of a truckdriver's life through his language the effort doesn't ring true. This passage is put in a book for the purpose of acquainting the reader with the argot of the truckdriver: "Suppose you had to drive a kidney beater like that dump truck of mine." [23]

It's just there. It lacks affect. It lacks the authenticity of dreariness of mile after mile of treacherous highway, the agony of trying to stay alert when your body demands rest, the joys and miseries of a feast-and-famine existence, the consequences of a nomad's way of life. The reader is unable to share the humor—or the heartache—that is part of all work activities. There is absence of detail. No children's book writer of today is doing for the truck-driver or any other occupation what Mark Twain was doing in the nineteenth century for the riverboat pilot. Hear Twain contrasting the mundane man of land with the man who worked the river:

> If the landsman should wish the gang-plank moved a foot farther forward, he would probably not say, "James or William, one of you push that plank forward please," but put the mate in his place and he would roar out, "Hear now, start that gang-plank for'ard! Lively now! What're you about! Snatch it! Snatch it! There! There! Aft again! Aft again! Don't you hear me? Dash it to dash! Are you going to sleep over it?" "Vast-heaving. I tell you! Going to heave it clear astern? WHERE're you going with that barrel! for'ard with it 'fore I make you swallow it, you-dash-dash-dash-dashed split between a tired mud turtle and a crippled hearse-horse!" I wished I could talk like that.[24]

So do I and every other reader, which is hardly the case with the truckdriver. There is not a clue to the knowledge that a truck-driver must have to ply his trade in the current children's books. Again contrast that with the twenty or so pages Twain used in his chapter: A "Cub" Pilot's Experience, or, Learning the River.[25] Here relevant information and authentic language add to the adventure. The Twain story could be enacted as a play, could be a launching pad for student improvisation. His is solid stuff, whereas

---

[23] Henry B. Lent, Here Come the Trucks, Macmillan Co., New York, 1954, p. 16.
[24] Mark Twain, Life on the Mississippi, Harper, New York, 1901.
[25] Ibid.

the modern writings are meringue. Do you still wonder why children aren't captivated by reading?

Those students who know truckdrivers begin to distrust the school. They know that Joe the friendly truckdriver does not always wave warmly to Pete the friendly cop—or, if he does wave, it is likely to be with one finger. The child from a truckdriver's family is apt to snicker when he reads: "Faster and faster it goes until the needle on the speedometer hits fifty. That is the legal speed limit—50 miles per hour. Although Eddy wants to get the milk to the city as quickly as he can, he never goes over the speed limit." [26]

Probably every six-year-old in this country has been in an automobile that exceeded the speed limit and often was passed by a truck going even faster. The task of building respect for law is one the school must accept. It is no easy job to perform successfully, but furnishing students with patent falsehoods and absurdities does not engender respect for law. It does, however, build disrespect for school. (How the school program can develop wholesome attitudes toward law and can develop appreciation of necessary restrictions upon individual behavior that are required of modern democratic society is discussed in detail in Chapters IV and V.)

Through role-playing, lecture, classroom discussions, and reading, the student should be made fully aware of the work world—its dimensions and its demands. The student should come to know the projections for employment in the future. He should know the skills that are required to function in certain activities and where this work is to be located.

As work changes from simple manual labor to the complicated, the technical, social, and the cerebral, the children born into poverty suffer the most from inadequate education. They, unlike the affluent, can get no meaningful information at home. Their parents are, if related at all, marginally attached to viable work activities. Only those children who from personal experience can learn something about the work in prestigious fields ever really learn what those fields are all about.

The protection of children from knowledge of the work world is a new thing. Not so long ago, when ours was essentially a family-

[26] Henry B. Lent, *op. cit.*, p. 16.

run agrarian society, very young children knew what work was all about. They discovered very early in life that farming wasn't all fun. They learned that much of the work was backbreaking, many of the smells were unpleasant, some of the skills required to do the job well were hard to come by and, as a consequence of their education, many of them ran off to more glamourous undertakings. The only real difficulty was that they hadn't had the opportunity to learn that many of the so-called glamourous activities weren't so glamourous either. The circus and its many glories were oversold: the work there was also backbreaking, unpleasant smelling, and required skills and dexterities often difficult to come by.

By the time a child is ten, eleven, twelve, he should have opportunities to experience what work is all about. Role-playing should simulate actual work experience. Youth should program data through computers. They should be involved in simulated human services. Knowledge of science, both physical and social, should be incorporated in the context of these activities. In addition to simulation, there should be many learning stations outside of the physical area of the school.

It is particularly important that persons currently employed in growth industries become actively involved in the education of young children. When children role-play doctors, an M.D. should be there to discuss and analyze their simulation. He should contrast their behavior with what he would have done, explain why a person's pulse is timed and what certain prescribed drugs are intended to accomplish. Similarly, an engineer could explain to a group of children how a bridge is built and the use to which arithmetic is put to accomplish this mighty task. An accountant can describe a business operation and the procedures used to maintain financial records.

The emphasis in the education of youth should be on diversity of activity. The child should have the opportunity to freely sample and savor the experience.

In New York they are considering locating a school in two stories of a skyscraper. The original plan calls for these two stories to be completely isolated from the rest of the building, with separate elevators to prevent the adult community from having contact with the children, and vice versa. This is wrong. The school should be distributed throughout the building at random. Students going there should be required to study in a room in, for example, the McGraw-

Hill Book Company, or in an office of the Merrill, Lynch, Pierce, Fenner & Smith investment house, or in the office of an optometrist, or in a department store or a welfare office. And all the learning that occurs in these stations should be incorporated into the total educational process.

In summary, the sequence of experience to increase a child's knowledge about work should develop in this order:

Primary Grades (ages 6–8)   The emphasis here is on role-playing and information provided through reading, storytelling, and small-group discussion. During these years there must be concentration on those basic skills that are required by the credentialed industries. In the primary grades it is expected that students be given a rudimentary orientation to the work world.

Intermediate Grades (ages 9–11)   During these years the student has developed greater sophistication about the "geography" of work. Through simulated work activities, discussion, reading, and lectures the student has become acquainted with the projections of future work and the skills that are required to perform the various projected tasks.

Junior High (ages 12–14)   By the time a student gets to junior high he should be sampling the work world. The education experiences should be deployed part of the day to work stations, and the learning obtained at these places must be incorporated into an integrated program of studies.

Senior High (ages 15–18)   In high school the student should be allowed to move into meaningful work, in which he is given responsibility and for which he is to be paid. The emphasis should be on sampling a variety of interests, while incorporating in this experience the activities that are designed to accomplish the other goals of education: democratic citizenship, culture-carrying, and personal competence.

A Closing Note on Career Choice

So much more needs to be said about education for work choice. I hope from what has been touched upon the reader has gained appreciation of some of the things that must be done. One need not be a thaumaturge to initiate change. We must begin by recognizing that education for occupational choice is a top priority issue. There will be those who will try to detour us. Some will want to reinstate ability-grouping. Some will generate new devices to determine the innate ability of people to work. Yet others will try to raise standards for admission to prestigious work, and many, whose intent defies categorization, will just add static through their ignorance and their prejudices. They can be overcome.

Much of what has been presented here applies in the face of current preoccupation with screening, evaluation, and testing. Current testing programs in the schools are not only irrelevant, but are unconscionable. The only justification for testing programs is that through such procedures deficiencies are discovered for which there is a strategy for correction. Testing programs should never be a cover for dereliction of duty. It is a far greater crime to deprive a child of the right to compete than it is to give him an opportunity to try—and fail. Even the onus of failure is displaced. It is the school that has stamped students as failures. It is the school which, in avoiding its responsibility, has stigmatized youth. It is the school which discourages honest effort, and, unless it results in notable achievement, there would be no need to curtail competition if the school would refrain from humiliating the loser. Maintaining an open educational system in which persons from all walks of life are encouraged and supported to aspire to professional status could change the character of human service, improve the quality of service to those currently deprived of adequate service, and, at the same time, offer pathways out of poverty and segregation.

CHAPTER III

An Educated Man's Responsibility to Change the Nature of Work

[In this chapter I analyze briefly current conceptualizations of work. I suggest that present formulations are basically flawed and that these flaws can be laid at the door of bankrupt scholarship. I introduce "New Careers" as a logical approach to unlimited career choice. I present in some detail a "New Careers" approach to education, and I conclude by reviewing some expert opinions about education's responsibility to the world of work.]

But I, being poor, have only my dreams;
I have spread my dreams under your feet;
Tread softly because you tread on my dreams.
        —William Butler Yeats

When lots of people are out of work, unemployment results.
        —Calvin Coolidge

What helps General Motors, helps the country.
        —Charles E. Wilson

Everybody likes and respects self-made men. It is a great deal better to be made in that way than not to be made at all.
        —Oliver Wendell Holmes

But as less and less work is required of the type that people in the . . . slums can offer, they will be increasingly isolated and exposed to unemployment, underemployment and plain exploitation. There is an ugly smell rising from the basement of the stately American mansion.   —Gunnar Myrdal

It was obdurate government callousness to misery that first stoked the flames of rage and frustration with unemployment a scourge in Negro ghettos; the government still tinkers with trivial half-hearted measures, refuses still to become an "employer of last resort." It asks the business community to solve the problem as though its past failures qualified it for future success.
        —Martin Luther King, Jr.

A good education does not attain its goal merely by preparing students for career choice in the work world as currently organized. The educator must use his knowledge and his influence to create a situation where a wide range of occupational options is truly possible. As a nation we have been trained to accept primitive notions about work. Many of us believe, to a point of nonreflection, that sufficient work is out there if only lazy louts would extend themselves to find it; or, if business was freed from governmental interferences, it would, in an orgy of appreciation, create work for all; or, work could be relegated to mechanical and electrical contrivances and man could be subsidized to pursue leisure-time activities; or, most depressingly irresponsible of all, this is a matter for divine influence, and, until that certain day, the poorly employed and poor unemployed will continue to be with us.

These primitive notions gain currency and prevalence because the allegedly educated add very little light or even heat to the subject of manpower utilization in a changing society. The academies imprison themselves in an ivory tower of Babel, unable even to communicate with each other, while outside are millions of unemployed, underemployed, misemployed, and unhappily employed. Economists contribute to the confusion. Their curious crypto-language sprinkled with "GNP's," "aggregate consumer demand," "Phillips Curve and Loop," "structural" and "functional unemployment," and "constant dollars" create an aura of discipline that isn't really there. Economists even believe their own statistics, which is unforgivable naïveté. They really believe that the Bureau of Labor Statistics periodic statement of unemployment rates is accurate. Economists as a group would have you believe that, through skill-training, the structurally unemployed could effectively be integrated into the labor force. Economists would have you believe that an increase in the growth rate of the economy (5% of GNP yearly) would lead to more purchases of goods and services (aggregate consumer demand) which, in turn, would lead to creation of jobs that would lead to vacuuming some of the currently unemployed into the lowest rungs of the work world. Economists would have you believe that a level of unemployment is necessary to avoid runaway inflation. Economists would have you believe that subsidy of business to train "hard-core" unemployables will increase employment. Economists of every persuasion have pet policies and panaceas, but, as a group, they only muddy the waters. With ex-

tremely few exceptions, the economists' concerns have nothing to
do with work *choice*. They rarely think beyond enough jobs to go
around for people currently looking for jobs. They are unwilling to
plan an ideal work situation. When they timidly dip into concern
about the *good life*, they sound more like poorly educated psychologists than the poorly educated economists that they are.

The psychologists are no help when it comes to analyzing
work. They are much more likely to ruminate about the psycho-
dynamics of those alienated from work than they are to design a
work world consistent with mental health. An apocryphal story
typifies their approach: A man knocks on the door of a psychologist, beseeching, "Please help me, I haven't eaten for days," to
which comes the reply, "You poor man, force yourself." Psychologists are preoccupied with developing tests to screen out potential
workers, or they try to "humanize" management, or they try very
ineffectively to repair the casualties of an imperfect work world.
The sum of their efforts is to justify the unjustifiable continuation
of abject poverty in an affluent world. Because they know so little
about economics or politics, psychologists are unable to even define the perimeter of the problem that needs to be addressed.

Sociologists, unlike the Cabots and Lodges, talk neither to
themselves nor to God. They justify their existence by comparing
themselves to psychologists or economists. Sociologists fail to treat
seriously the sociology of work. They, the degenerated descendants
of Mannheim, Weber, and Marx, who probed into the essence of
social structure, superficially analyze present work organizations
and offer trivial suggestions for change. They find themselves entangled in methodological concerns. They literally genuflect before
the computer. There was a time when sociologists thought big
thoughts; now they struggle to think small—and, even here, they
succeed but minimally. If anyone should ask you what success
has done to the sociologists, psychologists, and economists, answer
loudly and forthrightly—"Destroyed them"!

Political ideologies and policies reflect the bankruptcy of social
science. Concepts developed in the last century are still believed.
Unreconstructed Marxists hold to their view that alienation in work
stems from capitalist control—despite the evidence that unhappiness about work and among workers survives under Socialist or
Communist regimes. Whenever challenged on their beliefs, Marxists, if they respond at all, use the tired old excuse of football

coaches—the theory is good; it is the execution that is bad. Arrayed against the Marxists are an even more atavistic group of characters. Theirs, more a liturgy than an ideology, and stemming more from the bowels than the mind, is a proclamation of faith in business to provide jobs for all. It is sad how many of us are restricted in our perception. Jobs are not even part of the answer. Full employment is not the answer (even true full employment). The major reason that none of the conflicting ideologies arrives at a good answer is that they ask the wrong questions. The only concern of major contending political thought is for a stable, healthy *economy*. *There is no projected plan for a healthy and stable people!*

Look at some basic facts. In 1968, 77 million people were working in the United States (almost 81 million, if armed forces personnel are considered).[1] 111 million people are between the ages of 18 and 65 (probably a few million more who have not been enumerated by any census).[2]

This means that 30 million persons of work age are not working. Only a small percentage of these are unemployable because of infirmity. It is dubious that many of the employables among the 30 million have voluntarily chosen to be unemployed. Of the 77 million workers it is reasonable to assume that many, if not most, are not engaged in an occupation of preference. It is also reasonable to assume that many under the age of 18 would like to escape the yoke of adult oppression if work choice was available to them. We know very little about true choice because research in this area has always bound itself to current understanding of reality: e.g., if an uneducated person aspires to be a medical doctor he is invidiously diagnosed as unrealistic. The only way one could determine whether young mothers, for example, prefer to remain at home would be to offer them these choices:

a) Readily available, high-quality child care;

b) A wide range of work options;

c) A work ecology that is flexible in work location and hours.

The only way one could determine whether a 16-year-old black youth prefers the life of a "street hustler" would be to offer alternatives of:

---

[1] U.S. Department of Commerce, *Statistical Abstract of the United States 1968*, U.S. Government Printing Office, Washington, D.C., p. 215.

[2] U.S. Department of Commerce, *Current Population Reports,* Estimate of the Population of the United States by Age, Race and Sex, July 1, 1968, Government Printing Office, Washington, D.C., p. 5.

    a) Different forms of meaningful and personally gratifying employment with opportunities for advancement, or;

    b) Financial support for personally relevant education, or;

    c) Some combination of (a) and (b).

We have no alternative but to think big. We must recognize the backwardness and timidity of reforms that have been suggested up to now. Here I return again to the Kerner Report. I have previously criticized the recommendations for education; now look at its proposal for employment. The Commission allows: "Today there are about 2 million unemployed, and about ten million underemployed, 6.5 million of whom work full time and earn less than the annual poverty wage." [3]

The figure of twelve million identified as underemployed or unemployed excludes millions of others who are classified as unemployable or are out of the labor force but who, with different opportunities, could find work and would desire to work. Yet with the over twelve million persons who need better jobs, the Kerner Commission recommends creating one million new jobs in the public sector and one million new jobs in the private sector in the next three years. [4] The Commission recommends that private-sector employers be subsidized for their effort to create employment:

> To serve as an incentive to widespread business involvement the average amount of the reimbursement must exceed substantially the approximately $1,000 per year payment now made under federal on-the-job training programs and, for the hard-core unemployed, should at least equal the $3,500 recommended by the President in his manpower message of Jan. 23, 1968. [5]

The Commission recommends tax credits for businesses that create jobs, though there is no guarantee that this procedure will bring any benefits to the unemployed and underemployed: the Kerner Commission's recommendations would profit business.

The Commission's recommendations for employment have many weaknesses. The jumbling together of many proposals makes impossible the separation of mere nostrums from elements of true solution. But beyond the basic flaw of its eclecticism, the report has two major failings, which must be understood if we are to make

---

[3] *Report of the National Advisory Commission on Civil Disorders*, *op. cit.*, p. 414.

[4] *Ibid.*, pp. 420–423.

[5] *Ibid.*, p. 422.

progress in the world of work. First, the report is far too modest in magnitude; we need to create, in the next three years, many more than 2,000,000 jobs. Secondly, the report fails to illuminate the areas where work is most needed. The consequence of the latter failing is reliance on the private sector, although there is little likelihood of private employers creating new jobs unless they take over activities normally performed or subsidized by government.

Some historical perspective may be helpful here. As the following chart illustrates, *during the first decade of the 20th century, government expenditures contributed less than ten percent of the gross national product. Today, government expenditures are almost one-third of the GNP.* This growth has been continual and is seemingly influenced only by dramatic and total involvement in war. The party in power and its advertised ideology have seemingly little impact on the growth of government influence. (See Chart I.)

The relative growth in government spending has not been planned; it merely reflects a more complex society with unique demands. Because of lack of planning, the money has not been well spent. There has been great effort to keep spending down, to the detriment of education, health services, leisure-time facilities, air and water purification, etc. Much of the government spending has been deflected to subsidizing private industry. Selfish interests have operated against the common good. The Kerner Report suggests further opportunity for such misuse of scarce government monies.

Please remember that businessmen are not in business to create jobs. Businessmen are in business to make money (at least I, as a modest investor, hope this is true). The primary means by which business makes money is through reduction of expenses. Expenses are reduced when per-worker production increases. Management in its negotiations with organized labor has directed its fire against "featherbedding" (a term that connotes employment of minimally productive workers who enjoy job security). Business will not employ one more worker than is needed to do the job. If it needs the workers it will train them at its own expense. It is patently absurd to subsidize private employers to do what they would otherwise do without subsidy. There is a further danger— if there is not enough work for everybody and if black workers are recruited into situations where white workers previously had a monopoly, the inevitable consequence is further hostility between races. Ostensibly the Kerner Commission was opposed to height-

Chart I
Percent of Gross National Product
Attributable to Government Expenditure
1902–1966

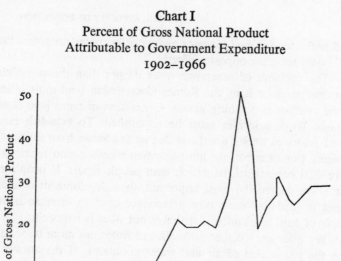

Year	GNP	Gov't Ex.	%	Year	GNP	Gov't Ex.	%
1902	24.2(a)	1.7(b)	7%	1940	100.6(a)	20.4	20%
1913	40.3(a)	3.2(b)	8%	1942	159.1(a)	45.6	29%
1922	74.0(a)	9.3	12%	1944	211.4(a)	110.0	52%
1927	96.3(a)	11.2	12%	1946	210.7(a)	79.7	38%
1932	58.5(a)	12.4	21%	1948	259.4(a)	50.1	20%
1934	65.0(a)	12.8	20%	1950	284.6(a)	70.3	25%
1936	82.7(a)	16.8	20%	1952	347.0(a)	99.8	29%
1938	85.2(a)	17.7	21%	1954	363.1(a)	111.3	31%
				1956	419.2(a)	115.8(b)	29%
				1960	504.0(c)	151.0(d)	30%
				1965	684.0(c)	205.0(d)	30%
				1966	743.0(c)	224.0(d)	30%

Source:
ª *Statistical History of the U.S.*, Stamford, Conn.: Fairfield Publ., 1965, p. 139.
ᵇ *Ibid.*, p. 172.
ᶜ U.S. Department of Commerce, *Statistical Abstracts 1968*, Washington, D.C., U.S. Government Printing Office, p. 312.
ᵈ *Ibid.*, p. 411.

ened racial tension and violence and yet it proposes programs that could only have the opposite effect!

The problem of manpower goes deeper than the superficial examination given it by the Kerner Commission (and most others in the manpower-planning game). Generation of mere jobs is not enough. Work priorities must be established. To establish manpower priorities we ask questions that up to now we have studiously avoided. For example, we must question whether auto repair is a more vital concern to the nation than people repair. If people repair is considered the most important, then development of manpower in medicine must take precedence over an increase in the supply of auto mechanics. Yet that is not what is happening.

We question whether pure air and water are more important than the production of air and water pollutants. If the answer is "Yes," then manpower planning should provide for more persons to be employed in air and water conservation and perhaps even place impediments in the path of cigarette manufacturing. A sizable tax increase on cigarettes could produce the revenue to employ persons in conservation, and might lead to a reduction of employment in the tobacco industry.

No manpower plan can hope to succeed without some definition of the goal of work in good society. There are three basic prerequisites: One, there must be enough work to go around. Two, top priority must be given to activities which are vital to the society. Three, the work must be compatible with nature.

If we maintain a nation in which there are insufficient jobs to go around, and if some jobs are so menial, so dead-end, and so low-paying that persons employed in them are locked into perpetual poverty, then even the perfect education is going to leave some people out. A good education and an imperfect employment system can only lead to many well-educated people being unable to find work.

The alternative is to educate for, and exercise leadership toward, the development of a truly full-employment ecologically defensible economy. There is certainly enough that needs to be done. Relief from insufficient air and water resources, lack of adequately staffed leisure-time facilities, deteriorating public transportation, dilapidated cities, deficient health services, paucity of services for the aged, deteriorating rural America, a decline in cultural involvement, and the correction of myriads of other problems could create employment for millions of human beings. The development of technology hasn't decreased the need for employment; it has only shifted the needs. The machine can do many of the things humans used to do to provide the basic necessities of life. The machine can take over the burden of goods-production and service, but in the process new demands are created. These demands, if the good life is to accompany affluence, have produced an almost insatiable demand for new kinds of work functions.

An Approach to the Good Life—"New Careers"

It is possible to devise a system of manpower utilization that can meet all the needs of a changing society. "New Careers" is that system.[6]

The complex of goals of the New Careers proposal includes the following:
1. A sufficient number of jobs for all persons without work.
2. The jobs to be so defined and distributed that placements exist for the unskilled and uneducated.
3. The jobs to be permanent and provide opportunity for lifelong careers.
4. An opportunity for the motivated and talented poor to advance from low-skill entry jobs to any station available to the more favored members of society.
5. The work to contribute to the well-being of society.[7]

There is grandeur and ambition in a full-blown New Careers program far beyond immediate accomplishment. But recognition of the promise is a necessary first step toward ultimate reality. Only with appreciation of what a New Careers program really means can developing programs be evaluated. New Careers in a limited sense can be viewed as a means to revitalize credentialed industries and meet acute manpower needs in specific industries. There is value in such restricted perspective—but only temporary value. The major problems of the society would be unaffected if such a narrow focus prevailed. New Careers in its broadest conceptualization has relevance to all the factors which cause alienation in modern man. Earlier it was postulated that bureaucratic intransi-

---

[6] See Pearl and Riessman, *op. cit.*, for further discussion of the "New Career" concept.
[7] Pearl and Riessman, *op. cit.*, p. 2.

gence, uselessness of person, segregation and nonredemptiveness
are major problems to which education must be directed. Work
organization is hinged to these disruptive factors. There must be a
dynamic interaction between work and educational change; New
Careers is relevant in this connection.

If more work is created than there are persons seeking employment, the greatest support of bureaucratic intransigence will be
removed. Once an employer has to compete for his worker, the
worker is in the catbird seat. No longer will he have to submit to
humiliating investigation; the reverse will more likely be the case.
The employee will be interested in the employer's Dun and Brad-
street rating, not the other way around. The employee will be in a
position to negotiate a contract based on individual concerns. Such
freedom would place enormous strain on bureaucratic restriction.

True freedom of such choice would also make redemptiveness
a possibility. Redemptiveness is always partially a function of a
full-employment-plus economy. Think back to World War II when
almost everyone, regardless of prior history or work record, contributed to the war effort. Little sixty-year-old ladies were employed as welders in the shipyards. There was almost instant
rehabilitation of skid-row derelicts. Persons with prison records
were given "fresh starts." The most-decorated war hero gained
that prominence after an almost equally distinguished record as a
juvenile delinquent.

Segregation by race and class is almost impossible to maintain in a full-employment-plus economy. The strain of worker demand overrides all other considerations. In the past segregated
ghettos broke down only when economic opportunity became more
attractive than the threat of outside oppression and when the value
of the ghetto resident as a producer overshadowed the prejudices of
those who resided outside. (Much more on this in Chapter VIII.)

Some economists (I fear the majority) insist that full employment would lead inevitably to inflation. Their argument is based
both on theory and empirical observation. It is true that an unregulated economy would undoubtedly cause an inverse relationship between employment and inflation. But unregulated economies
do not exist. Our economy is enormously regulated. It is regulated
by subsidies, tax schedules and interest rates, the nature of government expenditures, the prerequisite for government employment,
etc. The question that economists ought to ask is how can there be

full employment without inflation. The answer to that question will be found partly in economic planning and partly in education. The economics of noninflationary full employment would involve some restrictions on salary negotiations, prices, and profits. It would involve planning for a balance between monies spent on wages and goods and services available to the consumer. The educational phase would involve developing personal attributes that allow individuals to gain self-appreciation without surrounding themselves with things. This educational responsibility is dealt with further in the chapter on inter- and intrapersonal competence (Chapter VIII) and in the conclusion (Chapter IX).

Today there are among us selected populations who demonstrate the value of full-employment-plus. Certain groups are not queried about past indiscretions. Those who helped develop Hitler's rocketry are sought out by Hitler's erstwhile enemies—the Soviet Union and the United States—for related employment, with no questions asked. Other groups do not request interviews; the employers come to them. In years when college graduates were at a premium, IBM did its recruiting on the ski slopes of New England for the convenience of the Ivy League graduates they were trying to entice into this field.

New Careers hopes to accomplish, by plan, the advantages that have accrued, by accident, to some lucky few. New Careers is a means whereby unlimited options restricted previously to a tiny minority could be extended to the vast majority.

There are many gains from a New Careers program that are not readily apparent on a superficial glance. Through New Careers the education of poor children can be greatly enhanced. Earlier I criticized the approach to education of very young children because of its colonialism. I took issue with the allegation that poor children needed special preschool preparation. Poor children do, however, need support. They do have a handicap that no amount of school improvement will rectify—and that is their poverty. One major barrier to the education of poor children is the condition of despair in which they are immersed. Their parents, their relatives, their older siblings, the adults they meet in the street are locked into poverty with no conceivable avenues out. When children are in a daily press for survival, when they are surrounded by defeat, then education, regardless of excellence, must become in time, for most, a peripheral concern. At this point only two alternatives can be seriously entertained—either the child is totally removed from that environment and placed in a climate suitable for learning, or the atmosphere of despair in the environment is drastically altered. New Careers has relevance for both alternatives. By the creation of a full-employment-plus economy, *hope,* the vital ingredient that is lacking among the adult poor today, could be restored and, with it, the psychological support for children. For the small number of children (rich and poor) for whom home is intolerable, "New Careerists" could be assigned to adequately staff group life in youth homes. (There has been some minimal effort to establish such homes for "runaways" but these suffer from lack of funds and lack of well-trained staff.)

New Careers offers much more than the indirect relief from bureaucratic strictures, segregation, uselessness of person, and non-redemptiveness that come as a result of full-employment plus. Inherent in the concept is improvement of human service. A partial explanation of these distortions of life is inadequate staffing. Persons are treated bureaucratically when heavy work loads preclude more humane treatment. False economics contribute to other inhumanities. New Careers can be justified only on the basis of improving leisure-time facilities, health care, education, cultural pursuits, and the ability of man to cope with a complicated society. It is because these changes are so critical that political support for New Careers can be mobilized. Without these improvements it is doubtful if life in the future will be worth living.

New Careers will, when fully implemented, lead to changes in every aspect of higher education. The typical higher education procedure, consisting of a series of remote and unrelated experiences, will have to give way to a more coherent and organic relationship of theory and practice. The variety of disciplines and content areas of college departments will have to be recognized for what they really are: abstractions of convenience which, through the years, have outlived their usefulness. Through a connection between education and work, the student will have the opportunity to use what he knows. The New Careers idea is, however, not a mere updating of an apprenticeship model. It contains all the advantages of a good education. Modern technology and the utilization of modern media and transportation readily permit the instructor to go to the student. The work of tomorrow will require intellectual sophistication. It will be primarily mind work. Thus the training within the New Careers setting must stress conceptual development, analytical ability, abstract thinking, permissible inference, evaluation of experience—and thus should be consonant with the aims and emphasis of justifiable higher education.

The New Careers notion requires a new approach to instruction. In traditional education the teachers are far removed from the practice. But, because so much of the training in New Careers is job-situated, the practitioner can become involved in teaching. This is not only possible but desirable if there is ever to be a close relationship between institutions of learning and practice in the field. A variety of organizational forms can be used to bring the practitioner into instruction. One form that should be seriously considered is full-fledged faculty status for agency personnel. The job-related instruction should be considered a part of the faculty work load. The teaching practitioner should have all the rights and privileges of any faculty member. He should be able to exercise power to alter curriculum and instructional organization. If easy transfer between field and university staff is brought about, periodic change between stations may serve to keep communication open between the agency and the school, and may also prod both to change when change is necessary.

New Careers is no simple remedy. It is complicated. It requires educated leadership. In the past few years legislation has been passed which could speed up the development of the concept.[8] Progress to date has been agonizingly slow. Not the least reason for the sluggish rate is the lack of understanding of those designated to administer the program. Not too infrequently New Careers is merely a new label for an old, unsuccessful program. Even the best-designed program could be a New Careers development program only because an essential ingredient—more jobs than there are people searching for work—is not a feature of the existing legislation. But, even to qualify as New Careers development, the program must contain some critical features, the very least being:

1) The entry positions are available to all without either entrance requirements or disqualification because of prior record.

---

[8] At the federal level the Scheuer amendment to the Economic Opportunity Act represents such legislation.

2) The entry position is permanent and the worker is protected by seniority and has all other fringe benefits of a permanent employee.

3) The entry position beginning salary is pegged at a level far above that designated as standard for poverty.

4) The entry worker is guaranteed horizontal mobility in the form of salary increments for years of service.

5) The entry worker is provided training to enable him to become more proficient in his current assignment.

6) Vertical mobility is provided in the form of readily negotiated equidistant rungs in a career ladder.

7) The vertical mobility must be totally open-ended. The ambitious and talented worker should be able to advance to the highest rung in the ladder without either leaving the agency or incurring inordinate educational expense.

8) The training the employee receives on-the-job must not only be given college credit but the credit must be applicable to degree programs in the college and university. This step is necessary if the employee is to have maximum mobility to transfer to related fields; this also minimizes the possibility of imprisonment within the agency.

9) The education beyond job training must be tailored in form, style, content, and logistics to the special circumstance of the employee. The evaluation of student performance must also depart from the ritualistic and static procedures currently used in colleges and universities (e.g., an ability to find the "correct" response in a multiple-choice machine-scored examination).

New Careers, to be successful, will require carefully planned tactics and strategy. Education, which should be the fastest growing of all industries, which is the most critical for national survival, and which is the most plagued by obvious inadequacies, is a good taking-off place for an examination in some depth of the concept.

New Careers in Education

As the goals of education are further extended, the need for more persons in teaching roles will become increasingly clear. In the last chapter I suggest that one person in a teaching role to no more than ten students is probably the optimum arrangement. Given a world of increasing population and given the need for persons to go to school for much longer periods of life, it is possible that 20 or even 30 million people will be sought for teaching roles within 25 years in the United States alone.

These numbers can be successfully employed only if we reorganize what teachers do and how they learn to do it. The good school will require teachers with diverse competencies. It will be necessary to generate a means by which different skills can be categorized if that complex endeavor is not to break down into a shambles of aimless chaos.

New Careers is based on the assumption that the activities a teacher is called upon to perform range from complex matters requiring many years of formal training to activities that a person with limited training, skill, and experience can do quite well. There is an additional assumption that skills demanded of the expert teacher can be attained through life experiences which are at least commensurate with the learning gained at certified schools of education. (It is not beyond possibility that the *one* place these skills cannot be attained is *in* the schools of education as presently constituted.) There should be clear definition of skills required by persons at every level. The entry-level nonprofessional should be distinguishable from the highly trained professional in the following areas:

1) The extent of substantive knowledge. The professional should know more about the world of work, the limitations of nature, democratic principles and practices, the essences of culture, and the factors which impede or assist healthy human growth than could be expected from an entry-level nonprofessional. The professional should know more than the nonprofessional about the nature of skill development, especially those skills so vital to the "credential society."

2) The ability to relate to human beings. Education requires a trusting relationship between student and teacher—those at the top of the ladder must be more responsible and trustworthy than those at the bottom.

3) The ability to manage effectively and democratically a large number of students and staff. Obviously this skill should be more developed the higher one is on the teaching career ladder.

4) The ability to empathize with individual problems. If education is to rise from the low state to which impersonal bureaucratic organization has brought it, then those in teaching capacities must

be competent to accommodate individual needs and aspirations. The position a teacher holds in the hierarchy should be partially a function of his skill in drawing upon the strengths of students and staff.

5) The willingness to assume the responsibility of leadership. Those at the top of the ladder must have much more latitude of choice in decision-making than is allowed those at the bottom. This latitude cannot merely be a privilege of rank. If The Peter Principle of Incompetence is ever to be circumvented, then new standards for promotion must be established. Promotion to higher stations must become a function of demonstrated responsible leadership. The prime criterion for responsible leadership must be accountability. The measure of a decision must be the logic and evidence on which it is based.

6) The ability to evaluate educational practice. To overcome the meandering that so typifies current educational effort, there must be continuous assessment of programs. The greater the ability of the teacher to determine whether or not the educational activity is on course toward its goal (all other things considered), the higher the station he should occupy.

7) The ability to map and implement strategy. A true professional should be able to right the course of a process gone astray and introduce innovations into the activity without total disruption. The ability to perform strategic roles is but another way to distinguish the professional from the nonprofessional.

Any institution preparing persons to teach must justify its efforts by its ability to increase competence in these areas. At present the kindest evaluation of schools of education might suggest that they offer the graduate "delusional competence." The student is led to believe that he is prepared to teach, only to find after a day or two, in a slum school particularly, how completely mistaken he was. One short-changed, outraged teacher had this to say of one of the more prestigious institutions for higher learning: "Harvard assumptions, methods and approaches simply did not prepare me at all and are totally irrelevant to the lower class urban Negro children I am teaching." [9]

Through New Careers it would be possible to recruit hundreds

---

[9] Betty Levy, "An Urban Teacher Speaks Out," *Harvard Graduate School of Education Association Bulletin,* Vol. X, No. 2, Summer 1965.

of thousands of persons from underrepresented populations—black, Spanish speaking, poor whites, American Indians—into teaching. Almost overnight these persons could be assigned to a station commensurate with their ability, and could advance to positions of greater prestige and authority once they demonstrated the ability to take on more challenging duties.

There is an extremely vulgar and anti-intellectual distortion of the New Career concept, which reflects thinly veiled class elitism or racial bias and goes something like this: "I don't care what you say, I want to have a professionally trained medical doctor perform brain surgery on me and not some six-weeks-trained aide, and I also want a professional teacher and not an aide to teach my child." Nowhere in the New Careers theory is it even suggested that persons with limited ability be entrusted with sensitive responsibilities. It is always assumed that a highly trained staff will supervise the entire program. Moreover, if surgery is to be used as an analogy, an attack on New Careers in education makes little sense. There are many lesser trained persons working on a surgical team; without them the surgeon would be unable to function. Yet the surgical team is, however, not a good example of New Careers in action either. The lower-echelon members of the team have nowhere to go. They are neither evaluated for competence beyond their existing duties nor are they offered training to advance to a higher station. Medicine is particularly remiss in not offering intermediate positions between support staff and the prestigious M.D.

The New Careers notion of higher education minimizes the risk of professional incompetence. In New Careers, problems encountered in the job are used in the training process. Having defined the goals of education, the practitioner is helped to gain the skills needed to attain those goals. Under the New Careers concept, persons ascend in rank according to their proficiency; this is the only consideration for promotion.

New Careers is not a call for opening up the bottom of the profession so that the untrained can sneak in. It is primarily a call for upgrading the entire profession and can be expected to fully succeed only when the professional in education functions as a true professional. New Careers cannot be used to clutter up an already untidy educational scene. The nonprofessional *must* not be used for things that don't need doing or in activities that could be as well performed by a child.

The New Careerist should never be employed as a "cop" in the hallways. Once a school employs policemen the school ceases to be a school and all its functions are distorted. If education becomes so corrupted that students violently react to it then the underlying precipitating conditions need immediate correction. Failing to act responsibly at this point can only worsen the situation.

New Careerists should not be employed to collect milk money. Eight-year-olds can collect milk money and, in the process, learn many things consistent with legitimate aims of education.

An illustration of a New Careers sequence in education might help here:

Entry Level—Teacher Aide

Prerequisite: Six weeks on-the-job training or equivalent life experience.

Duties: Junior member of teaching team. Performs those duties assigned by team manager. Duties could range from clerical functions to classroom instruction. The aide would be expected to tutor individual students, lead small group discussions, supervise older students working with younger students, help students decorate a blackboard, work with students in programmed instruction, correct papers, and facilitate individual student inquiries.[10]

Postservice Training: Training on the job for which college credits are received (substantive content, classroom management, and interpersonal competence), concurrent with skill obtained from more formal seminars should be offered the New Careerists to advance their knowledge about social science theory, communication skills, interpersonal skills, and course content. The New Careerists should be encouraged to round out their education by taking liberal arts courses in the evening and during the summer.

Promotional Opportunities: Eligible for teacher assistant if trainee completes prerequisites or Aide II—more responsibilities in above-described duties.

Salary: Aide I —$4,200–$5,800
            Aide II—$4,900–$6,500

---

[10] In earlier works, e.g., *New Careers for the Poor, op. cit.,* Frank Riessman and I suggested more menial activities for low level positions but I have become convinced by my more recent work that minimally trained professionals possess capacity for service far beyond my original expectations.

Teacher Assistant

Prerequisites: Two years of appropriate college work or two years of service as aide with 36 units of successfully completed college credits for skills in theory and knowledge obtained on the job, or life experiences of a nature such as to obtain the skills required for the job.

Duties: Intermediate member of teaching team. Supervises teacher aides, conducts classroom activities which require substantial knowledge of subject matter. Helps plan lesson activities. Has complete responsibility for class under especially defined circumstances. Works individually with students who require special attention and assists in the evaluation of classroom activity.

Postservice Training: Continuation of program designed for aide— additional college work in theory, content areas, and liberal arts education.

Promotional Opportunities: Eligibility for teaching associate if completes prerequisites or Assistant II, which assumes more of above described responsibilities.

Salary: Assistant I —$5,800–$7,600
Assistant II—$6,500–$8,000

Teacher Associate

Prerequisite: Four years of appropriate college work or two years of service as assistant and 72 units of college work, all or partially obtained from credit offered for skills learned on the job, or life experience of such nature to instill the competence demanded by the job.

Duties: Senior member of teaching team. Principal tactician with responsibility for assigning and supervising lower-echelon staff. Specialist in substantive knowledge. Trainer of lower-level staff. Authority responsible for those decisions which must be made on day to day basis.

Promotional Opportunities: Eligibility for teacher upon successful completion of prerequisites.

Salary: $8,000 to $12,000

Teacher

Prerequisite: Master's Degree in Education or equivalent field, three years of service as an associate with 48 units on consultation supervision, evaluation, and continual specialization.

Duties: Chief strategist on teaching team. Responsible for planning of instruction and evaluation of long-range effects. The field instructor of aide, assistant, and associate. Consultant to lower-echelon staff. Specialist in content area (guest lecturer of teaching team), scholar in residence, and administration in context of an organization governed by democratic principles.

Postservice Training: Advanced degree program in school offering programs to increase above-mentioned competence.

Promotional Opportunities: Higher-level, administrative responsibility in local, state, or national structures, transfer to university setting.

Salary: $11,000 to $17,000

New Careers and the Quality of Teacher Preparation

The deficiencies of teacher preparation is a subject worthy of a book, and, as such, extends beyond what can be covered here. But a good portion of the atrocity of education is attributable to the education prospective teachers receive and therefore *something* must be said about this subject. It is not only the teachers of the disadvantaged who are ill-prepared for their assignments at the present time; many teachers are unable to provide the stimulation that students from all walks of life demand and deserve. One cause of teacher failure is the aimlessness of the system. Teachers do not have a clear picture of educational goals. In their training they have been subjected to platitude or to philosophies that were relevant, if at all, to a more primitive society. Very little is taught in schools of education that equips the future teacher to assist students to make career choice or to be committed to, and competent in, democratic decision-making, or to become culture-carriers, or to achieve psychological health.[11]

---

[11] Teacher training has vexed many concerned educators. The recently enacted Educational Professional Development Act is one manifestation of concern; the AACTE publication, *Teachers for the Real World*, Washington, D.C., 1969, is another. The author has some modest involvements with both of these developments.

The structure of schools of education also contributes to low-level teaching. It is not merely that schools of education know not what they do (and only a Jesus can excuse that); they don't know *how* to do what they know not what to do. As a consequence, many teachers energetically pursue policies that drive students from academic involvement, and, contrary to the Dr. Panglosses and Pollyannas who abound among us, the situation is getting worse.

Teacher education is organized to produce inadequate teachers. A New Careers approach can improve many of the negative characteristics of teacher-training programs. Teacher education fails because:

1) *The preparation is too remote from classroom practice.* A New Careers approach places the prospective teacher into immediate contact with the student. There is nothing fraudulent or artificial about the experience. Very quickly the New Careerist is able to discover if teaching is "his thing." He further has the option to choose another field before he has invested so heavily in education that he can no longer back out.

2) *Teacher education is based on low-level theory packaged to be applicable to the classroom.* New Careers places the challenges first. The theory is a direct result of problems encountered, and while this constitutes no ironclad guarantee of better and more usable theory, it at least increases the probability of such events occurring.

3) *Teacher education is plagued with a spoiled image and thus has to be content with the culls of the university system.* With New Careers it is possible for education to get first choice. The job first, education later feature of New Careers could at one level lure virile, alert males into elementary schools and attract others with talent who are discouraged by the dreary courses required for certification; and at another level it would make it possible for women to gain posts in administration where they are greatly underrepresented.

4) *Education draws teachers from too narrow a section of the population.* New Careers could attract into the field all those groups now underrepresented. While this has obvious significance for disadvantaged youth there is also promise of the recruitment of persons who could resonate to those middle-income white youth who are tuned to a different drummer but who aren't about to submit to a School of Education ritual.

5) *There is a lack of definition of the teacher role, and, included within it, are activities that the uneducated could well do; but also included is the repertoire of tasks that require enormous sensitivity, precisely defined skills, and thorough understanding.* The call for differentiated staff in schools, which is a vital, underlying component of a New Careers strategy, offers promise for revitalization of the training teachers. The practitioner can, in this altered set-up, receive training which is specifically designed for current responsibilities or for assignments which are imminent. The trainee is no longer reduced to passive dependence. It is difficult to have dialogue with the "expert" if he has all the experience on his side and the prospective teacher has only vague and growing doubts on his. Training and education built into a meaningful, active involvement with students can be tailored, not only to the specific duties to be performed, but also to the unique attributes of the trainee. In a New Careers set-up, individualized training is possible and a program can be developed in which "different strokes" can be fitted to the style of "different folks."

6) *Teacher education does not develop interpersonal skills.* It is impossible to develop much interpersonal competence encapsulated in a School of Education. There is very little contact with those persons the prospective teacher will have to "make it" with in the "real world." There is little meaningful contact with the children he will be required to teach. There is no contact with the administrators or the teachers with whom he is expected to work. Interpersonal competence is a multidimensional thing. There is no assurance that a warm, healthy relationship with students will necessarily ingratiate the teacher with his principal or with his peers. The ability to establish a relationship with one group of teachers may automatically put a teacher on the "outs" with another group. Only through meaningful involvement as a functioning member of a team is it possible to isolate interpersonal problems that should be rectified, and then, all too often, it is too late. New Careerists start in the school. The problem of relating to other people can be confronted as they arise. This mechanism for dealing with the problems here and now importantly distinguishes New Careers from more traditional training.

7) *Teacher education is a fragmented conglomerate of courses, resulting in much duplication and incompleteness.* The on-the-job feature of New Careers training offers a promise of integration of

all experiences. The New Careerist is in a position to evaluate the knowledge he receives, since it has immediate testability. He also is able to demand specific support when he encounters a situation he is not prepared to handle.

8) *Teacher education in a university setting defies rigorous evaluation.* A student in college takes many courses and participates in many experiences. Many years elapse before the student is asked to use the knowledge and skills he has acquired. It is virtually impossible to sort out these experiences and determine how much each experience has contributed to teaching skills. It is also impossible to assess the value of the total experience, since many other activities have entered into the life of the prospective teacher that could influence teaching ability. As a consequence, teachers are forced to submit to required activities of dubious merit, and change generally takes the form of accretion, i.e., the addition of more and more courses. Evaluation of New Careers training is much more readily accomplished than a university-based program. The value of an offering can be ascertained almost immediately. The evaluation can be ongoing and, if deficiencies are discovered, the training process can be repaired.

A New Careers intrusion into the present educational system is certain to create trauma. The traditionally prepared teacher will be challenged by the presence of the New Careerist. In many instances the teacher will be unwilling to delegate less demanding tasks to lower-echelon staff because it is only in such matters as bulletin-board design that the professional teacher has feelings of competence. Because teachers have been so badly trained many are forced to take refuge in minimal functions, and once they are liberated from them they are hopelessly lost. When this happens the New Careerist develops a disrespect for his superior. He accurately perceives that the higher-placed person has no more skills than he and he resents the differential in wage and status. If, as is so often the case, the higher-stationed person is white and the lower-placed person is black or brown the resentment is even more intense.

The realities of deficient teacher-training programs should not be used as an excuse for steering clear of New Careers experiments. But recognition of reality can reduce the pain that always accompanies radical reform. The programs should initially involve only the most receptive and capable teachers. This group, in turn, can be leaders in other programs as the idea gathers momentum. The professional teachers who are to be involved in New Careers programs must be given special training prior to and concurrent with the program. The idea that training is a process which never stops should be heavily stressed in the orientation of the program; otherwise disaster is almost inevitable.

The Politics of New Careers

All change is political. Not to understand that is to give away self-determination and allow others to make all relevant decisions. There has been sufficient political support for New Careers for some beginning legislation. The political support for New Careers has been more the allure of its rhetoric than the impact of a constituency. New Careers has been picked up in the backwash of legislative activity for civil rights and as a response to civil unrest. The future of New Careers is unclear.

The New Careers notion has been presented in detail here in a discussion of school activity designed to keep students eligible for work choice. New Careers could have been presented as vital to all other goals of education. In future chapters, New Careers will again be referred to as an important part of a strategy to help students become politically, culturally, and interpersonally competent.

There are many political obstacles to a New Careers strategy for manpower in education. Arrayed against it are powerful constituencies. Local school administrators tend to be cautious, often preferring the impossibility they know to the terror of some unknown venture. This, they delude themselves, is hard-headed realism. The diamondlike quality of their heads may be uncontestable; the reality is something else again. Teacher associations view New Careers with suspicion. They see in it the possible loss of hard-won standards and even a threat to already low wages. Parents, succumbing to the idea that only persons with advanced college degrees should be allowed into the classrooms, fear that their children's education will suffer if lesser qualified persons instruct their children (this is especially true for minority parents whose children have always been cheated educationally). But the greatest obstacle to New Careers is to be found in the university. The university is both resistent to change and sluggish even in those rare instances when change is deemed necessary. Yet it is here, where ignorance of current school problems is most prevalent, that all power for credentialing teachers resides. And if by some miracle a spark of life flared up spontaneously in some remote institution of higher education, national certifying committees, governed by manuals of operation, and state departments of education would be there to try to snuff out that spark.

The opposition to New Careers is powerful but not all-powerful. There are countervailing forces. It would be a tragic mistake to succumb to the notion that all is lost. None of the forces opposing New Careers is monolithic. There are administrators who have both courage and vision and they, though limited in numbers, stay in there. Some leaders in teacher associations see the paraprofessional, not as a threat but as an ally. Many minority parents want minority teachers and administrators and see in New Careers a means by which their desires can be attained without the loss of quality instruction. And even in those citadels of complacency—the schools of education—students allied with a significant number of faculty strive to bring about relevancy. With model programs serving as beachheads, a constituency can materialize.

Meanwhile, wandering in the wilderness are the so-called experts. To insure that students have a wide range of work options in a world that places formal education as the prime requirement for work eligibility, many changes must take place in education. Four major reformations have been suggested in the last two chapters. These are, to recapitulate: the grouping of students heterogeneously, the priming of teachers to expect success, the utilization of technological advancement, and the marked reduction of class size. However, continued eligibility in school is not in itself sufficient for career choice; the student must also know something about what is demanded by various endeavors. Here, too, education fails badly. It would be difficult enough to develop a wide range of options in the world of work if everyone recognized the importance of this goal. It becomes even harder to attain the goal swimming upstream. Much of the writing that either reflects or influences educational programs and policy runs counter to enhancing occupational choice.

Here is but a smattering of the outpouring of alleged experts in the field. In a book designed to assist teachers with maladjusted students, the author advocates ability grouping:

> Another approach to fitting the academic environments to pupils' varied talents is ability grouping, sometimes called homogeneous

or cluster grouping. This consists of placing children of similar academic potential in the same class. For instance, if a ninth grade is composed of six sections of students, those with the best past performance in mathematics will be assigned together in one classroom, those with the next best records to another, and so on until the least successful pupils are placed in the sixth section.[12]

Imagine the self-image of those in the sixth group. Whatever other adjustment problems these students might have had, they definitely will be maladjusted to the world of work. The author baldly recommends changing the environment through ability grouping for students, without any reflection on its possible negative consequences. There is no logically developed defense for the proposal or reference to any body of data to support the recommendation. Teachers are already disposed to sorting students; they need no further encouragement, particularly that which offers dubious procedures as if they are solidly moored to fact.

Look now how another "scholar" communicates an expectation about the disadvantaged: "Because of the slum children's emotional immaturity, certain of the prizes that appeal to them would never do for more sophisticated or mature children"; [13] or, "Children of the slums are often anxious or compulsive or both. Too much freedom may increase their anxiety"; [14] or, "We know that the attention span and degree of concentration of disadvantaged children are less than those of brighter people." [15]

Wow! There it is, out there for all to see. An expert—a teacher of teachers—instructs that slum youth should be prejudged as dull, immature, devoid of the ability to concentrate, and requiring protection from "freedom." Doesn't that conjure up images of the plantation master schooling his son for his imminent duties? Maybe now the antagonism of slum residents and students against the school becomes easier to understand.

The expert who recommends sorting or prejudgment of stability buttresses the argument for programs that limit career choice. There is another danger, and that comes from the expert who is silent about education's responsibility for career choice.

---

[12] R. Murray Thomas, *Aiding the Maladjusted Child—A Guide for Teachers,* David McKay Co., New York, 1967, p. 46.
[13] Helen F. Storen, *The Disadvantaged Early Adolescent—More Effective Teaching,* McGraw Hill, New York, 1968, p. 16.
[14] *Ibid.,* p. 18.
[15] *Ibid.,* p. 70.

John Holt is such an expert. He is an angry and perceptive critic of education. He has filtered his teaching experiences and has correctly identified much of the destructiveness of schools. He is right when he says that schools destroy youth by engendering fear of failure. He is correct when he attacks the essential dishonesty of schools.

He is correct when he accuses schools of rigidity, irrelevance, unnecessary restrictions, lack of spontaneity, adult domination, and coerciveness. But then he throws up his hands. He would not have teachers play a vital leadership role in changing this condition. John Holt would have each child determine his own educational goals: "Since we can't know what knowledge will be most needed in the future, it is senseless to try to teach it in advance. Instead we should try to turn out people who love learning so much and learn so well that they will be able to learn whatever needs to be learned." [16] He thinks that "School should be a place where children learn what they most want to know, instead of what we think they ought to know." [17] He ridicules a leadership role in teaching: "The most we can do is try to help, by letting him know roughly what is available and where he can look for it. Choosing what he wants to learn and what he does not is something he must do for himself." [18] He concludes: "In short, the school should be a great smorgasbord of intellectual, artistic, creative, and athletic activities from which each child could take whatever he wanted, and as much as he wanted or as little." [19]

John Holt is a good man, according to the way we all measure the goodness of man. He agrees with me about most things. He is for peace and freedom, and he is against poverty. In fact, he pretty much contradicts himself by his advocacy of social principles and his recommendations that a student should choose his own learning. The school he favors could not allow a student to choose that learning which would predispose him to be a racist, a jingoist, a waster of resources, or a selfish accumulator of wealth.[20] He thinks that

[16] John Holt, *How Children Fail*, Dell Publishing Co., New York, 1964, p. 177.

[17] *Ibid.*, p. 175.

[18] *Ibid.*, p. 179.

[19] *Ibid.*, p. 180.

[20] John Holt, "Education for the Future," in *Social Policies for America in the Seventies*, Robert Theobald (ed.), Doubleday, Garden City, New York, 1968.

persons can be educated to be above these frailties "By creating in the school an atmosphere of freedom, respect, and trust within which true kindness and generosity can be expected to grow." [21] When Holt considers peace, conservation, an end to racism and greed he ridicules the notion that schools should "Produce a generation and race of citizens who will understand that these things must be done and a certain body of experts who will have the skills to do them, the real job is altogether different. It has little or nothing to do with content, curricula or learning, and a great deal to do with the human heart and spirit." [22]

Here John Holt exhibits a combination of arrogance and anti-intellectual distortion of equalitarianism. Because he could not eliminate fear of failure in his classroom he assumes it cannot be done. Because that which is now taught in school is irrelevant he believes that it is impossible to identify relevance and teach it. I disagree! I believe that there is a body of knowledge to be taught to prevent racism and provincialism. I further believe that if future leaders are to be more adequate than the present crop we have elevated to august positions, then not only must we train for such leadership, but, even more importantly, we must also educate and train an *entire population* to recognize good leadership. I suspect that because of the failure of current education, Thomas Jefferson, were he alive today, would have been in the dock with Benjamin Spock, and Benjamin Franklin would be so busy warding off the House Un-American Activities Committee that he couldn't even get down to his serious concern with scientific and political business. But I stray afield; my major quarrel with Holt is the way in which he views the future of work. About work Holt believes: "There is likely to be less and less of it; what there is, is likely to seem less and less like work . . . today. Of those who do work, a great many find in their work little or no cause for self respect. We can expect this to become more so, not less." [23]

When it comes to the helping service endeavors that Holt does view as continuing to be important, he surmises: "Not many people, certainly not enough people will be interested in doing the kind of work." [24]

---

[21] *Ibid.*, p. 178.
[22] *Ibid.*, p. 175.
[23] *Ibid.*, p. 181.
[24] *Ibid.*, p. 184.

This, to me, is utter nonsense. I take issue with the thesis that work is being eliminated in modern society. To the contrary, I argue that a good society will always create necessary and rewarding work for its citizens.

Underlying the New Careers proposal is the thesis that a truly people-oriented society must provide at least as many opportunities for work as there are potential members in the labor force. . . .

There are many who argue that creating work opportunities is futile. The machine eats up jobs faster than man can produce them. This position runs counter to the New Careers approach. Advocates of New Careers foresee a future where work remains essential and, if anything, predict that the work needs of a society will increase.

Technological change will make education more and more a necessity for all segments of the population. Education will become a process that never stops. Accepting that assumption, there will be an ever-increasing demand for the services of adequately trained teachers.

Projected population growth will increase the need for health, welfare, and recreation specialists. The greatest population growth will occur among the very young and the very old. Both these populations require maximum medical attention, and educational, recreational, and welfare services.

If one goes beyond the myopic preoccupations of national concerns and takes cognizance of the world scene one faces the prospect of a world population doubling every thirty-five years. The projected needs for personnel to provide adequate health, education, welfare, and recreational support to this population is staggering.

If there is to be more leisure time in the future, if there is to be a shorter work life (earlier retirement), a shorter work year (more vacation and holidays), and even a shorter work week as some social planners request (and there appear to be some harbingers of these changes in recent labor-management negotiations), the need for recreation workers will increase proportionately. It is absolutely impossible to conceive of leisure without service personnel to make that leisure enjoyable. Music teachers, bowling instructors, boat repairmen, fishing guides, park rangers, and naturalists, etc. must be recruited to tend to the pleasure seekers. At the present time the thought of retirement is repugnant to many because of the lack of outlets available to the superannuated employee.

Every technological change that relieves the need for work in mechanical service or products produced in industry actually increases the need for manpower in human service! Every technological change that reduces the need for work in mechanical service and products-producing industries makes possible a greater investment of manpower in human service!

If the New Careers proposal is relevant to today's manpower problems, it's even more meaningful for tomorrow. If there is applicability to the United States, there is even greater potential in the newly emerging Asian and African nations.[25]

My disagreement with John Holt about a society's potential to create work is certainly debatable, since no society yet developed by man could be called truly people-oriented. John Holt is not on safe ground when he concludes that in the future people will be less able to gain self-respect from work than is now the case. He can only conjecture whether "many people will like" to be in careers that serve other humans. However, having been involved in a great many of the New Careers projects, I have found that the desire to help other humans is almost universal. Work in these areas can provide the worker a feeling of self-respect. There are other gratifications as well. Human service offers the helper a sense of usefulness, competence, and identity with the fraternity of man. Moreover, it *is* possible to design human-service operations so that almost everyone *can* play a useful role.

In league with John Holt is another celebrated critic of education—Edgar Friedenberg. He, too, quite rightly excoriates present practices of education, but after the flensing he offers little to replace what he has, with verbal assault, destroyed. He accurately disputes the excesses and corruption of the "credential society":

> We demand that the credential also tell us something positive about the incompetence that we require as a part of the candidate's qualifications—about what Veblen calls his trained incapacity, or a horse trader calls being well-broken.[26]

He amplifies the extent of the distortion of competence:

> A social worker must not only understand the dynamics of social stratification and of group work; he must be incapable of turning the poor on and using his skills to organize them into an effective political action group if he is to earn a good credential.[27]

There is power in Friedenberg's writing. Were I dean of a school of social work or education I would cower and plead

---

[25] Arthur Pearl, "New Careers: One Solution to Poverty," *ibid.*, pp. 81–82.

[26] Edgar Friedenberg, "Status and Role in Education," *The Humanist*, Sept., Oct. 1968, p. 15.

[27] *Ibid.*, p. 15.

"enough." But concern with corruption just isn't going to do it. The world Edgar Friedenberg hates—I hate. The petty bureaucrats who run it he despises and I, too, despise them. But his strengths are, as with all of us, also his weaknesses. He is, above all, an aristocrat. Work just doesn't concern persons preoccupied with grander things. And yet for most of us, work must come first. Only after we become economically secure can we consider other things—only then can we become concerned with art, music, and other cultural interests. What Friedenberg won't fully appreciate is that the enforced uselessness that ensues when a person is denied a credential leaves that person "up-tight." The restriction of dislocation from work hurts at least as much as inadequate preparation for honest interaction hurts the teacher in the classroom. Without hope for work involvement the poor are beaten down into apathy and sporadic rebellion. Without adequate preparation for available work the condition that Friedenberg describes reaches epidemic proportions: "Calm, gentle, long haired boys arouse genuinely pathological hatred in physical education teachers." [28]

One gets the impression from reading Friedenberg and Holt that they fervently believe that if we all ignored work—it would go away.

We turn now from the ethereal and look to the grubby-handed, hard-nosed innovators in the field, and we do not fare much better. Fantini and Weinstein in their book, *The Disadvantaged: Challenge to Education,*[29] decry the "phoney" school with its "antiseptic," "semiantiseptic," "nonessential," and "remote" curriculum. They want the school "with the real" to be for everybody:

> In fact, the assumption could be made that middle-class students fail to identify with the conventional subject matter curriculum because it is "phoney" to them also. Jobs and popularity are more real to them than goals which are defined solely in academic subject matter terms.[30]

Like so many others they see a basic truth:

> Our society, therefore, does not foster the social and economic mobility to the extent that we have believed true, nor does the school play an extensive role in fostering whatever mobility does occur.[31]

---

[28] *Ibid.*, p. 17.
[29] Mario Fantini and Gerald Weinstein, *The Disadvantaged: Challenge to Education,* Harper and Row, New York, 1968.
[30] *Ibid.*, p. 163.
[31] *Ibid.*, p. 169.

Edgar Friedenberg doesn't like the Fantini and Weinstein book. He dislikes what he calls its optimistic sentimentality. He reacts particularly violently to suggestions in the book that the disadvantaged should be shaped by the system in social behavior and language. He pooh-poohs their approach to changing the schools. They advocate that change agents funded by outside sources of power be introduced into the school. One of these agents (Type A) should be attached to administration, and the other (Type B) should be placed in instruction. They recommend that the real purpose of the agent—the introduction of change—be kept from the school personnel.

Friedenberg comments:

> As they described the game of Agent A and Agent B further I saw that the Ford Foundation must think of itself as the Cat in the Hat and that Agent A and B are really things turned loose in the school to make it fun on a rainy day.[32]

True, there is a James Bond quality to their secret agents and maybe the book should have been entitled "To Academia With Love," but Friedenberg is being overly snide. Fantini and Weinstein have written a useful book. Their approach to change may be callow and unreal. But all approaches to system-change designed now will, perforce, be insufficiently developed. Only as we learn from their inadequacies will we ever determine if the situation is really as hopeless as Friedenberg would have us believe.

Fantini and Weinstein define as one of the four major goals of education a work career.[33] They are extremely critical of current approaches to vocational education. They allude to the class, race, and ethnic bias in current systems. They suggest some learning by doing and earning for doing, but that is all they do—they suggest. When they describe new approaches to curriculum or descriptions of instructional processes they ignore work altogether. The school they suggest still appears remote, unessential, and antiseptic. In their chapter, "Toward a Relevant Curriculum"[34] and the follow-

---

[32] Edgar Friedenberg, review of Mario Fantini and Gerald Weinstein's *The Disadvantaged* in *New York Review of Books*, Nov. 21, 1968, p. 17.

[33] The other three goals, parental career, a citizen career and a career in self-development. These conform somewhat to goals identified here and references to Fantini and Weinstein will be found sprinkled throughout this book.

[34] Fantini and Weinstein, *op. cit.*, pp. 337–373.

ing chapter, "Toward a Content Curriculum"[35] the student seems to be going to pretty much the same old school with some gimmickry added to spruce it up a little. The student still is passive and is provided with only the slightest hint about how one connects to the work world or how that work could be rearranged.

A Concluding Note

Many readers may wonder why so much space has been devoted to work in a book about education. There is a simple explanation—economic security comes before everything else. Without economic security man cannot apply himself to more lofty ventures. Therefore it is essential that educated man direct his attention to creating a world of work designed to bring, simultaneously, maximum gratifications to worker and meet the needs of a continuously changing society.

There are many factors leading to alienation which impinge upon both education and work. As the world changes, accommodations to change must occur in both of these vital institutions. And yet it is clear that rather than moving closer together, there is increasing separation. Work organization must offer gratifications to the worker. Through work there must be the gratification that comes with a sense of usefulness, a sense of belongingness, and a sense of competence. Work as currently constructed inhibits persons rather than gratifying them.

There is a tendency, in the preoccupation of daily stresses, to do little more than try to manage crises. The crises that emerge are mere symptoms of much greater problems and yet they become the be-all and end-all of program planners. Once vision is restricted, then reality is restricted. The restriction on vision is partially explained by the failure of higher education to meet the challenge to provide leadership for change. There is too much encapsulation, in my opinion, and far too little testing of assumptive universes.

To change a world or any appreciable segment of it, leaders must know about that world. They must have historical perspective. They must know economics and political science. They must know how to devise and implement tactics and strategy for change. They must know how to evaluate whether programs have produced de-

---

[35] *Ibid.*, pp. 376–415.

sired effects. There is so much to do, and there is so little organized thought about these issues. In this chapter, I have introduced some issues, offered a theoretical perspective, and commented on how experts view the relationship between education and work. It is my hope that this has stirred some to reappraise where they are and others to action. The goals should be clear. Work and education must combine to bring fulfillment to the vast majority of the people while at the same time add to the necessary resources of the society.

CHAPTER IV

Preparation for
Democratic Citizenship

[In this chapter I present the thesis that preparation for democratic citizenship is more vital now than ever before. I submit that the school, rather than generating respect for democratic institutions, does just the opposite. The school does not build a respect for the Bill of Rights. It denies students expertise in judicial, executive, and legislative decision-making by making a farce out of student government.]

If a nation expects to be ignorant and free in a state of civilization, it expects what never was and never will be.

—Thomas Jefferson

I don't tell jokes—I just watch government and report the facts.

—Will Rogers

The dimmy cratic party ain't on speakin' terms with itself.

The raypublican party broke ye, but now that ye're down we'll not turn a cold shoulder to ye. Come in an we'll keep ye broke.

—Finley Peter Dunne

Did you too, oh friend, suppose democracy was only for elections, for politics and for a party name?

—Walt Whitman

While democracy must have its organization and controls, its vital breath is individual liberty.

—Charles Evans Hughes

It is terrifying that persons educated in this country know so little about democracy. And what is more frightening, they seem to care even less. About 44 million persons of voting age didn't vote in the presidential election of 1968; this is 13 million more than voted for Richard Nixon. And the 31 million who voted for Nixon would be hard-pressed to explain why—other than to say that he looked better than the other two in the running.

A democratic society can be only as good as the electorate. Only with mass enlightenment can there be evolutionary change in democratic practices and institutions. At one time persons with minimal sophistication about the working of government could perform their responsibility as citizens adequately. Not so long ago the system had enormous tolerance for failure. Today we have little margin for error, and citizens must know a great deal if national calamity is to be prevented. There are many aspects of a changing society that place dramatic challenges on the citizenship role.

Government of today bears little resemblance to government of as little as forty years ago. There is the matter of sheer size. Because many more people need to be governed, each of us has lost some of our representation. In 1964 the President represented 70 million voters; in 1932 the President was shared by less than 40 million voters. Because of the increase in the electorate, there are now six members of the House of Representatives for every million voters, whereas 30 years ago a million voters had eight representatives. At every level of government the representative is now shared by more people and will be shared by even more people in the future.

Mass media is having its effect on the democratic process. Through mass media the candidates have almost universal access to the electorate, but this contact is not reciprocal. Because of mass media the candidate can structure the issues, can generate his own questions, can resonate to the lowest level of understanding. Mass media is enormously expensive. Now, even more than ever in the past, candidacy for the highest office in the land becomes limited to those persons with access to wealth. The mass aspect of the media precludes serious debate—issues are treated superficially and minority interests are gobbled up in the sweep of the campaign. There is almost no opportunity for true negotiation among diverse groups with the goal of forming a real coalition. With mass media, it is possible to by-pass minority organizations altogether. Richard Nixon attempted to woo the "Negro vote" by generating a new slogan. Hubert Humphrey used "past history" as the basis of his appeal. Even George Wallace had the "Negro" interests at heart in his mass-media presentations. The relative merit of each position was never placed in disputation to be examined in depth by the electorate. The only role left to the organizations of the minorities was to affirm or reject. The more traditional organizations lamented the reduction of their influence. The emerging organizations were entirely excluded. Through mass media the candidate could make direct contact. As a consequence, labor leaders, for example, lost bargaining strength—they were no longer needed to deliver the labor vote. The same was true for geographical interests, religious interests, and fraternal interests. Whatever ideological issues separated the major parties were further obscured by the increasing importance of mass media in the election process.

Mass media has a more subtle influence in political process—it befouls the market place of ideas with trivia and overly simple solutions to complicated problems. It is against a backdrop of Western heroes shooting bad guys, secret agents shooting bad guys, and military anti-heroes outstupiding bad guys that a political education must take place. The mass media steals time and blows minds. It is both opiate and detractor. The political candidate adapts style and content to the standards of the mass media. Thus it is perfectly possible for a person possessing no more prerequisites than good looks and the ability to read a teleprompter to offer himself for candidacy for the most important offices in the land.

Ubiquitous bureacracy has an impact on democratic processes. Political organization has grown as the society of which it is a part has grown. Parkinson's Law governs political parties. They exist to expand. Their sole goal is perpetuation and aggrandizement—*as political parties*. They measure loyalty as devotion to party, and devotion to principle is viewed as naïve idealism. The major reason Richard Nixon remained politically alive after two disastrous campaigns is that he was a "good party man." There can be no other reason for Hubert Humphrey's nomination for the presidency.

That grand old pamphleteer of democracy, Thomas Paine, thought the bankruptcy of political parties stemmed from basically flawed governments. In particular, he thought political parties in those governments which arose over the people were sustained by:

> A set of childish thinkers, and half-way politicians born in the last century, men who went no farther with any principle than as it suited their purpose as a party; the nation was always left out of the question, and this has been the character of every party from that day to this.[1]

---

[1] Thomas Paine, *Rights of Man* (Winter 1791), C. A. Walls and Co., London, 1937, p. 124.

That two-century-old statement has a modern ring to it. It applies today because Thomas Paine failed to appreciate, as it is so easy for all of us to become lulled, that liberty won can also be lost and that a tranquil people can surrender, without thought, that which their ancestors fought so bitterly to establish. This will become all the more likely if the education process and structure violate the spirit of liberty and freedom.

The Peter Principle of Incompetence applies to politics. Those minimally competent survive to be considered for the highest posts in the nation, whereas the more competent who threaten the structure are shunted aside. The two most renowned scientists at the time of the Revolutionary War—Thomas Jefferson and Benjamin Franklin—were eminent in politics. It is inconceivable that, if they were alive today, they could have negotiated present political bureaucracies to equivalent importance.

Segregation distorts the democratic process. People insulated from each other are unable to communicate with each other. Many segments of the society who have mutual interests are unable to explore the basis for political coalition because they never get together. Instead, suspicion sown by separation leads to fragmentation of effort. The politically impotent—the poor, the young, the racial minorities—all separated by physical and psychological space—can, in the modern world, reach each other only through mass media. But mass media, because of its expense, is only available (except for rare special events) to the established. The politically marginal are driven to establish minority-interest newspapers and journals with limited circulation. These journals have a rich history and were extremely influential in politics of the past when that was the only means available to influence opinion and mobilize support. But now they are puny alongside the communication weaponry available to the politically dominant. The desperate effort to establish a base of political influence is divisive. A day-to-day struggle for existence can only restrict perspective and perception. It is at least to be entertained that the dreary old men who control both major parties are a formidable power group less because they are prominent than because of the inability of diverse oppositions to get together.

Government decision-making is more and more dependent on knowledge. The various approaches to international or domestic issues can be intelligently evaluated only by persons well schooled in history, economics, psychology, political science, demography, and ecology. Government decision-making depends upon access to information.

In the Vietnam war, for example, those highly situated in government tell us that if only we knew the facts we would agree that the policy followed is the best of all possible policies. Then they proceed to tell us that all the vital "facts" are classified and cannot be shared by the electorate. This is a frightening precaution. Things most vital to the public are kept from the public. The denial of access to information is joined with a reticence to seek information. Many persons are reluctant to learn things that will cause them to give up the comfort of their beliefs. They would like to trust as true what their leaders tell them because the alternatives mean a commitment of time, energy, and finances against established authority. This is not only expensive but also personally threatening. But unwillingness to pay the price of democracy ultimately means the loss of democracy.

Government is more remote from the electorate now than it ever was before. In the past, most of the concerns of government were local concerns. The voter had a basis for choosing alternatives because he was personally involved in the intricacies of a not very intricate decision-making process. But inexorably the locus of political power has moved toward larger and more distant bodies.

The chart on p. 114 gives an indication of the extent to which government has grown and how it has moved away from the local community. Since 1902 government expenditures have increased more than 150-fold. In 1902 about one-quarter of all government funds was expended by the federal government; by 1966 the federal government was spending far more than half the public funds.

The rate of change in government (both in growth and remoteness from local community) appears to be unrelated to political party or ideology. Government grew in size and away from the local community as much under the allegedly "conservative" Dwight Eisenhower as it did under the "spendthrift" administrations of Harry Truman or Lyndon Johnson.

The change in shape and size of government puts pressure on the electorate. The voter now knows intimately neither the persons involved in the decision-making nor is he familiar with the issues. As a consequence he grows suspicious of the operation. Today, literally millions of United States citizens look upon the federal gov-

Relationship Between Federal, Local, and State
Government in Funds Expended

% Of All Expenditures Which Are
Federal Government

Year

Expenditures in Billions of Dollars
Federal, State & Local

.4(a)	.7(a)	3.3(a)	4.7(a)	9.1(a)	39.6(a)	92.7(b)	134.4(b)
1.1(a)	2.3(a)	5.6(a)	8.4(a)	11.2(a)	27.9(a)	61.0(c)	94.9(c)
1.5	3.0	8.9	13.1	20.3	67.5	153.7	239.3

Sources:

a *The Statistical History of the United States,* Hargon Press, Inc., New York, 1968, pp. 719–720, 727.

b U.S. Department of Commerce, *Statistical Abstract of the United States 1968,* U.S. Printing Office, Washington, D.C., 1968, p. 378.

c *Ibid.,* p. 407.

ernment as an alien power. They hunger for the good old days. But they want what cannot be attained. There is no possible return to a government of simple decisions seated in the local community. Interdependency is a fact. All of commerce, transportation, and communication require regulation at state, national, and international levels. International relations are of such a nature that negotiation and decision-making must take place thousands of miles away from home. In the future things will be more, not less, complex and remote. If it is not possible to reduce the political workings of a society to the simpler mechanics of an earlier time, it is possible to educate an electorate which is capable of dealing with a complex world. This must be a major goal of modern education!

The Democratic Process and the Alienation of Youth

Involvement in judicial, legislative, and executive decision-making, undergirded by guarantees of individual rights, is the means by which humans are able to generate some measure of control over their fate in complex societies. Any groups excluded from such decision-making are likely to become disengaged from the dominant society. Youth are denied access to the political apparatus. In a variety of ways they bridle against second-class citizenship. This alienation of youth is not a new phenomenon. A. E. Housman described it half a century ago in his poem, "The Laws of God, The Laws of Man." Therein he decries a situation where man's behavior is always dominated by some external authority over which he has no control:

> Let God and man decree
> Laws for themselves and not for me;
> And if my ways are not as theirs,
> Let them mind their own affairs.
> Their deed I judge and much condemn
> Yet when did I make laws for them.

Schools continually demand of students strong and foolish exactments. Those alienated react in many different ways to their condition. An exceedingly large percentage of youth are up in arms against the schools. A large percentage are more passive in their opposition, and a depressingly large number willingly submit to authoritarian imposition. There is precious little effort made to understand these attitudes of estrangement. Many adults prate about the inappropriateness of youthful behavior, never once considering that the adult establishment is hardly in a position to complain about the illegitimate means of processing grievances if that community has not taken the pains to adequately teach youth legitimate means of processing grievances—or, even more basically, has never created a legitimate means for grievance-resolution. It is lamentable, but nonetheless true, that *a great many adults, including those within the ranks of teachers, school boards, and administrators will not even concede to the students the right to have grievances.*

Students' Rights—There Ain't No Such Thing

If the school is going to prepare students for democratic citizenship, the school must first recognize that individual rights are at the heart of all democratic institutions. Democracy begins with the right of citizens to be protected from the abuse of state authority. The school does not itself qualify completely as a democratic institution. Students cannot be expected to exercise complete self-determination, but nonetheless the school must be compatible with a democratic society—and there the school is a wretched failure. Conspicuous by its absence is a bill of rights for students. At best they suffer under a benevolent dictatorship; at worst they are subject to furious tyranny. It is actually possible, in an allegedly free society, for students to be harassed because the principal doesn't like the way they wear their hair. (There is only one possible explanation for such an act, and that is—principals, having so much trouble growing hair at all, become insanely jealous of youth that grow more than their share.)

None of the basic rights is respected by the school. There is denial of freedom of expression. Kindergarten students and graduate-school students both legitimately fear that an honest expression of opinion on their part will meet with recrimination by the authority and they will be without redress. A black twelve-year-old boy, in a "forward-looking" community that had desegregated its schools, in a classroom led by a teacher who took pride in his advanced racial attitudes (he had even invited a black colleague to Christmas dinner), was rewarded with a slap on the face when he insisted, in a discussion of racial characteristics, that the hair of black people was distinctly different than the hair of white people. This student, hurt and humiliated as he was, was even more concerned that no fuss be made over the matter, because, if that happened, the teacher would really get him.

Students are not presumed to be innocent nor are they offered a guarantee against self-incrimination. On the contrary. In the case of any transgression, students with reputations for wrongdoing are herded together, accused, and corrected by a teacher or administrator who serves as prosecutor, judge, jury, and executioner. The student is not allowed to present evidence in his own defense, nor is he allowed to remain mute. If he should respond to the indictment: "I know my rights, I don't have to answer that"—Bam!—He would be punished for the crime of insubordination. At this point some readers will protest, "He is overgeneralizing again." But I am not overgeneralizing!!! The response I am describing is so universal that any exception to it comes too infrequently to deserve comment. Even the rare teacher who respects student rights is more than neutralized by his colleagues. That teacher is forced to the defensive. If there is any student unrest, that teacher is accused of fomenting it. The student, libeled and labeled, is helpless. All too often he concludes, "If I have the name I might as well have the game!" Which translated means, "If they are going to convict me of all crimes, I might as well commit them!" A response rarely considered by persons who advocate erosion of rights as a means to reduce crime.

The lack of respect for rights of students plumbs to ridiculous depths. In every elementary school I have visited, something like this occurs. A teacher says: "No one is going to leave for recess until I find out who threw that spit ball."

That response is not what I like to think of as in the American tradition. It is modeled after the Nazis in Lidice. The whole town was to be held as hostage until the murderer of Heydrich was surrendered.

The student is denied even the most elementary respect for privacy. Adolescent youth, uncomfortable with their rapidly changing bodies, are forced to expose themselves to platoons of their classmates in shower rooms. If they refuse to "dress down" for gym they are flunked. In California, where the state law requires successful completion of a course in physical education every year, some seniors in the high school take as many as three hours of physical education every day to make up for past failures.

Violence erupted in one California school I visited because a crusading teacher burst into the girls' toilet in an attempt to apprehend students violating the law against smoking. True, smoking is against the law, and for health reasons it should be discouraged in the school, but aren't any limits to be placed on zealous law enforcement? Can't a student feel free from prying eyes anywhere? The absurdity of the teacher's action escalated into further absurdities. The surveillance of the many toilets on the campus taxed the investigation force beyond limits, so all but two of the toilets (one for each sex) were closed. The school faculty split into two evenly divided factions, to the point that they refused to talk to each other. They even set up separate eating quarters for lunch. Students were able to play one group against another. And of course outside the school six hundred billion cigarettes continued to be consumed annually. Children have almost unlimited access to cigarettes. They are told incessantly that cigarettes are things for which people will walk great lengths; that cigarettes have the freshness of spring in them, and that they live in a country where ruggedly handsome men smoke them. Despite some very recent limitations on advertising, cigarettes are still reputed to have marvelous properties. Against this backdrop a woman teacher storms into a toilet and peeps under a cubicle in order to catch a girl in the act of smoking. And there are still some people who wonder why children have lost respect for adult authority.[2]

Most heartrending of all is the response of the parents and other significant adult figures to the issue of student rights. A PTA group in a major city in the Northwest petitioned a school board to establish dress codes to improve the school image. The outrageousness of such a demand never penetrated the sensorium of the petitioners. On what pretense could one group of parents determine the apparel of *other* parents' children? I for one would be much happier with a school where children looked and thought like Albert Einstein than I would with a school where Pat Boone set the tone for attire and cerebral activities.

School officials also retreat to feeble excuses for the invasion of student rights. They far-fetchedly declare that the garb and hair styles of some students interfere with the rights of other children to learn. One justification for restriction on hair styles, very popular with principals, goes something like this: "Long-haired boys disrupt the classroom, provoking laughter and keeping other students from the serious business of study."

This statement is presented over and over again as a serious intellectual argument and represents probably, as nothing else does,

---

[2] Edgar Friedenberg describes a similar crusade against smoking in his book, *Coming of Age in America*, Random House, New York, 1963.

the bankruptcy of the educator's mentality. First, no educational activities should be so fragile that they could be disrupted by something as superficial as a student's dress or hair style. Second, the disruption is clearly a symptom of a student population not trained to respect the rights of others to be different. A well-educated student body wouldn't even notice the difference; they would, however, burst out laughing if, by some strange coincidence (as infrequent as monkeys with typewriters producing a great literary work), the whole student body would one day dress alike.

The educator often masks his intolerance for individual rights behind a solicitude for student welfare. His argument goes thusly: "I only insist that a boy cut his hair to protect him from physical abuse by intolerant students."

Now there is logic within a democratic context for you. The greatest advocates of the concept of law and order suddenly reverse themselves and say: "Because I cannot control the law-violator I must therefore restrict the victim."

Or, a variation on the same theme of concern for students is the idea that the student must be protected from himself. Here it is argued that dress codes ". . . are established because such standards are required outside the school and thus, when the school demands conformity in hair cuts and dress style, it is performing a public service. With long hair a boy could not get a job and by making him cut it off we're doing him a favor."

Here the authorities confuse rights and discretion. Every student has a *right* to a public education, and in almost all states his presence in the school is mandatory; that is where education differs from employment. No citizen is forced to take a job. One of the rights in a free society is the right to be a bum. A great many distinguished and celebrated Americans exercised this right before settling down to more socially acceptable behavior. Students can be encouraged into useful pursuits by the tactics outlined in the previous chapter, but the choice of whether to work or not still remains with the individual. Teachers, principals, etc. should indeed inform students about the world of work and the demands, foolish or otherwise, of prospective employers. But that is as far as adult responsibility should go; whether or not conformity to a superficial norm is too high a price to pay is a question only the individual student should decide. Teachers and administrators often are guided by a "domino theory" of student behavior. A great majority believe that if the students are not restrained in their dress and expression there will be no bounds on their behavior. Teachers have informed me that if they did not insist that girls be forced to wear dresses of a specific length, some girls would come to school naked. There is no evidence for such a dire prediction. But even if such an eventuality were possible, the time to act is when the situation occurs (or is imminent), not when the behavior is palpably innocuous.

Even the concept of democracy can be used to undermine students' rights. In this instance the adult authority insists that they are merely complying with dictums set down by students themselves. It is the student government that has evoked a dress code, and thus the matter is outside the control of teacher or administrator. How little is really understood about rights? Rights are not negotiable. They can neither be given up nor taken away. They are not created for the majority. Rights have always been needed by the weak, never by the strong. The essence of a bill of rights is that it offers protection to the minority from the tyranny of the majority. Students must be made to understand that they *have no right* to intrude upon the rights of others. In truth, this argument is a cover-up. Very rarely indeed do dress codes spring spontaneously from students. Behind the scenes there is almost always encouragement by the established school authorities for such standards. Even if all but one student in a large high school were of the opinion that the dress style of that person was inappropriate, unless there could be *clear evidence* that his behavior was truly exercising a negative influence on health and public morality, his right to be different must remain inviolate. And whether that dress code came into being through the duplicity of adults or whether it was the expression of the student body is of little relevance. All too often school officials stand placidly aside as vigilantism takes over. Not infrequently the lionized athletic society takes the law into its own hands and physically forces deviant youth to submit to the indignity of a hair cut they do not want. Even in such a prestigious institution of learning as Stanford University the student body president was, in the not-so-distant-past, so assaulted by a group of allegedly educated Stanford students. School staff, in some instances, actually encourages these behaviors and in other instances refuses to intervene when such outrageous acts against individual rights occur.

While *all* students suffer from deprivation of rights, it is the poor who are victimized. Affluent youth are far less likely to receive the scorn and abuse that beset the poor child. Suburban schools offer some semblance of respect for the student, even as slum schools take on the appearance of prisons. Affluent youth are able to draw support from the privileges accorded their parents. Affluent youth are offered something akin to due process in their grievances. The school simply wouldn't dare to treat the children of the rich the way the children of the poor are treated. It is possible for advantaged youngsters to avoid the rigid authoritarianism of the school. Their position in the society enhances their bargaining position and, in addition, they have maneuverability, which is not available to the poor.

Persons of means have choice of where they live (and often a deciding factor in this election of residence is the school system). They can pay for auxiliary education, that is, art or music lessons— and if the school situation becomes intolerable they have the option of a private-school education for their children. None of these alternatives is available to the poor and, in their absence, the oppressiveness of the school often becomes unbearable. A disrespect for democratic rights is very pervasive in our society. A public school does not enhance its image by compelling every child to look alike, nor does it improve its standards by expelling the students who need the education the most. The contrary is true; a school that respects its youth and respects the rights of individuals will, in that process, generate a loyalty from students, and, out of that loyalty, will come desirable behaviors that can never be obtained through oppressive measures.

The Beginning of Training for Democratic Citizenship
—Respect for a Student's Rights

Every student must have guaranteed rights which must be described specifically; these rights must be able to withstand the shifting political wind and must be clearly articulated to all of the relevant publics. The rights of students must be at least as difficult to abrogate as the rights guaranteed for adults in the first ten amendments to the Constitution. If that happens, the rights of adults will be more firmly secured. The rights that should be available to students are: the rights of free speech, free assembly, freedom of personal appearance, personal privacy, freedom from self-incrimination, freedom from cruel and unusual punishment, and—the most precious rights—the right to be treated with respect and the right to maintain a social identity. *If a school were to do nothing more than to introduce rights to students and respect and guarantee these rights regardless of income of parents, areas of residence, color of skin, or the language of parents—and did nothing else—the estrangement of students from school would be greatly reduced!*

Teachers and other school officials must continue to remind themselves and the outside community that every American patriot has distinguished himself by his nonconformity. Emerson in his essay on self-reliance (which is at least an important component of education) laid down a dictum that must be incorporated into the matrix of the educational process: "Whosoever would be a man must be a nonconformist!"

The adult authority in the school has but one permissible stance. *The right of the individual must be protected.* The teacher and administrator must articulate this position unambiguously and with passion, and must use all the power invested in their offices to insure that students' rights remain inviolate.

I have yet to visit a high school that guarantees students' rights. I know of none reported in the literature. Nordstrom, Friedenberg, and Gold, in their study in considerable depth of a wide range of high schools, found none that guaranteed student rights. Even the best of them was considered by the authors to be despotic.[3]

Jerry Farber doesn't put the college student in a much better light than the high-school student:

> Students at Cal State are politically disenfranchised. They are in an academic Lowndes County. Most of them can vote in national elections—their average age is about 26—but they have no voice in the decisions which affect their academic lives. The students are, it is true, allowed to have a toy government run for the most part by Uncle Toms and concerned principally with trivia. The faculty and administrators decide what courses will be offered; the students get to choose their Homecoming Queen.[4]

Thomas Paine in his *The Rights of Man* allows for only two kinds of government: one that arose "out" of the people, or the

---

[3] Carl Nordstrom, Edgar Friedenberg and Hilary Gold, *Society's Children: A Study of Dissentiment in the Secondary School,* Random House, New York, 1967.

[4] Jerry Farber, "The Student as Nigger," *This Magazine Is About Schools,* Winter 1968, p. 109.

other that was imposed "over" the people. Using England as an example, he claimed that man's rights are slowly, if ever, won in the latter condition:

> The English government is one of those which arose out of conquest and not out of society and consequently it arose over the people, and though it has been much modified from the opportunity of circumstances since the time of William the Conqueror, the country has never yet regenerated itself.[5]

Paine could not know that, just as it was possible for governments which come into being over the people to become in time "democratoid," so was it possible for the "out of the people" governments to be corrupted. The only protection against corruption is education—education that preaches and practices devotion to the rights of individuals.

Educational sophists do interesting things to the concept of rights. They tie it into responsibility. Over and over again teachers and principals tell me that students should have their rights only after they have proved themselves to be responsible. This is just flat-out wrong thinking. Rights come first, then responsibilities. That is the heart of the matter. Anything else is authoritarian. The only responsibility attached to rights is the one Thomas Paine identified, when the concept of rights was established as governmental guarantee: "A declaration of rights is, by reciprocity, a declaration of duties also. Whatever is my right as a man is also the right of another, and it becomes my duty to guarantee as well as to possess." [6]

To parents, teachers, and demanding taxpayers: Heed well— the rights that you fight to establish for schoolchildren may be means by which you salvage your own.

Democratic Responsibilities
—Judicial, Legislative, and Executive Decision-Making

A bill of rights is the prerequisite for developing competence in the citizenship role. It is not enough. In a truly democratic society, the school system must provide each student with extensive experience in judicial, executive, and legislative decision-making. A

[5] Thomas Paine, *op. cit.*, p. 37.

[6] *Ibid.*, p. 82.

student must be involved in the *development* of a bill of rights, he must have a hand in the preparation of the rules by which he must live. He must be involved in the judgment and disposition of students who violate those rules and he must have executive responsibility in the development of extracurricular activities and an advisory role on such matters as curriculum. An effective democratic society educates its citizens to a willingness to accept responsibilities. An interdependent society requires accountability from every segment of that society. Accountability, like any other complicated enlightenment, must be learned. This learning must take place developmentally and logically. One has no right to expect from a six-year-old the sophisticated decision-making of a sixteen-year-old. In actual practice the school operates opposite to any perceptible logic. The six-year-old is permitted to engage in much more independent decision-making than a sixteen-year-old. If a six-year-old decides that she would rather play with clay when the rest of the class is milking a yak, no one gets particularly upset, but if a sixteen-year-old were to engage in such independent decision-making the system would be thrown into a veritable tizzy.

Schools pretend to offer students opportunities in democratic decision-making. There are charades that are called student government. But with very, very few exceptions, what is paraded as student government is a farce. The student government's only function is to agree with the principal (who all too frequently is a football coach with four losing seasons). Rather than developing a commitment to, and a skill in, representative government the process has the opposite effect; it instills distrust rather than loyalty; ignorance in the place of knowledge.

The Tragedy of Student Government

Students in high school are encouraged to participate in democratic decision-making, but in the words of Tom Leher, "They don't live long if they try." Edgar Friedenberg in his book *Coming of Age in America* indicates what happened in a school when a group of "hoods" gained control of the student court. The administration of the school reacted by abolishing the court.[7] This is the typical response to student initiative. Students can't win! If they

---

[7] Edgar Friedenberg, *op. cit.,* p. 39.

disengage themselves from student activities they are berated as apathetic; if they engage they are criticized for their impetuousness. The student, in preparing for citizenship, confronts the same dilemma he meets in preparation for a job—he is denied a chance to engage because he lacks experience and he is unable to get experience because he is not allowed to participate.

A case study of a group of students attempting to generate a more real student government and the adult authority response might prove illuminating to those interested in understanding the alienation of youth from institutions run by adults. The study might also serve to help explain why democracy leads such a precarious existence.

In a rural community, approximately one hundred miles from the state's only major metropolis, a student leader initiated an attempt to revitalize the high-school's dormant student government. His platform was clearly anti-Establishment. But no element of that program exceeded what was permissible by statute. He was purely and simply for reform. He surrounded himself with a broad coalition of support. His main theme was a call for more student government. He enlisted as his running mate a leader of the "hood" (bad guy) population.

Specifically, his platform called for:

Student control over student monies;

More student control over the school newspaper;

Establishment of a publication which allowed for discussion in depth of student concerns—open to all shades of opinion;

Invitation to the campus of speakers to reduce the remoteness of the community;

More excitement and relevance in the school curriculum;

More student responsibility in the determination of rules which govern student behavior.

The adult authority response to this attempt at more student responsibility was predictable. They did everything they could to impede his progress. Here is a chronicle of the events that occurred:

First—The student leader was threatened. (This process in school terminology is euphemistically labeled "counseling.") He was warned that his behavior was jeopardizing his career. The ultimate threat was voiced—persistence in such foolishness could lead to dismissal prior to graduation.

Second—When the threat failed, the school officials became actively involved in student politics. They solicited "loyal" opposition to the "reform" candidate. Various student leaders were sought out and some were prevailed upon to oppose the reform candidate for the school presidency. Despite, or because of, administration opposition, the reform candidate received over 70% of the total vote; his "hood" running mate eked out the election by less than ten votes.

Third—The school administration charged that the election was invalid. Unable to dispute the landslide victory of the presidential candidate, the legitimacy of the victory of the vice-president was challenged. It was charged that the students had miscounted votes. The students countercharged that school officials had altered the election by pocketing some of the anti-Establishment votes. In a rerun of the election the "hood" candidate won again. The net impact of all of the administrative action was heightened enmity between adult leadership and student leadership and ruptured channels of communication between staff and students.

From Bad to Worse—
Or, How Adults Organize Youth to Actively Rebel

The school administration did not modify their stance after the election. On the contrary, the hostility escalated. The newly elected president was informed that his position was honorary. Although there were funds over which the students had ostensible control, in reality the principal could determine how much funds might be spent, while the student president could do no more than go through the formality of signing checks and vouchers. This did not set well with the student-body president. The most prominent of his campaign promises was independence. He would be no "rubber stamp for the administration." And now he was being asked to literally be just that. While things were not going well there was not as yet a *big issue*—even here the school administration was unwilling to let bad enough alone.

The new leadership wanted to enliven the educational process. They proposed, as a vehicle to accomplish this goal, the formation of a new magazine—*The Iconoclast*—whose title was to reflect its intent. Through the pages of this periodical the ritual that passed for rationality and the mythology that paraded as knowledge could be challenged. The students were circumspect. They adhered to the rules. They found a teacher who would act as sponsor and they cleared everything through the administration. However, the magazine, which was designed to be issued periodically, was never distributed—period. The first effort was completed and produced. All of its contents had been approved by the appropriate review bodies. But at the last second its distribution was held up. The district superintendent had prohibited its circulation. The lead article, which criticized the school's shop program, was decreed to be "libelous." Its offensiveness you may judge for yourself:

The Iconoclast, No. 1, Dec. 9, 1966
"Power Mechanics or Power Mania"

Power Mechanics in the past has traditionally been a course dealing primarily with the field of Automotive Mechanics. The students thought that this is what they would be studying when they enrolled.

Recently we were told that the administration wants us to be studying the basic theories of the internal combustion engine and working on the Briggs and Stratton engine, which is a small horse-powered lawnmower engine.

At this change some questions have arisen: (a) If we are not to work on cars in the future, why did the administration budget and approve the purchase of many tools that are, primarily, used on cars?

1)	a set of headlight aimers	$75
2)	a torque wrench	$45
3)	a timing gun	$65
4)	a cam dwell tester	$75
5)	two creepers	$25

(all of these prices are approx. and may deviate slightly from the price that was actually paid.)

All of these tools have very little if anything to do with the Briggs and Stratton engines but are primarily used on the car engines and other larger engines. Also I have never seen a lawnmower with headlights, let alone one that would have to have them aimed. It would seem as though the administration has bought around $300 worth of equipment so far this year that it has no use for in the new Power Mechanics way of doing things.

Is our administration planning its expenditures or are they using the trial and error method?

If they are using the trial and error method it would seem as though somebody is going to have to explain the $300 error.

All of the tools in our shop are meant to be used on car and other larger engines. There are very few tools that are small enough to work on the Briggs and Stratton engine. Actually there is not *ONE COMPLETE SET* of the recommended tools for the proper assembly and disassembly of this engine to be found in the shop at this time.

With this situation it may prove to be a bit of a problem for the thirty students enrolled to do an adequate amount of work required to pass the course.

Another problem in Power Mechanics is the amount of books that the administration approved for purchase. There are thirty students enrolled in two classes and only eight books, plus one reference book. These books therefore have to be shared among the two classes, which is common in more than one of the Vocational Courses. As a matter of interest the book that was budgeted, approved, and purchased for use by the class is called *AUTOMOTIVE MECHANICS.*

Again it is obvious that our administration has made another expenditure without planning ahead. According to the new way that things are to be done this book has been made obsolete in a little less than one semester.

Is our budget for new books so low that the school can only afford to purchase one book for every two students in the Power Mechanics course?

Why doesn't the school get a teacher for the course?

Since the first of the year the Agriculture teacher has been substituting as a Power Mechanics teacher. The administration did hire a teacher for the course, but after only *ONE DAY* he left for reasons unknown to us and has never returned. Could this be because the facilities to teach the course are inadequate?

With the Agriculture and Power Mechanics programs set up as they are at present are we going to lose any Federal Aid?

In the past the Agriculture program was set up on a full day basis. Now it has been reduced to only one-half of the day. We know that our school gets federal aid for having an Agriculture program, because we have gone over it in Modern Problems. As our school has reduced the program by one-half it only seems reasonable that the aid should be reduced accordingly.

This point is more or less for the parents, but many students now enrolled in our school system have paid taxes in the past.

What is the $6.00 charge for taking Power Mechanics going towards?

As near as I can figure, it is for any breakage, wear and tear, or loss of tools. Also it would go towards the purchases of any consumable goods such as the solvent and the alcohol (denatured) that have been purchased thus far for class use.

So far we have bought five gallons of solvent, one gallon of brake fluid, alcohol—one gallon, and a set of cylinder honing brushes for class use. Cost of these items could not amount to more than thirty dollars. This is about one-sixth of the total amount invested spent in about one-third of the school year. With no further expenditures on this account in sight, what is going to happen to the rest of the money? Are the students to get a rebate on their investment?

These amounts may seem trivial but this is only one class out of the school's many.

At present there is yet another problem to be reasoned out, preferably with more respect than seems to be shown towards the shop problem. At the first of the year we were given the Old Shop for use as a workshop. Then some questions came into being as to the suitability of this place:

1) The Driver's Education car has to be parked in this area from time to time.

2) The shop was being used as a garbage dump; this is a disgrace to the school and an insult to those students having to stay in the area during that time.

3) It is a fire hazard; true, it does have two doors but one of them leads to the shop area utilized by the maintainance crew and it is kept locked from the other side at all times during the day.

4) With what little room that we did have we came back one Monday morning to find that one-third of this area had been blocked off for use by the maintainance crew. This took place around the sixth week of school.

For any one or all of these reasons we were told that we could stay in the "garbage dump" or move into the Wrestling Room. It was the decision of the classes that the Wrestling Room was to be our new shop. All this was done about two weeks ago and as yet we still have not received any materials to finish building the shop. All that has been done at present is the moving of tools from one shop to the other. Also because there have been no electrical outlets installed and the shop is another fire hazard, we have temporarily discontinued working on it.

The *Iconoclast* affair did not end merely with its suspension. More serious consequences were to follow. Two faculty members' jobs were lost as a consequence of its abortive misadventure. Neither the magazine sponsor nor the teacher who provided information for the article had their contracts renewed. Their competence could not have been the reason for dismissal. Colleagues of the magazine's sponsor were lavish in their praise of his abilities. Some insisted that he was the best teacher they had ever seen and one appealed to a United States Senator to lend his assistance as a gyroscope of sanity in a corner of the world which had obviously gone off its rocker.

Nor did the harassment of the student-body president stop. He wanted outside speakers to come to the school, and, despite unanimous support from student representatives, this appeal was not honored. Finally after months of wrangling the president was suspended from school. The circumstances immediately preceding the suspension was an unresolved argument between the principal and the president, extending until late in the afternoon. At about five o'clock in the evening the student-body president, seeing no settlement in the picture, rose to leave. He was informed that if he left then without permission he would be insubordinate and the punishment for insubordination was suspension. He left and he was suspended. The next day the majority of students walked out of school in support of their president. And that is the stuff that student disorders are made of.[8]

Some readers are going to conclude that much is being made of one rare instance. But that is just not the case. What I have described is much more the rule than the exception. In school after school, student initiative is suppressed. One school administration becomes upset because students elected "Planned Parenthood" for their annual community service fund-raising. Another school rejects a student-initiated dance. Still another outlaws "peace buttons" on campus. A slum school attempts to disband a Black Student Association. In one form or another student government is emasculated.

I have described only one situation in which the "facts have been presented and only the names have been omitted to protect the innocent." The hero of my piece is obviously the student; the villains are the school administrators. The school administrators do not see it that way. They see the boy as an innocent victim, mesmerized by two adults. The indict the teacher who "derived a sense of personal power through the manipulation of children and got them to do his dirty work of undermining constituted authority" and they also indict the boy's father who, "everyone knew had severe personal problems," and they claim that the boy had become enmeshed in cobwebs that his disorders had spun. I, too, am blamed by the administrators. The boy had read a newspaper

---

[8] The strike was short lived and the president, realizing the proportion of explosiveness to which his modest efforts of student government had grown, "cooled it" and the semester ended with no further incidents.

article about me and, "impressionable as boys are," had accepted my "excessive statements" as "accurate prescriptions." I think the administrators' arguments should be considered. Assume that the boy was a Trilby and the teacher a Svengali. Assume that the boy has a troubled father. Assume all the arguments made; yet certain facts remain uncontestable. The student was elected by a large majority. The requests he made were consistent with a democratic society. And if he had all that trouble—did not the school have a responsibility to understand and help him? By no stretch of anybody's imagination can a student be called insubordinate if he desires to go home one and a half hours after school had been dismissed, particularly since he had not been detained for an infraction of a school rule. I believe there is but one responsible conclusion—the school officials did everything wrong! They overacted, *they libeled*, they suppressed. What should they have done?

The Appropriate Response to an Aggressive Attempt at Student Government

Start with a posture of good faith! Take all the students' positions at face value. Welcome more student initiative. Do not look for conspiracies. Don't insult a student by inferring that some behind-the-scene character is doing the thinking for him. If a youth is that impressionable, you, the administrator, impress him. If you can't get to him, look no further than yourself for the adult to blame. Remember this—in the search for conspiracy you create it. There is a little of Joe McCarthy in all of us, and, when inspired to engage in a witch hunt, read again Potter's book *Days of Shame.*[9]

Stay out of student elections! It is not the administration or faculty role to encourage or discourage candidates. The administration has no business even determining the eligibility for candidacy. If the student is enrolled in school he is a citizen and as a citizen he is eligible to hold office. If criteria are established which preclude any student from seeking office, the foundation of that system is endangered. If there is concern that the demands of the office might interfere with other school work, the staff should mobilize their efforts to insure that the student receives the necessary support to perform *both* his school work and governmental function. I would

---

[9] Charles Potter, *Days of Shame,* Coward-McCann, New York, 1965.

be less suspicious of administration in this matter of counseling youth against participation in student government if they were equally concerned about boys who possess physical prowess participating in athletics because such activity would interfere with their studies.

Don't get upset because the "wrong" people are going to get elected! Reflect a bit—recall some of the presidents the country has survived. The school will survive any candidates the students elect.

I mean—really stay out of student elections! Don't count ballots. Don't get involved in any administrative function. Render unto students that which belongs to students. If the administration has any concern about election procedures it should be expressed prior to the election. The only permissible attitude of the adult is technical consultant. In such a role it is legitimate to *suggest* to students that they might desire an election committee to supervise the election and some kind of structure to deal with any hanky-panky that might occur. Even here adults should be careful not to be overly aggressive in offering help. When students run to staff yelling "foul" the initial response must be to refer those students to the appropriate student committee. No activity of the staff could be more harmful than that which undermines student initiative by usurping its function. If there are problems in the system—*and there will be problems in the student government*—encourage the students to keep at it, then relax. Develop some tolerance for ambiguity. Consider what happens when you overact. Whatever were the motives of the official who overruled the first election for vice-president at the high school (and I assume that his motives were pure), his behavior fomented distrust. It wouldn't be difficult for students to suspect deviousness in his actions. Given the situation, they could have surmised that the adult acted as he did because:

1) The margin of victory precluded a challenge of the president's victory;

2) The vice-president could be challenged and it might be possible to replace him with a more acceptable candidate;

3) At a later date the president could be removed from office (persuasion or suspension);

4) The Establishment could again resume control.

There are, of course, exceptions to the rule of staff nonintervention in student affairs. There will be times when adults must interfere with student activities. However, in those instances the situations that would require adults to move in and the nature of their activity must be clearly articulated in advance. One of democracy's curious paradoxes is that the more it succeeds the more vulnerable it becomes. As the student begins to exercise more control over his life the more temptation there will be to pervert the process. I do not believe that it was a sudden conversion to the principles of Thomas Jefferson or even Woodrow Wilson that prompted Al Capone to activity in the Democratic party. I suspect that the relationship between government apparatus and his financial interests (bootlegging, gambling, prostitution, etc.) influenced his decision. In a petty way similar distortions can occur in a high school. If the students have control of funds, embezzlement is possible. Student government, with the power to direct student activities, influence curriculum, and even affect teacher tenure and promotion, could conceivably be corrupted. "Goon squads" could emerge to quell opposition, or there could be "ballot-stuffing" to win by deceit what could not be accomplished in open competition. (Many city machines owe their longevity to the efficacy of the slogan—"Vote often!") If the student government can, through its judicial system, exercise control over student behavior it is possible that extortion or bribery will occur. Even when such distortions take place students must be given ample opportunity to rectify the situation. They must not be told, in those supercilious tones that only educators seem able to master, "I gave you a chance and you blew it and now (*sigh*) *I* must step in and clean up the mess *you* made." Every adult authority should be humbled to this extent: every condition described above has happened in the political world of those who have attained their majority; the only *saving* grace is that no one moved in to take over (although in every generation somebody tries).

When transgression truly threatens person and property the adult authority must move in. When there is a condition of disorder the administration can legitimately declare "a state of emergency." This is a measure of last resort. The burden of proof rests with the adult. He must justify his behavior *to the student*. And even then, justified intervention is expensive. Enthusiasm for student government will diminish. There will be a bad taste in everybody's mouth. The students' confidence in themselves will be shaken. And when the condition of student government is reduced to such shambles, the anguish must be with the educator, because here, too, is but another indication of how *he* failed.

"Well and good," says the administrator, "but that is all theory, easy for you to say in your ivory tower, but in the *real* world where I live, the community wouldn't allow me to do that. How could I justify *The Iconoclast* and its charges of misuse of funds to the Taxpayers' League? How could I defend to the board the rebelliousness of the youth, how could I withstand the newspaper editorial that accused me of weakness? These are the groups to whom I must report, and if I don't satisfy them we don't get the money we need to run the schools. That, my friend, is the reality you choose to ignore."

The ultimate "cop-out" is always: "I'm as good as the *real* world will let me be." I have never been very sympathetic to that position. Current events—the failure of the Economic Opportunity Act to relieve poverty, the failure of the Elementary and Secondary Education Acts to assist the disadvantaged students, the failure of civil rights legislation to produce true integration, the assassination of Martin Luther King, Jr., and Robert Kennedy—have made me even more unsympathetic to the laments of the administrator. I have never considered his to be an easy job. But as Harry Truman once said (and this statement has even greater value since it is probably the only thing he ever said that was worth remembering): "If you can't stand the heat, get out of the kitchen!"

The superintendent is the educational leader. That is why he receives a relatively handsome salary. If he were only to follow orders of the community he should be replaced by a clerk. And what would have happened had he stood fast? What would have happened had the superintendent supported the student government and all of its activities?

He and the board might have been sued for "libel" because of the article in *The Iconoclast*. Possibly, but by whom? The article might have provided grist to the ever-grinding mill of the Taxpayers' League, who would have a field day over the apparent misuse of tax funds. Well—if the purchases of shop equipment were justified, the administration would have had to come forth and justify them. If an error was made (and errors are always made—the Ford Motor Company made a lulu in the manufacture of the Edsel), he would have to admit it and go on from there.

Parents might complain about the "uppityness" of the students and be joined by teachers who would feel that effective student government is undermining their power to control. All true. And if the superintendent supported the students his tranquillity undoubtedly would be disturbed. But how did he make out playing it "safe"? He did not remain free of criticism. In fact, the day the students milled around outside the school when they should have been in the classroom they brought to the superintendent precisely that kind of publicity that he had worked so hard to avoid. If pragmatism drove the superintendent to act as he did, he simply wasn't very pragmatic. He didn't win over his enemies. He didn't rally new friends. He didn't even analyze where his potential friends were.

One source of friends are students. Rarely do superintendents perceive students to be an important constituency. Yet they possess obvious attributes. Almost all students have at least one parent over whom they exert influence. Almost all high-school students will be voters within five years. If effectively mobilized five years ago they would now constitute a sufficient force to swing almost any election which pertained to school matters. Another source are teachers. Here again the superintendent in the name of expediency wasn't very expedient. In a school district with high teacher turnover, the dismissal of two teachers didn't elicit a feeling of confidence in those who remained. Although it is very difficult for many citizens to accept—and martyrs exist to give credence to the assertion that devotion to principle is unrealistic—there is still sufficient reason to believe that integrity and courage are not only vital to move education along, but are good politics as well.

There is one thing unusual about the case. The student leader was unique. But if we had an educational system that prepared students for citizenship he would be a more common phenomenon.

Preparing Students for Democratic Citizenship

If students are to be prepared for citizenship, they and their teachers must be doing very different things in the 12th grade than they were doing in the first grade. There must be continuity and logical development in the legislative, executive, and judicial decision-making.

Democratic Practice in the Primary Grades

In the first few years of school the student must become acquainted with rational order. During these years the teacher is totally in charge. There is no organized challenge to that authority. The teacher's primary role, in education for citizenship, is patently didactic. The teacher at this stage explains the necessity for the rules in the classroom and begins to establish an understanding of where the rights of one individual begin to interfere with the rights of another. The teacher might experiment. One day the class might be conducted without any rules at all—the next day the students could reflect on what happened. Another day, a class could be modeled after the Hitler *Jugend* and everyone would have to do exactly what the Führer demanded. That situation also could be analyzed and reviewed by the children. Instruction in democratic practice should include role-playing of judges, legislators, and executives. Through simulation, the very young can develop a sense of the parameters of democracy.

Training for Democracy in the Intermediate Grades

By the time a student enters the fourth grade he ought to be allowed to experiment with representative government. During these years students should be *randomly* assigned to governmental functions. The model should be the jury system, in which every citizen is obligated to serve. At this point the child is beginning to recognize that freedom carries with it responsibility. Every child, then, will get an opportunity to serve as legislator and make the rules. Every child will sit as judge or on the jury, to deliberate what should be done with rule violators, every child will help plan for student activities.

The initiation of youth into representative government by assignment rather than by election is preferable on a number of grounds. Elections based on ignorance can lead only to debasement of the process. The only basis for selection can be personal appeal. This is precisely what is corrupting the adult political scene. Premature attempts at elections will limit the experience in leadership to a privileged few. Excluded will be youth who are allegedly limited in ability; the economically deprived and the racial minority will rarely, if ever, get a chance to exercise leadership. They are doubly handicapped because when later in life they, as the under class, are asked to elect representatives they will have very limited knowledge of the specifics of the function and thus will hardly be in a position to make intelligent choices.

The teacher's role changes in this phase of development. The role requires active participation in the deliberation. The teacher will refer students to sources which will assist them. He will insist that they consider the possible consequences of their actions. The teacher must allow the students to make errors. He cannot allow the student not to learn from his errors. If things don't work well—a student activity becomes a shambles or a law meets with wide-scale violation—the teacher can convene the group and say, "Okay, what would we do differently if we had to do it all over? What did we learn from that experience?" and encourage the students to try again. If students become depressed he can restore their sense of humor. If they become overly zealous he can mitigate their authoritarian behavior.

Student Democracy in the Junior High and High School

Students in the junior high, the 12- to 15-year-olds, are now prepared to experiment with elections. They can be expected to nominate the candidate, campaign, and vote. They now have a measure of control over laws that bind behavior, treatment of law-violators, and student activities. The activities should include an advisory influence on curriculum and teacher behavior.

The sequencing of student control is important. Do not establish a student court if the students were not involved in the formation of the rules. Don't get students involved solely in the restriction of student behavior unless they are also involved in the good things of that society. Control can be appreciated only if it is deemed necessary for the *valued* activity. Flycatchers who used syrup instead of vinegar have understood this principle and yet it continually escapes those who analyze government.

The teacher's role now becomes that of a review authority. The teacher must make clear the latitudes of control which are available to the student. These restrictions should be announced in advance. The major function of the teacher is to return to the student, for reconsideration, actions which are internally inconsistent, which fly in the face of student rights, or which can be proved to lead to disastrous consequences.

By the time the student is in high school he should have matured to a point where he is a significant influence in the running of the school. His rights, as well as his responsibilities, have been clearly established. And in many areas the adults function primarily as technical assistants and consultants. If the system breaks down they have the responsibility to participate more actively. The same caveat mentioned previously in the suggestions to the administration in the high-school case must be repeated. The adults must maintain their cool, since precipitous intervention will seriously retard development of the citizen role.

Limitations to Student Government

Students cannot be expected to *run* the school. While they should have much more power than they now have, there are limits to their power. The school is truly a pluralistic institution, with many parties having legitimate claim to involvement. There must be accommodation among all of them. Teachers have rights, and they must be involved in the judicial, legislative, and executive decision-making of the school. Just as teacher oppressing student is an intolerable condition, so would be the reverse. Schools have a social responsibility. Local and more remote communities are entitled to *some* say in the education of youth. Because this influence has been abused and because these demands have been almost always excessive, inconsistent, and devoid of perceptible logic does not eliminate the legitimacy of community influence upon education.

Schools of, for, and by the students are not feasible. Students do not have the political, military, or economic potential to wrest authority from adults. Nor is there any persuasive logic to convince adults that they should relinquish all authority over the school. The call for elimination of responsible adult authority from the school is an antiintellectual posture. A sound education requires informed adults to transmit knowledge, focus questions, stimulate debate, supervise controlled experience, offer feedback and evaluation, and in myriads of other ways facilitate student growth. It is inconceivable that such leadership could be accomplished if either teacher or administrator is reduced to flunky roles.

The major hang-up to effective government is the way power is perceived. Almost always, power is seen as zero-sum. That is, all parties vie for more of what they believe is a finite amount of power. Thus it follows that whatever students gain must come at the expense of faculty, administration, or community. Efforts to establish student involvement in school government with a zero-sum approach to power can lead only to ugly wars of attrition. I do not believe there is necessarily conflict between adults and youth; nor do I believe that the essence of student government is to organize for a tug of war with adults for control of the system.

Power in a school consistent with democratic principles is *not* zero-sum. In fact the more power the adult shares with students the more power he has. Time is the only truly zero-sum game we play. Time spent on one thing *must* come at the expense of something else. Time spent by teachers establishing control over unruly youth must eat into time that could be used for legitimate educational pursuits. If sharing of power can reduce unruliness, the teacher gains time and, ergo, power to go on to other things. That this rarely happens is primarily because there is no consensus about educational goals. If youth and adults have markedly different educational goals, conflict is inevitable and the struggle for control is, indeed, zero-sum. There can be similar distortion when the means used to attain goals cannot be defended by logic or evidence.

If, however, there is basic agreement that education should lead to efficacy in the worlds of work, politics, culture, and interpersonal relationships, no battle for school hegemony need emerge. The goals offer boundaries for debate. Any action proposed from any quarter can be first questioned on its relevance to the goals. If its relevance is established, then negotiation only concerns implementation, and that discussion does not require polarization.

Student Involvement and Conditioning of the Environment

Student involvement in school decision-making will not result in a huge flap if adults in the community are prepared in advance for such eventuality. Before launching into a venture where power is shared with students, those who are to do the sharing must fully understand what is expected of them. The teacher, the board, and other significant adults should convene for a probing discussion of the implications and possible consequences of enhanced student power *prior* to embarking on the adventure. If the adult authorities are in disagreement, these differences should be resolved in advance of the undertaking (or the undertaking may have need for an undertaker). The various adults involved should be alerted to possible contingencies and to courses of action when emergencies arise. Because this doesn't usually happen, an unready community reacts violently against student initiative, and, in some instances, the student is reduced to an even more oppressed condition than that he suffered before he was encouraged to be involved in student government.

Inadequate preparation of students can also be disastrous. Educators ask for all hell to break loose if suddenly, without advance notice, they throw out an existing authoritarian system and announce that "students can organize a meaningful student government"! The students will conclude that they now have *total* control over the school. Any attempt to clarify the situation later will be interpreted as an about-face. The students will feel betrayed— worse, they will feel invaded. Power that once was theirs has been taken away. The friendly "good guy" educator who made the original pronouncement is now the vicious autocrat who is usurping their power. There will be far less turmoil if the limitation of power is clearly communicated to students at the very beginning. "Nice guy" administrators or teachers who are unwilling to recognize that there is power invested in their role that they cannot give away will only create problems for themselves.

There will be some critics and readers caught up in the romance of current revolutionary rhetoric who will renounce as revisionist all the limitations on student power that I have promoted in the previous few pages. They would have an all-or-none situation. Students who share power, they argue, are no better than those who have no power at all. Bushwa! ! This isn't even a half-a-loaf-or-none proposition, although half a loaf is always better than none, and only people who have never been hungry fail to appreciate the difference. The sharing of power is the only possible stable governing philosophy in a complex, multifaceted society. The throwbacks who argue otherwise and claim to be revolutionary are not. No one looking backward for models can rightfully call himself an advocate of progress. This is not to say that contortion and corruption of student involvement in school government is not possible. There is caducity in all democratic institutions. The students could be corrupted. They could be reduced to an illusory power. But if that happens then that, and that alone, is the condition which must be rectified. The misuse of adult power cannot be interpreted to mean that the only response is to remove the adult from any exercise of power.

Because our society as a whole, and our children in particular, have not been educated to accept democratic responsibility, very few will rush in to try.[10] There are too many threats to this initiative and too few rewards. A passive, dependent state does offer an illusion of safety. Many educators (and other adults) will be soured by the student response. They, like those who despair of student involvement because of adult takeover, will also despair because a minority of youth take over student government. They too, too often will prefer the perfect tyranny of adults to the imperfect involvement of students. It is they, not the students they condemn, who threaten student involvement in school government. Only as it is demonstrated that students can exercise power will students in large numbers strive for power. Only when the rewards for exercise of power far outweigh the rewards for renunciation of power will the majority become involved. Starting where we are, the development of a truly responsible student body will take some time. I, like so many others who are impatient, am unhappy about that. But I know that once student responsibility gains momentum its consequences may well be our salvation.

Whenever students exercise any degree of power, trouble is sure to result. There is some solace to that, because whenever students are excluded from important decision-making the inevitable trouble that results is much worse.

Knowledge Required for the Democratic Citizenship Role

There are at least two kinds of knowledge that a person adequately prepared for democratic citizenship must have. He must have a grounding in those substantive content areas that penetrate into the domain of politics. Political sophistication requires an understanding of economics, political science, psychology, sociology, and many, many other subjects. This kind of knowledge is

---

[10] See Erich Fromm, *Escape from Freedom,* Farrar & Rinehart, New York, 1941, for an analysis of a people's willingness to give up democratic involvement and subject themselves to authoritarian control.

discussed in the chapters to come, and therefore will be postponed for later consideration. There is yet another kind of knowledge a constructive citizen must possess. He must know something about the art of politics itself. He must know how to generate forces to bring about desired changes in social institutions.

The citizen must know about organizing constituencies. He must be familiar with the variety of means by which communication can be facilitated or impeded. There is a body of knowledge which has specific reference to political strategy and tactics. This must be taught to students. There are techniques and technicalities of political sophistication that, to be learned, require transmission of rather precise knowledge. Much that is needed to be known by the effective citizen unfortunately is not yet known. Even that which is known is not organized to develop effective citizens because so few educators have accepted democratic citizenship as a major goal. At this time I would like to elaborate only on how the ability to assess the impact of one's political efforts affects the citizenship role.

Newtonian Laws of Motion and Politics—An Analogy

Every action has a reaction. Isaac Newton argued that for bodies in motion, any action has an equal and opposite reaction. In politics, action also produces reaction. The reactions, however, are not always equal in magnitude or exactly opposite in direction. But that reaction may be a consequence to action must be taught to students. Understand that a complex society can operate democratically only if there is unlimited opportunity to mobilize constituencies and if the decision-making goes to those who have organized the largest constituent force. If the obvious can be accepted as true, it follows that an individual who mobilizes more people for the opposition than he does for his own side can hardly be called an effective political worker.[11]

Students are not apprised of the possible negative consequences of their actions (at least not in a manner that can be

---

[11] It is more complicated than that. There are many dimensions to political support; e.g., nature, intensity, salience, persistence and emergence of self must be considered when political impact is assessed. But the rule, while qualified, does apply, any activity which hurts more than it helps is politically stupid.

accepted as helpful). They are comforted by the conviction that right is on their side, and right somehow will always emerge triumphant. Once they find that politics does not always have a happy ending, many take a 180-degree turn and renounce politics completely in favor of mind-expanding drugs, hoping now that biochemistry can do what political action failed to do. A good education could have avoided all that recurring pain.

From a good education, students would have learned that neither psychoactive drugs nor half-baked campaigns will bring them what they want. They will have learned that some activities help them toward their intended ends, that others are worthless, and that still others harm the cause.

In California, approximately two years before this book was written, college students at a state college took on established authority in bloody confrontation. The grievances that precipitated the eruption were, in my opinion, legitimate. I do have some reservations about the tactics. They had every right to be angry. They had every right to feel frustrated. A turgid, procrastinating institution had piddled around promising much and delivering little. A governor had promised very little, but was too incompetent to deliver even that. The faculty, estranged from the students, got into the melee because of their own beefs. They were underpaid. They, at least compared to the more prestigious university faculty, were overworked. They, too, took on the Establishment. Who gained from that confrontation politically? It is my opinion that the governor gained, and further I argue that he needed the students and faculty to salvage his political career. Please allow for at least this possibility.

The governor was on the rocks. He had been elected on a platform of governmental efficiency that would pay off by reducing taxes while increasing services. Those who lionized him the most saw him stamping out all undesirable elements (criminals and bearded college students), much as he had dispatched them in the flicks. He had failed. Taxes were not down. Services were not up. Criminals were not crushed and there were even more shaggy college students in evidence on campus two years after his election than there were before. He, as governor, was a dud. The only thing that could save him was a commotion to which he could deflect attention from his obvious inadequacies. If this analysis is correct, the students and faculty at San Francisco State College were, in effect, organizing for the governor and reprieving him from a richly deserved political oblivion.

But there is yet another possibility worthy of study. It may be argued that the students did the only thing possible, and Newton's laws of motion may provide the basis for such a thesis.

A body in motion tends to stay in motion. It is possible to accept all of the above analysis and still defend the student and faculty activity at San Francisco State. If one perceives both political parties to be equally bankrupt and nonresponsive to student or faculty demands, the matter of Reagan's survival as governor becomes trivial, since his only possible replacement will come from a party offering no possible improvement. This analysis is based upon an assumption that it is the system and not the leaders which must be changed. Newtonian law offers some guidance for this group also. It could be claimed with some validity that inertia is the big problem. The body politic was at rest and needed to be set into motion because, once moved, it would remain in motion. The students could argue that the movement they had precipitated constituted a beachhead and mobilized a constituency strong enough to survive violent opposition, which would then move on to grow in importance.

Which of Newton's laws students should follow isn't really at issue. They should follow the one best supported by logic and evidence. What is important is that they are able to make a determination based on reason. This can happen only if a teacher is able to lead discussion, interject meaningful questions, and stimulate a concern for possible consequences.

Teachers should assist students in matters of ideology. Students should be prepared to debate relative merits of competing political thought and, in their deliberation, decide whether ideology is even necessary for modern Western man.[12]

Students must be prepared to analyze eventualities. They must be provided with the protocols of history-in-the-making, and, from this analysis, they will not only have a better understanding of political structure as it exists in reality but also a framework for assessing alternative strategy and tactics.

---

[12] Chaim I. Waxman (ed.), *The End of Ideology Debate,* Simon and Schuster, New York, 1968.

Summary

It is not likely that education will immediately transform itself into systems compatible with democratic principles. There will continue to be unfortunate denials of students' rights and corruption of student government. We will continue to deny youth the information they need for responsible behavior and berate them for their ignorance. But, if we recognize what we are about, there is hope we can change.

Change we must. The alternative to change is the hell Orwell described in *1984*. Each year the change must be perceptible. Next year there must be bills of rights in more classrooms. There must be more exciting experiments in student government. See for yourself how the school in your neighborhood now functions to obtain a bench mark against which next year's performance can be compared. And then make sure that *you* play a part in making next year different! ! !

CHAPTER V

Responsible Authority—A Model
for Democratic Citizenship

[In this chapter I stress the importance of the teacher as a model
of authority within a democratic context. I describe the attributes
of such authority. I distinguish between rules as ends and rules as
means, and castigate Max Rafferty on his confusion on this score.
I comment on the impact that leaders outside the school have upon
student commitment to democratic principles and I look at teaching "patriotism" in the context of preparation for democratic
citizenship.]

Many forms of government have been tried and will be tried in
this world of sin and woe. No one pretends that Democracy is
perfect or all-wise. Indeed, it has been said that Democracy is the
worst form of government except all those other forms that have
been tried from time to time. —Winston S. Churchill

Governments arise either *out* of the people or *over* the people.
—Thomas Paine

Many politicians are in the habit of laying it down as a self-evident
proposition that no people ought to be free till they are fit to use
their freedom. The maxim is worthy of the fool in the old story
who resolved not to go into the water till he had learned to swim.
—Macaulay

When a man hath no freedom to fight for at home
let him combat for that of his neighbors,
Let him think of the glory of Greece and Rome
and get knocked on your head for your labors.

To do good for mankind is the chivalrous plan
and is always as nobly requited,
Then battle for freedom whenever you can
and if not shot or hanged you'll get knighted.
—Byron

Patriotism is the last refuge of a scoundrel. —Samuel Johnson

Guard against the impostors of pretended patriotism.
—George Washington

The process of preparing a person for democratic citizenship is varied and complex. If the learning is to achieve the desired result the school must create an atmosphere that is supportive of individual rights. The student must have had considerable exercise in significant judicial, executive, and legislative decision-making. The student must be taught certain specifics about politics. The student must not only know a considerable amount about economics, sociology, psychology, history, and anthropology, but he must know how to apply this knowledge to the political arena. And yet all of this is not enough.

To be expert in democratic citizenship the student must observe leadership that is consistent with democratic principles. Only when seen in action does all of the training the student receives come together. Only then is it real. Cynicism is bred when a student sees a teacher preach one thing while he practices something distinctly different.

Democratic principles are confusing. A great many sins are committed in the name of democracy. As with nothing else, democracy has become a game of the name. Educators who prate about it really do not know whereof they speak. And whatever they mean by democracy does not conform to any acceptable standard.

Weisner and Hayes commented on the results of their survey of democratic attitudes of prospective and experienced elementary and secondary school teachers:

> They appear to have attitudes which they probably would not understand as, or admit to being, antidemocratic. They appear to realize the potentialities of change in our society—perhaps would even accept the need for change; but some would not provide for change through democratic means. They seem generally to have concern for the private rights of individuals, but many do not approve of the free exercise of means to bring about change. Many would not seem to be in accord with an idea expressed by the NEA Project on Instruction Report: "Differences of opinion are a continuing and important part of the life in a democratic society, they are to be respected, encouraged, resolved." The preoccupation of many teachers with authority over children arouses serious question. How many teachers are there who really understand and practice democracy? [1]

---

[1] John C. Weisner and James E. Hayes, "Democratic Attitudes of Teachers and Prospective Teachers," *Phi Delta Kappan,* May 1966, p. 481,

But bad as the teacher responses to questions about democracy are, their behavior is worse. And here we should be clear on what are the essentials of authority consistent with democratic principles. There are five components of authority within a democratic context. These include:

1) Appreciation of differences.
2) Accountability.
3) Negotiability.
4) Recognition that conflict is essential in a complicated society.
5) Recognition of rules as means rather than as ends.

1. *Appreciation of differences.* The teacher must communicate appreciation of a wide range of differences. The concept of rights becomes devoid of meaning if the teacher by stance or covert expression denies equal citizenry to those who are different. The nature of difference in one sense really isn't important—it can be style, appearance, religion, skin color, natural tongue, tempo, dress, sex, or physical handicap. If there is minimal appreciation for differences, there is minimal respect for persons who are exercising their right to be different. And yet the nature of difference *is* important. Some trivial prejudices can be ignored, but disrespect for persons because of skin color or political ideology cannot be ignored. Often we do an excellent job of convincing teachers to appreciate trivial differences.

There is no sure-fire way to produce appreciation of difference. There are tactics and strategies that are likely to improve the current situation. At every stage of preparation, and at every available opportunity, teachers must be impressed with the importance of respect for individual difference. Prospective teachers very early in their college career may be involved with tutoring; they should be challenged when they impugn the styles or language or dress of their students. Experienced teachers may receive the same kind of challenge in a summer institute. Every teacher, on a more informal basis, must continually face up to his colleagues when conformity becomes confused with education. The respect for difference must be applied when teachers are recruited. Stu-

and much the same impression is gained from Harmon Ziegler's, *The Political World of the High School Teacher,* University of Oregon, The Center for the Advanced Study of Education Administration, Eugene, Oregon, 1966.

dents will believe they have the right to be different when they see visible differences in their teachers. The groups from which teachers are drawn greatly influence the range of orientation and behavior of the teaching force. If the teachers collectively are to do what no teacher individually can be expected to do—respect the right of students to be different—then the New Career's philosophy expounded in Chapter III must be given serious consideration so that all diverse groups that make up a pluralistic society are represented.

2. *Accountability*. The teacher in a democratic context is accountable. Whatever he requests or requires must be defended. He must justify his activities to students, to parents, to taxpayers, and to administrators. Only logic and evidence, in the context of agreed-upon goals of education, can provide the basis for accountable action. Everything a child does within a school should be fair game for challenge, and the teacher should be able to explain the connection of the student activity and an educational goal.

Education is too complex for unanimity on any activity to be expected. Teachers must have the right to go their own way. They must have independence in decision-making. It is only when decisions can no longer be defended logically within the context of educational goals that teachers or administrators can be restricted. Only after teachers or administrators reveal their inability to become accountable should such persons be relieved of their duties. The concern for student rights can never become the excuse by which the rights of teachers or administrators are repudiated.

All the goals of education are compatible with each other. The teacher cannot say as a defense for violation of students' rights that such activity was necessary to accomplish another educational goal. And yet this is what frequently happens.

Operant conditioning is very fashionable in education today. Operant conditioning is a system by which behavior is reputedly changed by rewarding the student (subject or client) whenever he does something "right." Operant conditioning underlies programmed texts and "systems" approaches to the instruction of reading and other subjects. Operant conditioning is viewed by some as a major breakthrough. I am not one who has been converted to modern-day behaviorism. I think the adherents have too mechanistic a view of man. I think they have oversold their accomplishments. I think they suffer from the megalomania that accompanies cults. But most of all I think operant conditioning is not consistent with the goal of preparing students for democratic citizenship. Their terminology, e.g., "behavior modification or shaping," gives them away. They make no pretense of accountability other than the old saw that the ends justify the means. They argue that they know what is best for people and will reinforce those behaviors that coincide with their prejudices. There are behaviors they try to influence that are not subject to much dispute. Operant conditioning is used to correct speech defects; no group can object to that. But when youth with legitimate complaints and legitimate hostility that is derived from those complaints are coerced to comply with unequitable and degrading demands, this coercion is couched in scientific terms which give an illusion of justifiability. In effect what happens is that if youths submit to a demand of unnecessary silence on racial or personal slurs they are immediately rewarded ("reinforced") by candy or praise. If they resist sometimes they are ignored but often they are punished. Perhaps some of the efforts to condition the "socially and emotionally disturbed" into more acceptable behavior are justifiable, but precious little justification has taken place, and because of the almost continued effort of school to stamp out individuality, the accountability of the new-look social engineers must be questioned.

Sometimes the venture may be legitimate, but the demands that surround it cannot be defended. One advocate of a highly structured approach to reading instruction requires that his young charges jump up and down forty times before they begin their reading lesson.[2] There is no logic or evidence that reading is facilitated by up-and-down jumping.

Requiring children to do things not linked directly to an agreed-upon educational goal is a violation of accountability. Not only must the teacher be prepared to defend the major thrust of his requests; he must also defend the regulations that he attaches to the activity. Even spectacular accomplishments in one aspect of education cannot excuse the violation of other educational goals.

Accountability implies trustworthiness. A responsible authority in a democratic context must be trusted by those he is to lead. President Johnson had problems with his credibility, but he comes

---

[2] Sigmund Engelmann, *Encounter*, University of Oregon, Mar. 1969.

across as an honest man when compared with teachers. A major complaint of students is that they cannot trust teachers. It is not that teachers are viewed as "bad" people. It is more that they are "humanoid." They are not perceived as whole people. They do not indicate who they are or what they desire. There may be a human being hiding behind all those lesson plans, but students are unable to find him. Education demands that children change, and that is a scary business. If the teacher does not inspire confidence the student will shy away.

The minority student is doubly troubled. The teacher and administrator are distrusted not only because of the role but also because of race. It is exceedingly difficult to trust someone who represents a group you have learned from experience to distrust. School districts attempt to rectify the situation by placing persons with dark skins in positions of authority. This artifice fails because this person is often not accountable to students. One of the many names students have for him is "Oreo cookie," which means he is dark on the outside and white on the inside.

Whenever a teacher is placed on a job he cannot accountably perform, the ability to educate is weakened. Control in such a circumstance must be unilaterally imposed. The result will be disengagement of youth, and, in some instances, violent outbursts. Once student alienation is understood to be a direct reflection of the ability of teachers to be accountable and to earn the respect of the student, a solution to the problem will be within reach.

3. *Negotiability.* Education is never imposed; it always is the result of a negotiated contract between all persons involved in the process. The responsible authority is always ready to negotiate differences with students. Students should be encouraged to suggest alternative ways of doing things, and the teacher should be open to these suggestions. When the student and adult authority are in conflict (an inevitability), efforts to reconcile those differences are an important aspect of the education process. If serious negotiation takes place between students and adults, the student is being educated in the matter of conflict resolution. But negotiations are eschewed on many grounds, none of which is valid.

Teachers argue that the time consumed in negotiating with students interferes with instruction. The reverse is more likely true —the recitation of meaningless ritual interferes with the important learning that accompanies negotiation. Negotiation of differences has relevance to all of the educational goals. Negotiation is obviously a vital factor in work, in democratic citizenship, in learning to live with oneself and one's neighbors, in scientific investigations, and in the appreciation of the contribution made by diverse cultural groups.

Teachers argue that negotiations undermine their authority. This is true only if the authority is, by its nature, coercive. If, however, the teacher is a legitimate authority, if he possesses the leadership to govern, he gains authority through negotiation. If the teacher has no capacity to lead he *must* be encouraged to get into another business. The system cannot be grossly distorted to accommodate staff too inadequate to function in a democratic context. But this distortion is now standard practice. It is the coercive authority which receives support. All too frequently it is the teacher who is willing to negotiate who is encouraged to go into another occupation.

Negotiability must exist everywhere in education. The teacher-student relationship can be little better than the administrator-staff relationship or the board-staff relationship, etc. If a board imposes rigid nonnegotiable conditions on the staff—e.g., a dress code or a rule forbidding controversial speakers on campus—all others affected by this order are restricted in their negotiability.

The conditions that restrict teacher negotiability are generally very ambiguous and after the fact. It generally takes the form of support for status quo, regardless of merit of argument. Look at a typical situation. A social studies high-school teacher in a racially mixed inner-city urban school begins to take seriously the need for preparing students for democratic citizenship. He opens up for discussion critical current issues. His students become involved in research in areas of political controversy. His class departs radically from the usual highly controlled passive group of students to a group which actively inquires. The student response is uniformly enthusiastic. The principal of the school is distinctly unenthusiastic. He becomes even more negative when the students lampoon him in a creative multimedia presentation of authoritarianism in modern America. He accuses the teacher (now in his third year of instruction and therefore untenured, although highly praised on his performance in his first two years of teaching) of a multitude of serious offenses, among which were:

1) Inspiring students to show disrespect for constituted authority.

2) Inability to adequately control his class.

3) Irresponsibility (being late to classes and tolerating tardiness among students).

4) Feigning illness when actually well.

With very little notice the board met on these charges, none of which was substantiated beyond the unsupported statements of the administration. Students and parents rallied behind the teacher. The teacher was fired. The board's only defense is that they must support its "administration." Education cannot afford such support! An educational system that makes no more strenuous effort than that to negotiate differences will continue to disengage many of its students. The board had many options. To begin with, the members of the board had to recognize that variation in teacher behavior is to be encouraged not stifled. The board could have instructed the administrators to live with a variety of teachers and the teacher live with different types of students. No one will be loved by all. The same teacher who is worshipped by some students will be despised by others. All of this is fine. It sets the stage for all forms of negotiations, including assignment of students to teachers. If selection and deselection of teachers continues to be based on a willingness to conform blindly to administrative fiat, then the most alienated student will soon be without advocates or allies. The board could have sent the issue back to the school, suggesting that the staff (and students) meet in convocation and negotiate a means by which diversity could be accepted while necessary order was maintained. The board could have provided funds for a weekend retreat so that issues could be examined in depth, and they could have retained consultants who were expert in ameliorating tensions that arise when there is conflict.

The board could have considered reassignment. If the tensions between an administrator and a staff member may indeed be so basic and of such a nature that serious disruption of school activities is the inevitable result, the teacher (or administrator) may be reassigned to another situation. The board always seems willing to do this when incompetence is the issue (incompetent teachers never die, they just get reassigned) but never when insubordination is the charge. The message is very clear—no one really cares how badly a teacher teaches just as long as he doesn't challenge the system. If he challenges, he's got to go. There were other principals who would have found the accused teacher compatible with their philosophy and a valuable asset to their program. But the board could not consider this alternative because such action would be a "slap in the face" to the principal who wanted vengeance, and, implicitly, a transfer would imply an oblique criticism of the administrative skill of the principal. The board also felt that transfer would allow the teacher tenure and, if he indeed were a troublemaker, he would be teaching in the district forever. Tenure is not that powerful a protector. Teachers with tenure can be removed if boards want to take the trouble. Essentially what happened here is merely another manifestation of a board's desire to take the "easy way out"! To sort out truth from rumor—and ultimately the hard, tough business of negotiations—would require serious effort and much expenditure of time. Better for all to "dump" a dissident, oddball teacher and forget the whole mess. Fine, except that that just isn't going to happen. Ultimately the press upon the schools will reach such proportion to preclude sweeping problems under the rug—and when that happens, administrators will play hell trying to get back all those vital, questioning, exciting teachers they have driven out.

The board had a final option they never even considered— and that was to "slap the principal's face." He could have been removed. He could have been instructed in the function of duties of responsible authority. He could have been assisted in learning the skills required for his job. The same school district a few years before had another principal who was assigned to a ghetto school and who attempted to impose arbitrary and coercive control over the school. I had some minimal relationship with the staff of that school, but my contact with the school staff was discouraged because my "philosophy was so divergent" from the administration. I cautioned the central office administration that ultimately they would either have to help the administrator or remove him. As matters worsened they procrastinated, until two years later the change which had to be made was finally made. All that has happened in this country in the last few years has made even more intolerable the leaders who cannot sustain their position through negotiation. To forsake negotiation is to choose to crush all opposition. We can neither afford to win or lose such a battle with our youth.

To argue that only through strict authoritarian control can education function is to renounce any belief in democratic practices. If school personnel are unwilling to negotiate, they deliver to students the message that all the stuff taught in school about democracy is "baloney."

Of late, students have issued "nonnegotiable" demands. This "arrogance" is not welcomed by adult authority. I don't see why we as adults are either surprised or upset by the nature of the student demands. It only shows again that we taught them not wisely but well. The adult has taught students that important things are not negotiated but unilaterally imposed. The teacher has generated a stance that students have emulated. If we object to the student activity, shouldn't we intervene and alter the behavior of the adult models?

The issue of students' call for nonnegotiability is not one merely of student recalcitrance; there is also the question of rectitude. In some of their demands the students are on very solid ground. *There are matters which are not negotiable.* Student rights cannot be bartered away. Often students are placed in the ridiculous position of demanding what is rightfully theirs, and then they are attacked for their posture. One of the demands made by the Black Student Union at San Francisco State College was for unlimited enrollment in the school. This was opposed by the president, S. I. Hayakawa. He argued that admission of students with inferior high-school records would discriminate against those students who worked hard prior to high-school graduation.[3] This is missing the point completely. Black students are not denied college admission because they were lazy in high school. They are denied college because of all the factors discussed in Chapter I. To deny their admission is to deny them the opportunity to escape from poverty. Black and brown students not only have the right to demand unlimited enrollment; they also have the right to all the resources (financial, academic, and social) that are necessary for success. They also should have the right to be spared from the cavalier sillinesss that characterizes Dr. Hayakawa.

4. *Recognition that conflict is essential in a complicated society.* Not all differences can be reconciled, nor should they be.

---

[3] Speech before San Francisco Commonwealth Club, Oct. 1968.

Nothing would be more unnatural than to have all differences within a school resolved. And yet, differences are disquieting to school personnel. They do not like debate that is not well modulated and regulated. Only the exercise of debate is tolerated. If there is feeling, if the debate extends beyond the subscribed areas or takes forms that those in power find offensive, discussion is cut off. If the issues are personal, if they treat matters of social significance, there is inevitably some form of suppression.

In education there is an ungodly strain toward consensus. Pressure is put on all to conform. Faculties shy away from debate. When differences exist, in place of lively contention there is separation into two or more noncommunicating camps. Each group places blame on the other for the "cold war." None view the disagreement as inevitable, let alone essential.

Could it be otherwise? Nice, noncontentious people seek careers in education precisely because it is a haven from the outside world of noise, rage, vexations, confrontations, hurly-burly, violence. They go to a school of education that dries up a large measure of their vital juices. They serve with other teachers who rouse to life only to snuff out the spark that spontaneously bursts into flames in a colleague. Over them are administrators who pride themselves on their "well-oiled machine," "smoothly run organization," and willingness to *discuss* amicably all problems and act on none. I had a dean who epitomized that style—after every frustrating and nonproductive meeting he would, in smiling benediction, inform us that our rights to complain would always be welcomed and that next year, if still interested, we should bring up the matter again. And only a small minority of the faculty was furious at his attitude.

Once we recognize that dispute is desirable we will begin to make the necessary change. The means by which change in teacher recruitment and training and assignment can be accomplished has been discussed previously. (See again, New Careers, Chapter III.) What is added here are some of the dimensions to be considered when education for teachers is being planned and when persons are recruited for responsible positions in education.

We must go still further. When there is educational leadership that is consistent with a democratic society, when the pluralism of that society is acknowledged, and when conflict is judged to be inescapable, then mechanisms for independent resolutions of grievances *must* be established. The *willingness* of teachers and administrators to give up absolute control and substitute conciliation for despotism will do much to reduce the bitterness that now distorts so much of youth-adult relationships.

The problem of the principal and the dissident teacher discussed above is explained, at least partially, by an intolerance of controversy. Student unrest, which ultimately boils up into violence, would end up that way far less frequently if teachers had more than two strings to their bow. At the present time teachers and administrators are permitted either to coerce or to "cool out." Neither approach solves problems or educates. Coercion intensifies generational conflict, and "cooling out" (a phrase that connotes the illusion of compromise) only puts off the discontented, and, to paraphrase Abraham Lincoln, while you can cool out some of the people, you can't do it all of the time.

5. *Recognition of rules as means rather than ends.* Rules in the schools must be put into perspective. Students *are* violating school rules now, to an extent and with a style that they have never used before. This phenomenon should concern us all. What is happening in schools is a serious matter that requires some careful thinking-through and well-designed alterations in school programs. Not much serious thinking is taking place in the councils where the big decisions are to be made. In the place of serious thinking is cheap politicking and cries for vengeance. Student unrest is a windfall for grubby, power-seeking politicians.

Max Rafferty, former State Superintendent of Public Instruction in California, almost made it to the U.S. Senate by placing the blame for rule violations on "progressive educators" and tenderminded psychologists. His philosophy influenced much legislative and executive action, particularly at the local level. As unsavory as he appears to many responsible educators, Max Rafferty or any of his many counterparts cannot be ignored. But more important than a confrontation with Rafferty—or Ronald Reagan, another individual who is opportunistically benefiting from the unrest—is the need for understanding the forces which cause adult authority to act oppressively when students abrogate laws, and the factors which cause youth to disregard adult authority. The current mood would probably require that a Rafferty or Reagan be manufactured if a ready-made one had not presented himself to us. So many among us look always for the MAN to simply crush those who create problems for us. Because we are so unthinking about school problems we rally behind persons with neat slogans. Many of us would like to solve our generational conflict by "winning the war and getting out."

What must first be established in the minds of persons who gravitate to a Rafferty mentality is the illegitimacy and the un-reasonableness of the student effort. Students cannot be seen as driven to distraction by unresolved grievances, restrictions, stupidities. Never can the students be placed in the tradition of heroic opposition to oppressison (in league with other celebrated law violators such as George Washington, Thomas Jefferson, Benjamin Franklin, Wendell Phillips, and Martin Luther King, Jr.). The student unrest must be viewed as a conspiracy in which children are subverted by some shrouded evil.

Rafferty plays that conspiracy game to a fare-thee-well. He is gallant Lochinvar riding out of the West to save the day and spirit away fair education before she is wedded forever to John Dewey and his cadre of moral and mental weaklings. He identifies many forms of conspiratorial seductions perpetrated by the "progressive educators" who, like trichina, worked their way into the body of education during the 30's and have inflicted pain ever since. The "progressive educators" do their dirty deeds by:

a) Denying "positive and eternal" values.

b) Stressing "life adjustment and group acceptance" rather than "subject matter."

c) Downgrading the individual.

d) Catering to group interests and needs.

e) Categorizing memorization as a waste of time.

f) Stressing "experience" rather than reading and recitation.

g) Eliminating interindividual competition, and

h) Casting doubt on the free enterprise system.[4]

Rafferty conjures up images of rapacious youth (he likes to call them "punks" or "slobs") on the loose—ravaging and pillaging—while cowering in hidden corners are the pusilanimous teachers, for whom we self-sacrificing citizens have taxed ourselves into financial ruin.

---

[4] Max Rafferty, *What They Are Doing to Your Children,* Signet Books, New American Library, New York, 1966, pp. 76–77.

The conspiracy is portrayed as desperate, deep, and devastating. To become a teacher, one has to navigate through a school of education, and that, according to Rafferty "is the last defender of Progressive Education," [5] where the professor:

> . . . discourages and gives low grades to any of their student teachers who insist upon the organized, disciplined, systematic presentation of the subject matter as their principle interest and function. Now isn't that something from a person who insists that pupils' papers be handed back if they contain misspelled words and faulty construction that haven't been circled? [6]

> In countless professional journals they carry on a vicious and vindictive guerrilla warfare against any and all educational reformers who show any inclination to upset the cozy kingdom which those professors of education have built for themselves at the expense of both basic education and the taxpayer's pocketbook. [7]

In the Rafferty mind, while one insidious column corrupts the teacher, there is another working on parents. In this group are the psychologists who have undermined the parents' will to control their children:

> Things have changed of late in the field of discipline and more than somewhat. They started to change at home first back in the twenties and thirties. The prime mover in this change was the new psychology, which was widely publicized and which caused parents to seriously doubt their proper role vis-à-vis their children for the first time in recorded history of the human race. Fathers began to hear of the "Oedipus complex" and were urged to search their souls before whipping junior lest their real motivation be subconscious rivalry for mom's affection. Mothers were told of the "inferiority complex" and were frightened out of their wits at the thought of "repressing" junior. Both mom and dad were told sternly to get out of the way and let their child express himself unless they wanted him to blame his parents in later life for the traumatic psychoses that were almost certain to crop up.
> The result was the emergence of the least-repressed and worst behaved generation of youngsters this world has ever seen. Junior as a child played with toys but refused to put them away, threw spinach on the dining room floor but got the ice cream anyway, sassed his parents to their faces and got away with it. As a teen-

---

[5] Max Rafferty, *Max Rafferty on Education,* Devin-Adair Co., New York, 1968, p. 19.
[6] *Ibid.,* p. 75.
[7] *Ibid.,* p. 20.

ager, junior stole the old man's whisky and shared it with the guys, drag raced on the country highway at midnight with the family car, and told both the cop and the judge to go to hell when he finally was hauled in. He feared nothing and respected nobody because he had never been compelled to do either. The psychologists had been right in one respect, junior certainly had no repressions. He could have used a few.[8]

Rafferty's solution is simple. He would crack down, and hard, on rule violators:

> Common sense told us that discipline, like good manners had to be taught to a child over a period of years. Society disciplines its members through laws and penalties.[9]
>
> At any rate, once the two premises are accepted that (1) boys won't behave in school unless compelled to do so and (2) boys must be made to behave so that they can learn things that are essential to know then the whole paraphernalia of corporal punishment falls into proper perspective.[10]
>
> Why not outlaw profanity and bring back the good old soap-in-the-mouth bit for any youngsters who can't keep a clean tongue in their heads?[11]

Rafferty has a good thing going with his conspiracy thesis. He updates it and keeps it topical. When there is trouble on campus, "The conspirators are the white members of the so-called Students for a Democratic Society on the one hand, and the Negro members of the Black Student Union on the other."[12]

Rafferty is not alone in his call for a get-tough policy. Many teachers and administrators who actually function in the schools agree with him. Newspaper columnists throw in their opinions as if their lack of reflection is an ironclad guarantee of veridicality. Here is a prescription for the Portland, Oregon, high schools:

> Establish basic rules of accepted school conduct, and crack down hard to insure that students conform with the standards.
>
> The school system needs a uniform code of ethics for student behavior, and it must be enforced. After a few dozen student expulsions for repeated violation, the rest would get the idea.[13]

---

[8] Max Rafferty, *What They Are Doing to Your Children, op. cit.,* pp. 106–107.

[9] *Ibid.,* p. 53.

[10] *Ibid.,* p. 105.

[11] Max Rafferty, *Rafferty on Education, op. cit.,* p. 118.

[12] Max Rafferty, national syndicated column in *Portland Oregonian,* Apr. 3, 1969.

[13] John Guernsey, *Portland Oregonian,* Forum Section, Apr. 27, 1969.

Would that problems could be solved so easily. Would that lack of "discipline" was the work of subversives. Would even that there was evidence that a crackdown on rule-violators deterred the practice. Rules for schools are no simple matter, and anyone who believes that is either an ignoramus or a charlatan or both.

There are many factors that complicate the rules in school matters. There is the issue of justice. Rules rarely apply equally for all youth. There is a clearly discernible race, class, and ethnic bias in the formulation of rules and in their implementation. The very same behavior that gets a poor black child suspended draws an affluent white child no more than a reprimand.

There is differential reason to obey laws. The child who gets no satisfaction from school is less likely to discipline himself than a child who finds the experience gratifying. Rafferty, with his claims to patriotism, should know that from his study of the Revolutionary War. Rule-violation now, as it was then, is one way of informing establishments that "treading on will no longer be tolerated."

The plain truth is that getting tough with kids never has been effective. It didn't work in the good old days, when only the most motivated went to school. It won't work now. All that a crackdown will bring is heightened hostility—the educational hardliner should learn something from his parallel—the Vietnam hawk—before his foolishness leads to a parallel tragedy.

The whole picture is out of focus. The youth in school does not perceive himself in a permissive environment. The student does not see himself thumbing his nose with impunity at constituted authority, nor does he think he is having a ball at the expense of powerless adults. He sees himself in the precise hell that Rafferty recommends. To the student, school is a prison and the rules are merely excuses to be used to exclude or to humiliate.

Very few students (I have yet to meet one) deny the need for rules. They object to what they feel are unnecessary restrictions and enforcement which are discriminatory or brutal.

I, who believe strongly in the need for school rules, insist that the real issue of disorder is the perspective in which rules are put. What the Raffertys of the world choose to ignore is that rules are always secondary in a democracy. In a good society, man does not live just to obey rules. In a good society, rules are established because some behaviors must be regulated if more important goals are to be attained. *In a good society, rules are always means and never ends.* Only in totalitarian societies do rules become ends in themselves.

Too many school authorities subscribe to totalitarian doctrines. The teacher who places things in proper perspective, who places the integrity of the educational venture foremost will have little trouble with rule violators. It is the lack of relevance of school to career, to political, cultural, and personal matters that leads to breakdown of order. It is the lack of respect for the student as a responsible being which leads to breakdown of law.

The teacher who follows the Jeffersonian principle of ruling best by ruling least will avoid much unnecessary grief. Every teacher must keep this ever present in his thinking—every unnecessary rule leads to an unnecessary rule-violator. Never in the history of man has there been a rule established that some did not disobey.

The teacher must use judicial discretion in the treatment of rule-violators. Any ritualistic approach (mistakenly considered consistency) soon becomes totally unworkable. Teachers should be given the leeway to function as true professionals and be held accountable for their actions. Only then will either chaos or despotism be avoided.

Irresponsible Authority—Its Impact on Law and Order

Student unrest is partially a function of teacher and school administrator irresponsibility. Their lack of appreciation for difference, their failure to be accountable, their unwillingness to negotiate, their intolerance for conflict, and their imposition of rules as ends and not means have drawn a sizable proportion of students into overtly hostile acts against school personnel or property.

The educator is not solely responsible. He is probably only a minor player on the stage on which kingly characters' consciences are being caught. The leaders outside the school have an impact on students' behavior. Richard Nixon, Hubert Humphrey, and George Wallace, each in his own way, has contributed to the breakdown of "Law and Order."

Richard Nixon is a leader with a limited youthful constituency. He doesn't resonate with the concerns of the student who desires change. He is not allied with those who oppose a lengthy war. He has no appeal among those who want an end to racial injustice. He offers no solace to antipoverty fighters. He doesn't reach out to those who want humanization of depersonalized bureaucracies. To the contrary. He is cold, efficient, and businesslike. The students who identify with him don't suffer the alienation of powerlessness nor do they need exhortion to obey the law. Orderliness is their reason to exist. But what about the others—the minorities who see in his election an expression of majority insensitivity? Where do these persons go to find their leader?

This group of alienated youth can't reach out to George Wallace. George Wallace, regardless of his pronouncement, makes an overt appeal to lawlessness. His candidacy was an assertion that only laws that people agree with need to be obeyed. While he blasts away at "anarchists" he asserts the right to defy what the Supreme Court unanimously ruled to be the law of the land. He proclaims the right of any individual to impugn the motives of "pointed-head guidelines writers" or Washington bureaucrats and to act accordingly in defiance of them. He rejects accountability and negotiability as signs of weakness. There is a demand that those differing with him be crushed. He is all for a hard-line policy on rule enforcement (when he agrees with the rules), and these rules are seen as ends in themselves. The alienated youth who looked to Wallace were ones who lamented that the world walked off and left them.

The powerless at the other end of the political spectrum had only Hubert Humphrey to turn to for leadership for peace, equality, and human dignity. And here is real tragedy. The Humphrey candidacy had no credibility. He had been part of an administration that failed to attract youth. In fact, the dissent and the resistance movements emerged and grew as a direct consequence of that administration's policies. Humphrey had no popular following. He was rejected in primary elections. And don't forget that alienated youth tried to work for change in an orderly fashion and within his system. Many black and brown youth were attracted by the charisma of Robert Kennedy. Many far-out white youth cleaned up and knocked themselves out promoting Eugene McCarthy. But what happened? The renaissance of idealism was snuffed out in the ugly charade that the Democratic party tried to pass off as a nominating convention.[14]

---

[14] I think that many youth fail to interpret properly the events of the winter and spring of 1968. The Democratic party convention is viewed by some as proof that efforts within the system are doomed to fail, that the powers that be respect only force and disruption and that law and order are

The educator has to be in the forefront of all activities designed to revitalize the democratic process. He must be both in and out of the classroom—a model of exemplary citizenship. He has to infuse into the political process an intellectual component that is now sadly absent. "Law and Order" is an anti-intellectual response to complex social problems. But the most important issues placed before the American people are not decided on evidence or logic. Anti-intellectualism is, and has been, good politics. H. L. Mencken once commented that no one starved to death insulting the intelligence of the American people—politicians have made intelligence-insulting a profitable venture.

In such issues as the war in Vietnam, integration of schools, or sex education the expert intellectual appears to be more a political liability than an asset. Despite the overwhelming support of scientific opinion the odds are 5 to 1 against a public vote for fluoridation of water.[15] The reason for the ineffectuality of the intellectual in politics is not too difficult to fathom. The educator tends to be a political klutz. He allows others to choose the candidate. He allows others to make the headlines. When he tentatively offers his views he lacks power or clarity. He is easily lampooned. His style gives credence to the notion that education is gained at the expense of common sense. By his language and his tempo he sets himself outside of controversy. He is T. S. Eliot's J. Alfred Prufrock:

> Differential, glad to be of use,
> politic, cautious and meticulous,

means by which opposition to tyranny are crushed. Yet there is another possible interpretation and that is—the McCarthy enthusiasts succeeded with the following consequences—a President decided not to run for re-election, sufficient voters were attracted to win primaries, the platform reflected some of this influence, old-line leadership was forced to contend with challenges till this happened in a campaign that suffered because of its late start, its lack of effective coalition, its inadequate funding, its weaknesses of organization and its fuzziness of position.

That the campaign failed to culminate in the nomination of a President is not the mark of failure. The presidential nominating system is the least perfect of our quite imperfect democratic system. There, more than anywhere else, the electorate is locked out of the decision process. Delegates who win their positions through primary elections are more than neutralized by those who are selected by party bigwigs. If a campaign to nominate a President is to succeed, it cannot start the winter prior to the nomination. It must begin at least two years before, during congressional and gubernatorial elections which are crucial in the selection of delegates.

[15] See Robert L. Crain, E. Katz, and Donald Rosenthal, *The Politics of Community Conflict,* Bobbs-Merrill, New York, 1969.

> full of high sentence, but a bit obtuse
> at times, indeed, almost ridiculous.
> Almost, at times, the Fool.

The forces that push for repression of youth are vocal and have some organizational sense. They will continue to score political victories unless an opposition develops which is at least equal in organization and articulation. The teacher's failure to perform exemplar role models has contributed to a climate of anti-intellectual oppressiveness. The teacher's political passivity has contributed to the bankruptcy of existing political parties.

The Teaching of Patriotism

Preparing youth for democratic citizenship is interpreted variously, and this is a major rub. Very few quarrel with the general statement. A great many oppose the concepts presented here. A sizable number equate preparation for democratic citizenship with teaching patriotism. Notable among this group is the ineffable [16] Max Rafferty. Rafferty simply wants students to be taught to love the United States and its heroes. I find his approach to patriotism nauseating. He reduces love of country to the same plane advertisers use to sell body deodorants. I further resent Rafferty's self-deification. He has no corner on the patriotism market. Even by his own quaint definition, Rafferty is undistinguished as a patriot. Neither in war nor in peace can he defend the "super" status he claims for himself. On the basis of his record he is strictly bush league.

Rafferty's "patriotism" is repugnant for many reasons. It lionizes anti-intellectuality. Everything is distorted. The uncritical eulogizing of George Washington leaves no room for a Thomas Paine who questions only this of the country's father: "Whether you have abandoned good principles, or whether you ever had any." Adoration of Abraham Lincoln forces the censure of a man such as Thaddeus Stevens. There isn't the analysis necessary to appreciate that every man elected to office was just that—a man. None was without human failings. None was beyond criticism. None was elected unanimously. In every instance some citizens

---

[16] Ineffable is one of Rafferty's favorite adjectives. He attaches it promiscuously to everyone from James Bond to Adam Clayton Powell in *Rafferty on Education, op. cit.*

were denied representation and their grievances fell on deaf ears. Rafferty's "patriotism" is static and ahistorical. As a consequence of his teaching, those who have suffered indignity and inequality continue to suffer indignity and inequality.

Rafferty's approach to instruction in patriotism reinforces racism. It is racist by omission, glossing over injustice, slavery, genocide, and wars of aggression. It is racist by commission. An instance of patriotic heroism he cites is the pioneer woman fighting off the Apache murderer. His language doesn't allow for consideration of the Apache's complaints—that it was HIS home that had been invaded and that he was responding to one of the dishonorable acts in what Helen Hunt Jackson called *A Century of Dishonor*. Throughout, Rafferty equates "patriotism" with warriorism. He elevates bullies and sadists to heroic proportions. He defends "patriotism" by asking "What's wrong with love?" Nothing is wrong with love except to confuse it with hate. And hate underlies all of Rafferty's "patriotism." He hates the Supreme Court. He hates John Dewey. He hates American dissidents. He hates foreign ideologists. He would have us fight an enemy while he would deny us the right to understand that which we are compelled to fight.[17]

A sense of national purpose need not be perverted to jingoism. The school can and should play a constructive role in developing loyalty to democratic principles. This loyalty should be dedicated to perceiving hard-won virtues and eliminating persisting flaws in governmental structure. The only love that can be defended is the love and allegiance to principles of freedom. The manifestation of that love should be a constant struggle for equality at home and inspiration for those hungering for similar objectives abroad. I believe that that kind of patriotism will be best achieved when students have been afforded the knowledge and experience to function as democratic citizens.

The "Experts" and Democratic Leadership

Everybody tries to help the teacher prepare students for democratic citizenship. Most expert advice designed to help teachers play a leadership role in the classroom is dumb—the dumbness is expressed both in inarticulation and in unintelligence. Some advice

---

[17] See examples of all of this in *Rafferty on Education, ibid.*

is downright vicious. Some experts direct the teacher to disregard student rights and, for that matter, even question whether teachers have any rights to nonconformity.

Katherine C. La Mancusa is such an expert. She, in a book designed to help elementary teachers establish classroom control, puts it right out there: "Basic in a teacher's desire to establish classroom control is a commitment toward support and follow-through in this regulatory aspect of the school society." [18]

This formulation leaves no discretion to the teacher: "Theirs not to reason why, theirs but to do and"—you betcha—"die." Not once in 197 pages of caveats, homilies, anecdotes, prescriptions, and vignettes does the author allude to student rights. Never is there a flickering of recognition that race, class, and ethnic affiliation complicate classroom control. Pluralism is not mentioned or even understood. Thoreau's concern for those who listen to a different drummer is not given credence either for teacher or for student.

The author advises manipulation and humiliation of students, apparently for no other purpose than to secure the power base of the teacher. Examine the cute gimmick that the author calls "efficacious bouncing." A child challenges the teacher by refusing to come to the front of the class when ordered to do so, so the teacher manages to get the child out in the hall:

> Once outside in the hall, on a one-to-one basis and away from the rest of the students, the teacher may look at the child and say, "I do not understand why you acted that way in class. I want you to understand that the behavior you exhibited in the classroom will never be tolerated. I am sure you understand why."
>
> It is never wise to ask the child to "explain" himself in his actions, for he is too emotionally involved to think clearly. Also, nine times out of ten, by the time the child is outside in the hall with the teacher, he will break down in tears. There is something therapeutic and healing about helping him to wipe his tears away with a damp paper towel and allowing him to get a drink of water. Afterwards, he will doubtless have himself fairly well in hand. The teacher may say to him at this time, "I would like to talk to you about this after school." The child is amenable at this point and is willing to yield under the temperate and rather mild consequences. He had really expected a good deal worse.
>
> At this point, the door is swung open wide. All students look toward the door. They note that their errant classmate has been

---

[18] Katherine C. La Mancusa, *We Do Not Throw Rocks at the Teacher,* International Textbook, Scranton, Pa., 1966, p. 21.

crying. The child enters ahead of the teacher and walks to his desk. The teacher has a cross look on his face. For all practical purposes, it appears as though the teacher has had the final and victorious "last word." Why not? The child was crying, wasn't he? The teacher looked cross, didn't he? The boy came into the classroom, much pacified, didn't he? No doubt about it. He got his just desserts.[19]

That is ghastly!! Analyze what is being said. To begin with, why should a young child be forced to come to the teacher? Compliance with the command must lead to embarrassment. What prevents the adult teacher from going to the student? (And let's not hear the nonsense that the teacher has an obligation to the rest of the class—all of that has been washed-out while the above episode is being played out). Is the teacher's main concern the saving of face? If that is the issue then the purposes of education have been distorted beyond any reasonable defense. How about the child and his pride? Isn't that important? Shouldn't the adult who is paid to function as a professional be able to handle such a mild challenge without enlarging it into a big deal?

Consider now the conversation in the hall—the teacher's comments about not understanding the child are mind-boggling. In effect, the teacher is insisting on the right of the adult not to understand the child but is simultaneously obliging the ten-year-old to understand the teacher. If the teacher truly doesn't understand, or doesn't have hypotheses based on a definable theory of human behavior, what the heck is he doing in the classroom? If he does understand, why all the phony folderol? The assertion to the child that he understands why his behavior is intolerable is a great bit of one-upmanship. The child is accused of conspiratorial subversion of classroom activity and yet it is certainly possible and even probable that the child does not understand at all why his behavior isn't tolerable. It may be that he has many grievances and that *legitimacy of his grievances cannot even be examined because there is no legitimate apparatus for them to be expressed*. A case can be made that his behavior hasn't exceeded tolerance limits, but, rather, that *he* finds the class and the teacher *intolerable*. He may be denied opportunity to derive satisfaction from feeling intellectually competent (I bet that he has been labeled as "slow" and accordingly placed in a low-ability grouping). He may be barred from a sense of belonging (I bet that he has been relegated to an "outsider" social role where

---

[19] *Ibid.*, pp. 90–91.

recognition comes only from deviant behavior). It is highly unlikely that he is allowed to be useful (let alone essential) in classroom activities. If any or all of these demeaning conditions exist, then the constraints imposed on the child dun him fully for all the costs of conformity without offering, in exchange, any of the benefits. And that isn't the end of it. The teacher continues to exact flesh.

The child is manipulated into such a hapless, hopeless, help-less condition that the only thing left to him is to "break into tears." And he can't even be left to that limited satisfaction. He has to suffer more. He has to submit to the ministrations of tear-drying by the very person who made him cry. How can a poor ten-year-old handle that? Even the bitter gratification of hating the person who has defeated him is taken away. But, hold on—we are not done yet. There is still the ultimate torture. The child must go through the agony of the final, formal, ceremonial rite—he must be the crushed slave who precedes the conquering Caesar as they walk back into the classroom—living evidence that an important victory has been achieved.

The author makes it quite clear that "efficacious bouncing" is based on expediency. This is merely a means to win the day. Only when the procedures used rebound against the teacher should they be given up. For instance, the author advises against too much "hall bouncing" and "office bouncing" (sending students into the hall or to the principal's office) because these actions may cause the principal to question the competence of the teacher.

Katherine C. La Mancusa has more to offer in this vein. She is all for deceiving youngsters. She recommends punishment as the means to shape up the perennial offender (he is the one who doesn't "therapeutically bounce"). One way to do this is make him remain after school. However, crucial to his infliction is keeping the culprit ignorant about the teacher's true feelings:

> The saving factor in this situation is that children *do not know* how desperately a teacher wants to leave when the teaching day is done. A teacher must trade on this by saying now and again, "I have all the time in the world, John. I don't mind staying after school. In fact, I rather enjoy it. I have much time to get other things done." [20]

At this point I don't know whether to curse or cry. There could be no worse advice! Lying to children isn't going to get the

---

[20] *Ibid.*, p. 86.

teacher anything but further trouble. She is not going to pull it off. The truth will out, and then where is she? The whole thing is nutty anyhow—why should two human beings be forced to be where neither wants to be? And what will be the long-run gain from such foolishness? Will the perennial offender be rehabilitated? The odds are against it. The most likely conclusion is that the perennial offender will continue to perennially offend—receiving more and more severe treatment for his transgression until he is eliminated completely from the school system.

Using school as punishment makes no sense. That's one of the things wrong with school now—it is viewed as a bad place to be. School or school work should never be assigned as punishment. And, in fact, the concept of punishment should be eliminated from the vocabulary of teachers. There will be a time when a teacher will have to curb and regulate student behavior. When the teacher is required to restrict a student the action should be straightforward. There should be no gimmicks, no double-talking and no moralizing. The teacher should quickly get back to the business of assisting students to attain political, economic, cultural, and personal competence. The perennial offender and other hurting students will again occupy our attention when inter- and intrapersonal competence is discussed in Chapter VIII.

Whenever I lecture on control within a democratic context I provoke many teachers. I am told how naïve I am and that unless I followed some of the suggestions of Katherine La Mancusa I would be run out of the classroom. I have no illusions on the difficulty of performing a leadership role consistent with democratic principles. I am aware of my limitations. I also know that no teacher walks on water, and all teachers behave foolishly at times. Even if some of us begin to zero in on perfection the imperfection of the system would get in our way. All true. There will be children for whom education as currently performed and futurely conceived will not suffice. We just do not have the program for them. There should not be many of them and there should be no greater proportion among the minorities than will be found in the majority. We will have to exclude these few for the protection of the many. But when this happens it should humble us. It should cause us to redouble our efforts to improve, and that is far different from *recommending* stupidity as a desired standard operating procedure.

Most of the advice prospective teachers receive in class or from books is of the type Katherine C. La Mancusa gives. It comes from persons who draw upon teaching experience and it is generally very low level conceptually. The emphasis is on equating compliance with good citizenship. Most of it is harmless. The hazard is that teachers need very little encouragement to be authoritarian and they pounce on any proauthoritarian stuff that comes their way.

The Irresponsibility of Omission

There is another kind of expert to whom teachers are attracted. This expert doesn't offer advice on democratic control at all. He tends to ignore the entire problem. Such an "expert" is George Leonard. He has fabricated a highly lauded work.[21] In it he presents a cure for education's ills concocted of equal parts electronic devices, biochemistries, and staged confrontations. It is difficult for me to understand how the book gained any reputation at all. It is at best a slick shuck—a journalistic tour de force in which lack of profundity is camouflaged by innumerable references. However, the references only mislead and in every instance he oversells his product.

Of course the computer, the talking typewriter, and the programmed text are important to a good education, but the roles they will play are definitely subordinate. They will only make it possible for *good teachers* to be *better*. They will also, as is the case now, make it possible for *bad teachers* to be *worse*. Technology has contributed to bureaucratic intransigence and has fortified authoritarianism. More of it will not automatically reverse these tendencies. To the contrary, there must be well-enunciated strategies if technological advancement is to be restricted to advancing humanity. Mr. Leonard apparently does not see the necessity for these precautions.

The use of group encounters where people have at each other with no holds barred and break down inhibitions through contrived physical contact isn't where-it-is-at either. These activities may train persons to become sensitive, but it is quite clear, from years of evaluation, that most of this new-found sensitivity wears off quickly when the participants are returned to the "real world."

Leonard's fascination with psychoactive drugs is not very well balanced. He considers only the possible good things than can hap-

---

[21] George Leonard, *Education and Ecstasy,* Delacorte Press, New York, 1968.

pen. He discounts completely the possible horror. He ignores how drugs may isolate man from his social environments and may further involute an already too involuted psychological existence. The quest for an elixir to produce inter- and intrapersonal tranquillity and intellectual potency is as old as man. There is nothing in its dismal history to lend much encouragement for the future. Yet this is a major reed on which Leonard's education leans. (We treat drugs in much greater detail in Chapter VIII.)

Leonard is vague about educational goals and he is particularly sloppy when he discusses democratic citizenship: "To learn heightened awareness and control of emotional, sensory and bodily states and through this, increased empathy for other people (a new kind of citizenship education)." [22]

Leonard's new kind of citizenship education picks up all of the worst elements of the old kind. One of the things wrong today is the unwillingness of the school to open up, for honest examination, the flaws and failures of governmental workings. Leonard closes his eyes to brutal exploitation of man by man, to the domination of political processes by the very wealthy, and to abuse of power by those elected to office. He never deals with institutionalized racism. He is oblivious to the imminent threat of totalitarianism. His goal of citizenship education could have been surrounded by a balloon emanating from the mouth of the cartoon-strip character Mary Worth.

Nowhere in Leonard's book is there a recognition that dynamic leadership is required if democratic processes are to be kept alive for the limited number who now enjoy them and that even more intense effort must be made if the fruits of democracy are to be extended to the large numbers who have been denied the pleasure. Depersonalization of man through bureaucratic organization, segregation, uselessness of person, and nonredemptiveness (see Chapter I) are not going to wither away—nor is the oppressiveness of school going to magically disappear. Any expert who ignores these problems, as Leonard does, does a disservice to education.

The Leonard work, like so many of its genre, takes on the dimensions of a fairy tale because real problems are blissfully ignored. Nowhere does he deal with the problem of political control and the possible misuse of electronics, drugs, or psychological

---

[22] *Ibid.*, p. 132.

manipulations. He assumes that as man progresses technically he also progresses socially. History does not bear him out. He has composed a modern siren's song, one which many find as hard to resist as did the shipmates of Odysseus. He calls his approach to education ecstasy. He had made a common mistake. He has confused heaven with hell.

Is It All in Vain?

If Leonard can be called to task because he glosses over problems of preparing students for democracy, no such criticism can be leveled at Edgar Friedenberg. Edgar Friedenberg advances a most disturbing proposition. He questions whether training for democratic citizenship transcends mere difficulty. He questions the feasibility of democracy itself. He concludes that it is more accurate to reject the notion that democracy has become corrupted and perverted and recognize that "What is wrong with America may be characteristic of mass democracy itself." [23]

Friedenberg generates a cogent argument. He points to a record of nonresponsiveness to social issues: "In a society as open, invidious and competitive as ours, the kinds of people who succeed are usually incapable of responding to human demands; and the political power of the masses is used merely to express the hatreds and the envy, and to destroy anything that looks like genuine human satisfaction." [24]

According to Friedenberg we are presently on a collision course with disaster: "Tyranny has taken many forms in history, but the graceless vulgarity and egregious clumsy brutality of fascism are its most hideous forms; and these grow best out of the democratic process itself." [25]

Friedenberg is dubious of reform: "The present political structure of America is precisely what is wrong, and there is no a priori reason to assume that it bears within itself the seeds of its own reform." [26]

The hope of the future, according to Friedenberg, cannot now

---

[23] Edgar Friedenberg, "The Revolt Against Democracy," *Change in Higher Education,* May-June, 1969, p. 16.

[24] *Ibid.,* p. 16.

[25] *Ibid.,* p. 16.

[26] *Ibid.,* p. 17.

be accurately described, but whatever it is, it will fall outside the pale of established procedures: "But I am sure that if radical improvement in the quality of our national life can be made—and our survival depends on this—the devices by which it can be done will seem outrageous and will, indeed, cause widespread outrage." [27]

I concur with Friedenberg on the portentous nature of our times. I find little to quarrel with in his description. I differ with him on interpretation. If one perceives that education merely reflects dominant society, then Friedenberg's assessment is correct and (I believe) we are doomed. If one attributes some vitality to education and potential political power in a coalition of teachers and students, then there is hope.

Friedenberg attributes to repressive forces a consciousness which I think is not there. He believes that those bent on destroying democratic institutions know what they are doing. He sites as evidence of awareness the political leader and public responses to police brutality:

> The public does not accept discordant interpretations of reality anymore than a neurotic patient accepts an unwelcome interpretation: it was Walter Cronkite, not the public who learned from the experience. And the American political process *does* respond to the will of the people.[28]
>   . . . political leaders prattle of "law and order" as a remedy for "violence in the streets" as if they had not seen a dozen times by now that the violence in the streets is often committed by the forces of law and order.[29]

Of course they have not *seen* violence committed by forces of law and order. They have not seen it because they have not been educated to see it. Perception is functionally selective. People do tend to see, retain, and remember those things which coincide with group pressure, previous experience, and developed attitudes.[30] A major reason so much stress has been placed on preparing persons for democratic citizenship in this book is that training and education do influence how people politically interact with each other. If

---

[27] *Ibid.,* p. 17.

[28] *Ibid.,* p. 16.

[29] *Ibid.,* p. 17.

[30] There is a very rich literature on this; see for example S. Asch, *Social Psychology,* Prentice-Hall, New York, 1952; Muzifer and C. Sherif, *Reference Groups,* 1964; Arthur Pearl, *Decision Theory Model Applied to Perception of Person* (unpublished dissertation, 1960).

they have not learned to appreciate individual rights; if they have been removed from judicial, executive, and legislative decision-making; if they are unaware of the economic, political, psychological, and sociological facts of life; if they have never served under authorities who are consistent and committed to democratic principles, then they *will learn* to disrespect democracy.

Friedenberg's contempt of the common man's ability to perform the citizenship role concerns me. He alludes to a lack of capability. It is my view that mass democracy fails only because so little effort has been made to educate "the masses" for democracy. I believe that such education is possible. I believe that the masses are receptive to such education and I believe that of all the diverse groups in our society they have the most to gain from it.

Friedenberg's pessimism may be based on an accurate assessment of where we are going. I remain an optimist, because pessimism is a luxury I don't believe we can afford. The forces that oppose democracy are strong, and if those who support democracy are discouraged or half-hearted in their efforts, then certainly all is lost. One indicator of hope is that Friedenberg and I (at least at the time of this writing) hold positions of responsibility within the Establishment and have access to the public—although a case can be made that that merely reflects our lack of importance.

Summary

The issue of models of leadership within and outside the schools is crucial to the development of competence in democratic citizenship. The school must both reorient its existing staff and bring different kinds of people into education if this goal is to be attained.

The attributes to be looked for in the selection of staff are persons who:

1) Accept pluralism. The staff must itself be diverse enough to make advocacy of all the different groups within a school a reality.

2) Are accountable. No one questions the essentiality of rules and regulations, but the authority must explain the necessity for the restrictions, and the explanation must be based on logic and evidence.

3) Are negotiable. Differences between student and staff must be reconciled on a basis of mutual concern. The staff must be will-

ing to accept student suggestions for alternative ways of doing things.

4) Are aware of the inevitability of conflict. Teachers must not crush all who differ. They must learn to live with people who differ in values and goals.

5) View all rules as means and not as goals. The educator will be in far less difficulty if he keeps rules in a proper perspective. If rules are seen only as a means to attain a legitimate goal of education, then violation of the rule can be handled rationally.

The educator has yet an additional responsibility—he has to be an effective citizen himself. The blind-leading-the-halt approach to teaching of citizenship must be altered. If enlightened citizenship is to be obtained by the masses, it must begin with a politically enlightened teaching force.

CHAPTER VI

The Goal of Culture-Carrier

[In this chapter I examine the school's efforts to stimulate the student intellectually. I try to define culture-carrying competence. I claim that even from the most restricted view of culture, education fails. Students are not stimulated to master language, history, math, science, or art. The school leaves them bereft of social understanding. I single out language instruction for extensive examination. I identify particular problems and suggest methods to improve the quality of instruction.]

The great law of culture is that each become all that he was created capable of being. —Thomas Carlyle

Common sense is in spite of, not the result of education.
—Victor Hugo

I respect faith, but doubt is what gets you an education.
—Wilson Mizner

A nation's language is a very large matter. It is not simply a matter of speech obtaining among the educated handful, the manner obtaining among the vast uneducated multitude must be considered also. . . . I could pile up the differences until I not only convinced you that English and American are separate languages, but that when I speak my native tongue in its utmost purity an Englishman can't understand me at all. —Mark Twain

The notion that anything is gained by fixing a language in a groove is cherished only by pedants. —H. L. Mencken

Grammar and syntax are of no importance so long as one makes one's meaning clear. —George Orwell

It would appear indisputable that a major goal of education is to turn students on intellectually. The educational process should engender an unabating interest in art, music, literature, science, and math. Of the myriad of reasons why intellectual stimulation is important in school, at least two have paramount importance. Our society requires an intellectually sophisticated population in order for it to function, and the individual needs the gratification that comes from investment in cultural pursuits to retain his sanity. In a nation in which most of the activity is mind work, we obviously need people with working minds. In a highly complicated social environment, one that overpowers the individual with bureaucratic intransigence, one where the net impact on the individual is depersonalization and dehumanization, the individual must be able to attain that sense of self and those gratifications that come with the ability to involve oneself in intellectual and cultural activities.

A recurring theme throughout this book is that we have not generated the human leadership to contend with our technological advancement. Our society suffers because of the deficiency of this leadership. There is no way we can begin to develop human resources unless we radically change the nature of our schools.

We ought to be absolutely clear about what culture-carrying competence entails. As a result of schooling the graduate should be a disciplined thinker capable of weighing arguments and making decisions that he can defend with logic and evidence. He should be literate. He should have acquired a base of knowledge to assist him in critical discernments. He should be able to discriminate between faith (unsubstantiable judgment), opinion (unsubstantiated judgment), and knowledge (substantiated judgment). He should have an ideology. He should be able to filter his experience and alter his thinking and his behavior as a consequence of such analysis. He should base aesthetic appreciation on articulated theory. He should have developed a technique in one or more of the visual or performing arts. He should be able to derive deep, personal gratification from involvement in intellectual and cultural activities. He should not confuse mere association with cause and effect. He should know the boundaries of his knowledge.

The person who claims culture-carrying competence cannot be culturally isolated. He must be aware of the contributions of diverse groups in a pluralistic society. In particular, he must be aware of the contributions of the black, the Mexican, and the Native American. It is not that these groups are alone in their contributions, but, because of the unrelenting prejudice against them, their additions to American life must be given special emphasis.

Culture-carrying competence is both general and specific. Students should be encouraged to explore individual interests, to take the less traveled paths and accrue the benefits of that choice. But all students in a complex, interdependent society must share some common cultural activities—the very least of these would be to have the ability to communicate precisely with each other and to share an historical perspective. Because language and history have the additional importance of being the glue that binds together all cultural and intellectual experience, these two "subjects" receive expanded treatment here.

Even if the most limited view of intellectual achievement—a sprinkling of knowledge in written expression, literature, history, science, mathematics—is accepted as a legitimate goal of education, education fails. This failure is not readily perceived by students. *Life* magazine, in a spread (based on an intensive Harris poll of 2,500 students), "Collision Course in High Schools," found that students mainly complained about lack of participation in school decision-making (the kind of thing discussed in the two previous chapters), but were relatively content with what and how they were taught: "More students than teachers think education is valuable and stimulating. When it comes to assessing the curriculum, faculties and staff, the mutual esteem reaches incredible proportions." [1]

Life presents data to show that, of all subjects, students find English composition to be most useful, and a very small percentage suggest improvements either in quality or relevance of the offering. The lack of student criticism is more an indictment of education than it is a commendation. While it takes very little education for the student to recognize that he is powerless, it takes considerable education for the student to apprehend that he is being intellectually robbed. In the domain of power the student has a referent—the adult power structure. In the domain of intellectual activity there is no equivalent frame of reference. The student is content because he simply doesn't know any better—and that is the most ominous sign of all. The recognition of a problem gives hope of its solution. The failure to even recognize that a problem exists precludes any possibility of solution. I have no idea what the student is using for comparison when he gives approval to the school. The warm affirmation for school subjects does not correspond with my

---

[1] *Life* Magazine, May 16, 1969, p. 30.

observations. I believe that students are nagged by doubts about the value of school to a much greater extent than *Life* magazine reports.

"Education for Stupidity"

That young people should be ill-prepared for analytical judgment about school should, however, come as no surprise. At least one keen observer contends that students are educated to be unanalytical. The late Jules Henry, in an article, "Education for Stupidity," argues that "Children must be given subject matter that confirms legitimate stupidity and whatever challenges it must be withheld." [2]

Henry reviews a sample of high-school textbooks and singles out these specific areas where students are educated to be stupid:

a) "Stupidity about Negroes"—
The high-school student is fed information to convince him that the problems of Negroes are minimal, largely of the past, and fast being solved (and thus it follows that blacks should not get angry, because everything possible is being done for them).

b) "Stupidity about Labor"—
The student is informed that it was labor, through its efforts to organize, that *caused* rioting and bloodshed, that management insensitivity to worker concerns is now ancient history, and— probably most importantly—it is inferred that any militancy is suspect.

c) "Stupidity about Economics"—
The student is left ignorant about the economic workings of the society. He is instructed that depressions come mysteriously and just as mysteriously disappear.

d) "Stupidity about Poverty"—
Students are given neither the appropriate data nor an analytical scheme to make sense out of poverty, and often are trained to ignore its existence.

e) "Stupidity about Communism and the Soviet Union"—
The student has a problem that goes beyond mere lack of balance in presentation; he is faced with such a lack of relevant information that he is unable to understand the theory of Communism or the social structure of the world's second most powerful nation. [3]

---

[2] Jules Henry, "Education for Stupidity," in *Reason and Change in Elementary Education*, 2nd National Conference, U.S. Office of Education, Tri-University Project in Elementary Education, Feb. 13, 1968, pp. 117–134.

[3] It may be that China is the world's second most powerful nation—and students know even less about it.

f) "Stupidity about War"—

"Without exception" (in the textbooks Henry reviewed), "the analysis of the origins of the two World Wars is handled superficially, and United States complicity in bringing them about, and the possibility of any war at all being avoided are not examined." [4]

Henry concludes with a frightening assertion: "I have shown in this paper how the world is presented to children and adolescents in such a way that they do not get from school the information necessary to enable them to form an intelligent opinion about this world. College continues the work of instilling ignorance." [5]

The damage that school does to the intelligence of students is not restricted to controversial subjects. It intrudes into the basic and seemingly noncontroversial areas as well.

Some Allegations by Subject Matter

Students get short-changed in every aspect of their education!

The learning of "English" is especially difficult. Students are strait-jacketed at every possible turn. Rather than developing a facility with language, they are discouraged from written expression by rule-ridden instruction. The setting in which the student is asked to learn and the restriction he suffers militate against experimentation in form or content. As a result the language he learns is stiff, devoid of emotion, and very rarely applicable to "real life" situations. What passes for literature in the early years are clumsy abominations that are bad fantasy or misrepresentations of the outside world.

The study of "history" is every bit as dull as the study of "English." The student is saddled with some overly simple distortions. He is given the impression that history is little more than a compendium of names and dates, spiced with chronicles of wars.

Mathematics should be an area of inquiry with universal appeal. The knowledge obtained is essential for ordinary life activities. And people do learn it. The man in the street becomes quite skilled in determining if the change he received at the store is correct, or how much of a twenty-dollar bill has been faded in a crap game. He can worry his way through an income tax form. Moreover, mathematics is a relatively easy subject to master. The activities are pre-

4 *Ibid.*, p. 129.
5 *Ibid.*, p. 132.

cise, the language is specific, the laws are consistent, and the manipulations are uncomplicated. The simplicity of mathematics
pertains from its introduction to numbers through addition and
subtraction all the way to calculus.

Yet, implausible as it might appear, students have difficulty
with mathematics in school. The major reason for this is that they are
taught that mathematics is too much for them! Students are introduced to mathematics by elementary-school teachers who, by and
large, are desperately afraid of the subject. Rather than inspiring
confidence, teachers generate fear. Instead of communicating competence, the teachers communicate their doubts. In the teaching of
arithmetic, elementary teachers illustrate precisely the insulting of
intelligence that I claim all education is guilty of. When a little set
theory is introduced into elementary math the results are calamitous. Not only do the teachers share their trauma with the students,
but they further advise the students that the new math is so difficult
they cannot expect help from their parents. As a student progresses
through school the process becomes more and more confusing. One
set of manipulations and concepts is jumbled with another. Algebra, trigonometry, combinations and permutations, geometry,
and calculus are presented to the student as mysteries which will
become deciphered at some later date in much the same way that a
secret message becomes legible when lemon juice is applied to a
chemically treated paper. The poor youth who are not encouraged
to such a future learn that the secret message will never be revealed
to them. They *know* that there will be no effort to teach them the
intricacies of more developed mathematics.[6]

Over fifty years ago Alfred North Whitehead, an inordinately
wise mathematician and philosopher, said it as well as it has ever
been said, and still very few educators have heard the message. The
man who authored *A Treatise on Universal Algebra With Applica-
tions* questioned the importance of teaching students the solution to
a quadratic equation: "Why should children be taught their solution? Unless quadratic equations fit into a connected curriculum, of
course there is no reason to teach about them." [7]

Of the many valid points Whitehead makes, two have been

---

[6] See John Holt, *How Children Fail,* Dell Publishing Co., a Delta Book,
New York, 1964.

[7] Alfred North Whitehead, *The Aims of Education and Other Essays,*
Free Press, New York, 1929, p. 7.

persistently ignored. One is that everything taught must have immediate relevance. Any educational activity must begin with convincing the students of its *personal* importance. Because importance pertains to occupational, political, cultural, or personal matters, it will vary significantly from person to person, and this must always occupy a teacher's mind. If there is to be education in math

> Whatever interest attaches to your subject-matter must be evoked here and now; whatever powers you are strengthening in the pupil must be exercised here and now; whatever possibilities of mental life your teaching should impart must be exhibited here and now. That is the golden rule of education, and a very difficult rule to follow.[8]

The other lesson not learned from Whitehead is that education cannot be a disconnected experience:

> Instead of this single unity, we offer children—Algebra, from which nothing follows; Science, from which nothing follows; History, from which nothing follows; a couple of languages, never mastered; and lastly, most dreary of all, Literature, represented by plays of Shakespeare with philological notes and short analyses of plot and character to be in substance committed to memory.[9]

Whitehead asks the question, If what we do is obviously stupid, why do we continue to do it? And he replies:

> There is a traditional answer to this question. It runs thus: the mind is an instrument, you first sharpen and then use it; the acquisition of the power of solving a quadratic equation is part of the process of sharpening the mind. Now there is just enough truth in this answer to have made it live through the ages. But for all its half truth, it embodies a radical error which bids fair to stifle the genius of the modern world. I do not know who was first responsible for this analogy of the mind to a dead instrument. For aught I know, it may have been one of the seven wise men of Greece, or a committee of the whole lot of them. Whoever was the originator, there can be no doubt of the authority which it has acquired by the continuous approval bestowed upon it by eminent persons. But whatever its weight of authority, whatever the high approval which it can quote, I have no hesitation in denouncing it as one of the most fatal, erroneous, and dangerous conceptions ever introduced into the theory of education.[10]

---

[8] *Ibid.*, p. 6.
[9] *Ibid.*, p. 7.
[10] *Ibid.*, p. 6.

I cannot shed any further light as to the inventors of the notion. I do know that Whitehead's statement, written sometime prior to 1917, is as true today as it was then. The Max Raffertys of the educational world continue to fertilize the "dead instrument" approach by what they call "Education in Depth." [11] In truth, it is hard to know what education in depth is, despite the fact that Max Rafferty devotes a chapter in a book to the subject.[12] From that chapter I learned that "Education in Depth" is NOT "Progressive Education." And that isn't just me being snide—listen to Max:

> Californians are calling it "Education in Depth," and as is usual in such matters, it's easier to tell what it isn't than what it is.[13]

> It believes in the "three R's" right enough, but only as a springboard for vastly more complex subject matter.[14]

> Education in depth calls a spade a spade. History is taught as history, geography as geography and civics as civics.[15]

> . . . a reasonable amount of material must be committed to memory and there is nothing wrong with this. In addition, memorizing phrases and lines from famous works of poetry and prose should be encouraged as a means of perpetuating our literary birthright.[16]

> . . . it behooves the schools to assign literary materials carefully chosen from the children's classics and to see that this basic food of the mind is carefully ingested and digested before the less tried and tested items of current and popular taste are placed before the pupil.[17]

> The elementary instructor is going to have to tighten up and bear down. No more pupil papers handed back with grades of A but containing misspelled words and faulty constructions that haven't been circled.[18]

> Subject matter report cards graded A—B—C—D—F or a reasonable facsimile thereof are a must.[19]

---

[11] Max Rafferty, *What They Are Doing to Your Children,* New York, Signet, 1964.

[12] *Ibid.,* pp. 67–77.

[13] *Ibid.,* p. 73.

[14] *Ibid.,* p. 73.

[15] *Ibid.,* p. 74.

[16] *Ibid.,* p. 74.

[17] *Ibid.,* p. 75.

[18] *Ibid.,* p. 75.

[19] *Ibid.,* p. 75.

Rafferty isn't totally against Progressive Education—he condones it to this extent:

> The problem solving approach featured by Dewey was sound. It should be retained. So should the willingness on the part of the instructor to give reasons to the children for the many things he must ask them to do every day.[20]

Rafferty doesn't want "the baby thrown out with the bathwater" (he is big on clichés). I'm not quite that generous. I think everything Rafferty has ever said and done about education could be thrown out without education ever being the loser for it.

Rafferty is not holding back education all alone. He is getting help—and from quarters that would consider a likening to Dr. Rafferty to be odious. The behaviorist psychologists are in the same camp. The psychologists have effectively sold the bill of goods that identified specific skills can be learned through consistent reinforcement of desired behaviors. The reinforcement is immediate, so at a superficial glance it would appear that the "behaviorist" is giving utility to the learning process. Not so! The reinforcement is usually extraneous to the intellectual activity. The student is forced into a "token economy"! If he learns what the instructor desires, in the form the instructor desires and in the style and tempo the instructor desires, he may receive from the instructor "praise," a "blue star," or even a piece of candy (guaranteed only to melt in the mouth).[21]

A token economy distorts the education process. The reward becomes the end in itself. Both the immediate utility of the *knowledge* and its connection to a system of thought are perverted in the process. Operant-conditioning psychologists are wont to sneer here—"But we get results." However, this claim doesn't hold up under examination. The crucial factor in evaluation of effectiveness of a program is selection of the criteria. It is true that in some instances operant-conditioning techniques have improved student scores on standardized achievement tests. The problem is that the test performance bears little upon a culture-carrying competence. It is also true that almost any teacher commitment to students pro-

---

[20] *Ibid.*, p. 76

[21] For a more complete exposition of this approach to learning read Roger Ulrich, Thomas Stachnik, and John Mabry, *Control of Human Behavior,* Scott, Foresman and Co., Glenview, Ill., 1966, or any work by B. F. Skinner.

duces change in achievement on standardized tests. Herbert Kohl, whose lack of system defies all of the behaviorists' principles, reports one to two years of gain on standardized tests in six months.[22] The mere mastering of test-taking skills does not insure that the test-taker is literate, articulate, knowledgeable, or analytical. Because we rarely reflect upon this truth, persons without any of these attributes succeed to advanced degrees.

The fragmentation of effort and the lack of utility affect every level of education. The ease with which technology lends itself to specific skill development has furthered the disjointedness of education. The development of a credential society has contributed to the postponement of utility. Yet it doesn't have to happen.

Whitehead has no problem developing an approach to the instruction of algebra that has immediate relevance and connection to other life experiences and learning. If the essence of algebra is understood and its congruity to all intellectual processes realized, the nature of its instruction is also fairly easy to formulate:

> Algebra is the intellectual instrument which has been created for rendering clear the quantitative aspects of the world. There is no getting out of it. Through and through the world is infected with quantity. To talk sense is to talk in quantities. It is no use saying that the nation is large. How large? It is no use saying that radium is scarce—How scarce? You cannot evade quantity. You may fly to poetry and to music, and quantity and number will face you in your rhythms and your octaves. Elegant intellects which despise the theory of quantity are but half developed. They are more to be pitied than blamed. The scraps of gibberish, which in their schooldays were taught to them in the name of algebra, deserve more contempt.[23]

We run into much the same thing when we encounter science. Science should give students the exhilaration that comes from a sense of discovery, but do you know what the student discovers in science? He discovers that half-way through an experiment he has to clean up. He discovers that he has to memorize formulas and names. I don't remember whether it was Priestley or Lavoisier who discovered oxygen. I know we were breathing it before either of them was around. Science instruction in any depth and with any expectation of success is almost exclusively restricted to the elite,

---

[22] *Op. cit.*, p. 172.
[23] Whitehead, *op. cit.*, p. 7.

and in that discrimination the alienation of the poor and the minorities gains momentum.

Art and music education goes off in two misdirections. There are either art depreciation courses, or students are employed as puppets. In the former, students engage in such meaningless activities as slapping clay around an inflated balloon, baking the clay-covered balloon and passing off the product as an artistic creation, a bowl. This would make sense in an economy-minded ceramics factory in Hong Kong, but has very little to do with art education. There is no development of techniques, no opportunity to exercise creativity, no development of critical capacities. Jonathan Kozol describes vividly a similar destruction of creativity in what would pass for art education in the Boston schools:

> The Art Teacher's most common technique for art instruction was to pass out mimeographed designs and then to have the pupils fill them in according to a dictated or suggested color plan. An alternate approach was to stick up on the wall or on the blackboard some of the drawings on a particular subject that had been done in previous years by predominately white classes. These drawings, neat and ordered and very uniform, would be the models for our children. The Art lessons, in effect, would be to copy what had been done before, and the neatest and most accurate reproductions of the original drawings would be the ones that would win the highest approval from the teacher.[24]

The other distortion of art education occurs when students are exploited by a drama instructor or music instructor to perform carefully prescribed roles for the enjoyment of the adults of the community. The students do, in fact, derive some gratification from this activity. They perceive themselves as useful, they bathe in a rare experience of appreciation from significant adults, but the experience, nonetheless, is alienating for almost all. Some of the more independent students immediately raise objections to the limited latitude they have. But the long-range destruction of youth is what is most important. The student is unable to derive a measure of competence that can be generalized to other areas of experience. He is totally dependent upon the adult authority. Because the students have very little to say in the casting and very little opportunity for extemporaneous development, they cannot be expected

---

[24] Jonathan Kozol, *Death at an Early Age,* Houghton Mifflin Co., Boston, 1967, p. 2.

to generate much analytical ability or critical activity. In a similar way, student athletes are exploited.

How Not to Teach the English Language

The best way to insure that no language competency is attained in school is to continue what we are doing. Language instruction from the very beginning is unnatural. The instruction suffers from a preoccupation with rules, an insistence that the same words always be spelled the same way, limitation on the propriety of expression, and a preoccupation with real or alleged language deficiencies. All of these unnecessary impositions create tension, and tension, in turn, erodes the spontaneity of learner effort and also inhibits effort. There are many quite specific failings in language instruction that seem to resist educational innovation. Some of the most prevalent are:

1) Teach it as a static entity.

It is extremely difficult to communicate to English teachers at every level that language is dynamic and that it grows and changes as a society grows and changes. Language takes its shape, its tempo, its morphology, and its syntax from the predominant enterprises of the society. Language communicates thought, but also emotion. Emerson recognized the dependency of language on current life processes:

> If it were only for a vocabulary, the scholar would be covetous of action. Life is our dictionary. Years are well spent in country labors; in town; in the insight into taxes and manufactures; in frank intercourse with many men and women; in science; in art, to the one end of mastering in all their facts a language by which to illustrate and embody our perceptions. I learn immediately from any speaker how much he has already lived, through the poverty and splendor of his speech. Life lives behind us at the quarry from whence we get tiles and copestones for the masonry of today. This is the way to learn grammar. Colleges and books only copy the language which the field and work yard made.[25]

That language is a living thing came as a revelation to Herbert Kohl after some depressing experiences trying to teach language traditionally to sixth-grade Harlem youths.

---

[25] Ralph Waldo Emerson, *The American Scholar,* speech delivered before Phi Delta Kappa at Cambridge, Aug. 31, 1837. Cited from *The Portable Emerson,* Viking Press, New York, 1946, p. 34.

One day Ralph cursed at Michael and unexpectedly things came together for me. Michael was reading and stumbled several times. Ralph scornfully called out, "What's the matter, psyches, going to pieces again?" The class broke up and I jumped on the word "psyches."

"Where do you think the word came from? Why did everybody laugh when you said it?" Ralph, "You know, Mr. Kohl, it means, like crazy or something."

"The word psyche has a long history. Psyche means mind or soul for the Greeks, but it was also the name of a lovely woman who had the misfortune to fall in love with Cupid, the son of Venus, the jealous Greek goddess of Love." The children listened, enchanted by the myth, fascinated by the weaving of the meaning of psyche into the fabric of the story, and the character.

". . . look at the words in English that come from Psyche." I cited *psychological, psychic, psychotic, psychodrama*—the children copied them unasked, demanded the meanings; they were obviously excited.

Leaping ahead, Alvin shouted, "You mean words change? People didn't always speak this way? Then how come the reader says there's a right way to talk and a wrong way?"

"There's a right way now, and that only means that's how most people like to talk now, and how people write now."

Charles jumped out of his desk and spoke for the first time during the year.

"You mean one day the way we talk—you know, with words like *cool* and *dig* and *sound*—may be all right?"

Someone spoke for the class:

"Mr. Kohl, can't we study the language we're talking about instead of spelling and grammar? They won't be any good when language changes anyway."

We could and did.[26]

There is a tragedy to the Kohl story. He learned that language was vital, and, when treated as a live subject, students responded enthusiastically. He learned to treat his students with respect, but he is no longer teaching sixth-graders in a regular public school. The persons who teach language as an "old-fashioned" dead thing are still teaching.

2) Teach language as if all the rules were unamendable.

Regardless of what English teachers say, in practice rules are everything; and while here and there occasional exceptions emerge, the impact they have on English instruction is very slight.

---

[26] Herbert Kohl, *36 Children*, Signet Books, New York, 1968, pp. 23–25.

When a group of English teachers (ranging from elementary through high school) were given a composition to examine in a summer institute, *every one* red-penciled misspellings, grammatical errors, awkward phrasing, and the like. The director of the institute singled out one of the teachers and asked why she did what she did. Her explanation was that she was not about to violate convention. She would not engage in any action that would bring her under fire from other teachers, or parents, or administration.

Political expedience is not a valid justification for corruption of language instruction. Teachers cannot be permitted the excuse that they enforce rules only because they are forbidden to do otherwise. Leslie Whipp, who directed the above-mentioned institute, is crystal clear on that. "If it is a fact of life that one must play silly games in the classroom, one should not confuse that with teaching. And one should not pretend that one does it to benefit the child." [27]

But pretending and silly games do go on in the classroom. Teachers do delude themselves that children improve when errors in their language are brought to their attention. Whipp dismisses that contention:

> It is not that our corrections had no effect, although at times that seems to be the case. It is rather that our correcting does not have the effect we seek.
> It has instead the effect of inhibiting the child's use of language, of stultifying his fluency, of depriving him of the means of expression.[28]

There isn't any aspect of language that is safe from excessive fault-finding. Students are criticized for handwriting, for grammatical errors, and for misspelling. Teachers act is if there is but one correct way to spell a word. They forget that for a great many years communication took place without any standards for spelling.[29] Shakespeare had difficulty spelling. It is not that he lacked validity. His problem was not that he spelled

---

[27] Leslie Whipp, "The Child as Language Teacher," *Elementary English,* Apr. 1969, p. 470.

[28] *Ibid.,* p. 467.

[29] John Adams lamented in a letter to the president of Congress in 1780 (referring to Johnson's Dictionary published in 1755), "it is only very lately that a tolerable dictionary (of English) has been published . . . and there is not yet a passable grammar enterprised by any individual."

words differently from the way I think they should be spelled; he lacked reliability. He didn't spell the same word the same way all the time. One of the major reasons some doubt his existence at all is that he spelled his own name so many different ways. But he handled language reasonably well—at least as well as most English teachers.

I shudder to think what would have happened to William Shakespeare if he had been forced to go to public school in the United States today. By the time of age twelve he would be finished. Paper after paper would have been returned, fairly bleeding with red pencil: "misspelled," "misspelled," "To be or not to be," "Isn't there a less awkward way to express that?" It may be no accident that so many of our best writers (Twain and Melville, for example) had so little formal education.

Of course there must be standards in language, but rules of English are identical with the rules of social conduct—they are a means to an end. In the case of language the end sought is precise communication. If a person spells the word "eminent" when he means "imminent," he should be helped to learn the difference. If there is no confusion in the meaning, then there is no reason to offer aid. The preoccupation with committing to memory "correctly" spelled words is even more ludicrous when one considers that dictionaries have almost universal availability.

In many respects the English teacher treats language deviance as the police officer treats social deviance. There is minimal reflection on whether the crime is really a crime. There is a belief that the certain and severe crackdown on transgressions will produce "order." There is disregard for the evidence which shows that punishment is ineffectual.

In professional basketball there is a policy that "if there is no injury, there is no foul." It is unfortunate that English teachers have not yet attained this measure of common sense. It is lamentable, but true, that if baseball were taught like English is taught, students would spend twelve years discussing the infield fly rule and never get to bat.

3) Teach language as if skill is linearly related to time spent on routine exercise.

Language instruction is burdened by dreary repetitive exercises. Hour after hour, students mindlessly work to improve handwriting, memorize spelling lists, associate symbols with sounds, write essays, or read aloud. Some even become quite proficient in these skills, but the skills are not transferrable to other situations.

Skill development is dependent on overlearning, but that is an excuse either for drudgery or decerebration. In too many schools there is a distortion of emphasis. There is a belief that if five minutes of exercise is good, twenty minutes is better; and while vitamin manufacturers can get away with such nonsense, that is insufficient justification for similar stupidity in education. In almost all instances, when the student ceases to attend to the exercise he ceases to derive benefit from it.

There is logic of order in exercises which teachers rarely consider. In schools, ritual comes very early. The student learns that school is a dreary place before he has been convinced of the value of the exercise. Again we can learn from the wisdom of Whitehead. Whitehead argued that there should be a rhythm to education. The first stage of learning he called "romance." In this stage the intent should be to create ferment in which ". . . Subject matter has the vividness of novelty, it holds within itself unexplored connections with possibilities half-disclosed by glimpse and half-concealed by the wealth of material. In this stage knowledge is not dominated by systematic procedure." [30]

The second stage is "precision." "In this stage, width of relationship is subordinated to exactness of formulation." "It is evident that a stage of precision is barren without a previous stage of romance." [31]

The last stage of learning is "generalization." Now the student must find a place to apply his skill, to reflect on his performance, and begin the whole process all over again.

Too much of language training is barren precision without *either* a preceding "romance" or a subsequent "generalization." The school is in a much tougher position now than in years gone by. In pre-TV days the school had little competition, and "romance" really depended upon learning to read. Only through reading could a child flee the dreariness of his day-to-day existence by sharing the exotic life with Tarzan, the wonders of invention with Tom Swift, the rise to success with Horatio Alger's

---

[30] Alfred North Whitehead, *op. cit.*, p. 17.
[31] *Ibid.*, p. 18.

heroes, and triumphs with Frank Merriwell. Now, romance can be conjured up without benefit of precise skills, and thus it takes more doing to create the foundation for skill development. Rather than rising to the challenge, education has quit cold. There is very little spontaneous effort to generate the excitement which will make exercise palatable, and whenever there is some effort in that direction, someone like Max Rafferty shoots it down. (He calls it "frills" or "progressive education" and that is generally enough to kill it.) I don't think we should kid ourselves, "romance" is a costly business. Many 60-second TV commercials are multi-thousand-dollar propositions. If there is a true desire to set the stage for precision learning, there has to be willingness to pay the price.

4) Teach language as if one language is better than another.

Reluctantly, the school has been forced to recognize that we are a polyglot nation. But recognition is a far cry from appreciation or legitimation. The language of the school is presented as *the best language*, and children are told that other languages, conventions, or dialects are not acceptable. There has been considerable effort made to prove "scientifically" that the language of the poor, of the streets, of the blacks is inferior to that taught in the school.

Basil Bernstein, a British sociologist and linguist, makes a distinction between a formal language (the kind taught in school) and a public language (the kind uneducated people speak). The former is "elaborate," while the latter is "restricted." [32] An elaborate language has a complicated syntax and a rich vocabulary. It is precise; it is capable of abstraction. Any way you look at it, it is better. Middle-class children learn this good language at home and poor children don't; thus they, the rich, do better in school.

Black youth, Mexican youth, and some white youth in remote rural areas are alleged to suffer another language handicap—a dialect. Dialect is reputed to negatively affect learning to read because the words are sounded so much differently than they are spelled in print.

---

[32] See Basil Bernstein, "Social Structure, Language and Learning, *Educational Research*, 1961, pp. 163–176, and Basil Bernstein, "Language and Social Class," *British Journal of Sociology*, 1960, Vol. II, pp. 271–276.

Poor youth are hypothesized to learn this inferior language because of deprivation in verbal encounters in their early formative years. It is alleged that they do not get the "elaborate" treatment from their parents, nor are they within earshot of abstract expressions. "It can be said that for the middle class there is a progressive development toward verbalizing and making explicit subjective intent, whilst this is NOT the case for the working class child." [33]

Evidence is presented to prove that poor children have a poor language. Typical are the findings of a study conducted by Mildred C. Templin, who found in a study of children from 3 to 8 years of age that the children categorized as low socioeconomic exceeded the high socioeconomic group in only 13 of 230 comparisons. The poor preschoolers tended to be most inferior in sentence length, while their older comrades were retarded in articulation, grammatical complexity, and vocabulary. The difference between socioeconomic status exceeded differences found between levels of I.Q. or differences in sex.[34] Even authors who see positive features in the life and learning styles of the disadvantaged are apt to accept the assertion that their language is restricted. Fantini and Weinstein, who call for much-needed change in education, allow that the distinction is valid.[35] In doing this they ignore the inevitable consequences of that distinction. Because once it is assumed that the poor child has less proficiency in language, then all educational activity is influenced by the diagnosis. If the child is expected to know less, it is obvious that less will be expected of him, and it is equally obvious (as discussed in Chapter II) that he will also accomplish less. In time he will believe he is worthless (and so the cycle grows in viciousness).

The double handicap of a restricted code and a dialect is offered as *the* reason why black children fail in school. I find the argument and the evidence unconvincing. Another argument can be made, and that is that the inferiority is not in the lower-

---

[33] Basil Bernstein, "Social Class and Linguistic Development: a Theory of Social Learning," A. N. Halsey, A. Anderson and J. Floud (eds.), *Education, Economy and Society,* Free Press, New York, 1961, p. 238.

[34] Mildred C. Templin, "Relation of Speech and Language Development to Intelligence and Socio-Economic Status," *Volta Review,* Vol. 60, Sept. 1968, pp. 331–334.

[35] Fantini and Weinstein, *op. cit.,* pp. 47–54.

class language but rather in the language of the middle-class schoolteacher and researcher. Because they can't understand what is spoken, they knock it. Frederick David Erickson suggests that when communicants share a context of expression they use shortcuts. If the sociologist, or the teacher, or any other eavesdropper is "out of context" with poor blacks, he will be unable to pick up subtle nuances in their language and too often he will conclude it has no subtlety: "It seems that given a proper context, black dialect can be used to communicate abstractions with considerable precision. But in order for the researcher to realize this he must share the context of the speaker he observes." [36]

The dialect is viewed by some as a major impediment to language facility among blacks: "If the speech of Negroes is a charming and zestful adornment to dialect literature, it is also a tenacious and challenging problem for American pedagogy. If the grievous racial cleavage so lamentably characteristic of contemporary society is to be bridged, it is imperative that the radically deviant speechways of the Negro be eroded." [37]

The thesis that dialect increases racial cleavage is weak. It is much more likely to be the other way around—racial cleavage very likely contributes to the language differences. The right to speak a unique tongue has been one of the precious few rights that oppressed people have been able to secure. Today that language is proudly hailed as part of a social identity, as well it should be. It takes a hell of a lot of guts, after denying black people mobility, economic security, history, and education, to deny them their language too. Yet that is precisely what some precious, pompous, pedantic snobs would do. Please remember that there is no assurance that if the "Negro" gave up his dialect he would be any more accepted socially, economically, or politically. It would be fatuous to expect, as so many fatuous educators expect, that black people should surrender something that is valuable to them and receive nothing in return. (Before anyone says how much more employable blacks without a dialect would be, please refer again to Chapters II and III.)

---

[36] Frederick David Erickson, " 'F'get You Honky,' A New Look at Black Dialect and the School," *Elementary English,* April 1969, p. 495.

[37] Geoffrey D. Needler, "The Speech of the American Negro: A Select Bibliography," *The Negro Educational Review,* Oct. 1968, p. 103.

While "it ain't necessarily so" that the Negro dialect is an inferior language, it is certainly true that the language black people speak and the language spoken by middle-income whites is different. The differences can be found in vocabulary, in syntax, and in the patterning of speech.[38] The school does not even credit a Negro dialect to be a language. The student is denied access to primers and texts written in it, or teachers who speak it. Joan Baratz shows some of the barriers that the black ghetto student must overcome if he is to learn to read:

> The disadvantaged Negro must not only decode the written words, he must translate them into his own language. This presents an almost insurmountable obstacle, since the words often do not go together in any pattern that is familiar or meaningful to him. He is baffled by this confrontation with (1) a new language with its new syntax; (2) a necessity to learn the meaning of graphic symbols; and (3) a vague, or not so vague, depending upon the cultural and linguistic sophistication of the teacher, sense that there is something terribly wrong with his language.[39]

Teacher ignorance and insensitivity contribute heavily to student disorientation:

> . . . during the initial stages of learning to read, the disadvantaged child is confused and presumed ignorant and unable to comprehend concepts if, when he is taught the rhyming concept in reading, he responds that han' (hand) rhymes with *man*. When told he is wrong he becomes confused for he is right: *han'* and man do in fact rhyme in his speech.[40]

Baratz suggests that prior to teaching the black ghetto child a standard code he be taught to read in his native tongue:

> Such a reading program would not only require accurate vernacular texts for the dialect speaker, but also necessitate the creation of a series of 'transition readers' that would move the child, once he mastered reading in the vernacular, from vernacular texts to standard English texts.[41]

---

[38] See for example W. A. Stewart, "Socio-Linguistic Factors in the History of American Negro Dialects," *The Florida Foreign Language Reporter,* Vol. 5, 1967, pp. 4–5.

[39] Joan Baratz, "Linguistic and Cultural Factors in Teaching Reading to Ghetto Children," *Elementary English,* Feb. 1969, p. 201.

[40] *Ibid.*, p. 201.

[41] *Ibid.*, p. 202.

The linguists studying the blacks' nonstandard code are making valuable contributions. They are challenging with logic and evidence propositions of language inferiority that heretofore have been too readily accepted. But they do not go nearly far enough in their suggested solutions. The absorption system suggested by Baratz is unilateral. Ultimately the goal of the process is to get the poor black to accept the dominant white language. "Of course, success of such a reading program would be dependent upon the child's ultimate ability to read standard English." [42]

Baratz implies a sanctity for standard English which it should not have. It is not the platinum bar against which all yardsticks are gauged. There must be mutuality in the negotiations. There must be reciprocation between the ghetto codes, the basic codes, the Appalachian codes, and the standard code. As the language skill of the ghetto resident is facilitated, so is the standard language broadened and enlivened. Alternative expressions are credited equally. The two statements, "He is here all the time" (standard English) and "He be here" (black nonstandard), should be accepted as equivalents, much as, over a period of time, "don't" and "do not" have become accepted as equivalent and synonomous expressions without any loss of communication.

The resistance to acceptance of new languages and mutuality in negotiations of change is as old as the white man's settlement in the New World itself. Many of our national heroes got involved with it. Benjamin Franklin and John Adams in particular were concerned with adulteration of expression. H. L. Mencken, in his three-volume work, *The American Language*, traces the evolution of a language with distinct and unique characteristics. This language has gained a modicum of acceptance, but it has had to fight off the purists who have always confused sterility with scholarship (which explains why they produce so little.)

In 1816 John Pickering, a lawyer, politician, and pretender to scholarship, lamented the sad state of language usage and called for a return to purity:

---

[42] *Ibid.*, p. 202.

As a general rule, we should undoubtedly avoid all those words which are noticed by English authors of reputation as expressions with which they are unacquainted, for although we might produce some English authority for such words, yet the very circumstance of their being thus noticed by well-educated Englishmen is a proof that they are not in use at this day in England, and of course, ought not to be used elsewhere by those who would speak *correct English*.[43]

H. L. Mencken observes that Pickering's

theory is still entertained by multitudes of American pedagogues. They believe as he did that a natural growth of language is wild and wicked; and that it should be regulated according to rules formulated in England. To this end they undertake periodic crusades against "bad grammar," the American scheme of pronunciation, and the general body of Americanisms.[44]

Mencken cites a history of resistance to change, to flexibility, even to thought. Americanisms have been attacked as "lazy and unintelligible," for which atonement of "tears of shame and self-abasement" would be required. The same tone, the same stance, and the same smug claim to omniscience are found today at every educational level, but they have extended significance because they affect so many more people. All of the early efforts to maintain a sacrosanct language had very little social importance. Public education was run by the middle class (the rich sent their children to more expensive private schools). The aim of the school was to give the student a thin veneer of culture. The bias of that school was straightforward—it was an elitist institution without subterfuge.

Today the issues are confounded and class bias is interwoven with race and ethnic bias. It is no longer possible to talk about an American *language*. Now we must recognize American *languages* and appreciate what that recognition means for language instruction.

Joan Baratz touched lightly on one implication and called for creation of new primers and texts. I think that would have minimal and only transient impact. A langauge will attain legitimacy only when authorities in the school truly accept that lan-

---

[43] Quoted from H. L. Mencken, *The American Language,* Alfred Knopf, 1962, p. 50.

[44] *Ibid.,* p. 51.

guage. To date Stewart and a few others concerned with applied linguistics have tried to instruct English teachers on the intricacies of the black language. Their approach is neither efficient nor defensible. For all its good intentions it reflects colonialism. It harkens back to the missionaries who learned to speak a language of a heathen tribe only to convert it. An approach that treats all language equally would require that the spokesmen of those languages be distributed in proportion to their numbers in all positions of authority in the school.

The black and the brown, the Indian, and the rejected white will believe that the school truly respects their language when they see persons who speak their language (naturally and honestly come by) in important positions in the school. Here again we must return to a New Careers approach to staffing. One area of competence that could be used in lieu of formal education for eligibility to a teaching position would be expertise in a non-standard American language.

Children of the ghetto will believe that they "belong" in school when the language spoken there is their language. They will believe that they will be treated as equals in a suburban school when their "landsmen" serve as teachers, principals, and superintendents in those faraway places. Until changes in both places occur, neither a sense of belonging in the neighborhood school nor integration in a wide geographical context is possible.

There is yet another reason why schools should recognize the legitimacy of all American languages. Only when that happens will we come to appreciate more fully the deficiencies of the standard code. The language of the school is an inferior language. We don't look at its inadequacies, because only a small select group are allowed to evaluate it, and that group has been thoroughly brainwashed. For example, official school language eschews expression of hostility. "Nice children don't talk like that here." When language is outlawed, communication is impeded. When those who have the *responsibility* to teach communication skills are the very persons who *bar* communication we get to the ridiculous place we now occupy.

Emerson said it many years ago:

> Everyone has felt how superior in force is the language of the street to that of the academy. . . . The speech of the man in the street is invariably strong, nor can you mend it by making

it what you call parliamentary. You say, "If he could only express himself," but he does already, better than any one can for him. . . . The power of their speech is that it is perfectly understood by all . . . is always strong. . . . Cut these words and they would bleed; they are vascular and alive; they walk and run. Moreover they who speak them have this elegancy that they do not trip in their speech. It is a shower of bullets, whilst Cambridge men and Yale men correct themselves and begin again at every sentence.[45]

More than a century has passed since Emerson compared the language of the academy with the language of the street. Only two things have happened in the interim. The language of the street has improved, the language of the academy has gotten worse.

d) Teach language as if your real life role was as a minister of morality.

Language instruction is encumbered at every turn. The rules restrict, the language restricts, the dreariness of exercise devoid of "romance" restricts, but that is not where it ends. There is further restriction. Students are told which words of a language are acceptable and what themes are permissible. Almost all of this intrusion is capricious. To paraphrase the quotation, propriety and obscenity, like beauty, exist in the mind of the perceiver.

Reflect on what makes a word obscene. It all goes back to the year 1066 and William the Conqueror. If Harold had won—and he had more troops—all those nasty four-letter words would grace our primers and the Latin derivatives would be etched as graffiti on public toilets. If nine centuries later these "bad" words still have currency, and, furthermore, if children, who can spell little else can spell them, then we ought to recognize their validity. We also ought to recognize that an informal education is taking place outside the school that is more effective than that taking place within.

When teachers set arbitrary limits on the student's writing or talking, all too often they take the heart out of the communication process. Communication involves content! To keep students from talking about things important to them—sex,

---

[45] Ralph Waldo Emerson, *op. cit.*, pp. 3–4.

drugs, violence, race, anger—is to insist that students communicate about nothing. That is insanity.

Herbert Kohl found that when he relaxed the rigid rules, his sixth-grade children responded eagerly. They wrote voluminously and poignantly. They published a class paper *AND*— this paper was distinctly theirs. The class paper made the rounds. It appeared that he was over the hump. Such was not the case:

> Two days after *AND* had been distributed to the teachers and administration, and had been read and praised by some of the children's parents we got a visit from Mary Bonnett, a big, smiling, yet tough Negro teacher who considered herself the children's truest mother but who had the unenviable position of translating the principal's feelings into words the children understood. She entered the room smiling, a copy of *AND* and another class newspaper in her hand. The children quickly took their seats and snapped to attention—Mrs. Bonnett always commanded attention, but this time the children were even more alert—they cared what she thought of their work.

> I just read your magazine. It was really interesting, children. Robert Jackson, you really draw beautifully, only, Robert, why do you draw so much violence—child, your imagination needs to rest. Children, I don't understand why you talk so much fighting and stabbing. You can't possibly know about that. Tell me now, who knows what a junkie is? See, I told you no one knows. Newspapers and magazines aren't for that nonsense. Now look at this sheet, imagine it was put out by the fifth grade. Listen to this, you know how to do better:

> Shop with Mom
>
> > I love to shop with Mom
> > And talk to the friendly grocer
> > And help her make the list
> > Seems to make us closer.

> The children slumped into their seats demoralized.[46]

Children are continually told what *not* to say. It almost always has a demoralizing effect. It is ironic that our overconcern with morality should demoralize. Yet that's what happens. Students should be encouraged to communicate about a wide range

---

[46] Herbert Kohl, *op. cit.*, p. 154.

of subjects. If education succeeds, students will be interested in occupations, in politics, in culture, and in interpersonal matters. If we understand that student preoccupation with "depravity" is *caused* by inadequate education we turn to the antidote, which is to stimulate students to talk about other issues. If teachers stopped wasting so much time telling kids what they shouldn't say, maybe they could get down to the business of encouraging students to communicate about "better" things.

At this point some readers (particularly those who like to catch authors on inconsistencies) are going to triumphantly cry, "I got him!" Throughout this book I have stressed that racism in the school has to be extripated. O.K. Then it can be argued that if a teacher cannot forbid a student to say or write "fuck," how can the teacher object to the use of the word "nigger"? Let's get that in perspective. All words are merely symbols. It boils down to the difference in what both words symbolize. One merely offends convention; the other reflects a three-century policy of inequality. The responsible teacher communicates this distinction to students. The teacher has an obligation to point out that people in the community may take offense when students violate a convention and that the consequences of disrupted personal relationships should be considered. The teacher has the responsibility to communicate to students that a racial epithet is very serious. The students must be told that words inflame and that words are the means by which prejudice gains converts. There are teachers who see no difference between an alleged obscenity and a racial slur; I can only pity them. There are teachers who become incensed about obscenity and are sanguine about racial insults. I have nothing but contempt for them.

e) Teach language as if it is a separate discipline.

Language instruction suffers greatly from isolation and fragmentation. From the inchoate efforts at reading, through courses in English composition in college, language instruction is disjointed and without immediate utility. Almost everything about the instruction is artificial. The fracturing of language into many isolated pieces leads to many distortions. The student loses direction. For many, the passing grade becomes the only concern. They spend more time trying to "psych" out the teacher than they do trying to improve language skill.

Teachers have problems too. They lack context for meaningful evaluation. Students are graded by the pound. It is not un-usual for a college course in writing to require students to pro-duce ten 450-word essays. Anyone who falls short of that fails. There is no negotiability because there is no framework for negotiation. There is little accountability because isolation does not lend itself to acceptance of external criteria. A natural con-sequence of insulation is evaluation based on quantity of effort at the expense of the quality of the activity. The removal of language classes from other activities leads to oversimplification. There is a tendency to ignore the fact that a complex world re-quires diversity of expression. Classes tend to look for non-existent universals. Yet it should be obvious that different lan-guage skills are required for different situations. Language style, tempo, vocabulary, and affect must be altered, depending upon the intent of the message or the characteristics of the audience. The class doesn't lend itself to diversity—the primary audience for the student is a single person—the teacher.

f) Teach language so that the student is miserable.

Only a handful of students truly enjoy school. The rest gen-erally are there because it is the least obnoxious of all the ob-noxious alternatives available to them. Not to be at school means to be alone on the street, or working in a low-paying dead-end job, or home feigning illness. The choices aren't great. Language classes are like all others, only more so, because they are required. In class the student feels isolated, terrified, inade-quate, and useless.

The classroom can be a frightfully lonely place. The stu-dent is asked to improve his language skills all by himself. He sometimes reads in groups, but that can be the most lonely ex-perience of all, since he exposes himself to an entire class. If he goofs big, he is literally drowned in raucous derision.

The classroom harbors terror. It is a Poe story of a shrink-ing room and a swinging pendulum. The student can't know what the teacher wants because the teacher isn't sure. But the student does know that whatever he says or writes isn't going to be good enough. The student's luckiest day is the day the teacher forgets to call on him. The relief of escape is for many students the only real enjoyment of school—"saved by the bell," etc.

The student doesn't develop a sense of adequacy of language. To the contrary he sees himself as inadequate. Even students who succeed handsomely in school are afraid to venture out into either written or oral expeditions. They lack confidence in their ability. If they feel competent at all it is within the shelter of their limited experience. The student who has no such shelter (because his experience isn't honored in school) suffers from an even greater sense of inadequacy.

The language course doesn't engender a sense of usefulness. The student has no arena where he can put his skills to work. Bare literacy has no marketability. The student is not allowed to use his knowledge to help others. Some few in school do engage in useful projects: they write for school papers, tutor younger students, and prepare television scenarios. But even for these few there is lack of continuity. Some tragic few have a short moment of limelight (they produce a play or triumph on a debating team) only to be relegated to nonproductivity soon again. It may not be true that it is better to have a small moment of usefulness and lose than never to have had it at all.

How to Teach "English"

Good teaching starts with conceptualization. The instruction of language *must* be coordinated, interrelated, and systematic. A theory of instruction must be attached to well-defined goals. The approach must be complete. The instructor at any one phase of the activity must have in sight the ultimate goal of the instruction and an understanding of how his specific responsibility fits into the scheme of things.

The goal of instruction in language is true literacy! The student must be able to communicate in a wide range of languages and media to different audiences in different settings. The institution at any one phase must identify specifically the areas where knowledge attained is applicable. There must be evaluation of the activity at points along the way to determine whether that which is being sought is actually being obtained. The evaluation must logically fall within the theoretical perspective. It is not sufficient to know merely that the program is falling short. There must be sufficient information to understand why the program is failing and what needs to be done to rectify the situation.

Mere correction of existing errors isn't going to suffice. If language instruction was to free itself from its preoccupation with rules, if there was continual updating, if all American languages were equally accepted and persons who spoke them were equally represented in teaching positions, if teachers didn't act as censors, if within a classroom, language was considered an integral part of all activity, and if students were not denied a sense of competence, belonging, and usefulness, *the goal of true literacy would still not be reached*. In fact, if we did nothing but surrender our current preoccupations, there would likely be nothing left. To borrow from Oscar Levant, if we stripped from language instruction its exterior superficiality, we would only get down to its real superficiality.

Herbert Kohl's experience with his *36 Children* should give us pause. He managed to "make it" with his students. But it was more happenstance than design. He capitalized on his sensitivity, insight, wit, and dedication. He had no plan; he endured day by day. He had no evaluation scheme. He used informal feedback from his students and kept his antennae out for signals that indicated approaching danger or safe passage. And yet, for all that he accomplished, if he intended to keep his children in the school until they had attained the goals of education, he failed totally and abysmally.

One by one the students were overcome by the system:

> Robert is not the only one of the thirty-six children who is now close to being a dropout—John, Margie, Carol, Sam—I stopped searching, don't want to know the full extent of the misery and tragedy of the children's present lives. Recently one of the kids told me: "Mr. Kohl, one good year isn't enough." [47]

Herbert Kohl could not have known when the students had become educated, because he had no terminal goals. It is not right that Herbert Kohl should have to learn that after he began to teach. He was sent out without suitable equipment. He had no theory, and he needed one. He had no strategy or tactics to win allies within the system over to his side. He needed tactics and strategy. He lacked overtures to other instructors. He was in the best tradition of the American Western folk hero. He was there all by himself when both hands of the clock were at twelve—but life isn't like the movies (although Californians obviously don't understand that) and he, not the bad guys, died in the dust.

---

[47] Herbert Kohl, *op. cit.*, p. 205.

A good language program requires a political solution. A number of persons must share their power to make the program live. The alliance begins with a precise statement of goal. Only then can we even identify those who should be involved. The alliance must include almost all of the teachers who contact the student during a given day as well as the teachers who are likely to instruct him in the future. Those who want that good program had better tack their statement of intent to the wall and discover who is there with them. If the ranks are thin, they must plan accordingly. An ambitious program requires considerable support. Modest programs can help develop that necessary support, but not necessarily. Too often the teacher succeeds but the student dies, because the teacher has been above politics. If no other point has been driven home, I hope that I have convinced the reader that no educator can possibly be an island unto himself. The teacher alone in a system can do little more than Herbert Kohl. He can make his classroom succeed. But after that he has to make his accomplishments public. He must seek out persons with similar views. If there already exist a substantial number who share a common viewpoint, they must coordinate their efforts. A comprehensive language program will require coordination that is system-wide. I believe that we could be at that point quite soon if we—that is, all the persons who now share a common viewpoint—stopped acting like prima donnas.

A good language program is totally pluralistic. In it every language and every medium are respected. Pluralism isn't easy. Most teachers and most students lack the language for total communication. Some in the class will not understand others in the class. The more heterogeneous the class, the greater the likelihood of disrupted communication. It is possible that a teacher may be unable to understand one of the students. The teacher's first move is to ask the student for assistance. He can simply say, "I don't understand, please say it again," or, perhaps, "Say it a little differently." If there is still a problem, the teacher can turn to other classmates and ask for translation. If it is the reverse, then the student should feel free to first ask the teacher for help and then turn to others for translation. The teacher sets the tone for this freedom of inquiry.

A teacher must never use the guise of pluralism to affect a language that isn't his. Nothing is more phony than to have a middle-class, middle-aged, middle-bulging teacher try to act "hip." Nothing is less necessary. The key to the language program is not one teacher who is all things to all students, but rather a staff with sufficient diversity so that every student has at least one faculty member he can talk to.

Pluralism does not mean elimination of standards. It means a refinement of standards. The ability to communicate must also be evaluated in its proper context. A student has a right to know where he stands. He has a right to be graded, but the principles of accountability and negotiability previously discussed must apply. The grade must be defended by the teacher, and the specifics of its applicability made known to the student. The student may disagree with the grade, and, depending on the nature of the disagreement, a variety of negotiations may ensue. If the disagreement is in the student's performance in informal rhetoric (the ability to engage in persuasive dialogue with small numbers of colleagues) then the logical appeal would be to the target audience. If the disagreement is in comprehending a written passage, the student may request an examination before his peers.

Oral communication is the basis for all beginning language instruction; it remains the key throughout life. Other media should be continuously explored. The student should always be allowed to select his medium or media. Limiting communication to reading, writing, and talking makes little sense. The student should take full advantage of electronic transmittal. The McLuhan thesis that the medium is the message is overplayed, but a denial of the importance of television, radio, and records is a much more absurd position. The question of a student's ultimate *capacity* to communicate will undoubtedly slip into even the best of language classes. There is no answer except that everyone can communicate better than he does. It is imperative that teachers keep alive the idea that if a student can speak he can probably do everything else demanded of him. The most difficult intellectual accomplishment a human is ever asked to perform is to learn to speak. He must learn to take an infinite arrangement of sounds, put them under conscious control, attach meaning to them, and do all of this, generally before he is three years old. Nothing else is anywhere near as tough. I forget now who said this, but he made a point that every elementary teacher should always keep in the forefront of his consciousness the thought that "If children had to be taught to speak they probably would never learn."

The student must have avenues kept open for him. He must be

encouraged to experiment in content, form, style, and media. A good teacher keeps the student balanced between concern for discipline and concern for self-expression. If clarity of message was the only concern we would eventually sound like 1.5 billion David Brinkleys talking to 1.5 billion Walter Cronkites. If expression of self was the only concern, there would be no communication at all. The good teacher recognizes that a touch of hebephrenia distinguishes the stolid craftsman from the genius.

The language teacher opens up the world of literature to the student. The literature must be keyed to student interest. Contrary to the beliefs of Max Rafferty, it isn't the classics that will have the widest immediate appeal. In fact some of the alleged classics don't wear very well. Walter Scott, for example, leaves a good deal to be desired, and Jane Austen might be considered a little slow and not terribly relevant. The classic poets take a little getting used to. The literature of now has more appeal than the literature of the past. What Max Rafferty always overlooks is that the classics, at the time they were written, were often as poorly received as some of the literature of today.

Weinstein and Fantini describe a lesson whose principles could be incorporated into any aspect of a school program but which has particular relevance to language instruction and the study of literature: .

> The following lesson serves to summarize some of the major concepts we have attempted to develop in this book; here, "Do You Dig All Jive?" utilizes contact through the child's language. It also illustrates an approach to nonstandard dialect in such a way that the pupils feel that learning standard English dialect doesn't mean they must discard their own. It exposes children to the idea that poetry can "swing" and that some of the "swingingest" has been written by Negro authors. Its methodology is the inductive approach through questioning to challenge the imagination. Finally, it shows the way to vocabulary development through role-playing.
> In order to aid a teacher who asked how she might get her eighth-grade class interested in poetry, one of the present authors related his experience:
> "Sometime after I had been asked for aid, I was looking through my materials when I came across an anthology of Langston Hughes' poetry. I noted a poem entitled 'Motto':
> > I play it cool,
> > And dig all the jive.
> > That's the reason I stay alive.

> My motto, as I live and learn,
> Is: To dig and be dug
> In return.

I made about thirty copies and, with the permission of the English teacher, took them into her classroom. The children stared at me, probably wondering what I was up to. Without saying a word, I distributed the copies of the poem so each child had one.

There was a moment or two of silence while they read the poem. Finally, I heard someone mumble, "Tough!" followed by, "Hey now, this is really tough, man!"

Being familiar with their jargon, I realized they had paid the poem a supreme compliment, although it probably didn't appear that way to the other teacher.

"Hey now . . . this cat's pretty cool. Who wrote it?"

"Langston Hughes," I answered.

"Who's he?"

"He's a very famous Negro author, poet, and playwright." I saw that most of the class hadn't heard of him. "Do you know what this poem is talking about?" I asked them.

"Sure," they said.

"How come?"

"Well, it's written in our talk."

"Oh! Then you understand everything this is saying?"

"Sure," they said.

"That's good. Maybe you can tell me then what the first line means by 'playing it cool.' They had great difficulty in verbalizing the concept of coolness. "Are there any brave souls in here who would try something with me?" A boy's hand shot up. "Good! Come up here. Now I'm a teacher standing in the middle of a hallway. You're coming toward me down the hall, but you're walking on the wrong side. I'm going to tell you something, and when I do, I want you to play it cool. Okay?"

"Yeah," he said.

The boy started walking toward me, and I said in a very fierce manner, "Hey you! You're walking on the wrong side of the hallway. Get over where you belong!"

The boy, very calmly and without raising his head, moved with deliberate slowness to the other side of the hall and sauntered on as if I did not exist.

"Is that playing it cool?" I asked.

The class agreed that it was.

"I'll tell you what," I said to my volunteer. "Let's do the same thing, only this time show us what would happen if you didn't play it cool." Our little scene began again. But this time, after I had ordered him to move to the proper side of the hall he stopped angrily and said, "Who you talking to?"

"To you," I said.

"I ain't doin' nothin!"

He became very belligerent and a hot verbal battle ensued.

I stopped the scene before it got any hotter, and said to the class, "Well, what's the difference between playing it cool and not playing it cool?"

Finally, one pupil came up with, "When you're cool, you're calm and collected."

"Very good," I said, writing "calm and collected" on the board. "Anyone else?"

They were able to supply a few more words. I then gave them a few, such as indifferent and nonchalant. They were especially intrigued by nonchalant, and kept repeating it aloud to themselves.

"Now, how about this word 'jive' in the second line: 'and dig all jive?' "

One pupil said "It means jazz."

Another told how jive meant "teasing" in the expression "stop jivin' me."

Then a third boy chimed in with this incident: "I was in another city once, walkin' through a strange neighborhood. These guys were standing on the corner and one of them yells to me, 'Hey man, cut the stroll.' Now I never heard that before, so I turned and said, 'What?' That's all I had to do. If there wasn't a cop on the corner I might have been messed up good."

"Do you know what stroll means now?" I asked.

"Oh yeah. It's when you're walking like this." He proceeded to demonstrate. It was a walk with a limping gait or strut that I have seen our children use many times. It seemed to generate a "devil-may-care," or "watch out, it's me," attitude.

"It's like they were telling me," the boy continued, "that I was walkin' too big to suit them!"

"How does all this show what the word jive means?"

"Well, I just didn't dig their jive and almost got messed up."

"Then what's another word for jive as you have just used it?"

"I quess . . . talk, a kind of talk," he answered. "This here poem is written in jive talk."

"Do you think that 'all jive' in this poem could mean 'all kind of talk' "?

They nodded in agreement.

"What does dig mean?" Again we compiled our multiple meanings on the board. To dig someone is to like him; to dig someone later is to see him later; and to dig something is to understand it. When I asked which of the three meanings fit best with "dig all jive," they readily agreed that to "understand" was it.

We continued similarly to the end of the poem. The final interpretation was that "to understand and be understood in return" was the poet's rule for life.

"How many kinds of jive do you understand?" I asked them.

"Oh, we understand all of it."

"Well, let's see if you can understand my kind of jive. Okay?"
"Go ahead," they said.

I then proceded to give an elaborate oral essay, on the nature of truth, using some of the most complicated words I could think of. At the conclusion, I said, "Did you dig my jive?"

They looked at me blankly.

Then I said, "Now let's see if I can dig yours. Would you like to test me?"

They responded eagerly. Expressions were thrown at me. I was able to get five out of six, which impressed them greatly.

"According to Langston Hughes, who has a better chance of staying alive, you or I?"

"You."

"Why?"

"You dig more than one kind of jive."

"All right," I said, "I think I agree with Mr. Hughes, and I feel very lucky that I do understand many kinds of talk. In certain situations I'm able to use one kind of jive and in others, another kind. But you, sitting in this class, have, up to this point, mastered only one kind, and one that I think is very beautiful. But it is still only one. You've got to dig the school jive as well as your own, and also jive that might be needed in other situations. School helps you dig all jive and helps you stay alive."

Mrs. Baker, the English teacher, commented afterward that it was the first time she had seen the class so involved in a lesson. "I couldn't believe my ears. I saw some pupils participate today who haven't opened their mouths since the beginning of the term."

Shortly after that, various pupils asked me where they could find more of Langston Hughes' poetry. I allowed the anthology to circulate, and circulate it did. It was difficult for me to get the book back.[48]

The child, the adolescent, the adult can develop keen critical insights through discussion and analysis of popular lyrics. The nature of man-woman relationships can be examined through contrasting Otis Redding's and Aretha Franklin's versions of Redding's song "Respect." [49]

The use of popular songs is no sure-fire way to engender an interest in literature. There is a fine line distinguishing intellectual stimulation from pandering to intellectual laziness. To allow children to listen to songs at school that they listen to at home has limited educational value. There is value if the teacher uses the material as a basis for systematic discussion and the development of

[48] Mario Fantini and Gerald Weinstein, *op. cit.*, pp. 382–386.
[49] East-Time-Redwall Publishing, 1965.

critical faculties. There is value if the teacher can make contact by alluding to the familiar and then drawing the student out to ever-widening stimulations, interest, and involvement.

In Frederick Wiseman's film *High School*, a young high-school teacher is shown trying to teach poetry by reading the words and then playing a record of Simon and Garfunkel. The camera pans the class while this is occurring and it appears (at least during the interval shown to the audience) that she failed to interest the students. Two thoughts occurred to me while I watched the film. One, the class was structured very traditionally—the students sat very stiffly in rows; poetry was never meant to be appreciated in such an atmosphere. Secondly, she gave them no clues for analysis. It may be that criticism can emerge as it did in the "Motto" lesson described previously; but generally, students have a right to some help. The teachers should share knowledge and expression. The student can be introduced to "systems" of criticism. The work he is asked to review has undoubtedly been subjected to some "expert" criticism. The student can contrast a Marxian analysis with an existentialist critique. The student can look to form and to content. Subdivision into categories of work, politics, culture, and interpersonal relationship (the goals of education) may prove useful in analyzing literary output.

Language instruction is markedly influenced by classroom organization. It would be *impossible* to improve communication skills in a classroom organized to preclude communication. William Glasser in his book *Schools Without Failure* suggests three forms of discussion groups, all of which facilitate analysis of literature and improve communication skills. These are:

> 1) Social Problem-Solving Meetings—In these groups students work together to *solve the problems of living in their school world*. Over and above the value of learning to solve their problems through class meetings, students also gain in scholastic achievement.[50]

> 2) Open-ended Meetings—In the open-ended meetings the children are asked to discuss any thought-provoking question related to their lives, questions that may also be related to the curriculum of the classroom.[51]

---

[50] William Glasser, *Schools Without Failure*, Harper and Row, New York, 1969, p. 123.

[51] *Ibid.*, p. 134.

3) Educational-Diagnostic Meetings—These groups are 'always directly related to what the class is studying.' These meetings can be used by the teachers to get a quick evaluation of whether or not teaching procedures in the class are effective.[52]

These groups not only can be used as natural arenas for language development but also as means by which a "subject" can be handled as an integral whole.

A good language program will be guided by some rules. George Orwell suggested a few for political writers. They are probably as good as any:

(i) Never use a metaphor, simile or other figure of speech which you are used to seeing in print.

(ii) Never use a long word where a short one will do.

(iii) If it is possible to cut a word out, always cut it out.

(iv) Never use a foreign phrase, a scientific word or a jargon word if you can think of an everyday English equivalent.

(v) Break any of these rules sooner than say anything barbarous.[53]

If you write poetry, change the rules in order to get the desired imagery. Alter the rules if you want to break up monotony of expression. Change the rules or ignore them completely at other times, but when you do, do it knowingly and be accountable for what you do.

Summary

The schools fail to generate culture-carrying competence. The failure stems from many causes. Vague, shopworn goals contribute to the problem. Unwillingness to examine socially relevant issues contributes to the problem. Confusing "academic standards" with race, class, and ethnic bias contributes to the problem. The organization of the classroom contributes to the problem.

Cultural and intellectual competence depend on language, but language instruction is especially muddled. Students are discouraged

---

[52] *Ibid.*, p. 139.
[53] George Orwell, "Politics and the English Language," in *A Collection of Essays by George Orwell*, Doubleday Anchor Books, Garden City, New York, 1954, p. 176.

from expressing themselves. Capriciousness and precedent prevail over facility of communication in evaluation of student performance. A good language program would go far beyond mere remedy of existing abuses. A clear notion of purpose and tactics and strategy linked to that purpose is essential. Ultimately the reform of language instruction will require a political solution.

In this chapter, "English" was discussed in breadth and depth. Most of the criticisms and suggestions would apply equally well to any intellectual activity and should be read with that in mind.

CHAPTER VII

The Son of Culture-Carrying Competence

[In which I take a critical look at the teaching of history, deplore the "melting-pot" influence on American education, and reflect on the impact of mass media on the culture of the mass. I argue that a high level of culture-carrying is possible if teachers motivate students through feelings of competence, belonging, and usefulness and stop demotivating them through punishment or threat of punishment and misuse of grades. I argue against accepting either the extreme of mechanistic behaviorism or the extreme of anarchistic existentialism. I conclude by arguing that culture-carrying competence in students is predicated on culture-carrying competence in teachers and that we are doing very little now to entice intellectually alert persons to persist in teaching.]

So difficult a matter it is to trace and find out the truth of anything by history.   —Plutarch

What is history but fable agreed upon?   —Attributed to Napoleon

Perhaps there is only one thing worse than that the college student should forget his subjects; and that is that he should remember them.   —T. W. Hudson

A pupil from whom nothing is ever demanded which he cannot do, never does all he can.   —James Mill

All too often in the history of the United States the school teacher has been in no position to serve as a model for an introduction to the intellectual life.   —Richard Hofstadter

> When I'm dead I hope it may be said
> His sins were scarlet but his books were read.
>   —Hilaire Belloc

You can only explain the past by what is highest in the present. Only by straining the noblest qualities you have to their highest power will you find out what is greatest in the past, most worth knowing and preserving. Like by like! Otherwise you will draw the past to your own level.   —Nietzsche

Culture-carrying is a complex matter. It is also vital, affecting every aspect of life. Cultural and intellectual activity have value unto themselves, but they are also essential for an understanding of one's self and one's relationship with others, the work world, and politics. One basic ingredient of culture is language. The language must be precise. It must have depth. It must accurately reflect subtleties and complexities. The other imperative is history. Man is totally lost without an understanding of history. Santayana, a man who didn't know his history, asserted that those who didn't know history were doomed to repeat it.

In this chapter, history and its instruction are dissected, as are many other influences upon culture-carrying. Almost everything treated is worthy of an extended analysis which, however, transcends the purposes of this book. In the interest of brevity, many matters will be introduced, touched upon, and dropped. The reader is asked to perceive a large canvas while he, at the same time, functions in circumscribed areas. He is expected to integrate the ideas which are disjointedly presented here.

What is history?—E. H. Carr suggests that history has a dual function: "To enable man to understand the society of the past and to increase his mastery over society of the present." [1]

Carr later adds a third concern—the future—to his past and present: "Good historians, I suspect, whether they think it or not, have the future in their bones." [2]

Carl Becker suggests that "History acquires meaning and objectivity only when it establishes a coherent relation between past and future." [3]

Unfortunately, while historians talk ambitiously about the nature of history, they parade little more than trivia as history courses. At all levels of instruction, but particularly prior to college, the teaching of history is plagued by chronic problems that keep the defined goals from being achieved. Among the most persistent difficulties are:

a) A disconnected, time-locked, chronological approach.

b) Arbitrary restriction in the span of inquiry and limitations in competence of persons assigned to teach history.

---

[1] E. H. Carr, *What Is History?*, Alfred Knopf, New York, 1962, p. 69.
[2] *Ibid.*, p. 143.
[3] Carl L. Becker, *Everyman His Own Historian: Essays on History and Politics*, Crofts, New York, 1935, p. 173.

c) Undetected intrusions of race, class, and ethnic bias in textbooks or instructors.

d) Inadequate instruction in *method* of historical inquiry.

e) Cumbersome, and often downright dreary, presentation of material.

These problems need some further discussion.

Students justifiably complain about what they learn in history. A typical criticism by a group of low-income urban high-school students of history was that they never got beyond World War I. One high-school girl bitterly added that she couldn't see any reason to learn about cave men.

History, even in college, is limited by its organization. It is a great challenge for students to understand the past for present utility and future anticipation when so little in the instruction reflects these lofty purposes.

The courses are organized to give students some "facts" about specific historical eras or geographical locations. Colleges and universities are not immune to these artificial classifications. Look at a sampling from a typical university catalogue:

> Hist 411. History of Greece. (G) 3 hours fall.
> Political, social, and cultural history of the Hellenic world from the Mycenaeans to Alexander the Great.
> Hist 412, 413. History of Rome. (G) 3 hours each term, winter and spring.
> Winter: history of Rome from its earliest beginnings to the end of the Republic; spring: the period of the Empire.
> Hist 420. Historical Method. (G) 3 hours fall.
> Introduction to methods of historical research and writing.
> Hist 421, 422, 423. Middle Ages. (G) 3 hours each term.
> History of Europe from the decline of the Western Roman Empire to the Renaissance. Fall: to the Carolingians; winter: to 1100; spring: to 1300.[4]

The prevailing concern for "behaviorist objectives" in courses contributes heavily to this distortion of effort. The more the instruction is pointed to assisting students to pass an examination, and the more the examination is objective and nationally standardized, and the more publishing houses and "research" corporations can peddle programmed texts as an antidote for anarchistic professors or large classes, the more the educational function will be distorted to meet what little the tester or programmer knows.

---

[4] University of Oregon *Catalogue,* 1967–68.

It becomes virtually impossible for history teachers to meet the purpose of bringing coherence between past and present and future when neither course nor test objectives are compatible with that goal. There are two reasons why those who "huckster" programmed texts and tests are unable to generate material that will cover history's true functions. First, the questions that probe for anticipation or prediction of the future have no right answers. Secondly, the persons involved in the manufacturing of these materials are intellectually incapable of performing the tasks for which they claim expertise.

Very few who teach history have sufficient range to place their instruction into economic, ecological, political, philosophical, and cultural context. As a consequence, students receive a much too restricted picture of history, and history becomes descriptive rather than analytical.

What is not fully appreciated is that history is not, by itself, a legitimate area of study. *There is no such thing as history!* But everything worthy of study—everything that builds culture-carrying competence has a history! The development of a democratic political system has a history; progress has not always been even and there have been devastating setbacks, but the history of the idea of democracy and its difficulties in implementation are exciting and necessary to study.

When history is viewed as a separate area of study, crucial aspects of life are not treated historically. This is particularly true of the social sciences. Those who claim to be psychologists, sociologists, economists, and political scientists are often either nonhistorical (they don't know their history) or ahistorical (they don't care). A major reason for the rebirth of behaviorism in psychology stems from the psychologists' lack of awareness of the failure of behaviorism to change complex behavior fifty years ago. The distortion of sociology into nonideological "pure" science stems from its discontinuity with the past. A student truly immersed in historical context with the work of Marx, Durkheim, Weber, and Mannheim would operate much differently than the distant "scientific" sociologists who have attained prominence in universities today.

The study of mathematics takes on a much different complexion when accomplishments are viewed historically. Mathematics did not grow capriciously. It was no accident that Leibnitz and Newton happened upon calculus at about the same time. The world had generated problems whose solution depended on the invention of calculus. Mathematics is enlivened considerably as the student sees the evolution of a science and gets to know the people who did the breaking through.[5]

Every cultural or intellectual experience is a lesson in history. Every cultural and intellectual experience is also a language lesson. And that truth, while not beautiful and not everything you need to know, is very important, and you have learned a helluva lot when you have learned that.

What passes for history instruction in this country places far too much emphasis on the West. Those whom we educate today, as was mentioned earlier, will have much more contact with the East and the "nonwhite" nations of this world. Africa, Asia, and Latin America, now largely unknown to us, must become known. These areas of the world *will* impinge upon us, often to our internal discomfort.

Recent inclusions of black and other ethnic studies in the curriculum have been a partial remedy, at best. The effort to initiate such a change is a good example of how resistant to innovation educational institutions are. There is very little likelihood that the amount of change will be commensurate with what is needed. Racism has been described as our biggest problem, but the small changes that persistent minority students have won in valiant battle in order to alter this condition are not of the magnitude that the seriousness of the problem demands.

To the contrary, there is a great danger of tokenism. Remember that education has demonstrated an immunity to change. Through the years the little change that has occurred in education has been almost exclusively by accretion. New courses *are added* to the existing schedule, or a new sequence or department is added to the school organization. The old remains and it may even be more difficult to get at, covered over by superficial innovations. Change in education is considered *only after* the Establishment's systems are secured. The money for a new program must be in addition to that already committed to traditional programs. The required Western Civilization sequence must first be funded before there can be an allocation to black or Mexican studies. In "tight money" years

---

[5] See for example, E. T. Bell, *Men of Mathematics,* Simon & Schuster, New York, 1937.

(which is every year), innovations are always the first items cut. Everything in a modern school functions according to a priority schedule. If a program has low priority it might just as well not be introduced at all. Black studies in a white-dominated school is much like black workers in a white-dominated industry—the last to be added and the first to be cut. Unless large sums of money are suddenly made available (a highly unlikely occurrence), or unless there is willingness to do away with programs that have outlived their usefulness, ethnic studies may be seriously crippled by lack of adequate fiscal support.

Black and Chicano students patiently try to negotiate for program changes. They are frustrated by administrators who cry lack of funds, by faculty who solemnly declare that Medieval Poetry clearly has a priority over ethnic studies, and by politicians who evade the issues completely and yet somehow manage to cut off all the avenues of financial support. With such provocation, is it so hard to understand why some few students are driven to violent confrontation in an attempt to gain what they believe is rightfully theirs when no other means to attain their ends are available to them?

The issue of white and Western domination of history instruction runs deeper than problems associated with structural change in education. Other factors must be considered. When ethnic studies are beamed solely at minority youth there is a clear implication that the regular emphasis is appropriate for the majority. *But it is the majority who maintain and sustain white racism and they get support for their views from a distorted picture of history.* Infrequently, black and Mexican studies *are* appended to the curriculum of a suburban high school. When this happens it is because many adult authorities in the school have decided to "humor" student demands. Their feelings are that "last year it was the hula hoop, this year black studies and next year, who knows." Many teachers approach black studies like a fee-needing surgeon approaches a patient's appendix—he can hardly wait to cut it out.

Curriculum reform, while greatly needed, is not sufficient to eliminate racism in the instruction of "history." Instructor bias has an enormous influence on student learning (and assessment of learning). History instruction suffers from the identical malady that cripples language instruction—an inbreeding that results in consensus and allows mere prejudice to claim a status of scholarly knowledge. The solution is also the same—recruitment into teaching of the underrepresented (e.g., New Careers) and a thorough cleansing of those who now profess to be history professors.

The elimination of bias from history instruction is a prodigious assignment, but, when looked at historically, the solution emerges—educational institutions as political bodies will react only politically. The elimination of bias from instruction occurs when the goal of bias-free instruction is defined with sufficient precision that a constituency knows what they are mobilizing for, and tactics and strategy are generated as means to attain that defined end.

Neither demagoguery nor charlatanry will eliminate prejudice from history instruction. The former is often found in highly charged calls for destruction of existing systems with the guarantee that that by itself will automatically get rid of the problem. The latter either suggests simple-minded peripheral amendments—"a programmed text in black history"—or the addition of a "qualified" minority instructor to the faculty as a sufficient cure. Both of these types of responses are anti-intellectual and we must learn that there are no anti-intellectual solutions to intellectually challenging problems.

Educational institutions *can* be forced to change their curriculum and hiring priorities! But the effort will require that ecologically valid criteria be established against which different educational offerings can be compared. In place of traditionalism must come accountability. A course in the History of the Italian Renaissance must be defended as more important than a course in the "strategy and tactics of dealing with oppressors—a cross-cultural and historical analysis"—and the instructor must offer more than advanced degrees or published professional papers as evidence of his ability to teach. That struggle will be never-ending, but its end is not the immediate problem—our unwillingness to begin is.

The one pre-eminent reason to be studying history is that it provides the student with an opportunity to learn from prior mistakes. In practice we teach history so that students can learn mistakes, then later, as adults, make them every four years. In a rapidly changing world, a knowledge of history is indispensable. Misinformation and superficial analyses when presented as history are calamitous. The British historian E. H. Carr defines history "as a continuous process of interaction between the historian and his facts, an unending dialogue between the present and the past." [6] In the serious crises of today, causing the United States anguish both at home and abroad, a student will be absolutely lost without a thorough grounding in history.

Historians have come to realize that the teaching of history must include more than the memorization of meaningless names and dates. As Allen Brownsword indicates:

> History is interpretation centered . . . and in the last twenty years this has been the great new approach in the teaching of history. It has spawned by now literally thousands of books of readings crammed full of the most up-to-date historical thinking on important subjects.
>
> Unfortunately the students' responsibility in this approach is not much different than it has been with fact-related history—he still has to memorize. He now has to memorize interpretation where he formerly memorized facts. He doesn't have to reach interpretations himself, let alone think about them. Although this approach may get closer to the nature of history as we now understand it, it still makes history for the students a sterile exercise in memorization.[7]

And there is one of the tragedies of innovation in education.[8] No matter how radical the supposed intervention, in the final analysis what really emerges is the difference that makes no difference. The student remains as the student has always been—a passive recipient, where he was intended to be an active participant.

History instruction, more than anything else, is providing students with insight into the organization of data. It enables students to cull out the trivia and to identify the important. The study of history is a quest for truth, but certainly not a quest for the whole truth—no one can handle the data overload. The study of history stimulates a search for global social theory. History without theory reduces it to obscurantism, a "scholar's" search for a rare nugget

---

[6] E. H. Carr, *What Is History?* Alfred A. Knopf, New York, 1962, p. 35.

[7] Allen W. Brownsword, "What's with the Teaching of History," *California Social Review,* Vol. 6, No. 1, Dec. 1966, pp. 10–19.

[8] English instruction has gone through an almost identical process. Transformational grammar was to replace structural language instruction. It would replace irrationality with rationality and rigidity with flexibility. But in truth all that has happened is that one stupid irrelevant set of rules has been substituted for another set of stupid irrelevant rules.

of information that no one had discovered before.[9] That the information may have no consequence is often ignored. History with theory predisposes the historian to a predictable bias. A Calhounian interprets American history far differently than a Marxist; Spengler or Toynbee, with predisposition to cycles, see American history in an entirely different perspective than does a latter-day Parson Weems who views all events as links in a chain pulling us to a heaven right here on earth. The student at every level has to understand that ideology has influenced the interpretation of history. He shouldn't be afraid of it. He should be prepared to develop his own approach to life and to generate criteria which can be used to evaluate the validity of his ideological approach.

Martin Mayer has written a book, *Social Studies in American Schools*.[10] In it he severely criticizes what goes on in high schools in the name of social studies. History comes in for its share of the attack. From a survey of classroom texts he concluded (much like Jules Henry) that "Text materials for the first eight grades are uniformly dull and without focus, often inaccurate, almost always misleading." [11]

Much of Mayer's analysis is banal. Although critical of others for lack of focus, he has no focus. He believes in chronological flow and excoriates those who try to teach history from a current perspective. He ridicules the notion that the study of history has practical utility for planning. He lambasts Arthur Bolster for stating that "History is worth studying only if it predicts the future," which, Mayer claims, "is manifestly impossible." [12]

One very important reason for studying history *is* to predict the future.[13] Such prediction is not impossible at all. There will be error, of course, as there is error in every prediction, even in the most exact physical sciences. But the lack of precision does not justify renunciation of the activity. As the study of history advances, the ability to predict will also advance. What is needed is

[9] Some historians call this "antiquarianism." See Sherman Kent, *Writing History*, 2d ed., Appleton-Century-Crofts, New York, 1967, p. 3.

[10] Martin Mayer, *Social Studies in American Schools*, Harper Colophon Books, Harper & Row, New York, 1962.

[11] *Ibid.*, p. 7.

[12] *Ibid.*, p. 40.

[13] Some historians would prefer to use the word "anticipation" in place of prediction (see Carl L. Becker, *op. cit.*, p. 241), but this is a rather capricious distinction and doesn't distract from the points being made here.

a better understanding of a methodology that will make accurate prediction possible. Students are *not* given much insight into history as a *method* of inquiry. Here, Mayer's book is helpful. He cites examples of school programs that provide students the opportunity to engage in historical research. Mayer is particularly fond of archaeology and likes courses that allow students to dig into history through archaeological findings:

> Perhaps the most remarkable place in American public educa- tion is the Zilda P. Sibley Museum in the Walnut Hills School, otherwise an unremarkable modern single-story elementary school building, in Baton Rouge, Louisiana. The room was Mrs. Sibley's sixth-grade classroom . . . (which upon her death became the Junior Archaeological Society). . . . The society, says the preface to its magazine, *The Junior Archaeologist*, "is a scientific organiza- tion established for the study of man through archaeology, anthro- pology, and related sciences." Its faculty advisers, one of whom usually attends the two-hour Thursday-night meetings, are Fred Kniffen and William Haag of Louisiana State University. In addi- tion to the Thursday meetings at the museum, the society holds fairly frequent Saturday meetings and goes on monthly digging expeditions. Very few people know so much about Indians, or about archaeology as the two dozen young members of this society. . . . The product of these excavations inevitably found its way back to the classroom, and formal organization followed at the request of the students (who also contributed some of the boys'-club Indian aspects, with clans, secret rituals and handshakes, Chief, Shaman, Signal Sender, Wampum Keeper, Notch Maker, etc., as well as scholarly reports). . . . Everything is classified in a scholarly manner. Where examples of pottery or implements have not yet been found *in situ*, the boys, using tools the Indians used ("except we had a rolling pin for ceramics") have made them according to pictures in archaeological reports.
>
> A twelve-year-old takes the visitor around the room, pointing out first the Mexican material, then the collection of "projectile points" (serious archaeologists do not use the word "arrowheads"), gathered by the boys themselves. Every member must also make arrowheads, using Indian tools, to the satisfaction of his fellows. The various sites the club has dug are described—the Marksville site, Coles Creek, the Menefee site (named for the boy who found it on his father's farm, and thereby crashed into the society underage), Poverty Point. "Poverty Point," say a twelve-year-old, "was one of the most mysterious cultures we know of in the state of Louisiana." The remains of each site have been classified ac- cording to recognized culture patterns, and the boys have made enlarged drawings of the stratigraphy at the dig, complete to details of the pottery. ("Charley Waghorn and Toby Steiner are working

in this culture period.") At one of the sites, one pair of boys was lucky enough to find a full skeleton in a burial mound; it rests beside the front door to the museum, reassembled in a box of dirt with the artifacts around it, just as they were discovered. The first duty of the secretary of the society is, he says, "to read and keep up with all writing about archaeology, so I can advise members on the best proceedings." A library of about fifty books, and sets of half a dozen journals, takes up one corner of the room.[14]

History classes must offer students an opportunity to engage in library research; students must have access to original source material. Probably the most exciting form of historical research is "oral history." Students can tape-record interviews with persons who have made history—an old stevedore who was involved in the organizing of the CIO, a pipe-smoking Indian chief who recalls a brave's life of sixty years ago, a veteran Mexican migrant who can trace the changes in his life style that automation in farming has caused, a jaunty eighty-year-old feminist who recalls the excitement of the fight for the right of U.S. women to vote. The students then have to do what all historians struggle to do—they must sort truth from fiction, fact from interpretation, and significance from insignificance. *That individuals differ dramatically in their assessments is a powerful history lesson*! That the difference is conditioned by political ideology, ethnicity, and race is another important lesson. That their differences follow a pattern—there are some things on which everyone tends to agree—there are some things which "liberals" see entirely differently from "conservatives," and there are some matters of history about which there is absolutely no discernible pattern in interpretation. When students learn this, they are ready to attack history as a discipline. They are also prepared to identify what a historian has to do to keep subjectivity in history down to an absolute minimum.

History requires more than discipline in data collection and interpretation. There must be discipline in presentation. History with style and flair must be offered to students. Barbara Sizemore and Anderson Thompson, at Forrestville High School in Chicago, have generated an exciting approach to the study and presentation of history. They interested a number of students in a black ghetto school in a study of black history by having them identify with black heroic figures. The original group—"The Magnificent Seven"

[14] *Ibid.*, pp. 52–54.

—took the parts of Frederic Douglas and Martin R. Delaney, W. E. B. Du Bois and Booker T. Washington, Marcus Garvey, Malcolm X, and Martin Luther King, Jr. Each student studied his particular protagonist until he could live him. They poured through textbooks and archival material; eventually they committed to memory the important writings and speeches. They delved into the historical background. They went on tour and presented history on stage as a debate. It was good theater. It was also good history. But theater and history should never be mutually exclusive. The debates between "Douglas" and "Delaney" dealt with current crucial issues of separation and segregation. The problems of the slaves and the freedman in Reconstruction days were given a perspective. Impatience of young blacks with lack of progress becomes more understandable when seen in this context.

Three of the "Magnificent Seven" were to come to the University of Oregon to teach teachers how to teach. It was a fascinating experience. The teachers were drawn into the drama of history. It was no longer dead and something of the past. There was anger. The audience challenged "Booker T. Washington" to defend his submissiveness to white authority. One infuriated member of the audience demanded that "W. E. B. Du Bois" reconcile his 1919 position with his much later membership in the Communist party.

Some faculty and graduate students in the history department attended the session. A few spoke disparagingly of the lack of scholarship and of the "show biz" aura. It is unfortunate that too many historians (most that I have known) think that show business is no business. They have never accepted that they have an obligation to entertain.

History, more than most areas of inquiry, lends itself to the use of mass media. Films and television in particular are suited for presentation of history. To date these have been used atrociously. Even if McLuhan overstates his case when he argues that the medium *is* the message, it cannot be denied that media influences the message. When old-fogey traditionalists deny the obvious, they only impede educational progress.

The Teaching of American Political History

American political history is, on the face of it, exciting. None of the material presently shown on television sets can hold a candle to it, but such history is not currently being taught. American history is not only exciting but also controversial. All of our historical heroes in real life were boat-rockers. George Washington was not above the reproach of scandal. Many of his most intimate colleagues were overtly critical of his competence. Thomas Jefferson was not only a revolutionary; he felt that revolution was a necessary condition for a healthy state. He argued that "The tree of liberty must be refreshed from time to time with the blood of patriots and tyrants, its natural manure." Abraham Lincoln was unabashedly a dove in the Mexican War in 1848. He assailed President Polk for pursuing an "unconstitutional war," a position that cost him heavily politically.

American historical figures were flesh and blood. They were not the bloodless creatures that are presented in textbooks. If Emerson is right—and I believe he is—when he says that there is no history, there is only biography, then the single-dimensional presentation of historical figures is all the more indefensible. As students must learn the facts of life about the world of work (Chapter II) and the facts of life about the political structure of our society (Chapter III), so must they also learn the facts of life of American history. To delude them under some misbegotten notion that such is patriotism (when the reverse is true) is to miseducate them. To lie to them is worse than to miseducate them. As Thomas Jefferson once said, "Ignorance is preferable to error and he is less remote from the truth to believe nothing than he who believes what is wrong."

Today the knowledge of history is a matter of life or death for the nation. Without a knowledge of history it is doubtful that we can solve the racial tensions which are literally tearing this nation asunder or solve the international problems which at any moment could erupt and destroy us all. To understand what is happening internally, one must go back at least a hundred years. Important to the understanding of today's race situation is a re-evaluation of the role and reasoning of a man like Thaddeus Stevens. It is depressing to discover that so many allegedly educated people aren't even aware of Thaddeus Stevens. Stevens was one of the radical Republicans, and he, as Speaker of the House of Representatives, lead the impeachment proceedings against the then President Johnson. (I throw that out gratuitously, although I believe a President ought to be impeached every few years—just to remind him who he works for.) He was hardly alone in the matter, since, as you recall, the impeachment lacked but one vote of the necessary two-thirds majority of the Senate to remove President Johnson from office. Thaddeus Stevens, like other radical Republicans, desired a harsher treatment of the Confederacy. He argued that unless the control of the slaveholder was broken economically, politically, and socially, the Civil War would be fought for the next hundred years. In retrospect, his was an amazingly prophetic assessment.

Thaddeus Stevens and other radical Republicans have been treated shamefully by historians. Up until very recently his contributions were dismissed. His antagonisms to President Lincoln and President Johnson were interpreted as crotchety manifestations of his physical deformity (he suffered from a club foot); as a political vendetta because he had not been awarded a Cabinet post; or personal feelings because it was alleged that he had a Negro mistress. What seems to have been overlooked is that he was right. And in the lesson of Thaddeus Stevens and his times there are important implications for students today. He raised the issue of whether it is possible to treat serious social problems with moderate interventions. In 1952 Mort Sahl commented that Dwight Eisenhower was running for President on the grounds that we ought to go slow in civil rights, whereas Adlai Stevenson was stating that we ought to use moderation, and we, the American people, had to strike a mean between these two extremes. A student today must role-play and relive the past's agonizing days. In the process of understanding and evaluating the thinking of the moderates and extremists of the Civil War era and in the verifying of their assertions and positions against what has transpired since then, students would be obtaining meaningful guidelines for deliberations in today's turbulent times. They would gain a similar perspective if they could relive, through a variety of actors, the series of controversies and confrontations that have led to current tensions in the Far East, in Latin America, and in the Middle East.

How to Appreciate Diverse Cultures, or the Melting Pot Is a Lot of Rot

One of the most striking failures to appreciate differences (see Chapter IV) is in the area of diverse cultures. Teachers would like everyone to be "American." And "American" to many teachers, if not most, does not include much variation. The "American" is a white of European origin. He appreciates the same kind of music, art, and food that the teacher appreciates. He accepts the history of the United States that is recorded in the textbooks. Students who want to be different, e.g., black or Chicano, are forced into a mold. It would be a calamity if education succeeded in stomping out diverse cultures. Life would then lack seasoning. The "American" of the school is deficient in culture because he is a mere abstraction. He doesn't exist in the flesh. There is an alternative to this foolishness.

The school can become a place where all cultures that make up a pluralistic society are valued. It is not sufficient to have Negro history for Negro students to help their self-image. It is imperative that Afro-American history be a part of education for all students. It is not sufficient to alert the Mexican-American to the importance of the contribution of his ancestors to the development of the Southwest. That knowledge must be offered to everybody. The valiant, albeit tragic, fight that the various indigenous groups in this country have put up for their land must be told to all (the only reason that we call them Indians is that Columbus didn't know where he was). Their heroes—Crazy Horse, Cochise, and Joseph— must become our heroes. These teachings must be incorporated into a mosaic which includes appreciation of the white lower classes and the European immigrants. Appreciation must transcend mere identification of a roster of heroes. The music, the pictorial art, the literature, the life styles, and all other contributions must be included in a program of study. The melting-pot approach doesn't allow this to happen. And because we fail to look beyond our parochialism, we miss great opportunities.

In Oregon one of the school districts has a rare combination of students. A relatively large percentage of these students come from the migrant stream; they are of Spanish-American descent and speak little English. Another substantial percentage of the students speak only Russian. Their parents and grandparents fled Russia after the Revolution, wandered through China and South America before recently immigrating to Oregon. The traditional approach to such groups is to subject these two groups to remedial language classes to make up for their deficiencies in English. But they also have skills in languages that the indigenous "American" might find it well worth his while to learn. Rather than considering the Russians and Spanish-Americans as students with liabilities, they should be considered as students with rare and valuable attributes. In that school district they probably have more Russian teachers than exist in the whole state, maybe even in all the Western states. If the program could be so organized, every student of the district could, upon graduation, not only be conversant in English but also in Russian and Spanish. When we consider the sizable number of persons in the world who speak Russian and Spanish and the obvious growing importance to the United States of communication with people whose native tongues are Russian and Spanish, the value of such a training program for all students in that district should be clearly evident.

The melting-pot approach to education has gained momentum because of educational recruitment policies. Those who are allowed to teach are a very assimilated group. Far too often, they have been in the pot so long that whatever distinctive qualities they might have had have been fricasseed out of them.

In the recent past I was a strong advocate of the position that our task was to create a country in which a Negro would have the right to not be a Negro. I now realize that that position is indefensible. It has a nice humanistic ring to it, but it is naive, and, when examined critically, it is genocidal. Certainly a black person must have the *right* to first-class citizenship, to live where he wants, to work where he is qualified, to become qualified where he wants to work, to obtain a decent education for his children. But all these "rights" are woefully inadequate. A basic right is missing—and that is that *every black must have the right to be black!* The melting-pot philosophy that pervades school programs denies that right. That right will become accepted only when the school staff and administration trumpet it. Only when Negro teachers have the right to be black in school and only when Spanish-American teachers have the right to be Chicano, etc. will the school truly become pluralistic.

A black teacher told me the truncated evolution of her colleagues. At first they were solicitous in the best colonial tradition. They spared her assignments that were "beyond her competence." They were delighted by her performance in routine matters. Understand that this is a very competent teacher by any evaluative criteria. She is alert, charming, analytical, dedicated, and knowledgeable. Ultimately, her co-workers became aware of her considerable talents. One gushed, "I no longer think of you as a Negro, I think of you as another teacher."

White teachers who pride themselves on their "color blindness" really haven't evolved very far. Attitudinally, they are paleolithic at best. Of course, the teacher should be appreciated for her competence—God knows that happens rarely enough. But she has another valuable attribute that was going unnoticed, and that is her "blackness." The perspectives, the values, the experiences, the languages, the artistic expressions and critical analyses that teachers with a true social identity bring to the school transform drabness into excitement. Without the benefit of culture, teachers are not whole people. When teachers are not whole they become nonpeople. Teachers cannot achieve anything approaching integrity of self if they are no more than a loose collection of skills. This seemingly obvious set of facts completely escapes the advocates of "precision teaching" who want teachers to react to *every* student with exactly the same behavior. Mind you, this Barbie Doll approach to education is hailed as a major breakthrough, and teachers throughout the country are engaged in such stupidity as counting specific acts of students (not too many years ago otherwise unemployables were hired to count the number of automobiles that passed along a thoroughfare; later these marginal people were replaced with electronic devices. Now teachers are asked to do what the most expendable workers can no longer do, as this is called progress. O me!). "Precision teaching" has many flaws, but the one that has relevance here is the effect it has on washing out teacher difference. If a black teacher is required to do precisely what a white teacher does, that teacher might just as well be white.

Of course, a lot of slogans proclaiming black identity are empty rhetoric (although at this writing, the romance phase of the movement is giving way to much greater precision). But even if the most severe critics of "black nationalism" are right, and even if there is still some fuzziness in such phrases as "black is beautiful," it is a far better statement of role, goal, duty, and function of the black educator than the heretofore imposed restriction that "black is dutiful."

Pluralism is reflected both in the formal curriculum and in the activity of teachers outside of classroom presentations. Much of the earlier commentary about language and history relates to this former concern, but the latter is also extremely important if the goals of education are to be achieved. Education in some of its most profound aspects reduces to subtle interactions between teacher and student. In some instances a teacher is the role-model for a ghetto-lodged black. In another case a Chicano teacher in a suburban school alerts a middle-income white student to the plight of the migrant workers. Yet another teacher widens the students' range of interest in the expressive arts. It is impossible to conceive of a *teacher* who could inspire every student. But it is not impossible to conceive of a *staff* with diversity enough so that every student could select from it at least one teacher who represented him!

Reenter here New Careers. Diversity of staff is not likely if only school of education graduates are considered for teacher positions. But if persons are given credit for life experience, then a heterogeneous group can be assembled. The life experience skills that could be credited in lieu of college matriculation could very well be the natural accumulation of knowledge in the area of ethnic studies (wouldn't it be nice to have a course from a person who lived the history rather than from someone who had read a book about it?), or could be the ability to establish trusting relationships with alienated youth. A person with such attributes would receive college credits commensurate with his demonstrated capacity to perform. Only when that happens will pluralism in the school become a reality.

Mass Media and Culture-Carrying Activity

Fred Allen, the comedian, once said that television is called a new medium because nothing on it is well done. One of the reasons that television, although now older, has not gotten any better is that the nation has not generated a mass base for culture-carrying. The Ford Foundation can no longer be expected to subsidize intellectual and cultural activities. The patron of the arts never intended his support for the masses. The emphasis on mass enlightenment (and its implication for work, politics, and personal development) requires the development of new approaches to sponsorship. For quality mass culture, mass support is needed, but also, mass support depends on mass culture—and that's how dilemmas are made.

Mass media not only strains beyond capacity the wealthy's ability to perform a sponsorship role, it also undermines a group's efforts to generate cultural activities for themselves. The mass overwhelms the unique contribution of minority culture. Before the advent of mass culture, society did not have the means to discourage minority interests. Before the development of mass culture, in order for persons to be entertained, they had to entertain themselves. Any study of New York's Lower East Side of sixty years ago reveals gloriously rich cultural activities. There were music groups, theatrical groups, a variety of newspapers, writers and essayists, sculptors, painters, and much more. The persons involved were not rich. They had little formal education. They had nothing but themselves; they did not have one other thing going for them. They could not sit in front of a television set, stupefied, and allow others to entertain them.[15]

The virtual monopoly that electronic transmission has upon entertainment is insidiously destructive. The impact on the individual is ever-restricted choice and ever increasing passivity. The solution isn't for latter-day Carrie Nations to burst into bars and bedrooms and ax television sets. The solution is to build alternatives. Television doesn't offer much variety. Switch channels and you get more of the same thing. Right before the concluding commercial, a ghost, witch, or fairy maneuvers the anti-hero into a pratfall, or the good guy outwits the agent with the Russian accent or shoots the cowboy with the black hat and long sideburns. Late at night, viewers can choose between two or three untalented performers engaging in small talk with another group of relatively untalented performers.

A sufficiently educated population wouldn't tolerate such inanity. They would demand presentations that challenge the mind and extend aesthetic appreciation.

Television has the potential to be much more than it is. Through TV, theater of all kinds, pictorial art, music, intellectual discourse, and debate (not David Susskind and William Buckley trying to out-stupid each other), and poetry and literary criticism can be delivered to everyone—BUT here we run into a "Gresham's Law of Culture"—*bad culture drives out good*. Mass appeal is the *largest* common denominator appeal. Two factors alone determine whether an audience will be given an opportunity to view a television program. The majority of people must indicate a desire for it, and only a few can object to it. In other words, the major problem with television is that it is run just like the schools (except that they try some things on TV they wouldn't dare try to do in the

---

[15] See, for example, Hutchens Hapgood, *The Spirit of the Ghetto*, Schocken Paperback, New York, 1966 (although first written in 1901). The new edition was updated by Harry Golden.

schools). If we want more exciting television we must have more exciting schools.

The school must set out to repeal "Gresham's Law of Culture." The TV tube will cease to pander to books and busybodies only when the school has the courage to stand up to them. To establish a common denominator of tastes the school must compete with mass media, and, in the process, bring television into education and education into television. If ever there was validity in the idea that one beats an enemy by joining him, the education-television contraposition is that instance. Educators don't like to picture themselves in competition with television and would prefer a proclamation that would render unto education that which is education's and unto Sid Caesar that which is Caesar's. It will never happen. The gauntlet has been thrown down and there is no leaving the arena. The student knows that a battle is going on. An anecdote may illustrate who they think is winning.

Not so long ago I was asked to teach a class in a high school in rural Oregon. About one-third of the student body were from a nearby Indian reservation. The Indian students were almost uniformly failing their subjects. The instructor whose class I was asked to take over insisted that the students, their parents, their culture were at fault. The course was high-school psychology. I entered the room and found a distinctly unenthusiastic class. They arranged themselves centrifugally from me. They slouched in their chairs to physically communicate their disinterest. Some few bothered to hide their comic books behind textbooks. I asked the class to consider this proposition (one I hope the reader will entertain as well)— that all behavior is motivated. Which means that everything a person does, he does for a reason. Then I asked the students:

"How many of you watched *I Spy* last night (it was the big thing then) and how many of you did your homework for this class instead?"

All but one indicated that he had watched *I Spy*. I asked, "Why? Did any of you expect Culp or Cosby to be killed?"

There was no such expectation.

"Did you learn anything? Were you in any way inspired or exhilarated by the program?"

Again the answer was no.

"In other words, watching *I Spy* was a zero experience?"

Whereupon one of the "dumb" Indian kids in the back of the room stirred himself, looked up from his comic book and wryly commented, "Zero is better than minus. At least we were watching *I Spy* for *us* . . . we'd be doing homework for *him* (*pointing to the teacher*)."

At that point I asked the students to suggest activities that would be more meaningful than watching *I Spy*. From their comments it was clear that (1) they were intellectually alert, and (2) they were eager to participate in valid educational experiences, and (3) TV was not a true competitor for the minds of youth. Sure, education has been losing to TV. But this is only because education has refused to compete. In this particular instance, when the battle was joined the class was transformed—the air crackled with comments and reflections. Many of their recommendations clearly had educational significance. There was concern for physical ecology, literature, learning, and perception. And that concern is something that is spontaneous and now and individual. That's what schools have going for them and that's what, somehow, they always seem to lose.

Bringing Television into Education and Vice Versa

Television can be brought into the classroom in diverse ways. The "mech and tech" of television—its mechanical and technical aspects—is a fascinating area for study. Science can come alive as students delve into the mysteries of electronics and then unravel them. The technology of production adds dimensions to performing arts instruction. Television can be used for data collection. Students can videotape classroom activities for discussion of the dynamics of human behavior and bring a reality to psychological principles that case studies and didactic presentations rarely do. Although thin intellectual gruel, commercial TV periodically offers a show that has considerable educational relevance, and, whenever that occurs, teachers should pounce upon it for classroom discussion. Even TV at its egregious worst has educational value. It can be a contrast against which the classroom considerations and concerns are compared. The validity for the Wyatt Earp who reruns at midnight can be seriously debated. The Battle of the O.K. Corral could be the basis of a mock trial in which law, history, modern technology, performing arts are integrated. The creation of a newspaper could be combined with a discussion of Ned Buntline or William Randolph Hearst.

Television can influence education through its style and tempo. Because it is multisensory, television can do more faster than a single-sense presentation. And yet, logically, that is television's ultimate flaw—it is limited—it cannot influence tactilely or olifactorily. The school can do everything that television can do and more (obviously, since it can include television). Television has many drawbacks, which, in an effort to utilize its virtues, should not be overlooked. It controls the audience; the reader of a book can do what a TV viewer cannot do. He can determine pace, sequencing, location, and time. The cost of putting programs on television limits the range of its offerings. Television competes with more traditional modes of dissemination only if the institution perceives them as accomplishing identical objectives. If perceived as they should be, as complementary and meaningful only in the context of more profound goals, the issue is placed in proper focus—which is the identification of the appropriate means to accomplish the identified goal.

The intrusion of education into television is primarily a political issue. Television is the most political of all media. It is influenced by audience reaction. The school must generate a constituency which will demand more diversity and challenge in TV programming. Television is the melting pot's progeny. The school must develop at least this much tolerance—if you don't like a particular program, don't watch it, and if there isn't a program on any channel that you like, ask either for more channels or for a schedule that satisfies you, or both. Mull over the idea of whether there would be so many "crusades for decency," in which one group of citizens tells another group what they can view on television, see in motion pictures, or read in books, if the school wasn't constricted by a puritanical philosophy.

To repeal a policy and practice of low-level mass culture, beachheads must be established in television. Educational TV provides just such an opening. It is a shame that what is offered is so sadly lacking in quality. Much of it is the absolute worst of traditional education—lectures and insipid discussions, presented electronically. Even intellectually "heavy" stuff is victimized by shabby workmanship. Pedantry is confused with true intellectual value. There is a total lack of accountability. The scholar takes offense if it is suggested that he has a duty to convince the audience of the value of his offerings. When I, in a debate with the head of the English Department of the University of Oregon, said that a professor had to "package his product so that it was salable," I was told to "please have some respect for the English language." Educational television is very polite; in fact, it is so polite that it is neither seen nor heard. A little humor, a little life, a little raucousness, a little drama, and a dash of *ad hominem* debate could make a world of difference in educational television.

Students of every age ought to be encouraged to get into mass media. They have already shown a propensity to become involved in underground publishing. They should also be involved in radio (a resource now largely wasted) and in television. Every school should create at least its own radio station (at very modest cost), every school should be involved with television production (it could be at least shown as a public service on local TV at the "prime time" of 6:00 A.M.).

Creating an Alternative to Television

Even at its best, mass media encourages passivity. The schools must create an alternative to a recipient status. By developing skills and attitudes and creating opportunities for investment of energy and time, active involvement can be substituted for lethargic detachment. But it will take some doing, which currently isn't being done.

The school must become a twenty-four-hour-a-day, seven-day-a-week operation. Every school must be a community center serving all residents regardless of age. The closed, somber, almost Gothic-novel appearance of the school must be completely renounced. In its place should be open activity—readily available to all citizens. Every school must be both a museum and a studio. Every school must be a place for debate and for individual reflection and study. Every school must be a theater workshop, a political gathering place, a place for scientific discussion for development of technological innovation, a center for career analysis and training, and *the* community mental health center. Golf, tennis, skiing, chess, and bridge would be among the activities taught, and tournaments should be staged. The one sure-fire way to determine if there is a power failure in town in the years ahead is to look at the school—if there are no lights burning, there is a power failure.

Some readers might have wondered what would be done with three times the present number of teachers (see Chapters II and III). A school, dedicated to turning on all citizens culturally and operating around the clock will find that number a bare minimum.

Establishing a Climate for Learning

There is comfort in mindlessness. Television offers a therapeutic release—persons can escape into a threat-free environment. The threat of schools is unconscionable. In the place of encouragement, the school offers brutality and violence. Children, in this enlightened age, are still being subjected to physical punishment. Even projects designed to stimulate students to think fall short of this limited goal.

I had occasion to be a consultant to the Biological Science Curriculum Study Project. In this project a group of biologists had the task of generating a text for those students thought to be academically uninvolved and unmotivated. They concluded in advance that in order to interest the uninterested one would have to gear the level of inquiry downward. I prevailed upon this group to employ as consultants a group of disadvantaged youths. These were youths who had been involved in a project in which learning was integrated with work as practitioners in a child-care center, a settlement house, and as researchers to evaluate the performance of the other two groups.[16] To fully appreciate what occurred, picture the following: a covey of eminent scholars, professors from universities, and a select group of biology teachers in secondary schools from all over the country. They found their way to Washington, D.C., to present their way of thinking and to justify their approach and their product to a handful of disadvantaged high-school dropouts. The high-school dropouts had studied in detail the proposed new textbooks. The scientists were confident they had put together an important document; they thought they had developed a work that would interest and excite those currently disengaged from biological studies. They operated from a base of common sense and empirical knowledge. It was their belief that if students were actively participating in experiments they would become in-

---

[16] Community Apprentice Programs, Center for Youth and Community Studies, Howard University, 1965 (mimeograph). This was an early experiment to test out the validity of a New Careers approach and demonstrated rather conclusively that supposedly unmotivated and unable youth could perform very dependably and intellectually if given a chance.

terested in the process. Thus they proposed that students learn about the structure of reptiles through dissecting dead alligators. They were visibly shaken when they discovered that the youths weren't the least bit interested in cutting up dead alligators. They were further informed that dissecting live alligators would not interest them either.

The students continually emphasized a single point: the climate for learning was as important as the material to be learned. They continually chided the group of scholars for conclusions based on limited research and they pointed out the impossibility of generating a program when they were not acquainted with the conditions that students face every day. They asked, for example, how a student could really get involved in biology in one school in Washington, D.C., where all boys were required to wear ties. They didn't have to wear shirts! The vice-principal stood at the front steps and any student that approached without a tie was forced to remove the shoelace from one shoe, wrap it around his neck, and secure the lace with a bow if he wanted to enter school.

After such humiliating experiences, is a student really prepared to learn biology? One of the professors became surfeited with the steady diet of criticism about judgments that he operated without a research foundation. In exasperation he turned to one of the disadvantaged youth and belligerently asked, "After all this talk about research, just what is research?" To which the youth replied, "I believe research means that you're not so sure of those things you used to be positive of." There is much wisdom in that statement. The scientists *were sure* that the texts they had developed would radically change the so-called low-ability student's response to the study of science. As it turned out, the text was a valuable addition to biology. It presented in a more lucid way biological constructs and therefore had a positive effect on "able" students. Unfortunately, the disengaged students remained disengaged. My hypothesis coincides with the analysis of the disadvantaged youth. The climate of schools precludes student investment in learning.

Three Motivational Influences
—Competence, Belonging, and Usefulness
—Which Change the Learning Climate

Much prattling goes on in professional meetings about student motivation. The real issue is almost always ignored. Motivating students has never been the problem—demotivating them has been, and is, the issue. Or put another way this simply means, how do we keep schools from destroying the student's natural desire to learn. Learning is the process through which students acquire a sense of personal competence, group belonging, and usefulness. Only a few students now attain these gratifications. Some few are allowed to be intellectually competent. These are the "A" students. They usually have college-educated parents who often do their homework for them. They receive the accolades that the school offers, they get scrolls and their names in the newspapers, are selected to be valedictorians, and get scholarships to the university. The less-than-"A" student is a nothing. He is an anonymous nonentity. Some students, very understandably, would prefer to be recognized as competent troublemakers than to be ignored completely. If anyone really believes that there is joy in anonymity, as Cox suggests in *The Secular City*,[17] he should reread Baldwin's *Nobody Knows My Name* [18] and Ellison's *Invisible Man*.[19]

Only a few students are allowed to believe that they belong in school. These privileged few are the "brains" or the athletes or the "soshes" (high-school term describing the social elite—the popular kids). The adult Establishment extends a hand to them (although obviously different hands are offered to the athlete than to the brain). They are the "in" crowd. All others are "out." Yet man is a gregarious creature. If school will not allow him to belong, then resourcefully he will try to generate groups of his own. These groups are not necessarily anti-Establishment, although even there, little choice is afforded them. They develop styles, norms, and values of their own. Thus they become "heads," "hippies," "teeny boppers," "surfers" and "greasers" or "hodads," depending upon their proclivities and propensities. Some tragically cannot find their way into any group—these were the "punks" in the "gangs" of ten to twenty years ago. Today they are the "fringies." For them school is the loneliest place in the world.

The student is almost never given a sense of usefulness; even the few who are judged competent or who are allowed to feel that they belong are nonetheless locked into uselessness. Bureaucratic

---

[17] Harvey G. Cox, *The Secular City*, Macmillan Co., New York, 1966.

[18] James Baldwin, *Nobody Knows My Name*, Dell Publishing Co., New York, 1954.

[19] Ralph Ellison, *Invisible Man*, Random House, New York, 1952.

organization (which limits us all regardless of age and credentials) requires more than a decade and a half of school before a person can apply for work (Chapters I and II), and forces youth into a nongratifying role of passive dependency. In Chapters II and III a case was made for developing a sense of usefulness in the worlds of work and politics. Students can also be allowed a meaningful responsibility in more traditional classroom activities:

Developing a Sense of Competence

Robert White makes a big thing of competence motivation.[20] The concept he advances is really quite simple—people persist in things they do well (and thereby build personality and character) and lose interest in things they can't do well. Sprinkled throughout the book are suggestions for generating a sense of competence in students. Students can be given credit for the language they speak and for expression of culture. Beyond that, students can be enticed into exploring the unknown if they are assured that mastery of the activity is a realistic objective. A student who solves one of ten mathematics problems when, before, he could solve none, should be given credit for his progress. The teacher should help the student realize that if he achieved that much, more is certainly possible.

Given the variety of legitimate goals, teachers have almost unlimited opportunities to construct situations where competence can be demonstrated. Two corruptions of this policy must be studiously avoided. There is a tendency among some teachers, particularly in the elementary school, to give credit for nonaccomplishment. In effect, they tell children, "You are doing as well as a poor dumb kid like you can do." Children see through this phoniness and are put off, rather than encouraged, by undeserved compliments; only true accomplishment can be honored. The other approach that must be avoided is developing a sense of competence in many nonutilitarian activities. Rewarding students for behavior which is important only to the teacher will ultimately lead to tragedy. One of my many criticisms of mechanistic behaviorists is their insistence on determining the appropriate behavior and rewarding only that. Training a child to score well on a standardized reading achievement test is

---

[20] Robert W. White, "Motivation Reconsidered: The Concept of Competence," *Psychological Review*, LXVI, 1959, pp. 279–333.

a meaningless accomplishment. There is a further danger—the child may be deterred from "real" reading, which is the desire and the ability to seek out reading material for enjoyment and intellectual development.

A systematic approach to the analysis of behavior and a systematic approach to the distribution of rewards are obviously useful tools for teachers. But tools are valuable only if not misapplied. A hammer is of great utility in building a house; it has dubious value when used to beat someone over the head. Rewarding youth for nonprogress or nonmeaningful progress can be avoided only through teacher accountability. The justification for rewarding "competence" is the demonstrated relationship of the rewarded behavior to the goals of education. In the area of culture-carrying competence, the rewards must be linked to the specifics of culture-carrying that were outlined in the introduction to Chapter VI. It boils down to the ability of the teacher to answer the question, "Why do I have to learn that?"

Teachers tend to make the error of rewarding students for mere existence if they have no goals other than to make a child happy ("that's it, children, we will all sing merrily as we plunge over the cliff"). The error of reward for meaningless activity is a natural outgrowth of operationalism. Abraham Lincoln had a healthy disrespect for the "operational definitions" that cropped up in his day, as this story attributed to him illustrates. Lincoln was once reputed to have asked a farmer, "How many legs has a cow?" To which the reply came, "Why four, Abe." "If you call the tail a leg how many legs does it have then?" To which the farmer replied in puzzlement, "Why then, I guess he has five." "That's where you are wrong, calling a tail a leg doesn't make it one." Calling conformist mindlessness either intellectual growth or social development doesn't make it that either, something the operant-conditioning people either forgot or never knew. One of the grim horrors of today's educational scene is that almost all educational controversy reduces to a battle between the good-hearted, goalless humanists and the tough-minded, data-bound scientists. No matter who wins *that* battle— the children lose.

If students are expected to generate a sense of competence, teachers must assume the onus of failure. I emphasize to my students that I am paid to teach; if they are not learning, then I am not doing my job. It is amazing how often teachers who are unwilling to assume *any responsibility at all* for the learning of students complain about student irresponsibility. It is certainly helpful to point out progress when progress is made, but it is utter foolishness to deny problems when obstacles to mastery exist. The willingness to take on a share of the burden is the hallmark of a good teacher. In programs that I have run I am told by teachers, "I helped the student a thousand times (a small exaggeration; it is closer to four) with the problem, so what do I do now?" To which I reply, "Try a thousand and one—but alter your approach somewhat." A student who is eager and ready to learn has minimal, if any, need for a teacher. Teachers are for children who have difficulty. Pasteur was reputed to have a sign over his laboratory that read: "Nous Travaillons" (We Work). I believe that the dedicated teacher of today operates with the slogan "We Persist." A teacher who truly believes that when a child fails to learn he has failed to teach searches for new institutional methods and inspires the child to stay in there. Here, as everywhere else, teacher behavior has enormous impact on student behavior.

An examination can either be the means by which a student gains a sense of competence or the means by which he confirms his feelings of inadequacy. Tests are inevitable in education and, if appropriately used, add much to the process. Tests give a teacher feedback about failures in instruction. Tests inform the student of his present status. The taking of a test can be a learning experience. The test can be a means whereby the student consolidates his gains. It can also be a subgoal for concentration of efforts, a way station which, upon completion, can be used for reflection. But not as tests are currently used. Tests now are too ominous. Failure can have disastrous consequences. I take the threat out of tests. Students can test over and over again (or alternative forms) until they get the grade they want. Tests can have educational value only if the teachers are accountable and negotiable. Teachers must defend the test; they must be precise in preparing the students for an exam and they must be willing to negotiate items to be included in the test and the answers given to the test. In a summer institute for high-school science teachers, a professor presented some test questions that were "guaranteed" to stump every student. Such efforts to deceive the students can never be defended—and are exactly the means by which we drive students out of education and make them feel incompetent. The professor would have earned his keep if he had taught high-school teachers to construct examinations that truly tapped what a student knows and allowed him a sense of that much competence. He would have accomplished even more if he had instructed teachers in the art of asking students questions which students wanted to answer. Of infinitely more value to educational goals would be student evaluation of the *importance* of examinations than would be the *answers* to the questions.

I once debated an advocate of a highly structured, immediate reinforcement approach to education. He insisted—as it is crucial for all who are guided by such a philosophy to insist—that for every *instructional task there was but one right answer.*[21] I took, and take, the position that every *educational* task has no one right answer. In fact, every important scientific discovery has consisted of proving a "right" answer wrong. Education at every level consists of the teacher defending the importance of his question and the student defending the quality of his answer, and vice versa. Out of the proliferation of exchange between student and teacher, student and nonstudent, and students with persons neither student nor teacher, an honest sense of competence will develop.

To generate a feeling of competence the school must allow the student to stay with something long enough and intensely enough to truly get with it. Experience must be allowed to build upon experience. There is a beautiful book that describes such a school. The school is the Oruati School in New Zealand. The book is *In the Early World* by Elwyn S. Richardson.[22] The Oruati School's physical plant is dismal by United States standards, but that's where the comparison ends. The school's program turned on children intellectually. Everything a child was stimulated to do had ecological validity; the school was an integral part of the environment. The child in this context was encouraged and supported and challenged to attend to the environment and draw from it matters of intellectual worth. There was a strong emphasis on artistic creation— children learned to build ceramic masks and pots, make lino prints, write poetry; they also learned to express their thoughts in writing, study nature, solve mathematical problems, and generate aesthetic values. They did all these things without external pressures to dis-

---

[21] Sigfried Engelman, *Confrontation, op. cit.*
[22] Elwyn S. Richardson, *In the Early World,* New Zealand Council for Educational Research, Wellington, New Zealand, 1964.

rupt the rhythm, until they got good at them. All activities connected logically, and awakened new interests. Everything had a natural flow to it. The school's headmaster, Mr. Elwyn Richardson, elucidates the program through the description of the children's activities and reproduction of their products. The school takes on the shape of his concerns (I would have liked to have seen the school extend its ecological concerns to work and politics—matters which *perhaps* can be ignored in New Zealand but which are of immediate concern in schools in the United States). The book gains much of its beauty from the children's artistic creations. The development of skill was awe-inspiring. (The reader must make the effort to secure a copy of the book and fully appreciate what children can produce.) Language development was integrated into other forms of expression. Whenever children began to focus on an area of study, everything else was affected by that interest.

The teacher saw his job to be the ability to induce attitudes of awareness:

> . . . so that they became observers as well as appreciators of the world around them.
>
> Early one morning when the starlings began to chatter more loudly than usual three children went out to investigate and they found the plumbers clearing out various nests from the spouting and roofing iron. They collected the young birds in their nests and took them to a large hollow post where they rearranged them, and one mother bird continued to look after the nest, but the others were abandoned. We thought this was most unusual. The circumstances led the children to do a good deal of writing and some painting and lino print work. Rosalie wrote about the mother bird, "the pretty bird creeps on the tree nicely, softly and soundlessly." [23]

I can't help contrasting Richardson's children with Kohl's *36 Children*. Both educators struggled for an ecologically valid school. Kohl discovered that children gained a sense of competence as they brought the surrounding environment into the classroom. There was security in knowing more about what was already familiar. Richardson did the same thing, but he persisted. The "one good year is not enough" complaint that Kohl met did not apply. Richardson had support (there was never even a hint of board, staff, or parental hostility to the program). Because of lack of support, most of the

---

[23] *Ibid.*, p. 47.

36 children that Kohl wrote about appear to have been defeated by the system. Yet it is the world Kohl describes which is the emerging world—and Richardson's tranquil, sylvan world of solitude and slow time is disappearing. The challenge is to transform the continuity and opportunities for growth in the Oruati School into the bustling urban scene and thereby make competence available to the poor and to the minorities who are now among the most deprived, although *all* others feel increasingly the frustration of an impaired sense of competence. That competence could be attained in one school should, however, offer incentive to those who have not yet achieved a school of this type to keep at it until they, too, succeed.

A Sense of Belonging

Almost everything that happens in school influences a student's sense of belonging. Belongingness is enhanced by:

a) generating in students a sense of competence;

b) eliminating alleged ability grouping and removing the stigma that comes with a "low ability" label;

c) involving youth in legislative, executive, and judicial decisions of school life;

d) staffing schools with teachers who can exercise authority responsibly;

e) drawing into teaching and administrative positions representatives of the diverse cultural, racial, and ethnic groups which make up a pluralistic society;

f) respecting the language and traditions of all students;

g) building sufficient excitement and vitality in educational activities so that investment in them becomes a possibility;

h) dealing specifically with those things that estrange students from each other. (More on that in the next chapter.)

Even such seemingly peripheral concerns as hours of operation influence a student's feelings of belonging to a school. It is hard to feel a sense of personal involvement in a place that locks you out at 3:00 P.M. and on weekends (almost everything important in life happens after 3:00 P.M. and on weekends). A school will become a place where students belong only when it is operated for student convenience—a place to which a student is free to go for research in the library, work or consultation on a project, or for help with personal problems at any time.

To develop an institution in which the atmosphere and the style of operations reach out to every child will take extensive effort, but like everything else mentioned here, important steps can be initiated immediately. The traditional classroom, beset with restrictions and intransigencies, *can* generate a considerable sense of belonging. Individual learning assignments can give way to team learning. The teacher can stop seeing himself as a lone teacher with twenty-five students and can think of himself as a teacher with twenty-five colleagues. Students should no longer be kept from helping each other; instead they should be encouraged to help each other. Currently, when students assist each other they are very often accused of cheating. A good school would insist upon "cheating." If a student knows something that another doesn't, he should be required to share his knowledge. Contrary to some ignorant opinion, this is in the best American tradition. Rugged individualism was not the "American" code. It was not every-wagon-for-itself-going-West. When one pioneer got into trouble all the others pitched in and helped. Anything less than cooperative effort in the classroom in a highly interdependent world will also jeopardize survival.

A major criticism I have of "individualized instruction" programs is that such approaches foster a spirit of anarchism. The student who operates solely for himself will grow up to be emotionally and organizationally crippled. He will also be lonely. Students should certainly be encouraged to develop to the utmost their individual potential, but the core of the school must be interdependent group activities in which the student fulfills his social responsibility. Raucously and stridently, the conservatives of education bitterly denounce the irresponsibility of youth and yet they are equally acrimonious in their condemnation of efforts to build student responsibility. There is only one way to build student responsibility and that is to allow them to be responsible for something. Allowing students to be responsible for each other's academic progress also builds feelings of belongingness.

Belonging occurs when there is a true group to which a student can commit himself. There are very few groups in education. The word "group," is badly abused. Educators prate about reading groups, which have absolutely no synergy, interdependency, or group roles. These are not groups in any meaningful, psychological sense; they are mere assemblages of individuals acting as individuals. The group, to exist, must first of all have a goal to which all of its members subscribe. To call a collection of students who are reluctantly and resistingly complying with oppressive authority a reading group is equivalent to calling a work gang in prison a group (actually, groups often emerge out of these two situations, but the group goal is to frustrate the official function).

Each member of a group must have a specifically defined set of duties to perform for the group. If a member is absent, the group is hampered unless there is provision for such a contingency. The roles of all members of the group are dynamically interrelated. A change in the leader causes changes among all other members. Dramatic change among the membership forces change in leadership.

Not all roles developed in groups are educationally desirable. Even when the group's goals are defensible, some individuals assume or are assigned roles that degrade or restrict growth. A "flunky" is an example of such a role. Flunkies emerge as schools emulate industry. It is "efficient" to assign students to activities "commensurate with their abilities." The flunky does the scut work, and, in the process, establishes a sense of who he is and what he is expected to be. The "clown" is another limiting role. He provides comic relief to tedium and tension, but it is a tough role. He continually has to convince himself that the others are laughing with him and not at him. He becomes imprisoned in the role, finding often that no matter what he does or says provokes laughter. An infinitesimally small number of "clowns" parlay their role into life careers—for the others the role is tragically restrictive. Then there is the "scapegoat." He is the fall guy. He is the loser on whom every foul-up is blamed. Groups love to have "scapegoats"; they deflect criticism and the need for reappraisal of each individual's role. Why do "flunkies," "clowns," and "scapegoats" accept or assume their roles? Often they have no choice. But sometimes they even seek them out. These roles are better than nothing because they do provide a sense of belonging to the group. When teachers understand that students create their own groups whenever they are denied a sense of belonging or are offered only demeaning roles in established groups, some of the destructive attacks on youths in schools will come to an end. Man will go to great lengths to avoid nothingness. He will turn to drugs and establish a matrix of group roles in the process. He will turn to abuse and manipulation of other humans or conversely ask to be abused or manipulated if other choices are unavailable.

The teacher has enormous responsibility in the influencing of role-allocation, and this responsibility cannot be avoided. Lack of action by teachers will not prevent the formation of groups or the establishment of social roles. But irresponsibility by teachers will cause pain and limit choice. A person cannot achieve the goal of education—relative autonomy in an interdependent world—if he is curtailed in the social roles he is allowed to perform. A teacher cannot stand idly by and allow a student to be locked into being a "clown," a "flunky," or a "scapegoat" in socially approved activities, or to become saddled with such roles in socially disapproved activities (e.g., hustler, pimp, prostitute, mugger, acidhead, or pusher). The teacher must actively involve himself in the dynamics of the group. He can do this in many ways. In group discussions he can share observations with the group and ask them to be accountable:

> Once I was teaching (trying to teach would be better) poetry to a junior high school class. In the class was a clearly established "clown." Every comment he made was greeted with laughter. He had a field day with the poetry—mimicking and parodying every line. I stopped and asked the class to consider what they were doing. They had this poor youth locked into a role from which there was no escape and I wanted to know why they were doing it. There was no response to the question. But the next time the "clown" popped off, only one person in the class laughed. "I guess I still want him to be a clown," he said. The next time he spoke no one laughed.

The teacher can structure group activities to change roles. A flunky can be transformed into a leader if he is provided with leadership skills. Suggesting activities that coincide with a flunky's talents—for example, a discussion of a four-cycle combustion engine—can instantly turn a "dum-dum" into a "brain." Coaching a student and thereby allowing him to gain some unique skills can transform role and status:

> I once taught some high-school dropouts to calculate Pearsonian correlation coefficients (among many other research skills) on a desk calculator by summing the x's, y's, x^2, y^2 and xy's all in one operation. Some graduate students approached one of these drop-

outs and asked if he would instruct them in the operation. His
reply to the request was:

"Hell no, we're the only ones who know how to do it and
we're going to keep it that way."

While the response was not in keeping with a sharing of
knowledge advocated earlier as a means of building belongingness,
it is an indication of a desired social image. Actually the sharing
of information would continue to enhance a sense of self if continued growth of person is built into the program. If a student feels
that he is giving away the only thing he has, he will be understandably reluctant to give it away.

To fully create a sense of belonging the teacher must possess
the knowledge to orchestrate the strong points of each individual
in the development of a group which supports its members and
minimizes those processes which undermine the individual. He must
also compose group activities that utilize members' diverse talents.

Teachers withdraw from group responsibility with good
reason. They are not prepared for the arduousness of the task.
They have limited knowledge to use for analysis of group activity
and are almost totally without experience in the organization and
structuring of groups. Teachers are neither selected for their ability
to generate a sense of belongingness nor is there much emphasis on
developing such skills in a school of education (certainly, the school
of education has done very little to set an example for an educational program which inspires a sense of belonging in its students).
Here, then, are areas where change in recruitment procedures and
teacher preparation are clearly indicated.

School activities will likely generate a sense of belonging if the
students involved can aim for a precisely defined and tangible terminal product. Ideally, there should be projects that involve many
students in meaningful activities and an end result in which all concerned can take pride. Ten-year-olds preparing a first-grade primer
is one such project. A multimedia presentation of modern urban
life could be another. In this latter instance—a slide show with an
audio component could be developed from a combination of original material and literary research. Students could photograph
urban-life scenes, draw them, write essays about them, and tape-
record interviews with significant figures in the community. They
could comb through magazines and books for additional visual
material and use popular records for musical background. Many

talents and energies would be drawn into the activity. Producers, directors, painters, photographers, editors, photographic developers, layout men, interviewers, writers, and a variety of support personnel will be required to make the venture a success. The teacher's role would be to inspire, to present information when the students needed it, to question, to provide technical assistance or direct students to that assistance if what was desired was outside his area of competence. The teacher has to be careful that his commitment to the project doesn't reduce student involvement. He can't become the football coach whose ego-needs interfere with legitimate educational goals. Science, math, history, and language all lend themselves to such projects. Without such projects, fragmentation and resultant personal disengagement are very apt to occur.

A Sense of Usefulness

In one sense, all those activities that give a student feelings of competence and belonging also contribute to a sense of usefulness. But there is limited usefulness in assisting only one's self and one's peers. School programs should be developed which allow the student to help others.[24] The recommendation that very early in school life children should be involved in work activity will, in addition to gaining understanding of the work, give students the opportunity to be useful. Political involvement can do the same. Community organization is yet another possibility.

Usefulness can be generated in current school programs. One vital and relatively simple approach to usefulness is to have older children tutor and teach younger children. There is increasing evidence that this relationship helps both the student-teacher and the person taught. Every elementary school could easily include within its current structure the provision that for one hour of every day all students eight years or older should teach a student two or more years younger.

The use of older children in a teaching function can work only if teachers fully appreciate what such activities would mean to them. Without effective adult leadership there is little prospect of much educational gain. Without leadership, what is most likely

---

[24] Frank Riessman calls this the "helper principle" and he argues that it is a powerful motivation in the human service occupations. See Pearl and Riessman, *New Careers for the Poor, op. cit.*

to occur is a meaningless encounter between two children. Unless the older child feels competent in his task and senses that he is an integral member of a teaching team he can hardly feel useful or be useful in his teaching task.

The responsibility of the adult is to organize meaningful tasks for his tutors, The immediate goal must be understood by the child doing the teaching. He must also know precisely the tasks he is to perform. To gain the requisite skill he must engage in simulated activity such as role-playing. The teacher must arrange for monitoring the tutoring sessions and conduct "seminars" with tutors so they will learn from their experiences.

To make a cross-age teaching project work, the project cannot be merely an appendage to the existing program; it has to be an integral part of it. This requires planning and reorganization of time and the establishment of a new set of priorities. If the activity is viewed only as a frill, then its low priority dooms it.

The tutor needs to continually gain in skill and be given increasing responsibility. Otherwise, when the novelty wears off the value of the program wears out. Teachers argue that they haven't time for such additions, that their considerable responsibilities preclude this extra burden. This is nonsense. Time is like any other commodity. It can be invested. The time invested in developing an older-younger student teaching project will pay off in time gained at a later date. If time is not seen as a commodity for investment, no educational innovation will ever be accepted, because the system always demands that the old be maintained before the new is accepted.

Some parents object to older children "wasting" their time when they should be studying more advanced subjects. They object to younger children having nonexpert instruction. Neither objection is difficult to overcome if teachers are willing to be accountable. Parents can be convinced of the importance of giving feelings of usefulness. They can see the younger children learning lessons that they admit should be learned. The more that parents and other adults are taken into the teacher's confidence and the more the goals of education are explained and the means used to attain them are described, the less objection to educating by special programs there will be.

However, the techniques used to build competence, belonging, and usefulness can be perverted to mere gimmickry. The only justification for any technique to motivate children is that the activity is necessary or consistent with educational goals. If goals are lost sight of, the most exciting education is pure fraud.

Removing the Static from Education—Grading

I suspect that there is nothing which louses up education more than grades. Everything is distorted by grades: racism is supported, students are traumatized, and probably nothing is accomplished. "Experts" don't agree on grades. Max Rafferty says that vital to "education in depth" are grades of "ABCDF," although he never tells us why. William Glasser advocates the abolition of "ABCDF" grades:

> Because grades emphasize failure much more than success and because failure is the basis of almost all school problems, I recommend a system of reporting a student's progress that totally eliminates failure. That is, I suggest that no student ever at any time be labeled a failure or led to believe that he is a failure through the use of the grading system. . . . To keep a child working in school, we must let him know, beginning in kindergarten, that from the standpoint of grades or labels, it is not possible to fail.[25]

In place of the traditional system, Glasser suggests two evaluations, one for the elementary school (kindergarten through grade 6), the other for secondary school (grades 7 through 12). In the elementary grades students are promoted each year, and evaluation is in the form of written reports which, in positive terms, describe "what the child is doing and where he needs to improve." [26] Reports will cover language arts, mathematics, reading, social studies, and social growth. Parents will receive these reports from teachers at least twice a year. Reports are discussed with each student individually to help him fully appreciate exactly where he stands. Glasser believes that by "Thinking more deeply about their children so that they can write about them, teachers discover much more about them than they do using present superficial ratings." [27]

Glasser is willing to acknowledge superior work: "S." The written report card could include an additional paragraph in which the special accomplishments of the student could be enumerated:

[25] William Glasser, *op. cit.*, pp. 95–96.
[26] *Ibid.*, p. 99.
[27] *Ibid.*, p. 101.

It is important, however, that the superior (S) grade not be confused with the A of our present system.[28]

> For an "S" a student does extra superior school work on his
> own. If time allows, he may present his work to the class for both
> the enlightenment and the comment of the class. . . . In addition,
> when a student attempts an "S," he agrees to devote some time
> each week to those students who are not doing well.[29]

In the secondary school, where many teachers are involved in
different classes with one student, Glasser suggests a slightly different grading system. Students would receive a report card that
"differs considerably in emphasis and details" from the present system. There would be no failing grades. Students would either receive a Pass grade (superior students could still have one "S" on
this card) or the record would be left blank. It is a simple system
in which "Teachers set standards and pass only those who achieve
those standards." [30]

Glasser attempts to maintain the grading system. He would
like only to defang it. He accepts the notion of faculty-determined
standards and faculty-determined evaluation. There are many in
education who feel that the teacher-dominated educational system
is no longer defensible.

Neil Postman and Charles Weingartner oppose teacher domination of education. They have written a book—*Teaching as a Subversive Activity*—in which they advocate doing away with grades
entirely. They see all of the structure of education as insulting to
the student and good only for training students for playing the
trivia game. They want a "revolution" which will become visible
when "young revolutionary teachers" take the following steps:

1. Eliminate all conventional "tests" and "testing."
2. Eliminate all "courses."
3. Eliminate all "requirements."
4. Eliminate all full-time administrators and administrations.
5. Eliminate all restrictions that confine learners to sitting still in
   boxes made of boxes.[31]

---

[28] *Ibid.*, p. 101.

[29] *Ibid.*, p. 102.

[30] *Ibid.*, p. 103.

[31] Neil Postman and Charles Weingartner, *Teaching as a Subversive
Activity*, Delacorte Press, New York, 1969, p. 151.

And specifically (in a list of sixteen proposals), Postman and Weingartner recommend that teachers "Declare a moratorium on all tests and grades. That would remove from the hands of teachers their major weapons of coercion and would eliminate two of the major obstacles to their students learning anything significant." [32]

Rafferty, Glasser, and Postman and Weingartner cover the gamut on grading. Rafferty would keep the grades as they are—and eliminate the weaklings who falter in their enforcement. Glasser would eliminate negative grading only, and Postman and Weingartner would scrap grades entirely. *They are all wrong!* Of the three, Rafferty is the most destructive (he has been sufficiently treated already and nothing more about him need be said). Postman and Weingartner are the most seductive (and that in itself needs further analysis and discussion), and Glasser is the most "realistic," which, as you will come to recognize, is paint praise. All three fail to develop accountability. None establishes a basis for evaluating student performance in a broader social context. Because none has developed educational goals that make sense in a rapidly changing world, they have no legitimate basis for evaluating students.

I believe in the evaluation of both students and faculty (as I have indicated previously in this chapter). I believe that both not only need evaluation—both want it. But meaningful evaluation depends upon accountability and negotiability. A test has to be defended to students. Each question must be defended as educationally relevant. Each question must be upheld as a necessary link in the chain that leads ultimately to the goals of occupational, political, cultural, and personal competence. The student must be encouraged to exercise his right to challenge the teacher's arguments. If his "answer" doesn't correspond with that of the teacher, he, too, should be asked to be accountable. He, too, should be asked to defend his answer in the context of the goals of education. The classroom must become like the marketplace of Oliver Wendell Holmes, Jr.—where truth could be determined through open competition of thought. Assessment which is fundamental to this competence requires negotiation. A social contract needs to be established. There is no possibility of contract if there is no commonality of goal. But even agreement on goals does not assure meaningful

---

[32] *Ibid.,* p. 138.

negotiation. There is also the elemental issue of power. Again, Oliver Wendell Holmes offers legal advice that has relevance to the classroom and grading procedure. If open competition of ideas from which grades are to be given is to become a reality, then there must be the understanding that freedom of contract begins where equality of bargaining power begins.

The student must have access to binding arbitration and conciliation. In my classes, students can always ask for ten students, drawn at random, to determine the legitimacy of their grievances—either about tasks to be performed or evaluation of the worth of those tasks. Glasser does not allow for such negotiation. Nor is there any effort to justify the assignments to students. He talks quite a bit about relevance—"something that the children do in their own lives outside of school," [33] but he fails to play a leadership role; he doesn't establish domains of relevance. He is unable to place education in relation to *changing* reality. Glasser is content to change the processes of education without examining its purposes. Therefore, schools without failure are also schools without occupational or political relevance (although one can make a case that his recommendation would have some relevance to personal and cultural growth).

Even in the area of grading policy per se, Glasser errs on the side of conservatism. There can be no possible justification for negative grades—no one should be worse off for taking a course than if he had never been in the course at all. Glasser recommends either a passing grade or no grade (as if the student hadn't taken the class), but only the teacher has the authority to set the standards for grades. I believe that standards should be negotiable and that grades should either be "Pass" or "haven't passed yet." It makes little sense to me that a person who almost passes a course has to take it over, or that everyone should have to pass a course in exactly the same period of time. Why can't some students complete this work two weeks later than the others in the class and still receive full credit for their efforts? Suppose an agreed-upon standard for a class is to determine the ingredients in an unknown chemical substance. A student may not have deciphered the problem by the semester's end—but if ten days later he finishes the job, is there any earthly reason why the student shouldn't be given a Pass for

---

[33] Glasser, *op. cit.*, p. 49.

his accomplishment? Of course not. The supposedly radical Glasser isn't for any of these rational approaches to grading. He is at bottom a traditionalist (at least for the high school): "A student who does not achieve the standards set by the teacher is eligible to take the course again." [34] "If he does not pass after two tries, he must petition a faculty committee to allow him to take the course a third time." [35]

Students who get no credit for their years at high school do not escape a sense of failure. There is no sense of accomplishment, belongingness, or usefulness for nonaccomplishment. Glasser falls back on the most retrogressive of suggestions for nonsuccessful students. He exhibits complete ignorance of the emerging world of work, and he recommends ". . . courses at a simpler non-college preparatory level. These courses encompass vocational training and skill training in both the prevocational and vocational sense." [36]

Glasser's book has many excellent recommendations, and, for those, teachers will find it useful. His program is coherent but insufficient for elementary school; but in larger context, it falls completely apart when applied to the secondary school.

Now to Postman and Weingartner and their approach to grading, or, more accurately, their headlong retreat from it. Postman and Weingartner develop their philosophy about grades and their book on two basic assumptions: "(a) In general, the survival of our society is threatened by an increasing number of unprecedented, and, to date, insoluble problems, and (b) that something can be done to improve the situation." [37]

Clearly, though more by implication that explication, Postman and Weingartner argue that one of the essentials for deflecting the world from its charted course to doom is a markedly changed school. They find all the things wrong with schools that have been mentioned here—dreariness, irrelevance, sterility, brutalization, etc. —but they present a solution which is markedly different from that advocated here and which warrants a discussion (albeit that discussion is tangential to the topic: "The static that grading brings to education").

---

[34] *Ibid.*, p. 104.
[35] *Ibid.*, p. 108.
[36] *Ibid.*, p. 108.
[37] Postman and Weingartner, *op. cit.*, p. xi.

A Digression—Do We Improve Education if We Merely Substitute Questions for Answers?

There is a group in education that recommends "inquiry training" as a reformation and alternative to current educational emphasis. Postman and Weingartner identify themselves with this group. They believe that they have hit upon something new and vital. They think that what they have is of the electronic age.

Inquiry training can be identified by the following characteristic teacher behaviors:

> The teacher rarely tells the students what he thinks they ought to know.
>
> His basic mode of discourse with students is questioning.
>
> He encourages student-student interaction as opposed to student-teacher interaction.
>
> And generally he avoids acting as a mediator or judge of the quality of ideas expressed.
>
> He rarely summarizes the positions taken by students on the learning that occurs.
>
> His lessons develop from the responses of students and not from a previously determined "logical" structure.
>
> Generally, each of his lessons poses a problem for students.
>
> He measures his success in behavioral changes in students.[38]

What's wrong with this behavior? Nothing really—and everything really! Nothing is wrong because the teacher behaviors are all desirable attributes, and everything is wrong because what is depicted is insufficient. The behaviors are not connected to educational goals. They represent processes without reference to outcomes. It is not possible to even guess what a student can *do* about saving the world from its impending disaster as a result of the described teacher behaviors. The teacher is postulated to be a part of a process designed to produce enormous change, yet he is without even a map specifying where he is and where he is trying to go. What Postman and Weingartner will not recognize is that they have generated a system which is every bit as anti-intellectual as the

---

[38] *Ibid.*, pp. 34–36.

"fact training" they oppose. In both instances the teacher is not projected as an *intellectual leader*. I sympathize completely with the criticism of "right answer" oriented education. It *is* sterile and ritualistic. Teaching students how to pass examinations has limited utility. The information gained is not useful in the solution of real problems. Even in that rare instance when the information can be put to use, it is almost always learned in such a way that it is minimally transferrable. All of this is true, and Postman and Weingartner neatly dispatch the advocates of performance goals. They are brilliant, devastating, and witty in their denunciation of the "tough-minded" fact-dominated dolts who are gaining ascendancy in schools. But in their desperate effort to avoid Scylla, Postman and Weingartner *become* Charybdis. There is a romantic, recurring notion that powerful and valid criticism of existing conditions automatically leads to relief from those conditions. Persons who hold such a belief stubbornly refuse to learn the lessons of history. The most reasonable and probable result of criticism without a defensible alternative is a change that really is no change. I'm afraid that that is all we have to look forward to from Postman and Weingartner. The only thing subversive about their book, alas, is the title.

Question-asking can be just as sterile and ritualistic as question-answering. In fact, Postman and Weingartner warn us against this eventuality. (Page 81.) But warning against sterility is no big deal. Everyone who favors a question-answering approach to education also opposes sterility—in fact, it can be safely said of *everyone* in education (particularly the most sterile)—that they are against sterility. In practice, the warning against *stupidity* in education by educators is the *ritual* that exonerates the practice of stupidity and allows education to exercise it with total impunity.

For good education, the student or the teacher (an arbitrary distinction) can neither a questioner nor an answerer be, all the time. What-he-is-when is determined by the goals of the enterprise. To solve man's heretofore unsolved problems, the student must have an enormous number of facts at his command. He must continually apply those facts to the high-priority ecological puzzles. The problems must be analyzed so that manpower concerns (both from the vantage of the individual and the greater society) are treated. The political issues (and *all* important problems will require a complex political solution) must be considered, the substantive knowledge of man must be applied to solve man's struggle for survival in such a way that the dignity of each individual is kept within the learner's consciousness. And while it is true that no important question has but one right answer, it is also true that some answers are more right than others. It is disputable whether the answer to "who discovered America and when?" is "Columbus in 1492," but that answer is more accurate than "George Wallace in 1968." The answer regarded right (or extremely right) affects greatly how a student attacks man's major challenges to survival.

Contrary to Postman and Weingartner I believe that a good teacher *does* start off by telling students what he thinks they ought to know—but he then has to defend to students why he believes what he believes. He not only must be accountable to them, he also must be willing to negotiate with them. The negotiation can have meaning and be something more than a senseless tug of war for power only if there are agreed-upon goals that keep discussion within bounds. In the context of his functioning as an accountable authority, the teacher questions, answers, debates, disputes facts, and summarizes. He *always* has a logical structure in the form of a plan which can be amended or even abrogated, but only when a *better* plan more consistent with educational goals is forthcoming. Without continual reference to goals, without "factual" support for arguments, without new concepts introduced by the teacher, the student will wallow in his prejudices and his ignorance. It is inconceivable that an accountable educational system can or should avoid an evaluative system. The student has a right to know where he stands. Postman and Weingartner actually concede such a point relatively early in their book and then vehemently deny such at the end. Their call for elimination of conventional texts and a moratorium on grades (pages 138 and 141) doesn't jibe with an earlier call for measurement of student success. Some of the following are quite conventional, easily operationalized, and, in the context of educational goals (and only so), are a defensible approach to grading students:

> The frequency with which they ask questions; the increase in the relevance and cogency of their questions; the frequency and conviction of their challenges to assertions made by other students or teachers or textbooks; the relevance and clarity of the standards on which they base their challenges; their willingness to suspend judgments when they have insufficient data; their willingness to

modify or otherwise change their position when data warrant such a change; the increase in their skill in observing, classifying, generalizing, etc.; the increase in their tolerance to diverse answers; their ability to apply generalizations, attitudes and information to novel situations.[39]

The major reason Postman and Weingartner confuse readers is that they are obviously confused. The call for measurable indices of success isn't held with much conviction because it is not believed by the authors that man can really communicate very much, let alone measure anything. The main thrust of the book is a plea for recognition that man's isolation from others is inevitable and essential:

> We now know that each man creates his own unique world, that he, and he alone, generates whatever reality he can ever know. But this is not exactly a cause for unqualified celebration. It turns out, for example, that John Donne was wrong. Each man *is* an island entire to itself. The purposes and assumptions and, therefore, the perceptions of each man are uniquely his, and there is no one else in the vast sea of the universe who shares them in every detail. Among other things, this means that no man can be absolutely certain of everything. The best anyone can ever do is to say how something appears *to him*. The cosmos offers no absolute confirmations. Relativity and the uncertainty principle are more— much more—than technical terms in physics. Each one of us must live with them every second of our lives.[40]

Postman and Weingartner are not only bad poets but worse scientists. The distortion of psychology and physics to make some dubious point can never be justified. Because no man is identical to another in no way disproves Donne's basic claim that man is interdependent. That truth *is* hard to come by, that some things can only be approximated; that measuring-instruments contain error can never be used to argue that science doesn't exist. Man is much less an island now than three and a half centuries ago when John Donne, in one of his *Devotions,* pleaded with us to recognize that every man is a "peece of the *Continent,* a part of the *maine.*" Only when each of us becomes "involved in *Mankinde*" will those unsolved problems get solved.

---

[39] *Ibid.,* pp. 36–37.
[40] *Ibid.,* p. 99.

The reference to a law of relativity and a principle of uncertainty is also specious. That physics amends its laws is no denial of scientific truth—it is a part of a development leading to greater precision and a better statement of the truth. Heisenberg is less a renunciation of Newton than he is an evolution from Newton. That statements need to be made probabilistically rather than deterministically (that is, one calculates the odds of an event occurring rather than absolutely proclaiming it) make that event no less lawful.

Postman and Weingartner add a few wrinkles of their own to "inquiry training." [41] They are all entangled in the silliness of Marshall McLuhan. Because they are unable to divorce process from purpose, they assert as unassailable truth the palpable falsehood that the medium is the message. *The medium is not the message.* The medium is subordinate to the message. A message must have content. Not only must something be said in a message, but that something, if it has educational value, must relate to important problems. And here is where the "inquiry" boys fall apart. They cannot make a commitment. They are unable to take sides because they cannot tell right from wrong. Weingartner and Postman in their approach to language and perception stress only subjectivity, imprecision, and privacy. In the end they defy all that they claim to believe. In a book that demands that teachers be limited to "three declarative sentences per class, and fifteen interrogatives" (p. 138), they string together hundreds of declarations and offer no interrogatives. They are shallow where they should be deep, slippery where they should be forthright, and cynically humorous where they should be serious.

Postman and Weingartner have written a book that starts with a bang and ends with a whimper. They start off with a powerful first chapter. That chapter, entitled "Crap Detecting," suggests that students must learn in school to separate importance from trivia and truth from misconception. It is unfortunate that they did not heed the advice they offered in that first chapter. If they had, they would have written no more.

Certainly, teachers should declare less and inquire more; certainly, teachers should stimulate students to question more and

---

[41] See Richard Suchman and Hilda Toba for different emphases in inquiry training.

answer less, but "inquiry," like any other tactic, remains just that. To elevate it to what it is not, to call it the essence of education, to label it the *new* education is to do education a disservice. The ends of education should influence the means. Any educational process that fails to tie itself specifically to a long-range outcome (cultural, political, personal, and occupational) is not only inadequate but probably worthless.

The Role of Punishment in Intellectual Stimulation

There is no room for punishment in education! There is no place for bullies or sadists in the teaching profession! Any activity whose purpose is to inflict pain, embarrassment, or to cause guilt must be eliminated from schools.

For the protection of the enterprise and for the protection of other students' rights, some children's behavior will have to be restricted, and, in very rare instances, some children will have to be removed from the classroom. The incidence of restriction should be much less than it is now, and, when required, the children affected must be insured due process.

The need for restriction will markedly decline when teachers generate classroom activities that are intellectually stimulating and educationally defensible. When students are taught that only through intellectual endeavor will they gain the skills to survive and only through investment in cultural activities can they add excitement to their lives will they respond positively to school.

Control of a classroom, without punitive measures, is possible when teachers learn to motivate students through "competence," "belonging," and "usefulness"—so that all students partake of the gratifications. Some tender-hearted, light-headed educators would call this manipulation. I say that, if accountable and negotiable, the teacher is only exercising the leadership we pay him for.

It Takes an Intellectual to Stimulate Students Intellectually

It is inconceivable to consider turning on students with turned-off teachers. The public-school teacher is usually not distinguished by his involvement in intellectual affairs. At best he skips at the periphery of intellectual matters. He is hardly a culture-carrier. His reading habits include *Reader's Digest, Life,* or *Look,* some paperback novels, perhaps *Vogue* or *Sports Illustrated*—and not much more. He may belong to the Book of the Month Club. In grades K through 12, we find teachers teaching science who are little interested in science; history teachers with a minimal investment in history; math teachers who are virtually terrified by math; art and music teachers with the same lack of enthusiasm and/or knowledge. In colleges and universities the same anti-intellectualism prevails, only now it is disguised by more flowery phrases and intellectual-sounding rhetoric.[42] The whole educational process has produced a cycle of mind-reduction. Wherever students are, they are confronted with teachers who are intellectually uninteresting because they are intellectually uninterested. These students in turn find their way through all the obstacles, and eventually end up with a credential. This final accomplishment is less a tribute to their perseverance or their talent, and more a reflection that they have neither the wit nor the courage to do anything else. Once on the track, in a manner similar to a rat negotiating a maze, they endure until they reach the end. That student in turn is sent forth to bore the next generation.

Where, then, is the cycle broken? Everywhere and anywhere. Through new approaches to recruitment, intellectually stimulating persons can be brought into teaching (through procedures described in detail in Chapter III). Schools of education can be forced to replace low-level offerings with less counterfeit activities. Administrators can become intellectual leaders rather than stifling bureaucratic managers. Teacher associations can become accountable and place their demands for improvement of teaching conditions in a context of educational goals. All of this is possible because the current system cries out for creativity and innovation.

The teacher cannot be expected to be a Renaissance man. He can be expected to be intellectually alive and he can be expected to be part of a staff made up of diverse talents who prod each other into continual growth. The revitalization of the culture-carrying activities of education is going to be difficult to achieve. There will be many casualties, there will be many more slaggards. Many times we will be called upon to paraphrase Senator Dirksen: There is nothing

---

[42] A projected sequel to this work is the *Atrocity of the Social Sciences,* and while allusion to that sorry state has been made here, further elucidation is needed.

so discouraging as a man who will not die when his time has come. We will have zombies with us for a long time in education. But if we examine the obstacles we can make the headway so urgently needed.

Creating a Climate for Intellectually Stimulating Teaching

It should be obvious—although apparently it is not—that it is impossible to create a climate for learning in a climate unsuitable for teaching. The teacher is not in a position to help students realize a sense of competence, belonging, and usefulness if the teacher is unable to derive such gratifications himself. Face up to it—as currently constituted, teaching is a mediocre job. The pay isn't particularly good—insurance brokers and TV repairmen make more than teachers, and also make fun of them. Taxpayers indicate their opinion of them in budget and bond elections. Administrators try to tyrannize them; legislators try to investigate them. And to top it all off, teachers don't like each other very much. They have little pride of accomplishment. Only the most gullible and stupid are able to accept the goo that they are "miracle workers entrusted with the inspiring responsibility of educating our most precious possession— our youth," which the superintendent utters when he welcomes them back each fall.

Taxpayer revolts, behaviorist-oriented programs, and attacks on controversy in the schools may worsen an already bad situation. We cannot afford to let that happen!

We must recognize first, however, that there are no cheap solutions to expensive problems and we must expose frauds for what they are. The revolutionary who opposes taxpaying isn't really the problem—he will continue to exist. The problem is the dearth of constituents who are devoted to education. That constituency doesn't exist because there is not now a school that is deserving of devotion. Again we encounter the classic dilemma—the lack of community support discourages dedication among teachers, and the lack of dedicated teachers discourages community support. Intervention on either side would alter that situation.

The behaviorists, with their insistence on precision in teaching, restrict teacher behavior, and, as a consequence, stifle intellectual activity. The teacher is forced to structure activity for the *one* desired answer. Behaviorists argue that seeing children succeed gives the teacher a sense of competence. And in a sense they are right. But the sense of competence is as a *technician*, not as a teacher. Some teachers probably can master no more and a rigid program would offer more both to them and their students than the chaos that now prevails in their classes. However, these teachers should be eliminated from education or relegated to less than professional activity (see Chapter III), rather than allow a whole system to be distorted because of their deficiencies. Most teachers are capable of doing much more than they do. Expectation of teacher stupidity will have the same effect on their accomplishment that similar expectations have on student performance. (See Chapter II.) Teachers can do more if they are given the freedom to be true professionals and given the training and education that that requires.

One increasingly popular suggestion is to reward competent teachers with "merit pay." Teachers have good reason to be wary of the suggestion. They ask: "Who will make the decision on competence and upon what criteria?" The answers are never very clear. If the Peter Principle of Incompetence governs promotion, why wouldn't a similar procedure be used to reward meritorious teaching? If the administrator is to make the decision, or a committee of his choosing, what is to prevent the worse kind of politicking from going on, with rewards going to friends and loyal supporters?

Teachers will generate a sense of competence in intellectual matters when the "system" prizes intellectual competence, and the "system" will prize intellectual competence when teachers as a group respect each other for it and convince others of its importance. And that process can begin anywhere.

Teachers will have a sense of belonging when they function as true teams. Team learning, learning in diverse sites, long-term student projects, and integration of all learning activities require teacher cooperation. The teacher will function as a member of a group when he eliminates the need for "scapegoats," "clowns," and "flunkies" from his ranks and builds instead a system of mutual reliance. Divisiveness, petty and personal, can be found at every level of education. It more than self-defeats the individual teacher; it eats away at the vitals of education. The warring factions are both a symptom of a goalless education and a cause of aimlessness.

Teacher organizations devoted to educational relevance will do much to engender a sense of belonging among teachers. No group has as much potential power as teachers. But that potential is now largely wasted because it is either not used or, when used it is often for very selfish reasons.

The more the goals of education can be specified, and the more these goals are related to man's struggle to survive, the more teachers can derive a sense of usefulness in their achievements. The climate for teaching thus is identical to the climate for learning—the changes suggested for improving culture-carrying competence in students will, if implemented, do much to encourage culture-carrying competence among teachers. And conversely, change in teachers could do much to speed up the quality of culture-carrying activity in the classroom.

Summary

In the wondering and wandering that has occurred throughout this chapter, one point, hopefully, was driven home—the schools must be changed radically if the goal of universal culture-carrying competence is to be achieved.

Hopefully, also, the reader has come to appreciate the necessity for universal culture-carrying competence. The problems facing man will not be solved by a mere handful of the educated elite. Only with sophistication of the mass will we be able to come to grips with our most pressing problems. Only with relevant, high-quality education will man be able to:

> Provide sufficient food, air, and water for a population expected to double every thirty-five years (or, to develop programs which will prevent this dire prediction from coming true).
> Develop alternatives for intra- and international disputes other than the one traditional and intolerable response—war.
> Generate social systems that do not stifle or depersonalize the individual.
> Make justice and equality of opportunity more than empty phrases and hollow slogans.

In short, only with universal culture-carrying competence will man learn to think the thinkable. The solution of all ecological problems depends upon man's attaining a thorough understanding of communication processes and a skill in the use of living languages. (Students should also be allowed, for their personal satisfaction, to learn dead languages, e.g., Latin, Greek, and "English".) Man's struggle for survival depends on possession of historical perspective and extensive knowledge of the physical and social sciences. For enjoyment of life, man must be able to appreciate fully and participate fully in aesthetic activities. Many suggestions for reform have been presented here which are consistent with the end of culture-carrying competence. Among the most important:

> Carl Becker's notion that every man become his own historian should be taken seriously by schools. Students should be allowed to experiment in collecting historical information. They should interpret their findings and present them to a variety of audiences.
>
> The melting-pot orientation that prevails in the schools should be junked. In its place should be a philosophy of respect for all the cultures of a pluralistic society. The respect for pluralism will be demonstrated only if all populations are represented on teaching and administrative staffs.
>
> The mass media, which sets the tone for culture-carrying activities, must be considered in school programs. The school can both improve the quality of mass culture and offer alternatives to it.
>
> The goal of universal culture-carrying competence will be more nearly obtained if students are permitted to gain gratifications from competence, belonging, and usefulness in legitimate educational activities.
>
> The goal of universal culture-carrying competence will be more nearly obtained if barriers such as punishment and irrelevant and demeaning grading procedures are eliminated from the schools.
>
> Gimmickry and cheap solutions only muck up educational problems. Both the extreme of mechanistic "one right answer" behaviorist programs and the extreme of "open-mindedness to the point of empty-headedness, 'no right answer'" inquiry training should be eschewed.

And finally, and probably most importantly, the school will attain the goal of culture-carrying competence only when intellectually exciting and liberated persons are recruited and allowed to function as teachers.

Maybe between a modern poet and a seventeenth-century scientist, I can summarize the summary. The modern poet, Richard Brautigan: "A friend came over to the house a few days ago and read one of my poems. He came back today and asked to read the same poem over again. After he finished reading it, he said, 'It makes me want to write poetry.' " [43]

The seventeenth-century scientist, Galileo Galilei: "My dear Kepler, what would you think of the learned here, who replete with the pertinacity of the asp, have steadfastly refused to cast a glance through the telescope? What shall we make of all this? Shall we laugh, or shall we cry?" [44]

Or, shall we stimulate people to look through telescopes, and shall we write so that others will want to write?

---

[43] Richard Brautigan, *The Pill Versus the Springhill Mine Disaster*, City Lights Books, San Francisco, 1965, p. 66.

[44] Quoted in Giorgio di Santillana, *The Crime of Galileo*, University of Chicago Press, Chicago, 1955, p. 5.

CHAPTER VIII

The Goal of Inter- Intrapersonal Competence

[In which I look at the growing alienation of people. I question the wisdom of school policies of segregating the emotionally disturbed, the training of school personnel to work with the unhappy and the uncomfortable, and the theory with which experts operate. I suggest that we have become a centrifugal society and that this affects dramatically the family and other socializing agencies. I propose that the school become an institution which has centripetal influence on people's lives. I discuss specifically the problems of loneliness, scapegoating, racial separation, drug abuse, and attitudes toward sexual relationships. I conclude with a discussion of leisure time, activity, and staff appropriate for the goal of education.]

Nothing so needs reforming as other people's habits.

—Mark Twain

Loneliness does not come from having no people about one, but from being unable to communicate the things that seem important to oneself or from holding certain views which others find inadmissible. —C. G. Jung

I laid my heart open to the benign indifference of the universe. To feel it like myself, indeed, so brotherly, made me realize that I'd be happy, and that I was happy still. For all to be accomplished, for me to feel less lonely, all that remained to hope was that on the day of my execution there should be a huge crowd of spectators and that they should greet me with howls of execration.

—Albert Camus—*The Stranger*

I thought for a minute that I saw her whipped. Maybe I did. But I see now that it don't make any difference. One by one the patients are sneaking looks at her to see how she's taking the way Mc-Murphy is dominating the meeting, and they see the same thing. She's too big to be beaten. . . . She lost a little battle here today, but it's a minor battle in a big war that she's been winning and that she'll go on winning. We mustn't let McMurphy get our hopes any different, lure us into making some dumb play.

—Ken Kesey—*One Flew Over the Cuckoo's Nest*

> But to go to school in a summer morn,
> O it drives all joy away;
> Under a cruel eye outworn
> The little ones spend their day
> In sighing and dismay.

—William Blake
Schoolboy

Education ain't just what comes out of the books, but it's everything that goes on in the school and if you leave school hating yourself, then it doesn't matter how much you know.

—H. Rap Brown

Learning to live with one's self and with one's neighbors, like so much else, reduces to choice. Of all the possible people a student can become, what are the opportunities, the experiences, and the knowledge he needs to be able to choose to be the kind of person he can be happy being? What are the opportunities, experiences, and knowledge a student must have so that he can work harmoniously with others? How much of this knowledge, how many of these opportunities and experiences is the school responsible for? How many can be delegated to the family? The church? An employer? Some leisure-time activity or acquaintances? What body of theory can we rely upon to help us develop intra- and interpersonal competence? What group of "experts" is qualified to assist in the process? What impediments are there to the attainment of social and personal competence? What kinds of persons are particularly vulnerable to disturbance, what symptoms are likely to occur in malfunctioning people, and how do we deal with these alienations? This chapter is devoted to answering the above questions in detail, although in the previous chapters there has been much said that has relevance to this matter of psychological well-being.

Interpersonal competence at one level reduces to the ability to feel competent, to belong, and to be useful to others. At another level intrapersonal competence is involvement in a healthy society. A healthy society does not require some individuals to be destroyed so that others can find fulfillment. A society that requires war for its citizens to have a social identity does not qualify as a healthy society, nor is there psychological well-being if males, to attain a sense of competence, belonging, and usefulness, must gain these gratifications at the expense of females—or whites at the expense of blacks. Nor is a society healthy if major problems of that society are left unattended because people are unable to find a way to get together to solve problems. Nor is a society healthy if the organizational structure of that society achieves economic and governmental function by overwhelming and depersonalizing its citizenry.

How bad is our situation? Terrible! Look first at the indicators of personal unhappiness.

We come now to the supreme irony of modern American life. Despite affluence, despite unparalleled prosperity, despite technological advancement, Americans are hardly an untroubled people. There is a prevalent feeling in America that although money isn't everything and "it can't buy happiness," it can buy everything that produces happiness. And then, paradoxically, Americans proceed to create a society which clearly demonstrates that money can buy misery to the same extent that poverty does.

By every conceivable index, man is having increased difficulty living with himself and with other human beings. This is especially true for youth. And while the conditions of personal competency are influenced by social background, the inability of a person to come to grips with himself or his neighbors is not restricted to the disadvantaged or to the minority. There can be no denying that we are an up-tight, hung-up people. The rate at which Americans commit suicide is increasing. College youth, those with the most going for them, knock themselves off once every three hours. Crime and delinquency are increasing. The incidence of marital breakup is increasing. The incidence of drug abuse is increasing (and there is no greater indicator of inability to derive a sense of self-sufficiency than the dependence upon some chemical substance for a feeling of contentment). Dependency on psychoactive agents is by no means a problem restricted to the youth or to the deviant. Drug abuse cuts across all social and age categories, and, as a consequence, there are six million chronic alcoholics in this country.

When we look to broader social relationships, the situation doesn't improve. Man's inhumanity to man is reflected in his inability to live at peace with other nations and his inability to resolve the problems of racial tension and conflict at home. Americans are among the most "learned" people of the world; they have invested heavily in the education of their children and yet there is no evidence that this learning has led to improvement in racial or international relations. Westinghouse may have made it possible to live better electrically, but no agency has assisted us to live better interpersonally. Least of all in helping the situation has been the school.

The School—A Major Culprit in the Destruction of Inter- and Intrapersonal Competence of Youth

Schools destroy youth. Largely because of schools, youth are denied a sense of social worth, a mastery over their environment, a feeling of belonging, or a sense of usefulness. The school's failure in these areas has been described in considerable detail previously. These are general failings and need no further explication. There is, however, even more tragic destruction, and that occurs when students are singled out for special treatment because they have been diagnosed as mentally unsound or socially and emotionally disturbed. When this happens the most vulnerable students are sought out and mercilessly deprived of self-respect and social competence. Mind you, this is done in the name of therapy and concern for mental health. It is done callously. Its devastation is largely without design or intention. Like everything else encountered in school, the horror is not the result of viciousness but rather of stupidity. One reason for the school's failure to produce interpersonally and intrapersonally competent persons is that the approach to the problem is half-hearted and timid. Another major failing is allegiance to obsolete theory and practice.

Segregation of deviants (regardless of kind) into isolated compounds is characteristic of institutions that want to play it safe. And while all institutions historically operate with minimum risk, no institution has been as ventureless as the school. And the school has been the most careful with its "emotionally and socially" unfit. The school advocates segregation of the disturbed with multitudes of appeals. Segregation of the unfit has an aesthetic appeal—the "adjusted" are spared the sight of disgusting antics. Segregation has an economic appeal—the efficiency of the classroom is not impaired by disrupters. Segregation has a humanitarian appeal—the afflicted are protected from abuse. Segregation has a therapeutic appeal—those who need special attention can be placed where specialists can examine them. All of these justifications are specious. The mass production of look-alikes and act-alikes is the perversion of aesthetics, not its preservation. Segregation *always* leads to increased costs and *never* leads to more efficient accomplishment of educational goals. And rather than being helped, the segregated are always hurt in the process. But segregation continues to be the primary institutional response of schools to those labeled as disturbed. These youths receive treatment equivalent to those stigmatized as mentally "slow" and retarded. In the name of rehabilitation and treatment they are removed from the mainstream of education, ostracized, villified and taunted, and, in many, many cases, are driven out of education altogether. One of the atrocities committed by schools is the wholesale manufacture of "disturbed children" who got that way solely because of the school and its segregation system.

The segregation of the "maladjusted" reflects yet another kind of timidity—and that is timidity in dealing with persons who question the legitimacy of the system. The socially and emotionally disturbed are almost exclusively those who "act out." They are the ones who cause a fuss. They make noise. They are unruly. Disproportionately to their population they are male, impoverished, and from an ethnic minority. But increasingly of late they are children of educated parents. The labeling of the antisystem student as mentally unfit relieves the school of any obligation for examining grievances. By curious logic the school, through its typical indirection, defines mental health as blind conformity. Thus, ultimately, the school's sole aim is to create persons who will do what they are told. This approach to adjustment means that independent spirits—those who question totalitarian direction—will be crushed.

In a very real sense, the isolation of the "disturbed" student is an effort to camouflage the battle for classroom control. The concern for the student is flimflam; the teacher wants that troublemaker out—and any diagnosis to bring that about will do. The teacher is the equivalent of Ken Kesey's Big Nurse. She, too, demands subservience and she, too, is bound to win. The classroom all too often becomes a battleground in which the only thing at stake is hegemony. The cost for the student who is willing to fight is loss of self-respect and a crippled relationship with others. He is fearful, closed, and devious, where his survival requires him to be secure, open, and honest. The McMurphys, the uncommon few with the talent and wit to win in a fair fight, are very likely to wind up (either figuratively or actually) as the original did, lobotomized. The student who defers to overwhelming authority pays dearly for his conformity. He, too, loses self-respect. He, too, ends up fearful, closed, and devious.

But far worse than all the horrors committed by the school are those things left undone. School programs allow *neither* the nonconformer nor the conformer to develop as persons. This stunting of growth of youth is the ultimate horror. The school's greatest destruction of youth is its fishbowl climate and structure. Students are so restricted that they are not allowed to grow beyond the limitations imposed on them and then, unprepared and unprotected, they are cast out into a world that demands that they function in complex organizations, work with diverse groups, and respond nonstereotypically to new challenges (although these demands are not recognized by nonschool institutions either).

The classroom does not allow for experimentation with different selves. The student cannot try out new roles or new ways to play those roles. A student is rightfully afraid to assert himself in different ways. If he fails to pull it off he will be ridiculed, or if ridicule doesn't bring him into line, harsher measures will be employed. He is *continually* told that there isn't time for him to learn to know himself or others. The school doesn't budget time for reflection, self-assessment, or for examination of the impact of the self on others.

But even if time were allotted, the school structure inhibits personal growth. The social organization of the school is primitive. The every-man-for-himself structure eliminates complex social functions. Students are not provided the opportunity to work with others in a variety of duties and roles. There is no opportunity to learn to trust others, to share responsibility, to gain a sense of strength through interdependent activities. The nonredemptiveness of the school militates against personal growth. The school and its efficient record-keeping assures that once a student is labeled a troublemaker he is forever labeled a troublemaker, and that contorts growth.

The lack of connection to outside school activities negatively affects social growth. The roles that students learn in school can only rarely be transferred to life situations. This was poignantly revealed by Herbert Kohl in his *36 Children*,[1] when he reflected that the one student who had developed a social self compatible with the school was least well adapted to her own people. The inability of students to transfer social skills from school to community has an analogue. The "street-wise" youth cannot put his skills to work in school. He becomes the school's enemy and the out-of-school tormenter of school conformers primarily because the school refuses to allow him to employ his skills within the system. The most successful rehabilitation programs have allowed for transfer of skill. Programs that employ group leaders in delinquent-prevention programs in the school or those that use offenders as leaders of treatment within a correctional institution have learned the value of allowing for social-skill transfer.[2] Efforts to bring the school closer to the community and to blur the distinction between school and community are still very much the exception. And because the community is a changing concept, and because, like everything else in our society, it has become centrifugalized, the nature of community-school institutions needs more careful analysis than it has been given by educators. (More on centrifugality of society later.)

The structure of schools feeds xenophobia. The student is taught to be frightened of persons who are different from him. This is most apparent in race, class, and ethnic differences. The machinations of society to keep the school racially isolated informs the student (as no other instruction can) of the terrible consequences that will result from commingling. Segregation by any other means sows similar suspicion. What that does to the suspected is fairly clear. He already has self doubts—could it be otherwise? He has been told he isn't fit for normal instruction. But think now about the student who has been "favored." First he is denied an understanding of the person who is different. This lack of sensitivity can come back to haunt him in many ways. He will be handicapped in his future dealings by his limited social interaction. His fears build

---

[1] *Op cit.*, p. 223.
[2] See for example: Charles N. Cooper, "The Chicago YMCA Retarded Worker; Current status of an action program in *Juvenile Gangs in Context*," Malcolm W. Klein (ed.), Prentice Hall, Englewood, N.J., 1967, pp. 183–194. Doug and Joan Grant, *The Offender as a Correctional Manpower Resource*, The Institute for the Study of Crime and Delinquency, Sacramento, Calif., 1966 (Mimeo).

barriers to communication. Because of his favored status he is very apt to be, later in life, a social scientist or to work in human services (a teacher, lawyer, doctor, or social worker), and when that happens his paranoid reflections are paraded as scientific knowledge. I firmly believe that much of the distortion of school programs is a direct consequence of the limited social experience that leaders in education have personally had.

School staff are not prepared for complex social interaction. Those presently employed could not, given their experiences and their training, open up the system and not be engulfed by it. But rather than developing a teaching population that can exercise leadership in a school which strives to enable individuals to grow psychologically, the emphasis is on ritualistic credentialing and teaching mechanistic skills. Clearly it is impossible to even contemplate a school which is psychologically health-producing with a staff whose heads are screwed-on wrong. Now move that up a notch and think about how impossible it is to turn out psychologically healthy teachers when their eligibility for teaching depends upon their surviving instruction from the insulated fools who dominate schools of education. (More on staff for mental health later in this chapter.) The failure to produce psychological health cannot be blamed entirely on school climate, structure, and staff deficiencies. There is also gross inadequacy in the theory which governs practice.

Devotion to Obsolete Theory

The underlying prevailing theory of mental health is the notion that the sickness is in the individual and not in the basic systems of society. If a person is classified as intolerably different it is postulated that there is something wrong with him, but there is an unwillingness to fix responsibility on governmental institutions. The school in particular is relieved of responsibility. Theories of mental health polarize into two distinct camps. One is historical and looks to early experience to explain alienation. The other is ahistorical and looks to reinforcements of behavior to explain why persons behave abnormally. Each camp views the other's leader as the antichrist. Both are right! Both the Freudians, and their derivatives, and the behaviorists share one fatal commonality—neither group is able to look at mental health in the context of a broader society. They are unwilling to examine the essence of a society.

One factor neither the behaviorists nor the psychodynamicists is willing to acknowledge is the centrifugalization of our society. The behaviorists' lack of understanding reduces their effort to control behavior (rewarding only the socially acceptable) to childish games. The behaviorists are unable to reach out to the diverse influences of a pluralistic society. They are unable to sustain gains because of the lack of continuity between one agency of the society and another. Changed behavior in the classroom cannot be carried over into the community or to the job. Making a person more "employable" in a society with insufficient jobs leads only to bloodshed and, if not extinguished life, extinguished skills. The range of ignorance of the behaviorists is enormous, matched only by the erroneous knowledge of the psychotherapists. Both groups rely heavily on an antiquated notion of the family. The behaviorists see the family as a vehicle to provide reinforcement for appropriate behavior. The Freudians and their motley offspring view the family as the wellspring of the difficulty. Naming the family as both cause and potential cure of emotional disorders are concepts which need to be looked at critically.

The notion that the family has the sole responsibility for developing character is widespread. Both scholars and laymen believe that children are taught their social values in the home, and they argue that the home provides the persuasions and restraints that develop personality. Many persons zealously and jealously insist that the family and the family alone must retain *all* jurisdiction over mental health matters. Look back a few chapters and recall Max Rafferty railing out against "life adjustment" classes as the creation of old devil John Dewey himself and his infernal progressive education.

I, for one, would eagerly assign to the family all responsibility for developing inter- and intrapersonal competence if only the family could perform. I believe, however, that the family—even the intact, "middle-class," well-educated, nuclear family—no longer has the capabilities to function in this capacity. And that because of important changes in the nature of our society, the school must assume responsibilities for personal development and, pardon the expression, life adjustment. The failure of school programs to recognize that the family is no longer able to perform its traditional role serves only to aggravate antagonisms between parent and child. The increased tension in turn leads to a wider breach within the family and attendant guilt and other unhappiness.

The Decline and Fall of the American Family

The change from a centripetal society to a centrifugal society must be understood. Because of technology and complex social organization, changes in the nature of work, in population deployment, and changes in transportation and communication, the family no longer *can* be the center that gravitationally pulls to it all things relevant to a child's life.

The family not so long ago was *the* basic unit of the economy. All economic ventures of any significance were centered in the family. The family worked the farm or ran a small business (and that took care of most of the economy). The huge industrial complexes which have, in the last century, grown to enormous size and significance, were, in their growing stage, small family-centered activities. Children were integrated into economic activity very early in life. The father and mother had skills that the child emulated. Many kinds of relationships developed because of economic interdependence—the parent was vocational educator and boss and he was also available for consultation in personal matters. He was an ally against common enemies. The precarious nature of the economic enterprise bound the family together. It was not always tranquil, the family discussions were sometimes violent, but strong forces pulled them together and the problems that individuals developed could be traced to struggles within the family. *That* family could offer its children some psychological security and stability. It *could* provide the essential reinforcements to modify behavior.

Today the family as an economic unit has almost been completely replaced by impersonal bureaucratic organizations. It is the foreman, boss, dean, or manager who now plays the surrogate parent role. For poor children the family is an economic liability. Poor parents lack: (a) knowledge about the work world; (b) the capacity to enable their children to get the credential required by the employer; and (c) the "contacts" to sponsor their child. Affluent children are also estranged from their parents, not because their parents are unable to supply knowledge or unwilling to give economic support in college or be a sponsor for a job but, rather, because the work they do is not gratifying. Large-scale organization overwhelms, depersonalizes, and frustrates the desire of youth to find himself. Both rich and poor parents are mystified by their children's attitudes about work. Neither appear to understand that the change in the *nature* of the family has contributed markedly to estrangement.

The separation of family from work leads almost ineluctably to separation of adults from children. This happens in many ways. The replacement of unskilled laborers by the machine has changed the concept of maleness. The child can no longer look to the father as an "ego ideal"; the father has been automated out of that role. The decline of clearly definable sex roles and work roles and how they relate to each other leads to subtle, and some not so subtle, abrasions at home. These tensions between adults cloud the relationships, as each parent tries to ease his own guilt by placing blame for the difficulty on the other.

The change in the nature of work that precludes much opportunity for youth to work leads to intrafamily squabbles. The young person is constantly "hassled" by his parents about his indolence. Young people are incessantly reminded by parents of all the wondrous things accomplished "when we were your age," and the nagging only makes a bad situation worse. The adult, and most importantly the social scientist, fails to appreciate that Bob Dylan is right—"Times, they are a-changing," and that being young is now a handicap because laws and customs have made young people virtually unemployable. But work is not the only factor changing the nature of family life.

Once the family was a social unit. The family was forced to interact with each other because of the lack of other contacts. In a rural society, sparsely populated and limited in transportation and media transmittal, children depended on the family for almost all social intercourse. The family's geographical location had impact on all personal matters. For example, the family was able to exercise considerable sway over the children's dating and mating. The choice available in these matters was restricted, and since colonies were almost homogenous by religion and heritage, the pressure for perpetuation of family tradition was overwhelming. Again there were exceptions that led to violent outbursts, but the pull was to the family.

The family was a powerful force in determining ethical and

moral values. The church and the family worked together symbiotically, but youth are no longer dependent either on family or church for values because neither has the power to exercise control. Mass media and transportation have changed that. The record industry, television, and motion pictures challenge family-held codes. The child is bombarded with ideas that contradict those cherished at home. The mass media dangles skeletons before the eyes and ears of youth that adults thought were safely locked in the closets. Adult leaders in responsible political and business positions are revealed as liars, hypocrites, and thieves. It is difficult for youth to revere hard work and believe that there is honest concern for others in our society when driven into their consciousness are images of: a senator's misuse of funds; a general's participation in "black market" operations; a group of business executives' involvement in price-fixing.

The media tends to distort—it presents the unusual as the representative. Only sensational events are newsworthy. If this leads to cynicism in youth—which unfortunately it does—it also has a destructive effect on adults. The adult view of youth is mangled. He sees violent mobs mindlessly tearing down the bulwarks of organized society. Mass media arouses the adult against the youth. The adult is unable to comprehend what is happening, and he is organized not to understand. Many adults have become convinced that on the campus militant youth have besieged outmanned faculty and administrators. This distortion further tears up a society, prolongs the dispute, and heats up the hostility. This spinning-out fractionates our society, and the family is in no position to draw the warring parties back together.

Transportation, particularly the automobile, has attenuated adult supervision over adolescent activities. Automobiles are universally available; adolescents use their own autos (or those that belong to others) for a variety of purposes. The automobile is a social club, a badge of status, a mobile hotel room, a place of business where narcotics are trafficked, a retreat for confidential discussions. All of these things erode family influence. All of these contribute to a way of life that is nomadic and disjointed.

The changes that have occurred in the world are irreversible. Technology has forever destroyed small organizations. Autonomous settlements tied to the family have been replaced by large-scale organizations. Both the family and the school must adapt to this emerging world. The school can assist the parent in understanding his child and also prepare the student for a more complex parental function. The school can begin by removing unnecessary pressure from the parents, and, hopefully in the process the parent can be enlisted as an ally in the education of youth.

A New Kind of Relationship
—School and Family Allied as Advocates for Youth

The school and family now are engaged in a conspiracy against children and youth. The child in trouble at school is also in trouble at home. The school makes sure of this. Typical is the following:

> A bright, eager exceedingly well-intentioned teacher of the first grade had a six-year-old in her class who was unrulier than usual. He hit other children, tore papers from the bulletin board, threw erasers, and pulled hair. In desperation the teacher sent the boy to the principal's office. The boy, rather than obeying, went directly into the yard in search of a rock (showing that he was an advanced biblical scholar). The principal called the child's mother. The mother came to the school and gave her child a whack on the back while calling him a "bastard" and telling him to get into the car.
>
> That parent didn't need to be told that her child was causing trouble at school (all of the staff "knew" his mother was unfit anyhow). The child didn't need to have his mother attack him. Then and in the future the child would blame the school (with good reason) for getting him into trouble at home. Remember, this was not a monster. It was a little unhappy six-year-old. He had reasons to be provoked by his classmates. They teased him, told him he was dirty and smelled bad. The teacher did not unequivocally indicate her disapproval of these actions. The child needed an advocate in school. The teacher could have been that advocate. Certainly she had to protect the person and property of other students—but there are many restraints that could accomplish protection short of banishment and tattling. There was nothing to be gained by telling the parent. The threats to the other children were minimal. The nuisance he caused was minimal, but the teacher's acts led to a destruction of him that was total! Like Anthony Newley, he had no one to turn to when the teacher turned away.

There are lessons to be learned from this anecdote:

1) A teacher should never tattle to a parent about a child's problems unless he has a specific course of action to recommend

and the assurance that the parent has the talents and the temperament to do what is suggested.

2) A teacher or principal should never invite a parent to the school solely to inform this parent of the child's transgressions.

3) A teacher should never place on the parent a major responsibility for the education of a child. No student should be *expected* to receive help at home.

For a child's mental health the home must be a sanctuary. It must be the one place where the student feels he is safe. The school should do *nothing* to set one family member against the other. To the contrary, the emphasis must be to encourage parents to support their children and listen to them. The adolescent doesn't want to fear his parents, nor does he want, when he is most alone, to be unable to communicate with his mother and father, and yet this happens today with increasing frequency. The home can reestablish itself as a vital force in modern society when it is a refuge for the family member who needs a refuge. Parents can be supportive if school personnel stop enlisting them in conspiracies against children and if school personnel encourage them to be supportive.

It should be emphasized that parents, in order to be open and supportive, need not embrace actions or principles not their own. They gain neither respect nor influence if, to demonstrate solidarity, they join their children in deviant acts. It is possible for adults to support, love, and accept a child and yet disapprove of some of the things the child does. All of the essences of responsible authority discussed in Chapter V are relevant to the assistance a school can give to parents. Certainly the extent to which the school refrains from insisting that parents do what they cannot do (or should not do) and assists the parents to do what they can and should do, the more that family can become a comprehensive, "real," and constructive influence on a child's life.

Bringing the Parent into the School

Antagonism between parent and school personnel has been heightened both by erosion of family function and by bureaucratization of the school. The insistence that teachers undergo many years of specialized training to be credentialed renders most parents ineligible for teaching activity. Even the few who are allowed to participate as volunteers or aides are placed in clearly subordinate positions. And the rare parent allowed to assist with the teaching helps only the young child (who is the minimal threat to the family). The older the child is the more removed from education the parent is. If the school is organized to include the parent in the instruction process, every effort will be made to extend activity to involve parents in the education process.

One means by which the parent can be involved more in the education process is by hiring parents as New Careerists. The parent, particularly the minority or poor parent, can be drawn into education through employment. And while only a small number of parents could participate through *full-time* employment, a great many could participate in education as part-time teachers and consultants.

Schools can become an effective antidote to the dis-ease that centrifugalization causes. The school can be a force that could restore a sense of community. Currently there is much talk about community control of schools. The talk isn't real because a true community does not exist. At most, persons who reside in a circumscribed area possess only one thing in common—a common enemy —and they perceive the nature of the enemy in so many different ways that they are unable even to effectively coalesce against it. Misplaced emphasis on the community-school relationship fails to improve the situation. The community (whatever that may be) will not control a school (whatever that may be) because there is a lack of direction in both parties. Those urban communities that have any definition at all got their identity primarily in their efforts to secure a voice in the management of schools. Important as that is, it is not enough. The school must take the initiative in the making of a community.

A school that achieves the goals of career choice, competence in democratic citizenship, culture-carrying, and inter- and intrapersonal competencies *will*, in the process, create a sense of community. Only as the school becomes intimately entwined in community activity can career choice be achieved; only in interchange between all groups can political competencies be achieved; only through respect, based on valid exchange of information, will there be culture-carrying; and only as individuals gain competence, are useful to others, and function in groups based on mutual respect will there be true personal development. The school thus is not an agency to be controlled by the community, nor is it an institution that determines community, *but* it is a force, an entity that can draw the community together.

The school, to achieve its centripetal importance, must cease to be a place where youth are merely deposited. As long as a school is seen as a storage place for youth it can play no more important a role in community development than a bank does (perhaps even less). Once education is perceived as a process that never ends, when the goals of education are as valuable for the adult as they are for youth, and persons of every age are encouraged to attend school, then and only then will there be a true sense of community.

Understand that the generation gap has widened because youth and adults share nothing in common. Schools are one of the few *places* where young and old have any contact with each other, but no sense of community emerges because the school lacks a commonality of purpose. *That can all be changed!*

The development of career-carrying competence (discussed in Chapter II) provides a variety of means whereby youth and adults can function together. There can be continuity of effort from beginning instruction and orientation by community figures about the work world, to later involvements in learning, beyond the physical boundaries of the school, to paid work assignments which allow for a variety of experiences, to, ultimately, New Careers positions. Each of these developmental activities provides a basis for multiage interactions.

Political activity provides another basis for community synthesis. The school can be the place where persons of all ages come together for discussions of community issues, for active interchange with elected local, state, and federal representatives, and for the preparation of initiatives and petitions.

The school fulfills its culture-carrying responsibility when it generates activities that have widespread appeal. The respect for pluralism does not mean the imposition of segregation. Segregation by age is, on the face of it, absurd. There is no six-year-old history, art, music, or science. There is no twelfth-grade multiethnic appreciation.

A sense of community can develop when persons work together on community projects. A feeling of community almost always occurs during a calamity. People work together during a flood but not during low tide. Positive activities have unrealized

potential. Community theater, art, and music are all projects that
can bind people together.

A sense of community is developed when those things that
divide residents are faced up to with a resolve to improve the situation. The key is *commitment to solution*. Mere airing of differences
leads only to increased hostilities. Too often psychologists, in particular, and other self-proclaimed experts recommend, *ex cathedra*,
meetings in which all parties gain "catharsis" through outpourings
of feelings. I insist that rather than leading to solutions for racism
or other community chafings, aimless discussion only worsens already bad situations and leads to further fragmentation of the community. The net result is warring sides that rip apart any feeling of
community belongingness. (Later in this chapter I will discuss
racism further and its implication for community development.)

Meanwhile Back at the Counselor's Office

All allegedly different approaches to "helping" students learn
to adjust to school share, to some degree, the same feeling. They
want the student to make the change. Even those theoretical approaches that give lip service to environmental change are so
vague about the nature of change that concrete suggestions based
on these theories are totally lacking. Counseling theories are particularly remiss in dealing with the work world, political processes,
bureaucratic organization, racism, nonredemptiveness, delinquent
behavior, and drug abuse—or, to sum it up, if it is important the
counseling theorist has nothing important to say.[3]

The theories of counseling are grossly inadequate—like "The
flowers that bloom in the spring, Tra-la, [they] have nothing to do
with the case." Counselors very rarely operate with a base of
articulated theory, although it is not difficult to explain what counselors do. They rid the system of "troublemakers." In Erving Goffman's terms, they "cool out the mark." [4] They do what every con
man does—they try to convince the victim that he shouldn't cause
trouble for the system. They use any tactic necessary. They per-

---

[3] A detailed criticism of counseling and therapy theories is beyond the
scope of this book. But the reader may, if he desires, peruse something like
C. H. Patterson's *Theories of Counseling and Psychoanalysis,* Harper &
Row, New York, 1966, and make his own assessment of the counselor's
theoretical approaches.

[4] Erving Goffman, *Stigma, op. cit.*

suade or threaten. They are friendly or distant. But in the end, they and the institution "clean up" at the expense of the person who is asking for help.

The counselor is able to table consideration of solutions that require system change. Consider a student who is so angered by what he perceives to be unfair treatment that he or she reacts violently—"acts out" is the term the counselor like to use. He or she may hit someone, throw a book, wear an arm band or a button —even raising one's voice qualifies for counselor treatment. If the counselor can't get the offender to see and mend the "error" of his or her ways, he has no alternative but to recommend transfer, suspension, expulsion, or referral to an extra-school agency (e.g., a mental hospital or a training school for delinquent youth). When that happens the one who complained is gone. The threat to the system is extinguished. Everything is "cool."

The counselor is easily seduced to play this inelegant role because he has been so inadequately educated. His meager knowledge of the work world, of politics, of culture leads invariably to inadequate knowledge about the inter- and intra-aspects of personality. Generally the counselor fails even to qualify as Herbert Marcuse's one-dimensional man. A person without dimension is simply not qualified for leadership in the school.

The counselor, when he isn't "cooling things out," is supposed to be guiding the student's vocational future. A kind of "cooling out" takes place here also. The counselor, in deference to reality, advises only some of the students to consider college. This advice somewhat reduces the pressure on the system. The college-directed students correspond roughly to the ability of colleges to absorb and the ability of "credentialed" industries to hire. The process obviously reinforces all the class, ethnic, and racial biases, but, in fairness to the counselor, he is unaware of his prejudices, *that* being probably the most savage indictment of all.

The counselor promotes inequality because he is taught to be a racist and class elitist. He directs almost all of the upper-middle-income white students to college-required careers and almost all the poor minority youth to "vocational training" or to jobs that require little education. He *believes* that there is a difference in ability, motivation, culture, and socialization between the two groups. He has "research" to prove it. He isn't a bigot (by faith, he cries); he is a scientist and a professional. His suggestions are based on what he has been taught. The concepts of "cultural deprivation" (membership in social groups whose values and norms disparage intellectual development and commitment to discipline); "accumulated deficit" (children who are victimized by limited intellectual stimulation in their very early years, from which they can never recover); and "constitutional inferiority" (children who are judged to be genetically inferior and lack the "smarts" for anything but low-level marginal contribution) are well accepted by counselors.

The arguments for "cultural deprivation," "accumulated deficit," and "constitutional inferiority" have been met and, hopefully, exploded previously in this book. But counselors still believe these classifications to be valid. They believe them because they are encouraged to believe them. These "theories" are promoted in schools of education, medical schools, and departments of social sciences. Counselors believe these theories because it is economically advantageous for them to believe them. If counselors were to discard these explanations, they would have to change the system that employs them. That can be expensive. Ultimately, however, it must be understood that challenging the system is the only choice available.

All school personnel must begin to change the school so that the school becomes a place where a child can learn to become the person he would like to be and learn how to work out wholesome relationships with a wide variety of other people. Let's look at some particular problems and suggest some logical approaches.

The Run of Long-Distance Loneliness

Schools are lonely places, and teachers must work to rectify that condition. A teacher can begin by reducing the feeling of threat in the classroom. A student will not be alone if he feels that the the person up front is on his side. A school will not be a lonely place if every student can ally with *someone* on the faculty. Each teacher can (with minimal risk) widen his base of support. Teachers can also initiate procedures to widen the range of persons teaching. (All this has been covered in the discussion of New Careers and needs no further elaboration here.)

Teachers must confront students when they insult other students. Refusal to intervene when one student is tormented by others is tantamount to approval of the action. Teachers must recognize that most taunting and teasing is "kidding on the square!" The tormentors truly mean to hurt and the victim truly feels the pain. The "kidding" is the "clean-up." It is the excuse used when they are asked to be accountable. How many times have we heard a group of children heckling another child, and when the child broke down and cried after a continuous barrage of insults he is accused of being a "baby." Here he was, outnumbered, with no way to escape and not even allowed to surrender. Often the teacher sides with the tormentors and argues that this is merely a part of growing up. Nonsense! That is merely part of hating school. Only bullies support such activities.

> Once I worked with a number of high-school dropouts, one of whom had mannerisms which provoked attacks on his manliness. He came to me and said he would no longer go to group meetings and asked if he could instead work with me on some statistics. I asked him if he would accompany me to the next meeting and I pledged that if he wasn't comfortable I would leave with him. We worked out an arrangement for communicating our feelings.
>
> I attended the meeting and confronted the group on their behavior. I asked that they defend it. The chief tormentor argued that he "was only trying to get the person over his timidity." I pointed out that the methods he used were precisely the methods that school personnel had used to help him with his "stupidity." Immediately the hostility was directed toward me (and I, the person paid to exercise leadership, certainly should be better prepared to deal with hostility). I communicated in a language that all understood that to get at the boy they wished to ridicule they had to get past me. For many reasons they didn't want to do that. I discussed the matter with them. I offered an explanation of their behavior which was too powerful for them to dismiss and which did not enhance their self-image at all.
>
> I stayed with the issue. Doggedly I forced each student to be accountable and in a few weeks the situation had changed. Where once they had found the boy to be a "loner," now they welcomed him into the group. This in turn led to changes in his behavior which made for recognition of his contribution to the group. In time he became one of their leaders.

Loneliness is almost always a function of problems that school personnel would like to ignore. Loneliness stems from matters that motion pictures would restrict to "mature audiences only." Fears about sexual identity and competence contribute heavily to loneliness. The school and the broader society restrict sexual roles. Even the lauded athlete and the sought-after sex goddess often suffer from restriction and they, too, experience loneliness. The favored few are always haunted by the fear that their success is transient. They are often unable to break out of stereotyped behaviors.

The unattractive, the slight, the uncoordinated pay dearly for their impediments. The large, ungainly girl; the frail, unathletic boy sometimes bear for life the scars of exclusionary tactics. (Max Rafferty claims that his unprepossessing physical appearance made *him* into the man he is today.) [5]

Race and class distinctions contribute to loneliness. Programs advertised as desegregating and apparently blessed (hell, demanded) by the Supreme Court can leave the minority student with the sinking feeling of solitary confinement in hostile territory. The muddle-mindedness of policy without regard for the impact on individuals crushes the most vulnerable. The counselor again offers little in the way of solace or assistance. Typical is the following:

> An elementary school had two black students—a brother and a sister. The boy was popular. He was attractive and a good athlete. The girl was unpopular (which is both euphemistic and synonymous for *alone*). She was *not* attractive. She had no apparent valued attributes. She had many qualities which were not highly prized. She was quarrelsome and aggressive. She reacted violently when teased. She particularly objected to being called "chocolate face."
>
> The counselor (with urging from the parents) tried to convince the girl that she had to adjust to the *reality* of the dormant culture of the school. She had to recognize that there was no harm meant by the teasing—you know, "Sticks and stones may break my bones, but names will never hurt me." The counselor pointed out to her that she brought upon herself the difficulties she experienced because she was so uncompromising.

The counselor by his behavior was contributing to her loneliness. He was also rejecting the girl. She didn't need another person to point out her failures. She needed friends. The counselor could have been her friend, but to be her friend, he had to challenge all the persons who were making her miserable. He had to intervene when she was ridiculed. He had to take up the cudgels with the faculty. When he opted out he became her chief tormentor. When I suggested to the counselor this other role he was shocked. It never entered his mind that he should be an advocate. Nowhere in his training was this idea advanced. When I suggested that the girl had been thrown into a situation that shrieked out "black is inferior to white," and had, in desperation, generated a strategy that al-

[5] *Rafferty on Education, op. cit.*

lowed her the delusion that the rejection was due to factors which she could change (her nasty disposition) rather than factors over which she had no control (her skin color), the counselor again was dumbfounded by the naïveté of that suggestion. He was certain that if he played the role I advocated he, too, would be rejected and isolated, and then he would no longer be effective. His dilemma is the dilemma of most decent "liberal" educators. Unfortunately, most end up taking the path of least resistance and becoming the "cooler out" described previously. The few who do play the advocate are often isolated and are unable to influence policy. Because neither alternative is acceptable, children are miserable and education is an atrocity.

Schools frequently try to deal with the loneliness that stems from social isolation by hiring black teachers and black counselors. This tactic leads to a particular form of "cooling out" that, rather than decreasing the pressure on the minority student, has the opposite effect. Some black counselors place unrealistic demands on black students. The black student is asked to behave so that the counselor can look good. The student's grievances are ignored lest the counselor be embarrassed. The student is called into the office and "read out" by the counselor for acting like a "nigger." The student is placed in the most intolerable of positions—he is not allowed the limited solace of being wronged by racial prejudice. It is not the white administrator who tells him that there is no bigotry here—the lot falls to the black staff, and the student is told that *he* is "lousing things up" *for blacks* by his behavior. The injustices he feels fall by the wayside. The bigots go scot-free.

The black authority who irresponsibly imposes his will on the black student leaves no place for the black student to go. That particular type of black teacher fights against any white support for black students.[6] If a white teacher is willing to be an honest teacher —an advocate of black student rights (that white authority, although rare, has cropped up throughout history. He was the abolitionist, the stationmaster for the underground railway, and the civil-rights warrior)—he is subject to attack by the black counselor or teacher. To practice his precarious role, the black counselor must attack the white advocate. He must convince the black students that not only is the white advocate no friend, he is the *real* enemy.

---

[6] The black defender of white oppression appears to be vanishing, but it is still sufficiently important to deserve comment.

The culmination of this theater of the absurd is a black staff member *defending* the most brutal racist on the staff and *attacking* the white staff member who is relatively free of prejudice and willing to stand on principle. The identical charade is played out when other factors contributing to loneliness are confronted. The female turns on the female, the poor on the poor, and those characterized as different on others similarly characterized.

The structure contributes to loneliness. The student will be less lonely if he is a valued member of the learning team. The *more indispensable he is to others, the less he will be alone*. Teachers can build such interdependencies by insisting that every member of the class contribute to the educational project. The teacher can insure that the student gain his measure of colleague respect by providing the necessary support for success. If a student is failing to meet other student demands, the teacher must become involved. If the demands are unreasonable, the teacher lets that be known. If the demands are reasonable but unfulfillable by the student, the teacher assists the student. Frequently the teacher must reorient the students. When perceptions and relationships deteriorate the teacher must bring his concerns to the attention of the group. Gerald Weinstein suggests one way that students can learn to appreciate the valuable attributes possessed by each other. One of the more inventive practices Weinstein uses is a game he calls "Mr. Goodpoint":

> Mr. Goodpoint is played by having each member of the class identify positive features in their classmates. A student describes a valuable characteristic he perceives in himself. Every other member of the group adds to the list by singling out another desirable attribute.
>
> It is amazing how students who feel alone and worthless can be turned around by this technique. The teacher should begin with a student who has some positive self-image. The teacher must be prepared to interject an attribute if there is none forthcoming from the class. The teacher must be honest in his interjection. One consequence of this game is teacher re-evaluation of the students.[7]

Mr. Goodpoint, while a valuable tool in overcoming loneliness, is also a means by which students can learn to develop critical literary judgments and sophisticated categorizations of personality. It can also be used to deal with another destructive feature of today's classroom—the need to identify a scapegoat.

---

[7] Described by Gerald Weinstein in a tele-lecture to the University of Oregon Teachers Institute, Summer 1967.

Ain't It a Shame, but if Things Go Wrong,
There Must Be Someone to Blame

The school mirrors the greater society, and by doing so perpetuates one of our most destructive infantilisms. We must find a fall guy when things go wrong: "Herbert Hoover caused the Depression." "John Dewey destroyed education." "Earl Warren is the criminals' best friend," etc. Each of us has heard those bromides and many more like them many times. The same kind of statements occur in the classroom; now, however, they are directed to little children whose names mean nothing to us.

There is an almost overwhelming desire in every aspect of our society to simplify all problems through the identification of the bad guy. The school is no different. Hitler was reputed to say that if Germany had had no Jews he would have been forced to invent them. The classroom without its scapegoat might be driven to equally desperate measures. The alternative to a bad guy is more penetrating analysis and more complex hypotheses.

Teachers must be encouraged to look to something more profound than a "bad seed," a provocateur, an agitator to explain school disruption. Rather than accepting such simple-mindedness, teachers must be encouraged to search in the program for failures to offer competence, belongingness, and usefulness to the student.

Teachers complain about lack of support from administrators when administrators refuse to punish troublemakers. Those administrators are half-right. They must refuse to accept scapegoatism —true. But, in addition, they must exert leadership. The administrator must set an example and he must also support the teacher who is generating a program that respects all students, rejecting the one that singles out some for destruction.

To eliminate scapegoatism in the classroom, teachers must first eliminate scapegoatism in the faculty lounge. When teachers forego fingerpointing among themselves, then it will be possible to discourage such practice among students.

The solution to scapegoating begins with *one* teacher!

To Integrate or Not to Integrate Is No Question

Mental health is impossible in a racially divided nation. Despite laws and exhortations, racial divisors persist and even increase. We as a nation have embarked on a national policy that can lead only to tragedy. We call it desegregation. Desegregation is a far cry from integration and is based on a foundation that can lead only to a worsening of race relations.

The *raison d'être* of all desegregation programs is that racial insulation is *bad for black children*. It is *they* who suffer because they cannot associate with *us*. The laws in effect say that our good white children have to put up with those dirty blacks so that our goodness can rub off on them. And on the basis of that thinking (?) a policy is generated that nobody wants.

The whites are not happy with desegregation because at best it waters down the content of education and slows down their children (the liberal lament); and, at worst, it subjects their children to physical abuse and a premature exposure to sexual relationships (the reactionary rant).

The blacks aren't buying desegregation because the argument that mere association with a white skin will assist a black student to learn has decreasing credibility, and the deployment of blacks into schools with white majorities dilutes the limited power that blacks have to influence school policy. Of late, blacks have substituted a call for desegregation with a call for local control of schools.

I believe in integration. I do not believe that segregated schools can survive. I believe that further segregation along racial lines will destroy the country; the result will be constantly warring factions. But integration, to be accomplished in schools, must proceed according to a rational plan.

Integration is based on mutual respect. All arguments of racial superiority—i.e., constitutional, environmental, cultural, or social —must be rejected. Integration must be presented to blacks as a means by which they can *add* to the education of a society. Integration must be presented to whites as a means by which the education of *their* children will be enhanced, not retarded. If integration is to be sold as something *beneficial* to *both* black and white (Mexican, Anglo, and Native American), then there must be a total strategy and a synchronization of different components in a logical order. *Integration begins with integration of staff, is followed by integration of curriculum, and concludes with desegregation of students.*

Integration of staff demands a marked increase of black,

brown, and poor whites in every level of school staffing. In particular, the minorities' representation must be enhanced in the upper-echelon of the schools. The minority staff member must be clear as to his role—he is there as advocate, not as "cooler out." His presence in the school unequivocally proclaims that the minority staff in the heretofore white school is the pioneer. He will gain friendships and sponsors who will lead interference for his move into the neighborhood. Only with total devotion to a New Careers strategy will the first phase of integration be accomplished.

Integration at the level of curriculum has been amply covered previously, but schools still hold back, and most wait until the demands for change come from the minority students. Often it is argued that blacks and other minorities will object to development of curriculum without their participation. Of course minorities will object to curriculum developed *for* them. However, an integrated curriculum is not developed *for* minorities; it is for all students. Moreover, the minority staff recruited in the first phase of the integration strategy should be involved in the formation of the curriculum. And yet all this misses the point. The curriculum, no matter how well developed by the staff, will be imperfect. The student should be encouraged to suggest refinements and improvements if curriculum is perceived as something that needs constant revision. The argument that *any* group is prohibited from exercising leadership falls apart. The black student is not very likely to object to the curriculum if there is accountability. If the school program is defended by logic and evidence, the criticism is likely to follow a similar course. Educators are far too thin-skinned about their contributions. If it is on a solid foundation, a curriculum can survive criticism. If indefensible, it ought to go down. Educators have rejected criticism and critics and have paid dearly for their own arrogance.

The third phase of integration is the easy phase. The furor and the acrimony about busing, Princeton plans, or educational parks will be reduced to barely audible whispers if there is success in the first two phases of integration.

Governmental activity ought to encourage integration. School districts should be encouraged by federal grants to hire minority staff. Federal grants should be readily available for curriculum revision. The cost of student transfers should be borne by federal grants. Governmental threat only adds to opposition, whereas gov-

ernmental inducement could do much to establish exemplar programs and models that others could emulate. Only after districts
refuse these blandishments should proscriptive measures be used.

The Opiate Is the Religion of the People

Drug use and abuse is a major problem for youth. Public policy
has made matters worse. In fact, much of the justification for drug
use *is* public policy.

Police have been given the responsibility for dealing with drug
problems, but police have no competence in this area. Drug abuse
is not a police problem. Drug abuse is a health and education problem. Because police are in the game, educators and medical practitioners have been forced out. Police and police-oriented agencies
have made outrageously false statements about drugs; these in turn
have provoked almost equally outrageous statements in defense of
drugs. Because narcotics-enforcement police have continuously
sought to evade the laws of evidence, the narcotics offender has
been elevated into the curious position of crusader for justice.
Arguments for drug use gain credence *only* because the arguments
against drug use are so ludicrously devoid of logic. Thus, in truth,
we have come full circle—the opiate has become the religion of the
people.

Some things are known about drugs—but much is unknown.[8]
We can differentiate between addictive and nonaddictive drugs (the
distinction is relative). Addictive drugs lead to physiological dependency. Heroin is a highly addictive drug. The body builds up a
need for the drug and goes into violent withdrawal symptoms if
suddenly denied access to the drug. Cigarettes are mildly addictive;
heavy smokers complain about a "nicotine fit" following abrupt ab-
stention. Marijuana is minimally addictive; there is no evidence of
physiological distress if a person who uses marijuana suddenly
stops using the drug.

Almost all drugs are habituating. The individual takes drugs
because psychologically he derives pleasure from them.

Some drugs can induce death. An overdose of heroin will kill.
Barbituates are one of the most commonly used means of committing suicide. Death from an overdose of ethyl alcohol is ex-

---

[8] Many recent publications deal with these issues in some detail. See,
for example, Margaret O. Hyde, *Mind Drugs,* McGraw Hill, New York, 1968.

tremely rare (not so from methyl alcohol), and death from acute marijuana poisoning is, as far as we know, nonexistent. However, alcohol and marijuana can lead to loss of motor or cognitive control, which, in turn, can lead to fatalities.

Most of the current outcry about drug use centers around marijuana. Claims of its devastating effects and its value are equally outlandish. Those who insist on its illegality argue that: (1) it causes people to commit crime and (2) leads to involvement with more serious drugs. Those who favor its use argue that: (1) it is less dangerous than alcohol or tobacco; (2) heightens artistic appreciation; (3) improves interpersonal relationships. The truth is that we *know* very little about marijuana use. True, some persons using marijuana commit violent crimes, but there is no assurance that the same persons wouldn't commit crimes if they didn't use marijuana, nor is there any reason to believe that some persons were deterred from violence because they were lulled into passivity by marijuana. The argument that marijuana leads to the use of more heavy drugs lacks proof. There is ample evidence that many, if not most, marijuana users are content with that drug. There is also testimony that many heroin users completely by-passed the more innocuous psychoactive agents.

The arguments for marijuana are also faulty. There is no evidence that marijuana is less harmful than alcohol or tobacco. The comparison is absurd. The chronic effects of alcohol (cirrhosis) and nicotine (cancer or heart diseases) can rightfully only be compared with the chronic effects of marijuana, and we know almost nothing of the effects of regular, long-term use of marijuana. The law discourages such research. We are just now beginning to learn the long-term effects of marijuana on infrahuman subjects. But there is always danger of generalizing for humans what has been discovered in white mice. The dangers of alcohol are exaggerated by the marijuana-user. Moderate alcohol-users constitute little threat to themselves or to society. Raymond Pearl established years ago that the longevity of moderate alcohol-users exceeds both abstainers and abusers. About six per cent of the alcohol-users in the United States are alcoholics. That is to say, only this group are so negatively affected by alcohol that their social and economic lives are disrupted. Probably a comparable percentage of marijuana-users are "marijuanics"—people who are in trouble because of their inability to handle the drug and are unable to receive help for their disability.

The magical features of marijuana are also exaggerated. There is no evidence, or for that matter logic, to suggest that *any* drug heightens artistic accomplishment or interpersonal communication. That persons still hold to such myths means only that they desire a cheap solution to complex social problems. They want a drug to substitute for hours of disciplined practice or for extension of self to other people.

If looked at from a larger perspective, all the preceding discussion of drug use (dreary or interesting) is irrelevant. The major problem of drug use is not the *drug* but the *user*. The misdirection of concern has led to misdirection of public policy. Promiscuous drug use of any kind is either wasteful or pernicious, but not for the reasons trumpeted by law-enforcement officials. Such use is harmful because it feeds social irresponsibility. The drug-user is turned inward. He looks for solutions to *his* problems within *himself*. *There* is the major risk. Important interpersonal problems can *only* be solved interpersonally. Interpersonal problems are *never* resolved by drugs. There is no inexpensive solution to man's alienation from other men. The *illusion* that drugs can help is the problem. Those who call for persons to drop out of interpersonal arenas, where all decisions vital for man's survival are made in favor of the happiness that drugs bring, are being flat out irresponsible.

The survival of man depends on his ability to communicate openly with a wide range of his fellows. Legal policy concerning narcotics inhibits free communication. But so does the narcotic—anything that affects cognitive functions is a deterrent to honest communication. Only if we radically change our laws and approach to narcotic use will it be possible to change youth's attitudes about narcotics.

The first level of attack on narcotics must be in the classroom. Students must be informed about the natural consequences of narcotic use. The student must be provided with facts—cold, objective information—about the impact of airplane glue, amphetamines, barbituates, marijuana, LSD, morphine derivatives, etc. on the central nervous system. All scare techniques must be scrupulously avoided. A teacher must have the background to answer questions. He can't afford to bluff. If he doesn't know, he must have access to experts. Teachers should periodically attend workshops to update their level of understanding about drug use. Today many elementary-school teachers know less than their students about drugs and their properties. It is also frightening to know how little the drug-user himself knows about the properties of various drugs. The teacher who pretends knowledge is a fool. Yet very few schools of education equip teachers to lead discussions about narcotics. The teachers' lack of knowledge about drugs can lead to hilarious spoofs:

> One elementary school had a drug scare. In wastebaskets in the school, "reds" (seconal) mysteriously appeared. The police were immediately called. The students were lined up and frisked. It was a solemn, weirdly frightening occasion.
> The "drugs" were analyzed. They were red, true enough. But they were also vitamin pills. Imagine the delight of the prankster who could so disrupt a school because no one in the school could distinguish between a dangerous drug and a vitamin pill.

The treatment of the addict, glue sniffer, or "marijuanic" needs drastic revision. The best drug-treatment program would probably never even mention or even allude to drugs. The best drug-treatment program recognizes that drug use is a "way of life." The only alternative to one way of life is a better way. No one will ever give up drugs of any kind unless he can derive satisfaction (competence, belonging, and usefulness) without drugs. One of the little-understood aspects of drug-peddling is that some persons are unable to derive any sense of social importance *except* as drug dispensers. To threaten such a person with prison is meaningless. He has nothing else going for him. The best, and today the only, legitimate career for former drug-users is in the treatment of other addicts. A variety of treatment programs have emerged which allow the former "doper," "hype," "head" a sense of social worth through his work with others similarly afflicted.

Unfortunately, there are insufficient opportunities for rehabilitation of drug abusers through what Frank Riessman calls the "helper principle"—persons who derive pleasure from helping others.[9] Or, to paraphrase A. E. Housman, Them it is their helping helps! Doors must be opened which allow the former addict to attain gratification in drug-free environments. He must be provided the social, economic, and educational support to new careers

---

[9] Synanon is perhaps the most highly publicized, but other programs varying greatly in philosophy have been developed.

that he finds gratifying. Drug rehabilitation in the final analysis is conversion. Treatment of drug-users all too frequently "fails" because all other avenues are closed to the addict. And that brings us to yet another problem of mental health—the nonredemptiveness of our society.

Dummy, Doper, Troublemaker, Clown
—Once They Get You, They Keep You Down

The drug-user, like all others with spoiled images, is locked into ways of life from which there is no escape. Teachers and school programs can change this lamentable condition. Every classroom can strive to be a place for "fresh starts" and "clean slates." It is not enough to eliminate ability groups, special classes for emotionally disturbed, or I.Q. scores on permanent record cards. The identical segregation and humiliation can take place within a single classroom. The teacher must exercise leadership to generate an open society. The teacher must demonstrate the responsible authority discussed earlier: appreciation of difference, accountability, negotiability, recognition of the inevitability of conflict, and common sense in the application of rules in the treatment of deviants.

The teacher must recognize that redemptiveness starts with students having the opportunity to belong, to be useful, and to be competent. Only with continual challenge to teachers, only with the constant exposure of the barriers placed between students and education, only with clear alternatives to current practice will teachers exercise the leadership required. Redemptiveness for teachers is a prerequisite for redemptiveness for students. Teachers get locked into demeaning roles; they, too, suffer from bad "reps." They, too, once they have the name, might just as well have the game. The teacher suffers from labels of troublemaker or dumbbell. The school will be seen as a credible institution with concern for all youth only when it extends openness to staff.

The redemptive society will, like everything else deemed desirable in education, be difficult to attain. Teachers, in coalition with other friends of education, can get it—but only if they are dedicated to change.

Programs generated in schools can be generalized to other institutions (the reverse is also true). Teachers can play leadership roles in securing the following:

Laws which forbid any public or private employer from requesting any information about activities that occurred more than five years previously. There is evidence that persons with criminal records who remain free of extralegal involvements are no more likely to be reinvolved in crime than persons who have never been convicted of a crime.

School records which are the property of the student and his family. Students and family should be able to handle school records like bank accounts are handled. They should be able to deposit all information they want recorded and withdraw all information they do not wish to have recorded.

Elimination of any correctional program based on punishment. Teachers must offer intellectual leadership in convincing the public that there is extremely limited power to deter deviance through punishment or threat of punishment. The opposite is more likely; the more the deviant is punished, the more deviant he is likely to become.

Many teachers truly believe that punitive measures are effective. They recount testimonials of students who many years later came back and thanked them for prior punishments. These of course are the successes: the lawyers, doctors, congressmen, and ambassadors. There is much wrong with that kind of thinking. The most glaring deficiency is that such a sample is not representative. The failures don't come back; the welfare recipient and chronic criminal, the alcoholic or the deadbeat don't show up at farewell banquets and reunions and tell the teacher that her harsh treatment made *them* what they are today. If they do tell their story, the teacher conveniently forgets it. Unfortunately, teachers are like gamblers at Las Vegas. They remember only the winnings and that's why gambling houses are economically successful and why punitive policies remain in effect.

In School, Sex Is a Three-Letter Void

There can be a no more senseless objection to a school activity than the objection to sex education. The arguments in opposition to sex education include all of the inanities discussed or alluded to previously. Here is found lack of tolerance, disregard for the rights of others, specious logic, provincial prejudices, meager foundation of knowledge, and limited historical perspective.

Unfortunately, arguments *for* sex education often suffer from the identical deficiencies.

Schools *must* offer sex education. Sex education is necessary if population control is to be achieved without resorting to abhorrent totalitarian impositions. Sex education is necessary if man's inhumanity to man, in general, and man's inhumanity to women, more specifically, are to be reduced. The ability to live with one's self and one's neighbors hinges considerably on educated attitudes on sex.

As a nation the United States has generated norms and values about sex that are, to paraphrase Richard Brautigan, attitudinal Hiroshimas. Those who preach "morality" may be among the most immoral. Those who promulgate "liberation" may be among the most enslaved. Both groups are unhealthily occupied with sex, and while for one there is terror and for the other ecstasy, neither can think, talk, or write about much else. Be clear on this, no child in this land is free from stimulation. Our national heroes *are* sex symbols. The media are brazenly sex-arousing. Parental embarrassments about sex *do* create in their children strong desires and strange fears. Children titillate each other everywhere they meet. Even if only dimly conscious about what they say or do, they know it's "naughty" and are excited about *that*. An increasing number of motion pictures, magazines, novels, TV shows, and newspapers exist solely to sexually arouse and thereby sexually "educate." That being the case, schools must either get with reality or continue to pursue a course of irrelevance.

The only questions facing educators about sex education are: What should children know? At what age should they be taught? Who should do the teaching? How should it be taught? The answers to these questions are: Everything. The younger the better. Teachers. Straightforwardly.

Children should know all there is to know. They should be informed about the physiology of sex and the ecological consequences of sex acts. If there is conflict about values and norms regarding sexual experience, students should be able to tune into all sides of the controversy. No child should be so ill-prepared for adult roles that he is entrapped into them solely because of ignorance. Increasingly, children must be made acutely aware of the awesome responsibility of bringing children into the world. No unwanted child should ever be born. Overpopulation can no longer be dismissed with "God's will be done." Overpopulation can only be understood as "education's work undone." The misery of adults transferred ad infinitum unto future generations because of un-enlightenment must be stopped. The misery can be reduced by vigorous, well-planned sex education programs.

No child is too young to learn about sex. Almost from birth he has been exposed to prejudice and misinformation. The younger he is straightened out, the better. The same kind of absurdities are encountered in sex education that are encountered in education for work or politics. Solicitous souls, some few of whom are even well-meaning, want again to protect the innocent from the seamy and the sordid. One need not be a Freudian to recognize that young children are not so innocent. Sylvia Ashton Warner found that sex and violence were central concerns of very young Maori children, and these children had been spared the artificial stimulation of television and motion pictures.[10] Uninformed children find them-selves enslaved very early in life in tragic situations: undesired pregnancy, homosexual involvement, abuse by an adult (suffering from his own inadequate sexual education), an unfulfilling mar-riage. Discussions postponed for a more appropriate date somehow just never seem to materialize. Parents "lay on the table" questions about sex and all too often their child is "laid" before the questions are answered.

Teachers should bear the major responsibility for sex educa-tion. Of course they should utilize all the support and resources available to them, but, as educational leaders, they are in charge of the classroom and should perform the leadership role. Medical doc-tors can provide assistance in the area of sex education. But the ar-rogance of some members of the medical profession who feel that they alone are competent enough to instruct about sex must be challenged. Some of the medical profession here (as in other areas) should be counseled, "physician heal thyself," because doctors also are the psychological victims of poor and distorted sex education. It should be remembered that sex education involves attitudes as well as biology.

Teachers can lead discussions about sex, but they need better preparation. Neither their preservice training nor their in-service training has been adequate. Clearly, preparation for sex education must become a high-priority teacher-training item. Workshops and institutes should be developed immediately. But in the interim,

---

[10] Sylvia Ashton Warner, *Teacher,* Simon & Schuster, New York, 1963.

sex education should go on and common sense should prevail. Some teachers should not be asked to talk about sex now or in the future. Their hang-ups and embarrassments need not be communicated to the children. The concept of differentiated staff that has been a recurrent theme throughout this book has relevance for sex education. Teachers should do only those things they do best, and persons on the staff most qualified to speak should do the talking. Because sexual values, norms, language, and behavior *are* influenced by race, class, and ethnicity, the instruction should be sensitive to these differences.

The instructor must be honest, open, and candid. Euphemisms and deceptions instruct the child that there is something fishy about the proceedings. Sex education is not personal hygiene, preparation for parenthood, or biology. Obviously, it is a part of all these, but we clearly don't have as much trouble discussing dental caries, family budgets, or bird and bee procreation as we do sexual activities of the human being. Open, straightforward sex education will provoke community opposition, but so will subtle and sneaky approaches. Here, as everywhere else, the educator must be accountable; he must defend his program with evidence and logic. Here, as everywhere else, the teaching force must be the first to be brought on board. Teachers must be given the encouragement to engage in open debate. They must be intellectually responsible. Currently the fears of teachers reflect to a large extent the prejudicial ignorance of the larger community. Schools of education are particularly loath to deal with sexual attitudes. Schools of education reflect the same kinds of mindlessness *and* gutlessness with respect to sex that they demonstrate in political controversy. The safest and easiest place to begin the change in sex education is in the schools of education programs for elementary-school teachers. If we don't begin there, then the atrocity of education will be reflected in sexual maladjustment. To successfully implement a program of sex education, schools must avoid the moralist trap and the liberation trap.

The Moralist Trap, or Sex Education Belongs in the Home

Those who claim to be moralists on sex education simply are not. They suffer greatly from a lack of truth in advertising. Included in a very mixed bag are:

The opportunists who see political hay to be made from opposition to SEX taught in the schools;

The paranoids who see every innovation as a part of a giant conspiracy to steal away their children;

The poor, confused souls who just don't know what is happening and wish that school, like everything else, could be restored to something familiar and easy to understand.

We have met most of these folks before. They are the same crew who oppose politics on campus, organize against integration (BUS may even be a dirtier three-letter word than SEX), want dress codes for students, are horrified by "obscenity," are against increasing teacher salaries, and want to keep foreign federal governments, such as our own, from influencing school policy with their dirty dollars.

There is only one way to deal with this group. Stand up to them! Follow all the rules of responsible leadership. Be accountable. Justify all aspects of the program with logic and evidence. Be negotiable. Incorporate suggestions into the program. Be willing to accept exceptions because of uniqueness in values and norms of substrata of the population and be calm and rational when irreconcilable differences do occur.

To date, proponents of sex education have behaved irresponsibly with their "supermoralist" opponents. They have tried to placate and co-opt their adversary. This effort is dishonest. The moralists will not be taken in by such silly subterfuge. It has just the opposite effect—it encourages them. The lack of candor in treatment convinces them that there truly is a hidden agenda in sex education proposals. The retreat from principle is correctly perceived as lack of courage and the willingness of proponents to retreat when intimidated and threatened. Over the long haul those who support defensible programs for sex education are deserted by administrators who try to woo the enemy. When that happens all is lost. The program acceptable to the opponents of sex education is so replete with contradictions that no honest educator could support it. And those for whom all the distortion has taken place are moral to the end—they resist the seduction. They attack as furiously the compromised version of sex education as they did the unadulterated original proposal.

How should proponents of sex education proceed? Proponents should recognize that sex education, like everything else in education, is political. Only when a constituency is rallied behind a program and is educated to understand the issues can there be any true educational reform. Sex education will succeed when proponents organize their friends. This will take enormous energy and devotion. There is no time for appeasing opponents. Ultimately the two forces will clash, as they should, in the political arena. The clash will occur in elections for school boards, in school budget and bond elections, in public forums and debates. When that happens sex education will be incorporated into school programs. *All* of the logic, the evidence, and common sense are on the side of well-designed sex education programs. To date, opponents of sex education have gained headway, less because of their political savvy but more because we who want progress have been politically inept.

The Liberation Trap, or "Anything Goes"

Freedom is a little-understood word. Because of the breakdown in education, very few people are able to relate freedom to the distribution of the earth's resources or to work choice or to political decision-making or to a range of opportunities for cultural expression, personal development, and social identities. This limitation of perspective leads many people to think of freedom solely as a release from inhibitions. This distorted concept of freedom has considerable relevance for sex education.

Be absolutely clear on this: *The school has no organized movement for the surrender of all sexual inhibitions*; only the most paranoid could "invent such a preposterous conspiracy." But there is a highly organized educational effort going on outside of the school. Motion pictures (particularly "skin flicks"), television, magazines, underground papers, and records ever increasingly let it be known, with very little left to the imagination, that sex is the world's most pleasurable activity. (It is increasingly clear that night baseball will *not* replace it.) The sex media didn't generate the movement out of the blue; seduction has been around for some time and an ideology to justify it every bit as long. So what is new about Hugh Hefner or his counterpart on the *Berkeley Barb*? Five hundred years ago Robert Herrick, in suggesting that one gather his rosebuds while he may, had the same intent and at least as much talent. But new or old, irresponsible hedonism has been inadequately handled and it's time we get at it.

The reality of the appeal for sexual license cannot be ignored by school personnel. They must be prepared to deal effectively with what appears to be a very attractive proposal. This is particularly difficult because a few teachers are genuinely attracted by the notion, while even more are genuinely repelled by the insensitivity and the sometimes demagoguery of the moralists. If this latter group is unable to generate a stance of their own they give the student the impression by their silence that they support sexual liberation. The appropriate activity of the teacher with respect to any organized or unorganized approach to sexual behavior is to treat those views as all controversial issues are treated. *Teachers should teach.* The teacher should examine with students the underlying assumptions of the approach and its likely alternatives and consequences. If students are reluctant to look at the possible negative effects of sexual liberation, the teacher is obligated to put those issues on the agenda and stay with them through hoots of derision and seemingly interminable silences. The teacher must insist that students be aware of the coercive influences that are disguised by the call for sexual liberation.

Whenever the suggestion for surrender of sexual inhibitions is organized, either as the value system of a social group or through mass media, there is the danger of a cult. In cults, minority views are met with suppression. In such a cult, the modern hedonist, in order to convince himself, has to convince everyone of the rectitude of his position. In this context liberation becomes nonliberation. The disrespect for pluralism leads to an intrusion on the rights of others. The true believer in sexual liberation is always hitting on the square. He is trying to help the nonaligned square dude out of his "old-fashioned bag" and to help the square chick "into the sack." He is generating groups to help "sensitize" the insensitive and thereby rid him of his sexual "hang-ups." (One of my criticisms of George Leonard's book *Education and Ecstasy* is his seemingly unqualified endorsement of such group pressures.)

Adolescents are particularly vulnerable to the appeal of freedom from sexual inhibitions. They are torn by hormonal influences. They are subjected to passionate entreaties. They want to act grown-up and they think that sex alone allows that opportunity. They have few adult confidants. The only contrast to the allure of the liberalists is the unconvincing preaching of the moralists. If the teacher is to fill that gap he must specifically explore two possible unhealthy consequences of unbridled sex: reinforcement of sex and race inequality.

Much of the call for sexual liberation fails to even consider the continual exploitation of women in our society. Women *are* relegated to second-class citizenship. In education, for example, women are the "niggers"; they predominate as elementary-school teachers, are very rarely found as "slavemasters" (principals), and even less frequently make it into "the mansion" (superintendents). There is no more effective way in our society to neutralize the aspiring female than to seduce her. There is no more effective way to exploit or manipulate women than through sexual domination. Those who campaign for sexual liberation would argue that their activity is an important step in the liberation of women. They insist that they are for the elimination of a double standard, for an end to hypocrisy, and for equal sexual rights for women. All this appears to be on the side of sexual equality. I find this argument unconvincing. I think completely missed are the structural and economic factors that relegate women to less-than-equal status. There is a lack of critical thinking about cause and effect. Sexual restrictions are a consequence of economic and other discriminations against women. The woman who is "free" in sex and not "free" in the educational and economic world is only set up to be exploited sexually.

Sex liberation is often a mask for hostility. One particular hostility is masked racial anger. Often the sexual relations between black males and white females reflect only hate on the part of one partner and guilt on the part of the other. Black women are doubly offended by this "think black—sleep white" activity. They are placed in an unenviable and exploitable position. Their options are reduced and their loneliness is increased. The gambit of black males with white girls is convincing them that unwillingness to engage in sex relationships is proof of racial prejudice. This tactic has no counterpart in black girl/white boy relationships. I am sure that many are based on wholesome attitudes, just as I am sure that many all-white relationships are basically unwholesome. But the underlying motivation of all relationships needs to be understood. It is patently false to say that hate and guilt will be worked out in bed. If that is the basis of the relationship, the *only* conclusion is personal tragedy.

In no sense is unreflecting sex "liberation" (living only for the present moment) truly hedonistic. The immediate consequence of unrestricted sex acts may bring pleasure to one partner while bringing pain to the other. But the long-range effects may result in pain to everyone involved. For those who view themselves as "studs," sex can only be a zero-sum game where male pleasure is derived at the expense of the woman. Sophisticated versions of the same kind of relationship do not relieve it of its unwholesomeness.

It is not only the male who inflicts pain under the guise of love. The reverse situation is equally known. Sexual intercourse may be the trap for devastating relationships. Only involvements that are socially responsible and, in the most true sense, moral, should be advocated.

Those who call for sex liberation tend to be shallow. Often they allow themselves to be carried away by rhetoric. They do not permit true discussion of cause and effect. They use the identical tactics of those they most condemn.

Young people must be made aware of their sexual motives and their behaviors. They must know why they are doing what they are doing and what are the probable consequences of a variety of alternative actions. The "moralists" have worked hard to foster shame and guilt. The liberationists have not stressed social responsibility sufficiently. A good sex education program stresses social responsibility without generating guilt.

Leisuring More and Enjoying It Less

Leisure is an important concern for modern Americans. If nothing else, leisure is economically important. Millions of dollars change hands because of it. With all that activity, someone ought to be enjoying it. In theory, at least, the modern American has won the right to more leisure time. Inexorably the work life, year, and week have shrunk over the decades. Because of negotiation and legislation, workers are guaranteed earlier retirement, longer vacations, more holidays, and shorter work weeks. But despite such liberation, enjoyment has not come easily. In fact there is good reason to doubt whether the average ordinary never-had-it-so-good U.S. citizen has gained a whit of happiness for all his affluence.

Leisure time actually represents yet another way for a person to learn to live with himself and with others. In one sense, leisure represents the activity that allows for maximum options. Even the best work would impose limitations. Work is organized for purposes external to each individual. It is conceivable that, for some, avocational interest and vocational pursuits will totally overlap. Hopefully for all, work will be compatible with interests and tastes. A good society can never demand that man live solely to work. A good society is governed by the principle that man works in order to live. Living must allow for pleasure—and each of us must have the opportunity to explore that which uniquely gives us pleasure (restricted only by intrusions into the rights of others for life, liberty, and the pursuit of happiness).

Several years ago, the theater critic Walter Kerr wrote *The Decline of Pleasure*.[11] In that book Kerr concluded that pleasure was fast disappearing because it had been undone by utilitarianism. Because man was coerced into doing only those things that had demonstrative social value, he was left incomplete. Kerr noted that "We are vaguely wretched because we are leading half lives, half heartedly and with only one-half of our minds actively engaged in making contact about us." [12]

According to Kerr, usefulness has become so dominant in the philosophy which governs our lives that man cannot engage in any nonutilitarian activity without paying the price of guilt or anxiety. Kerr's argument, while diverting, doesn't hold water. Man can and does engage in nonusefulness without evidence of anxiety. He can sit transfixed before a TV set without feeling the need for rationalizing the value of the time spent. It is not that man is driven to *justify* his leisure time which causes him so much consternation. He is anxious and guilt-ridden because he cannot generate a sense of *usefulness in his work life*. The decline of pleasure is not the result of any philosophy. Rather it is the absence of philosophy which has led to the destruction of enjoyment. Pleasure is a major casualty of Topsyism—a system that just "grow'd."

If Kerr had written a book entitled *The Decline of Usefulness*, he might have hit upon something. The American feels empty because he is unable to convince himself that he is useful. In previous chapters I have suggested means of promoting a sense of usefulness. But man is entitled to more than a life of drudgery. To be psychologically healthy, man must enjoy himself. Many factors con-

---

[11] Walter Kerr, *The Decline of Pleasure,* Simon & Schuster, New York, 1962.
[12] *Ibid.,* p. 12.

tribute to his inability to find happiness. Among the most important is that he hasn't learned how to enjoy life.

Learning to enjoy life was a natural process in an uncomplicated society. But just as complexity of work, politics and culture and interpersonal relations have led to new challenges for education, so does complexity place strains on pleasure-seeking activities. Centrifugality of a complex society impinges on enjoyment. Kerr pinpoints one casualty of a centrifugal society. In more primitive social organizations the artist could influence the mercantile mind. In the not-too-distant past the poet and the businessman commingled:

> When Dr. Johnson marched off to the club—only later identified in a more limited way as the Literary Club—he meant to spend an evening in conversation not only with the scribblers whose working problems be shared but also with an assortment of clergymen, doctors, lawyers and statesmen. These men, in turn, meant to spend the evening with Johnson and Goldsmith, Garrick and Reynolds; they were even prepared to be patient while Johnson dictated to them, and not on matters of syntax but on matters of statesmanship. To arrive at something comparable in our own time, we should have to imagine that William Faulkner, W. H. Auden, Aaron Copland, Frederic March, Willem de Kooning, Lyndon Johnson, Robert Oppenheimer, Thomas Dewey, Reinhold Niebuhr, Dr. Dana Atchley, and one of the vice-presidents of Merrill, Lynch, Pierce, Fenner and Smith, perhaps with Leonard Lyons as their Boswell, were to meet regularly, drink heartily, and at all times give their greatest deference to the voices of Auden and Faulkner.[13]

In context of the total society, Kerr's ecumenism was extremely restricted even in its heyday. Only the elite were allowed to participate. Those in the mines, which are "dark as the dungeon and damp as the dew, where the dangers are many and the pleasures are few," weren't invited; nor were the beggars, the field hands, the tradesmen, or the craftsmen. But there is in the proposition (for all its provincialism) a germ of an idea which is essential to a good life. For man to gain pleasure he must have access to the talented and to the creative thinkers of his society. To deny him those avenues is to restrict his options for enjoyment.

---

[13] *Ibid.*, p. 69.

Tom Wolfe looks at the desperate and the despairing in their quest for pleasure. *The Pump House Gang* [14] ranges far to find the worlds of "happiness" people make for themselves, and *he* thinks they have succeeded: "What struck me throughout America and England was that so many people have found such novel ways of just that, *enjoying*, extending their egos way out in the best terms available, namely their own. It is curious how many serious thinkers—and politicians—resent this obvious fact." [15]

I think I qualify as both a serious thinker and as a politician. I find Tom Wolfe to be witty and scathing, but his lacerations barely break the skin. His pleasure-seekers don't come across as having much of a good time. Hugh Hefner, who created his own "status-phere"; the Pump House Gang, middle-class dropouts who surf almost all the time and kill themselves only sometimes; Britishers who act as though they are Americans; Carol Doda, who asked the question, Can a girl with a 35-inch bust find happiness in America? and, having answered in the negative, pumped herself up to 44 inches; owners of a taxicab company who make it big as Pop Art connoisseurs; society folk who delight in four-letter expletives; Columbus, Ohioans, who speed on motorcycles—none quite pull it off. Sure, they are out there doing their different things, but none come across as truly gratified. What Wolfe describes as a synthetic enjoyment. The people he describes did not get where they are through reflection or through sampling different kinds of enjoyments. They got there as a reaction to even less gratifying alternatives. Only a tiny minority among us will find genuine pleasure rebounding from one dissatisfaction to another. The majority will learn to enjoy only if there is opportunity to explore and savor. The school is the logical place for such experiences.

Every aspect of school should be pleasurable. Preparation for work roles, citizenship roles, and culture-carrying roles should be personally gratifying. In no instance should a student be made to feel that school is a cross he has to bear.

Traditional vocational education is more likely suited for avocational pursuits. Walter Kerr is sore annoyed because some modern business big shots find themselves only when they are building a spare room on the house. If a person can weigh a large

---

[14] Tom Wolfe, *The Pump House Gang*, Bantam Books, New York, 1969.
[15] *Ibid.*, p. 19.

variety of enterprise and find that through carpentry he gains a sense of competence, usefulness, and personal wholeness, what's wrong with that? My quarrel is that many persons aren't given that choice. If they are in "college prep" in high school, they are either forbidden or discouraged from taking shop.

Every student should be given the opportunity to explore art in its multivarious forms. Each community should have its artists in residence—persons who would be encouraged to inspire by example, encouraging others to become involved in aesthetic activities. One of the most memorable experiences for me was to watch Diego Rivera paint a mural in the 1939 San Francisco World's Fair. Every community should have access to funds with which they could entice poets, or novelists, or sculptors, or composers, or painters, or other virtuosos. The contract negotiated between the community representative and the artist would require accountability from both parties. The community would provide the base of operation, the opportunity for the artist to develop his art. The artist in turn would pledge to be a member of the community—to participate in community activities and to be available to discuss with others *his* aims, *his* aspirations as well as respond to the concerns of others in the community. Twenty thousand such artists in colleges, high schools, and grammar schools could be obtained for 2.5 million dollars a year, which is considerably less than one week's cost of conducting the war in Vietnam.

Counselors and teachers should be trained to work constructively with students who are at loose ends and, while not miserable, are not happy. The absence of happiness should be of concern to all school officials. And while the school cannot or should not protect the student from life's harsh realities, there is no reason for allowing anyone to be overwhelmed by them:

> At the time of writing this book I launched another career. I decided to run for Governor of the State of Oregon. One of the intents of the campaign was to make politics enjoyable. I specifically requested of persons interested in my behalf that "no masochists need apply." A colleague at the University became infuriated (he even wrote a letter to the local newspaper). He argued that political matters were too serious for enjoyment. It really is very much the other way around. If political activities are so designed that only a very few can find pleasure in involvement, then governments of, by, and for the people will disappear from the face of the earth.

The essence of enjoyment requires a change in school perspective. But more than changes in attitude are necessary. There must also be augmentation of leisure-time personnel. One reason so many among us are unable to find pleasure is that there isn't anyone available to help. We are restricted to lonely and sedentary existence because there aren't enough naturalists, ski instructors, bowling instructors, discussion group leaders trained or employed.

The vacation that one anticipates for a year can turn out to be the identical rat race from which escape was sought. Our national parks are crowded and understaffed. Parents cannot be carefree, because young children need constant supervision. Adolescents may be bored because of the limited range of activities. Amateur fishermen do not have the expert advice needed to catch fish. None of these disappointments is necessary. Every national park can be a place of total enjoyment. Crowding can be reduced through creation of more recreational facilities. Every park can provide for total family enjoyment. A well-staffed day-care center included in the resources of the park can give children the things they want. Naturalists can open up the excitements of ecosystems to inquiring minds. Well-staffed marinas can make boating and fishing available to all. Guides can open up the wonders of wildernesses and also protect them from being spoiled. The New Careers notion is critical to a leisure world that would bring pleasure to everybody.

The Staff for Life

If the school is to become a place where students can learn to live with themselves and their neighbors, then the attitude of the staff needs to be considered. The school cannot combat loneliness, scapegoatry, prejudice, drug dependency, and unhealthy sex attitudes unless there is a staff prepared to deal with such matters. Nor can it be expected that students will find enjoyment in school when the teachers are miserable.

The teacher need not be without hang-ups or problems, but he must be helped to deal with his own difficulties and at least be in control if he is to assist others. He need not be highly trained in psychiatry, but he must know how to use specialists for technical assistance and consultation. The teacher must be encouraged by his administration to be warm and supportive. He must feel free to experiment, while at the same time he must be required to be accountable.

Recruitment, pretraining, and in-service training of staff must focus on developing trust and openness in the teaching staff. They must also be educated to understand how a changing society changes all kinds of relationships. It is not sufficient merely to be sensitive technicians; teachers must also be scholars. They must learn how to question the nature of interpersonal relations and to struggle for new and better answers.

Summary

One cost of a more complicated society is the complexity of intrapersonal relationships. Only as the school keeps up-to-date will it be possible for persons to truly enjoy life. Those attitudes which separate people from themselves and others must be confronted.

We have generated systems that destroy and overwhelm individuals. These are difficult problems, and we have run away from adequate solutions. Basically we have isolated and segregrated, stigmatized and ignored. The school has not been helpful; frequently the school only adds misery to those already unhappy.

People will be happy when they have freedom to explore and access to persons who can help them weigh alternatives. The school can become that place.

Everyone must be allowed personal renewal. People need advocates and advisors. They need statutes of limitations to protect privacy. They need limitations on statutes to guarantee freedom. They need staff to make leisure worth the time it takes. Without immediate attention to these concerns, gains made technologically will be more than offset by growing alienation.

CHAPTER IX

Making It All Fit

[This, the finale, is a synthesis of the four goals. I discuss the dilemma of coherence in education and particularly the difficulty of making education coherent over time. I suggest that *education for survival* in this time of ecological crisis is the umbrella under which all of education can be covered, and I conclude with a statement about the nature and organization of administration in schools which are directed to the achievement of competence in work, politics, culture, and personal well-being.]

Unless we can be surer than we now are that this generation has a future, nothing else matters. It is not good enough to give it tender, loving care, to supply it with breakfast foods, to buy it expensive educations. Those things don't mean anything unless this generation has a future. And we're not sure that it does.   —George Wald

All of this boils down to a few elementary facts. There is not enough food today. How much there will be tomorrow is open to debate. If the optimists are correct, today's level of misery will be perpetuated for two decades into the future. If the pessimists are correct, massive famines will occur soon, possibly in the early 1970's, certainly by the early 1980's. So far most of the evidence seems to be on the side of the pessimists, and we should plan on the assumption that they are correct. After all, some two billion people aren't being properly fed in 1968.   —Paul H. Ehrlich

God first invented idiots, that was for practice, then he made school boards.   —Mark Twain

Proceed to educational administration, a subject and a profession that imagination has touched even less than intellect.
    —Kenneth Eble

What is defeat? Nothing but education. Nothing but the first step to something better.   —Wendell Phillips

> Drugs nor isolation will cure this cancer.
> It is now or never, the hour of the knife.
> The break with the past, the major operation.
>   —C. Day Lewis

We need change—dramatic, wide-reaching total change. The poets write about that need. They communicate the feel, the sense of urgency. But their writings are not making it. The Chrysler Company and its Plymouth automobile *are* "making it." The poet describes, he doesn't prescribe. The poet is an outsider looking in and is repulsed by what he sees. But his detachment is his undoing. He writes laments for the half-living and then is driven to a half-life himself.

The educators who are poets compartmentalize themselves. The poet that is in them is kept aloof from the unpleasantries of administrative affairs.

The educators who predominate are not poets. They pride themselves on that. They are beneath such foolish sentimentality, and because in this world of reality where up is down—they flourish and they thrive. How do we combine a poet's sensitivity with a scientist's analytic ability and penchant for data and give that combination the stick-to-it-ivity and the persuasiveness for political effectiveness? The answer is the educated man I have been writing about. The person with these attributes has attained all four goals. How all four are tied together into one comprehensive whole is the concern of this final chapter.

Education—A Matter of Balance and Coherence

Assigning different periods for work preparation, citizen preparation, cultural development, and interpersonal growth would be as inappropriate as are the present systems of separate classes for art, music, history, language, algebra, etc. Education does not lend itself to that separation. Therefore it is impossible to provide a recipe or a blueprint. To the contrary, what is needed are activities which can be defended as appropriate to educational goals. The teacher as team leader has the responsibility for insuring balance and continuity. Everything done must be reconciled with immediate and long-range concerns. The student must perceive how everything that happens hangs together. If he is unable to appreciate the relationship, then his concern must be handled through the negotiation process described previously.

The school, to be a centripetal force in our coming-apart society, must: (1) provide a continuity for the present disconnected experiences, and (2) at the same time, provide continuity for future

existences. These two distinct responsibilities are not easily reconciled. Some educators are only future-oriented, while others are
concerned only with the student's present existence. Unless both
kinds of continuity are established there can be *no* worthwhile education.

There are many ways imaginative teachers can bring a unity
into education. Most of the classification used in education is arbitrary. Concepts offered in one place or time could just as readily
be presented elsewhere. Using this book as illustration, the following things could be changed without ruining the sense of the message:

The implicit bias in intelligence assessment which was presented as a problem of career choice could just as easily have been
discussed in the chapter on culture-carrying competence.

The attributes of teaching within a democratic context, which
were included in the chapter on Responsible Authority, are equally
applicable to *any* other aspect of education.

Whitehead's insight into the rhythm of education is a concept
that is as pertinent to the development of interpersonal competence
as it is to the learning of language, where it was offered.

The developing of a constituency of support, which was expli-
cated under sex education, could have been subsumed under education for career choice.

The particular staging and phasing of any educational activity
would have to accommodate the style and talents of the staff, as
altered through negotiation with the student and further amended by
pressures from other interested parties. This, of course, is what happens now, but because there is no clearly defined goal the process
breaks down totally in the exchange. Issues are not decided on educational merit but purely on the ability to wield power. However,
if the goals are clearly articulated and if all controversy is referred
back to the goals, then many widely different paths may be taken
without any distortion of the educational process. The process must
be examined periodically to determine whether all parties are satisfied that progress is being made, and here there should be great
precaution taken against the very likely possibility that *all* the participants have deluded themselves by their enthusiasm. Every effective teacher *must* believe that he is accomplishing something
worthwhile. But unfortunately, merely believing that something
good is happening does not make it so. The self-delusion of edu-

cators, which later becomes educational policy, stands as one of the great barriers to reformation.

Making Today Continuous with Tomorrow

The balancing of today's educational activity with preparation for tomorrow's world is exceedingly difficult; at best we must rely on tenuous prediction. The lack of certainty is used by educators to avoid responsibility entirely—thus missing one of the important lessons that comes from the study of history. Because I believe that tomorrow is what we, who live today, will make it, I take a dim view of educational programs that are only "now" oriented. George Dennison describes a school concerned only with the problems of today in his book *The Lives of Children*. The book is a description, a defense, and a treatise of an experimental school, and, because many forward-looking educators are taken with the ideas advanced in the book, I would like to critically review it in the context of all that has preceded and use the criticism as part of a summary. George Dennison believes "That the primary concern of a primary school is not education in a narrow sense, and still less preparation for later life, but the present lives of children—a point made repeatedly by John Dewey, and very poorly understood by many of his followers." [1]

Lives of Children is an account of the First Street School in Manhattan. The book is both a log of school activities and a discussion of educational philosophy. The school is the "mini school" that Paul Goodman advocates. In the year it existed it served 23 children, almost all poor, but otherwise diversified by race, ethnicity, and sex. The children ranged in age from 6 to 14. The school was staffed by three full-time teachers (all women) and one part-time teacher-director (a male). A philosophy of "freedom" undergirded all school activity. Drawing from A. S. Neill, Leo Tolstoy, and John Dewey, the director interpreted freedom as: (1) "Some true organic bond" that exists "between children's wishes and their actual needs"; and (2) By acceding to most of their wishes, children are encouraged into responsible decision-making (page 21).

---

[1] George Dennison, *The Lives of Children,* Random House, New York, 1969, p. 190.

The director (who is also the author of the book) is pleased with the results of the First Street School: "We were obviously doing something right and I would like to hazard a few guesses at what it might have been. All instruction was individual and that was obviously a factor. The improvement I am speaking of, however, was not simply a matter of learning but radical changes in character" (page 96).

The gains are attributed to the "now" orientation of the school, the elimination of conventional routine (especially those that give to the school a military or prison appearance), and the abolition of traditional administration. The author is adamant on this last point: "The present quagmire of public education is entirely the result of unworkable centralization and the lust for control that permeates every bureaucratic institution" (page 9).

I just wish that Dennison was correct. But I don't believe that the staff of the First Street School did many things right. I believe that they were less culpable than the staff in an ordinary public school. And while there is some solace in not "messing over" children to the same extent that occurs in regular school, that just isn't enough. Temporary relief from terror is not an acceptable goal of education. And that, I'm afraid, is all that the First Street School accomplished. At the end of the story there was no First Street School and children and staff had gone their different ways and the world, it was the old world yet. Dennison absolves himself of any long-range responsibilities: "Teachers have asked us what 'long range effects' we produced. People who have worked among the poor do not ask this question" (page 269).

Says who? That's one of the first questions I ask and that's why I have never been satisfied with demonstrations and pilot projects I have directed. None has ever produced the "long-range effect" sought. They did not eliminate, or markedly reduce, poverty, racism, neglect, etc. I now believe that unless a project is seen as part of a total strategy it is dubious if it has *any* value whatsoever. To me the distinction between a beachhead and a typical educational project is the commitment to long-range effects.

The First Street School differed from most elementary schools. It was loose and natural, there was much improvisation interspersed with conventional lessons, particularly in reading. A great deal of the activity was student-initiated. The staff was supportive. The school was a haven. Children had the opportunity to help others.

It was a school of tours, confrontations, games, melees, and honest and warm tender groping for each other. It was a school where savage hatred and hostility were expressed. It was a school without restrictions on language. It was a school of pouting and horseplay. It was a physical school. Students and staff hit and fondled each other. It was a school with minimal inhibitions.

Dennison ticks off the school's strong points. Children who heretofore hated school came willingly to First Street. Children who had failed to score at all on standardized achievement tests scored higher than their grade level. Students who had been terrified of other children learned to play happily. Children learned to handle their hostility. A Puerto Rican boy and a black boy whose racial hatred in the beginning erupted into violence (which could easily have escalated into mayhem) became close friends by the end of the first year. I was moved by the description. However, I've seen it and heard it all before. It is the story that Maxwell Jones relates in his therapeutic community.[2] Fritz Redl and David Wineman have done much the same thing with very aggressive youngsters.[3] I haven't been impressed by the evidence of the past. I am not excited by its rediscovery now. The approach is deficient in its understanding of the nature of man and in its interpretation of the lasting impacts of oppression. In Chapter VIII, I argued that theory which looked clinically at victims of poverty, racism, bureaucratic intransigence, an nonredemptiveness was obsolete. I'm afraid that George Dennison operates with such a theory. He continually interprets the behavior of his students with a clinical perspective. His school sets out to repair the accumulated ravages of a hostile environment. Over and over again Dennison characterizes the students as "unstable," "disordered," "ignorant," "defeated," and "impoverished in sensory experience." He views adjustment to the streets as essentially pathological. The one truly indigenous staff member, a Puerto Rican youth, had to be let go because he had been ruined by his environment:

> He's a good athlete and is lively and outgoing, but his only models are the public-school authorities and the waddling cops of the PAL who can't even pick their noses except with aggressive and threatening gestures. In short, he's too much a product of the

---

[2] Maxwell Jones, *The Therapeutic Community*, Basic Books, New York, 1953.

[3] Fritz Redl and David Wineman, *Children Who Hate*, Free Press, New York, 1951.

streets, too prone to push the boys around and be censorious in a
narrow and terribly authoritarian way.[4]

There is distortion and nonredemptiveness in a program which
postulates accumulated deficits from poverty existences. I do not
romanticize squalor, inequity, overcrowdedness, unemployment,
unbearable summer heat and winter cold. They take their toll. They
leave their scars. But it is not all negative. Much that is vital and
valuable is learned in the struggle for survival. When only the
pathological is emphasized the nonpoor are granted an exalted
status that inevitably leads to their missionary stance toward the
"unfortunate." Even when poverty *causes* a pathological response
the disability may be neither accumulative nor chronic. That is,
when the pressure is removed the problem ceases. I believe that
very many of the symptoms associated with poverty will disappear
—if not immediately—very quickly, if poverty is eliminated. Black
feelings against whites are much less the result of the years of accumulated bigotry and much more due to the pervasiveness of current injustices. The black is angry because he is denied his rights—
today! He is angry because he has a worse education, poorer health
services, a lousier job, a more dilapidated house, less access to
leisure, and more humiliation—*now*—than his white counterpart.
Eliminate the injustices and the hate will also be largely eliminated.
Dennison implies both chronicity and accumulation of effect in the
students. Therefore he is able to explain away continued maladap-
tive behaviors. He never questions whether his school provided a
true environment for healthy learning—and that some children
could not respond to it at all and some others partially—or whether
the lack of total response was because some of the inequalities of a
racist society were incorporated in his school. From my own experiences I believe that the expectation of disability led to a perception of disability which, in turn, led to lowered intellectual challenge
and a kind of colonialism in the school that I feel is ultimately
defeating.

The school was to a large extent nonintellectual. One form of
nonintellectuality was in the assessment of teaching qualities. Dennison agrees with Paul Goodman that adults who are literate and
well-intentioned possess all the knowledge necessary for the educa-

---

[4] Dennison, *op. cit.*, p. 232.

tion of small children, and if they have to be trained at all, they should be trained in group therapy, because those skills are the only ones that are useful. I will not defend teacher preparation (as presently constituted). I agree that any literate adult would not be any worse in the classroom than the ordinary teacher. But that misses the point. We don't need a new or different category of inadequate teachers. We do need well-trained teachers who themselves know a lot about subject material and the unique pressures placed on different children. Some of this knowledge might come naturally, and, if so, it should be recognized and credited. But most persons need help. They need education and they also need training. (Review again Chapter III.) Even the best of us has glaring faults that need correcting. The staff of the First Street School had many unique and desirable talents. They also had some shortcomings. For example, they could not incorporate people with different attributes (a young street-educated Puerto Rican boy) into their staff. They didn't even have a plan for helping him. All they had was a negative set and a vague hope: "But we must give him a chance to get the hang of our style" (page 232), and after a bit they fired him. The dismissal was a strange contradiction because Dennison had earlier criticized school systems for not developing indigenous leadership in the school.

> I believe, too, that a Puerto Rican, at home in both English and Spanish, and familiar with both cultures, could have helped José far more than I. This is so obvious, and there are so many mixed up Puerto Rican children in the city schools—whose average of intelligence, according to my impressions, is remarkably high—that one can wonder why this large-scale training and recruitment of Spanish-speaking teachers has never taken place (page 180).

Large-scale training doesn't take place for precisely the same reasons Dennison didn't engage in small-scale training. The Puerto Rican isn't considered because whoever does the selecting rejects him because of his limitations. (Being "too much a product of the streets" is one such ascribed limitation.)

Dennison is nonintellectual in his approach to research in education. He mercilessly castigates Jerome Bruner because of his "mere intellectualization" (pages 249–256) and his "absorption" in "bureaucratic research." It is true that educational research is barren and not only unproductive but often downright silly. It is not an overstatement to describe educational research as pompous answers to trivial questions. But Dennison's rejection of research leads him to an unquestioning attitude toward his own work. And that is every bit as fatal as retreat into "scientism." It is also a manifestation of an identical malady, a disease of the mind that leads to sloppiness, imprecision, aimlessness, and misplaced self-satisfaction. Dennison is convinced that his First Street School was on the right track. He would have us emulate his efforts—at least as a first step. He thinks it quite simple. All that is needed is a healing environment in which are placed teachers who are well-intentioned, mature adults. But what kind of an environment heals? "Precisely the ordinary one of children at play among themselves" (page 212).

In the end Dennison sounds just like those hawkers of educational wares he despises. And, like them, he hasn't proved the worth of his product. We only have his word for its value. We don't know what would have happened to the children if First Street had not been available to them. I suspect that creating a natural healing environment is not as simple as he makes it sound. But go beyond that—assume that we could duplicate the school and assume further that the results attained at First Street are desirable, it is still not likely that, if attempted again or even if maintained in operation, the same good things would happen. There is such a thing as the "Hawthorne Effect." And this effect is a considerable factor in educational innovation. Almost always the good results of an experiment evaporate over a time or when atttempted again. That is one of the reasons educational innovation always works but education never changes. The experiment is done under optimum conditions never again repeated. Excitement and spirit accompany something novel. The experiment has a staff that is markedly different from run-of-the-mill teachers. The students feel the importance of the experiment and respond to it. The students are not representative of the target population. All of these factors may explain First Street's apparent success. Dennison allows that *his* enthusiasm was waning. He turned down an opportunity to go with staff and students on a summer trip. "They want me to go along, but I don't think I will. I've had my fill of children for a while." (Page 245) There was uniqueness in First Street; the staff very clearly had talents far beyond most mature and literate adults. And even the children may not have been typical school "rejects." The typical school "reject" might have resisted recruitment. There is a popular notion that once schools are subjected to careful evaluation the good in them is lost. Dennison, I fear, believes that, and therfore he is able— without a single conscience pang—to avoid research altogether and get in gratuitous cracks against researchers at the same time.

Dennison's most glaring fault is his lack of concern for intellectual activities in the curriculum of the First Street School. He doesn't believe that he has a responsibility to challenge the children. Children graduating from such a school would be educated for the stupidities Jules Henry says students cannot avoid in regular school. They would be stupid about "Labor," "Economics," "Communism," and "War." They would know something about "Negroes" and "Poverty," but the information might not be useful. If the goals presented here are used as standards, the First Street School comes up short in many areas.

The First Street School falls down completely in the matter of career choice. In many ways the school was overwhelmed by its surrounding poverty. Although priding itself on its reality orientation it was totally unreal about work. Neither the qualifications for existing work choices nor for an ideal work world were ever discussed. As a consequence of this oversight, 13- and 14-year-old youths were pointed to lifelong deprivation and economic isolation.

The First Street School was far more adequate in preparing students for democratic citizenship. The school was based on respect for students' rights, although even here there is not the consolidation of learning that I would like. Using Whitehead's notion of rhythm in education, First Street generated the "romance" of student rights but was remiss in the "precision" and "generalization" phases. The student at First Street did engage in important judicial, legislative, and executive decision-making although again, the means used were informal and primitive and thus were not transferable to out-of-school political systems. In fact, the obvious distaste of the staff for the dirty, corrupted world of American politics, particularly big-city urban politics, communicated to the students a defeatism and cynicism that they just could not afford. The staff of the school appeared to function as responsible authorities. They did appreciate the differences in the children, were accountable to them and their families, negotiated program changes, recognized the inevitability of conflict, and tied rules to legitimate

ends. In fact, the relationship of staff to students is the most com-
mendable feature of the school, but this is not surprising, since the
author insists that this relationship is the *only* important factor in
the education of the child.

In culture-carrying, the First Street School was obviously better than most inner-city urban schools. The student was not reviled
as an uneducable stupe—but he was not challenged either. It is
difficult to determine what happened intellectually in the school,
since those activities were never described and only through sketchy
allusions was the reader given any clues at all. This can be interpreted (I think validly) that "cultural activities" were not very important at First Street. But that is not the total picture, because the
school obviously benefited from the staff's natural propensities.
They were a thinking group. Indirectly the importance of thought
was communicated to students through informal discussions and
other interactions. The formal structure, particularly the teaching
of reading to those who were far behind, was pedestrian and the
results were equally unspectacular. José, the Puerto Rican youth
with a reading problem, never was able to gain any true sense of
competence in reading, nor was he ever able to see himself as belonging to a literate group, and he could not find many arenas
where his limited skills could be put to use. The individualized
nature of instruction, one of the school's most prized procedures,
may have contributed to the problem. The lack of any extensive integrated group *intellectual* project shut José out from any opportunity to see himself as a reader. He was either confined to remedial
study or was not participating. Neither alternate is acceptable, but
I believe those are the only choices which schools run according to
the First Street philosophy offer.

First Street struggled hard to assist students to become inter-
and intrapersonally competent. The stupid rigidities which keep
students from knowing each other in a typical school were eliminated. But the lack of intellectuality of the school hampered true
personality growth. The efforts of students to overcome racial
prejudices, for example, is certain to be futile if the work world demands that for survival those in the under classes must compete
against each other. Willard, the black, and José, the Puerto Rican,
at the end of the school year attain an arm-over-each-other's-
shoulder friendship after a violent and seemingly irreconcilable enmity at the beginning, but I fear that their friendship is doomed to

be short-lived. Back on the streets, going their separate ways, José and Willard, given the limited understanding they have about the relationship of credentialism and economics to racism, are certain to be caught in pressures that will destroy any good feeling they have for each other. They are owed something more than that! A good school would have helped them analyze who indeed each one of them was and why external forces shaped relationships and what was necessary for true and lasting friendships.

First Street lacked an integrating experience. It denied students knowledge about the very real threat of extinction. The student didn't know that man was burying himself in his garbage (even in the midst of a garbage strike, that fact could not be known). First Street students were not *informed* that population growth, plus consumption of resources, plus pollution, were bringing mankind to an imminent catastrophe and that population, consumption, and pollution must be studied, understood, and controlled if man is to survive.

Ecology—The Integrating Course of Study

It is possible to achieve education that is balanced, internally and externally, *if*, and only if, the central theme of study is man's survival. The study of ecology—the relationship between living organisms and the environment—must become education's binder. The study of ecology is the umbrella under which an intelligent review of work, politics, culture, and personal well-being becomes a coherent possibility. By relating all of education to the salient issue of man's survival, the chronic school plagues of dreariness, fragmentation, irrelevance, and humiliation of students can be bypassed or overcome.

The study of ecology provides a solid basis for supporting quality education for all. Education for everybody has a limited appeal to the "middle American" because the request has an altruistic ring to it. In effect, those with means are asked to pay for an education for those less fortunate than themselves. They, however, have been educated to believe that those for whom they are asked to sacrifice are unworthy, shiftless, and incapable of learning. Altruistic appeals are losers: Apart from some small tax-deductible donations, nothing much comes from them. But the ecological crisis changes all that. Now the appeal for universal education is based on self-interest—and that's a winner! The average well-situated citizen has no alternative. He *must* support quality education for all because *his* survival depends upon *everyone* having the competence to deal with the forces that threaten human existence.

In approaching the study of ecology, children from their very initiation into school must be told the truth about the crisis. The basic equation of survival as a function of population limitation, consumption of resources limitation, and pollution abatement must be introduced early in a student's education career. This formula:

$$S = f\left(\frac{I}{\text{pop.}} + \frac{I}{\text{consump.}} + \frac{I}{\text{pollut.}}\right)$$

must be encountered and dealt with in greater sophistication through a lifelong educational process.

From the very beginning students must be provided the following about population growth:

The 3½ billion people now overcrowding the earth will increase to over 7 billion within 40 years.

The *rate* of population growth is increasing rapidly.

Population growth is more rapid in so-called underdeveloped countries than it is in technologically advanced countries.

The very young must be told the following about consumption of resources:

The United States, with less than 6% of the world's population, uses at least 50% of the world's resources exclusive of food.

Every year there is an increase in per capita expenditure of air, water, food, and land.

Much of the per capita increase in consumption of resources is for manufacture of products which are not necessary for man's survival or even for his comfort.

Even a toddler must be aware that:

Air resources are being destroyed by automobile exhaust and other pollutants that are the result of industrial, agricultural, and irresponsible individual acts.

Water resources are being devastated by detergents, inorganic fertilizers, pesticides, nuclear-powered reactors, and industrial waste.

Space (particularly arable land) is being covered with concrete and further despoiled by litter from solid waste materials.

Students must reckon with Paul Ehrlich's three possibilities for the immediate future—two of which lead to nuclear war, the third "happy" solution being a callous participation in programs (famines, wars, and diseases) that will lead to a reduction of the world's population to 1½ billion by the year 2100 through systematic elimination of Asians, Africans, and Latin Americans.[5]

Students at every age must accept Ehrlich's challenge and try to create alternative scenarios and defend them with logic and evidence. They must devise the tactics and strategies to implement their solutions to the environmental crisis.

At every level of school the student must grapple with:

The impact that pesticides have had on bird life, livestock, and water resources—and come up with alternatives to their current use.

The devastation that hard detergents have had on water supply, and again propose solutions.

The consequences of a dam on the Nile River to the fish population of the Mediterranean.

The impact of gasoline combustion engines on air— and what do we do about that?

The problem of storing waste from nuclear-powered electrical plants, and compare that difficulty with the problems that crop up where other efforts to generate electricity are used, and discuss alternatives to all of that.

The student has to generate plans to limit population, consumption of resources, and pollution and defend the feasibility of those plans.

And if that weren't enough he must go beyond deliberating about the threat to man's survival. He must deal with the social problems that are directly related to the ecological crisis. The student must become aware of a "social ecology," the relationship that man has with man. He must generate solutions to war! Each student must be asked to derive a theory of peace in which he stipulates the necessary conditions for a world without war, the means by which this end can be attained and he must, in that light, assess the activity of his own and other countries as peace-preserving nations.

---

[5] Paul Ehrlich, *The Population Bomb,* Ballantine Books, New York, 1968, pp. 72–80.

Race antagonisms! The student must formulate the ideal race relationship—defend that ideal in open debate and devise a plan to achieve the goal.

In much the same way the student must think through problems of sexual relationships, class antagonism, generational conflicts, and every other form of human interaction that historically has been perverted and leads to exploitation and manipulation.

Periodically students should be asked to demonstrate what has been learned. One way the student can do this is to present a plan (in some rare instances this could be a solitary effort, but almost always a team venture would be preferable) for a model community. The plan should be complete. It should include the physical as well as the social dimensions of life. The plan must be defensible ecologically. The buildings and transportation systems must respect nature's precious resources. The social, cultural, work, and political projections must protect against the usual and persistent inhumanities that men practice on other men. This plan should be defended before adult experts—architects, economists, psychologists, and the like—and before peers and more advanced students. The exchange between the student and his diverse mentors should be open, honest, and without colonial subterfuge. If pursued this could be the most valuable education the student experiences.

Ecology and the Goals of Education

Many ecologists have difficulty relating their concerns to school activities. The teaching of ecology is not immune to the distortions presented in this text. And in addition there is the particular problem of failing to go beyond the description of impending doom. The implications of the ecological crisis to the world of work, politics, culture, and personal well-being have not been sufficiently thought through and thus discussion of the environment often is as artificial and ritualistic as any other matter deliberated in school.

Ecology and Preparation for the World of Work

The way work is organized in our society contributes enormously to ecological imbalance. Over the years, work and nature have become increasingly incompatible. The devotion to the notion that continued economic growth is absolutely necessary has further alienated work from a livable environment. Such a notion has justified the plundering of the earth and the destruction of its sensitive ecosystems. In fact, destruction and progress have become synonymous terms. Man's work requires him to ravage our resources. He plunders the earth of its water, air, iron, oil, rubber, and soil—and after he has done that to a fare-thee-well, leaving everything with unhealable scars, making his world ugly and barren, he moves on to devastate neighboring areas. We call that civilization and brag about it. Whole nations have been wiped out solely because they hadn't exploited the land to the fullest extent possible.

Sad as that is, it isn't the half of it. Even more tragic is that the worker who plunders is employed in the main to make things that are not necessary for life. The tobacco he grows, cures, manufactures into cigarettes, warehouses, transports, and sells is very likely hazardous to health. The electrically powered toothbrush or shoe-shine kit he builds require a similar prodigal use of manpower and unnecessarily drain electrical energy. Those big, garish automobiles he builds and foists upon us use far more oil, iron, rubber, and glass than is necessary for convenient travel. And even those new suits and dresses he makes for us aren't necessary, since last year's purchases are still serviceable.

Through the years work has been its own justification. Only a few art and literary types carped about the philistinism inherent in the organization of work. But since their mutterings were heard only in arcane gatherings, they bothered nobody and nobody bothered them.

The Marxists were far more public in their complaints about work; they bothered and were bothered. But their concern was almost exclusively the exploitation of the worker by capitalism. At least implicitly, Marxists believed that progress was dependent on continued economic development which, in turn, required an ever-increasing depletion of the earth's resources. Other than a condemnation of the exploitive nature of private ownership the Marxists have had little to criticize about a "thing-oriented" society. They have a faith that, once profit is removed from enterprise, people will no longer desire goods they do not need. There is little evidence that such faith is warranted. Some ideologies go even farther and insist that the concern about the environment is a capitalist ploy. They argue that there is no real overpopulation problem—it is an artificial conception created by bourgeois scientists to divert the proletariat from his true revolutionary responsibility.

The technologists have also obfuscated what work must be in an ecologically balanced society. Among those most readily taken in were the educators. Not too long ago *the* going myth was that work was soon to be obsolete. Machines would do all those things people through the years were forced to do. Robert Theobald was perhaps the most articulate spokesman for the new utopia. Completely ignored was the impact that automation would have on the earth's resources. Almost everyone eagerly sought that morrow when electronic wizardry would bring surcease of sorrow and bless each and every one of us. No one calculated the expense—the cost in iron, concrete, and water, and the destruction of the environment that would accompany the increased use of power (no matter what means would be used to generate it), and so it came to be that technology became our Frankenstein monster and it, probably more than anything, has led to such rapid increase in per capita consumption of resources. Two overriding considerations must govern all references to work in school. We must stress:

1) All work must be justified. The goods and services produced must be vital for human survival or comfort, and;

2) All work must be respectful of nature's resources. The only economic system that can be applied is that which uses resources as the measure of value.

No longer can a counselor or a vocational educator defend his recommendations by saying that that's what the employers "outside" request.

Students must deliberate various approaches to work. One clear implication is that our survival as a nation and as a world depends more and more on supplanting a products-producing economy with a service-producing economy. Thus, the New Careers notion presented in Chapter III as a means of offsetting poverty and racism and at the same time generating more competent staff for health, education, and welfare, takes on an even greater significance when it is reviewed in the context of the environmental crisis.

Given the credential society, those most negatively affected by the worsening situation are forced to be its most ardent supporters. The workers in the mills, the minorities locked out of the construction trades, the mothers receiving aid for dependent children are compelled into a support of a goods-producing society. They react against their own interests because they are denied eligibility for credentials and see only traditional work as a means of escape from poverty and because they believe that the wealth of nations is calculated in the number and elegance of the things its citizens own. They have not only been educated to believe this, they have never encountered any opposing thought. They also believe that only the elite could perform as doctors, lawyers, scientists, or professors. The following anecdote illustrates how effectively people have been educated to pursue a path that can lead only to their own doom:

> I decided one day to escape from the "effete corps of intellectual snobs" (my colleagues at the university) and lunch with a group of construction workers who were in the process of erecting a new law school. We got into a discussion about a proposed nuclear-powered electrical plant and I took the position that such a development was not in the interest of the people of Oregon. They, to a man, disagreed with me.
>
> "We can't stop progress," one said. "We need a nuclear plant because of the construction jobs it offers" and because "the new industries it attracts will bring even more jobs," said another.
>
> There were many other comments, most of which reflected upon my questionable sanity or my alleged sexual propensities, but all contained this essential element—if there was no further development of electrical power, there would be no work for them.
>
> I suggested that instead of their thinking of themselves as lifelong construction workers devoted to building law schools that others were educated in, why didn't they think of themselves as lawyers. I then introduced to them the notion of New Careers in law. I pointed out that it wasn't such a radical departure from history. Abraham Lincoln didn't go to law school to become a lawyer—he was able to attain that status by first being apprenticed as a law clerk and then he received his education about law. Except for some gratuitous and erroneous cracks about Lincoln's attitudes toward blacks—they couldn't respond. They had been so totally educated to believe that they were good for only certain tasks that contrary suggestion dumbfounded them. I am convinced that only when offered a real opportunity in service activities will the notion of a service-oriented society have any credibility to them or any others who share their life style.

Students must spend time in school designing ideal work situations, allocating the functions and assignments, calculating the costs, ascertaining how many persons will be employed by devising career ladders and designating the procedures that will be used for training.

Work, as we now know it, must be adjusted ecologically. Such a change, while significant and earthshaking, is not nearly sufficient. There is a companion responsibility. The planning for an ecologically balanced society makes new demands upon manpower. Population limitation is dependent upon adequate sex education, repeal of laws that prohibit abortions, universal distribution of birth-control devices, and provisions to impoverished populations and those victimized by racism opportunities for equal participation in our society. Each of these antidotes to overpopulation has an employment component. There is a need for staff to teach about sex, staff to provide safe and inexpensive abortions, staff to assist women *and* men in appropriate use of birth-control devices, and staff to overcome racism and poverty. Again, the student must be drawn into the planning phase and he must be prepared to work in these vital areas.

Ecology and Preparation for Democratic Citizenship

Man's survival is a political problem. Every variable in the equation requires mobilization of a constituency and legislative, judicial, and executive decision-making. Population limitation, reduction of consumption of resources, and pollution abatement are influenced at every level of political activity. For each there must be enactment of laws, development of regulatory authorities, and appropriation of funds.

Ecologists as a group have been distressingly naive about politics. Often they have been deceived by the most unscrupulous self-seeking officeholder or office seeker. Ecologists frequently are oblivious to the fact that a politician mentioning environment or condemning pollution does not commit himself to a program for change. The same politician, without pausing for breath, will appoint the primary polluters to an environmental control board or direct funds required to overcome pollution to a less vital military project and never think twice about it. Ecologists tend to be slow movers, rousing only after considerable erosion of the environment has taken place. They don't assign politics a very high priority in their personal commitments. They are neither prepared to exercise political leadership themselves and announce for office nor are they willing to back wholeheartedly people with talent and a dedication to the environment.

Of late, ecologists have become political at least to this extent. They have sounded a clarion call. But it is easy for their impact to be muted. Ecologists lack organization. It is quite common, in any ecological controversy, to find pitted against each other two equally eminent scientists: Agronomists debate the value of DDT; gynecologists, birth-control pills; physicists, nuclear-powered electrical plants; and botanists, sustained-yield timber supply programs. The debate is not only between scientists, it goes on *within* the scientists. Sometimes it is virtually impossible for the ecologist working for the government to be sure in his own mind whether he is a dupe—the window dressing for an administration that allows him to do his own insignificant thing while everyone else is involved in ransacking the earth for themselves and their friends, or whether he is the wave of the future establishing the base from which will emerge the dominant theme and features of the administration. Tortured by his doubts he cannot find solace from friends or relatives, who aren't attending because they are so busy stuffing their pockets; or from his wife, who felt from the beginning that he had sold out his integrity for an opportunity to rub shoulders with big-time operators. Worse, he knows that he can't make a decision. He has no place to go—he is on leave for a year. He has sublet his house. The children are in school. And even if he could extricate himself from all of that, there would be the questions and the need to explain that he quit and that he wasn't fired for incompetence or disloyalty. But if he did take a stand, could he ever again get a grant to do his research?

The scientist's role in government should be weighed carefully in school. In a world that depends for its survival on the availability of expert advice, the scholar must assume ever more importance in those high councils. What should be the extent of his decision-making? How should he be chosen? What protection should he be given from officials or opportunistic elected leaders? At what point does his influence step over the line and become oppressive? How can the public detect the real intellectual from the counterfeit? How can he overcome the deep-seated anti-intellectualism which is reflected in public distrust of eminent scholars? Students must go at these questions. They must analyze current situations, generate simulated experiences, develop models that use scientists in a variety of ways in government. These activities should, as has been suggested for everything else, be developmental. After a dozen school years the student should have advanced to a point that he could evaluate the scientist's role and be prepared to function in the lower rungs of such a career ladder.

The school must not only generate the talents and appropriate models, it must also generate public understanding. There can be no denying that the average, ordinary, run-of-the-mill American citizen holds the fate of the world in his hands. Those 70 million-plus American voters who will go to the polls in the next major election are likely to make it or break it for everybody. What does education do to help them choose the lady not the tiger? What school activities must be generated to prepare them for the choice that perhaps could end all other choices? What leadership can we expect from ecologists?

Science and politics are not new to each other. Today's crisis may be more total, and disaster more imminent, but the scientist as molder of public opinion goes back a long way—and a glance at that history isn't reassuring. In fact, if the past is any guide to the future, the prospects are downright grisly. Scientists as a group have had tough sledding in politics. The pope crushed Galileo. Darwin couldn't hold up in Dayton, Tennessee, and he is having troubles even today in California. Sigmund Freud, for all his puritanical attitudes, was severely battered for his prurience. Even gentle Albert Einstein didn't escape unscathed. Pasteur made handwashing in hospitals a subversive activity. The tragedy is that political decisions aren't determined on the basis of scientific evidence. Political decisions are determined by mobilization of opinion through an active constituency. The best scientific argument can be a political disaster. Sure, truth wins out—in time. Galileo *was* vindicated, but first he had to pay for his revolutionary advocacy of the Copernican theory of the solar system. And the question must be raised, can we today afford to lose first and win later? Do we have the time? Many of our most concerned minds say no. What, then, can we learn from prior activities that can help us now? Is there any way that political decision-making can be more influenced by knowledge, and can this be done quickly? These are questions that need immediate answers and further study. Students had better be doing both.

Ecologists have not been much assistance in plotting the political isomorph for a livable world. They haven't mocked up the model. They haven't priced out the costs to produce zero population growth, zero consumption growth, and the elimination of pollution. They haven't devised a public-education program. They haven't postulated the attributes required for executive, legislative, and judicial leadership in an ecologically balanced world. They haven't even assured the feasibility of proposed current solutions.

Education for political competence on the matter of man's survival must get down to some very fundamental considerations—wealth and power. There are those very high up in government who believe that the environment can be saved without any fundamental change in distribution of wealth and power. They hold out the hope that survival doesn't even require any major shift in priorities. They believe that some repairs are needed—that's all. A $2-billion-a-year program can clean up the waterways. Air pollution can be solved by passing the costs on to the consumer. Solid-waste pollution can be eliminated by requiring deposits on bottles and cans. Such proposals are patently absurd. The environment, even more than the school that is a part of it, is beyond repair. At the very least, wholesale reformation must take place. There must be a total reordering of priorities. Given the urgency of the situation, a $20 billion military budget is probably more than we can afford. (And what great threat is there in a foreign power taking over the world if there is no world to take over?) There can be no hope for the world if the vast majority are denied any opportunity to influence the decisions that affect their lives. We face again the alternatives: reform or revolution. With revolution the wealthy would be removed from power and their possessions confiscated. I see no immediate hope for, or value in, revolution. I am for reform. Reform would *require* drastic overhauling of the tax structure of the society. The rich would have to shoulder the primary burden of the cost involved in survival. Rather than the consumer the persons least able to pay for pollution control—those with the strangle hold on the economy, the extremely wealthy producer—must take on that responsibility. Every tax loophole, subsidy exemption, and special-privilege allowance must be reexamined in the context of man's threatened tenure on earth. Every *penny* of governmental money not allocated for vital life-stuff production, reduction in consumption of resources, population limitation, preservation of air, water, and soil must be rerouted to where it is needed. Discussion

of the alternatives of repair, revolution, and reform and what each
means in distribution of wealth and power and the establishment
of priorities must be the stuff that school curriculums are made of.

The politics of ecology are extremely complex. True, there are
some relatively simple problems. Effective regulatory legislation
with substantial staffing of executive authority can go a long way to
cut down pollution. But population and consumption control are
much more difficult to achieve than pollution abatement. We need
much more than laws—the government must also generate a climate of hope. The bulk of the world's population is mired down in
such ecological imbalance that for the perspective of those who
have been "down so long" there is no possibility of going up. One
political dilemma in the survival business is that ecological balance
in the future is at least partially a function of concentrated efforts
to achieve ecological balance today. The economically underdeveloped countries with the least capacity to produce food now have the
fastest-growing populations. The people now starving cannot be expected to exhibit concern over future overpopulation when they
have no future. There is no immediate political solution to ecological imbalance (apart from mass annihilation that destroys people
but leaves plant life unimpaired. Perhaps that is why some of our
leaders insist that such horrors as nerve gas continue to be manufactured and stored in the United States). The wherewithal to feed,
clothe, and house all of the world's 3½ billion people just doesn't
exist. But in the absence of the current resources, there must be
perceptible commitment. In place of indifference to starvation
there must be a world-wide crusade to stimulate food production
(without destruction of air and water resources). Political leadership must be credible. Those who are now without hope must see
about them evidence that every possible effort is being made to
bring the world back into ecological kilter. The leadership of the
United States is incredibly uncredible. Neither Richard Nixon nor
Spiro Agnew can present themselves as leaders concerned about
the plight of the poor or the minorities within the United States—
let alone the world. There can be no effective appeal to the blacks
in the United States to join with the whites in a common cause of
zero population growth when there is no visible effort to offer the
blacks a fair share of employment, education, health, and housing.
Expect most blacks to be unenthusiastic or apathetic to such appeals. Expect some blacks to be extremely hostile, believing the

call to be a form of "genocide." Remember that the black is continually reminded that a major reason he is without political power is that he is an isolated minority and that his only political hope rests in his outbreeding the whites. Don't go to other victims of racism with your plea for smaller families and expect much support. The Mexican American in the field doesn't want to produce fewer children. He needs every one he has to eke out his meager existence in the fields, particularly since he still is not covered by minimum-wage law, industrial accident compensation, or health statutes. The political problem of population is entwined with the age-old concerns of racism and poverty, and it is dubious if any progress can be made with the former crisis unless simultaneously there is renewed activity against those latter chronic social maladies. Here we run into an interesting phenomenon. The concern for the environment has driven out of the public eye the wars against poverty and racism. There are hardly any remnants left of the civil-rights struggles of the early 60's, and even less of value is left from the war against poverty.

Fadism should occupy considerable attention in classroom discussions of the politics of survival. Disheartenment has been the all too frequent legacy of the altruistic youngster in his political encounters. What, if anything can be done to mitigate these unwelcome consequences must be a matter for school discussions.

The solid, silent American must also be challenged in the classroom. He must at least be asked to consider whether his political success will not in the near future destroy *him*. He may continue to vote his prejudices and his candidates may gain office, but his may be the ultimate in Pyrrhic victories. He may have managed to go to hell on an eight-lane highway paved from money obtained from gasoline taxes, riding in his overpopulated, lavishly outfitted, pollution-producing handbasket.

The political mechanisms used to support a products-producing economy at the expense of a service-producing economy need to be studied thoroughly. Government isn't neutral in these matters. The automobile industry is given enormous encouragement by government. The highways are built with tax dollars, and auto travel is given a tremendous advantage over alternative forms of ground travel. Imagine how many people would be interested in buying automobiles if there were only 1890 gravel- or cobblestone-covered one-lane roads available for travel.

Consider what would happen to sales of electrical appliances if government imposed the lowest utility rates on those who used the least power and charged the highest rates for those who used the most.

Suppose government refused to allow *any* profit in military-related ventures, how interested would some of our larger private industries be in a continued increase of military expenditures?

Suppose government did not lower taxes and made credit more available in periods when there is diminished economic growth, what would happen to the goods-producing sector of the economy, particularly if, instead of stimulating that aspect of the economy, billions of dollars were appropriated for additional manpower in health, education, welfare, recreation, and conservation?

Suppose government, in addition to passing legislation for health services to the aged, also appropriated the funds to generate the staff and provide them with education and training in a newly designed system for delivery of services—would it then be necessary to: (1) Place a ceiling on the fees doctors charge (which will probably result in the aged getting no doctors at all); (2) Lock out minorities from equal representation in the medical services; (3) Pay the prohibitive costs of welfare, crime, and segregation that always accompanys large-scale unemployment?

Conversely, consider what would happen in a society that appropriated 50 billion dollars for hiring 8 million more teachers and these teachers would work in an educational system where man's salient concerns were discussed, significant problems were solved, and persons of every age would find ways of filling the void in their lives with something other than things? Or ponder the consequences of a cutback in governmental support for health, education, and welfare? The jobs lost in these fields can be picked only in the "thing-producing" sector of the economy; so, to forestall a recession, incentives are given to manufacturers to make things no one needs and to consumers to purchase them with little down and a long time to pay.

The government policy and program regarding consumption of resources must be studied, and students should be able to intelligently address the issue and formulate a plan in which the government reinforces a healthy economy without encouraging the destruction of nature.

The ecological crisis forces us to reexamine the nature and extent of rights in a free society. In Chapter IV I questioned the school's activity with respect to traditional rights. It appears that survival depends upon an extension of the concept of individual rights. There is a need for guarantees now that were unnecessary in the past. Man did not need a right to breathe clean air or be free from somebody else's garbage. He did not need protection against overcrowding. He did not need assurance that there would be water to drink. Those rights are needed now. Currently in Congress there is a variety of proposed constitutional amendments to extend the concept of rights. Similar discussion needs to be taking place in the schools. A good takeoff might be the rights Paul Ehrlich lists on the back cover of his book *Population Bomb*. He comes up with this proposal of "mankind's inalienable rights":

1) The right to eat well.
2) The right to drink pure water.
3) The right to breathe clean air.
4) The right to decent, uncrowded shelter.
5) The right to enjoy natural beauty.
6) The right to avoid regimentation.
7) The right to avoid pesticide poisoning.
8) The right to freedom from thermonuclear war.
9) The right to limit families.
10) The right to educate our children.
11) The right to have grandchildren.[6]

These rights need to be debated. Machinery needs to be developed for their implementation. Model communities need to be established where these rights are respected and studies made of the impact that such guarantees have on interpersonal behavior and social organization.

Ecology and Culture-Carrying Competence

Added to the stupidities students are educated for must be education about environment. Part of the destruction of the environment stems from stupidity about "economics," "war," "Communism," "racism," and "poverty." But over and beyond that there

---

[6] Paul Ehrlich, *op. cit.*, back cover.

is the specific stupidity that comes from not analyzing the consequences of economic advancement. Students are taught not to analyze consequences. And this lesson may well be our undoing.

Now contemplate—we did not set out to destroy our world. Whatever other intentions those who led in the shaping of our destiny had, it was not to rob the earth of everything valuable. Each one of our esteemed leaders of industry had heard about that fool who killed his goose that laid golden eggs, and each one *knew* that that allegorical tale did not apply to *him*. Those advocates of nuclear electrical plants may be power-mad, but they really believe "electricity builds progress." Those automobile manufacturers don't really want to pollute air or space. The chemical magnates who developed pesticides didn't have in mind the extermination of sea birds—nor did they desire to make water undrinkable through nonbiodegradable detergents. Very few among us anticipated such horrible consequences. (I think back now on my activity on behalf of fluorides in the water and wince.)

The single most glaring deficiency of the school curriculum is the absence of discussion about possible effects of different courses of action. It is only in areas of minimal controversy that anything resembling such discussion takes place and that discussion is both banal and nontransferable to matters of ecological importance.

Schools fail to generate culture-carrying competence in yet another way. The formal school program does not assist the student to distinguish a stupid question from an intelligent question. The idea that a truly educated person is one who can phrase and defend his questions doesn't penetrate into the school. We haven't even developed a system to evaluate answers—and this is less a measure of the quality of intellectual performance than it is a measure of conformity. Answers are evaluated favorable if they coincide with the authority. The threat to survival provides both a basis for evaluating the importance of a question and the impetus to a change in educational orientation. The immediacy of extinction can and must serve as a break against educational inertia. We can no longer tolerate stupid questions. We must, in the name of survival, discourage economists, for example, from asking the inane question, "Won't a full-employment economy lead to inflation?" and get them instead to ask the intelligent question, "How do I devise a full-employment economy that is not inflationary?" The first question leads inevitably to answers which are geared to a products-producing economy and to juggling interest and tax rates and to defining the government as employer of the last resort. The second question leads to development of new categories of workers; new kinds of delivery systems for human services, updating of training; career ladders; and government as employers of the first resort. I really don't have to tell you that the economists who are influencing government policy are asking the stupid questions and are even doing a dreadful job of answering them.

The culture-carrying competence for human survival requires all that was described in Chapters VI and VII. Unless there are universal broad-based communication skills and unless there are historical perspectives and universal sophistication about biology, other sciences, and mathematics, we are finished. But that alone would give the whole of education a pragmatic cast that would carry it far off its desired course. And that, too, would be an example of how lack of concern for consequences leads to disastrous ends. We have generated a way of life in which we are dependent on "things" for enjoyment. This way of life feeds upon itself and grows larger and more controlling. It is never enough to prohibit or restrict a way of life. It is also necessary to offer a substitute way and to provide the support during the tenuous period of change-over. A request from the President to buy less or stay home or stop smoking would have at best a transient effect. And this would be true if HE, too, "bought less," "stayed home," and "stopped smoking." If buying, touristing, and smoking are all people know how to do, that is what they will do. Conversion to a new way of life requires dedicated leadership, well-thought-through programs, *and* large-scale investment of funds. The alternative to a goods-oriented society is one in which people can derive gratifications from social projects and from art, music, literature, and the theater. The decline in the importance of active participation on the performing arts leaves people no alternative but to be sucked into a mire of "things." This point, which should be obvious, is continually missed.

Only if proposals advanced throughout this book are put into effect—only with the development of artists in residence in every city, only with the support of people as *participants* in leisure, only as schools become lifelong, around-the-clock-operations can people renounce a way of life that is dedicated to consuming the earth's resources and embrace a way of life that is harmonious with nature.

Every "traditional" educational activity can be translated into something that has ecological validity. It is the perversion of liberal arts education into its current ritualisms and formalisms that has divested it of vitality and has driven people into wasting nature. Twelfth Century French Poetry can have ecological importance if it is "taught" in such a way that it has a sustaining effect on a way of life. If the student of Twelfth Century French Poetry can gain through the experiences a sense of competence, belonging, and usefulness, he could give up that extra, large automobile or that electrical appliance or that trip to Hawaii which had no purpose other than to generate something to talk about with friends and members of the club.

Ecology and Inter- and Intrapersonal Competence

A society which has developed a culture, a politics, and a work world disrespectful of nature has a devastating impact on the individual. The dynamic interrelationship between the four educational goals has been emphasized throughout this book. Man out of harmony with nature has to be out of harmony with himself and his fellows. Martin Buber has emphasized that human relationships become distorted from a human "I-Thou" to an impersonal "I-It." Ecological imbalance forces us to regard others as Its. The three scenarios Paul Ehrlich presents leave no alternatives but to regard the victims of nuclear holocaust or continent-wide starvation as "Its." The dehumanization of man is partially a function of a world out of harmony with nature. But it works the other way also. A culture that has become preoccupied with "things" shapes the nature of human identity and relationships. It is very difficult for a person to escape the life style that every social institution defines for him. Martin Buber, while he touches on it, doesn't emphasize sufficiently how dependent on things we as persons are. We don't even have I-It relationships. We have "thing-thing" relationships in which my things come in contact with your things. The most gratifying encounter our society has fashioned is an automobile accident. Through an automobile accident, intensive involvements are generated. The accident inspires social definition, status, unending conversation, activities with doctors, insurance adjustors, police, garage attendants, friends, and relatives. Seriously, though, for many persons, an automobile provides the only mechanism for a sense of competence, a sense of belonging, and even a sense of usefulness.

A society in which we define ourselves by our possessions needs considerable study and analysis. We are shaped by our goods-orientation, partly because of a lack of development of inter- and intrapersonal competence; "goods" fill a void. But partly, also, the goods are a protection against threats to security which are real and external to the person. Affluence is only one face of America's life style. The side it doesn't show to itself is fear that prosperity is ephemeral and failure is impending. We have built very little security into our society. The income of older people can be wiped out by inflation and property-tax increase. Sickness can bring about financial ruin. An accident can economically devastate a family. When a person surrounds himself with much more than he needs (and by so doing extracts more from the environment than is necessary) he is, given the realities of this world, purchasing a form of insurance against calamity. Students must question what would happen to life style if an old age of threat-free leisure was guaranteed, if every citizen had a right to health care, and if there was full employment plus.

The person who is inter- and intrapersonally competent is also a person who is compatible with nature—and the student who is involved in experimenting with the variety of selves he can be comfortable being must always evaluate those selves against the backdrop of ecology.

How Many Administrators DOES It Take to Get a Pound of Brains?

Some critics of education feel that we can eliminate administrators and that education will not be worse off for their departure. This is a theme that both Dennison, in his book *Lives of Children,* and Postman and Weingartner in *Teaching as a Subversive Activity* stress. Certainly we do not need the type of administrators that now predominate in education. The current administrator is not an educational leader; he is much more a businessman in a sheepskin. And those who dictate educational policy, the business-dominated boards, decree that that's how it ought to be.

Tough-minded businessmen have always leaped to the conclusion that fuzzy-minded idealists muddle education because they lack the reality orientation of tough-minded businessmen. This theme crops up periodically in education and it goes something like this—if only we ran our schools like we run our businesses we would be out of trouble! The problem is just the opposite. It is the business ideology that has gotten education into its greatest difficulty.

Raymond Callahan, in a bitter denunciation, summarizes the damage the business mentality has inflicted on education:

> The tragedy itself was fourfold, that educational questions were subordinated to business considerations, that administrators were produced who were not in any true sense educators. That a scientific label was put on some very unscientific and dubious methods and practices and that an anti-intellectual climate already prevalent was strengthened. As the business and industrial values and procedures spread into the thinking and acting of educators countless education decisions were made on economic or on non-educational grounds.
>
> The whole development produced men who did not understand education or scholarship; thus they could and did approach education in a businesslike, mechanical, organizational way. They saw nothing wrong with imposing impossible loads on high school teachers because they were not students or scholars and did not understand the need for time for study and preparation, the training had been superficial and they saw no need for depth or scholarship. These were men who, when designing a college, provided elaborate offices for the president and the dean and even an elaborate student center but also crammed six or eight professors in a single office and provided a library which would have been adequate for a secondary school. They saw schools not as centers of learning but as enterprises which were functioning efficiently if the students went through without failing and received their diplomas on schedule and if the operation were handled economically.[7]

Callahan traces the route of educational interest to the all-powerful efficiency deity. Under the auspices of "scientific management," educational leadership became somewhat ineffectual in the first three decades of the twentieth century. But with courageous leadership there was a brief rally against this influence in the 1930's

---

[7] Raymond E. Callahan, *Education and the Cult of Efficiency,* University of Chicago Press, Chicago, 1962; first edition, pp. 246–247.

and 40's; now with a renewed onslaught, the position and condition of educational leadership may have plumbed to its nadir. Business was not in such a good position in the 30's that it could present itself as a model to the American people. As Babe Ruth commented, when questioned whether it was right for him to make more money than President Hoover, "But Hoover didn't have a very good year." The same factors which led to the destruction of educational leadership then still prevail. Callahan cites the following as factors which were more than education could handle:

> Undoubtedly the sheer number of students to be educated, plus the great moral commitment to educate all the children to the limit of their ability, would have created stubborn educational problems even if Americans and their educational administrators had not been economy-minded and had not developed a mechanical conception of the nature of education. But fifteen years of admiration for the mass production techniques of industry on the one hand and saturation with the values of efficiency and economy on the other had so conditioned the American people and their school administrators that they allowed their high school teachers to be saddled with an impossibly heavy teaching load. The American people not only allowed this to happen but their insistence on economy forced it upon the schools. And just as some of the leading school administrators did not repel but actually *invited* lay interference, they not only did not resist this increase in class size but actually initiated the steps, advocated and defended them, and put them into effect.[8]

Conditions are worse now. The problems to be overcome are even more complicated. Funds are more difficult to come by, sources are more diverse, and the procedures necessary to obtain these funds are increasingly more cumbersome. The cost of education continues to increase. The lay public is more demanding but not better informed. Students are more unruly. The "sheer numbers to be educated" have increased. The moral commitment to educate everyone has been joined by an economic necessity. The additional problems brought on by technology and urbanized society have brought with them problems of interpersonal relationships that confound education and perplex educators.

For the new issues as well as for the old, those that lead in education offer only the same tired old declarations of faith. At a time in history when business must look to education for its lead-

---

[8] *Ibid.*, p. 232.

ership, there still is a devotion to the principle that ignorance should govern education. And yet on reflection, how could it be otherwise? In the absence of precise goals, how can education be intelligently evaluated? And what standards can be used to judge programs or leadership? Under those conditions, efficiency seems to be as good as any other standard for judging education.

The administrator, to be an effective educational leader, must have attitudes similar to those described for effective teachers— only more so. He must be trustworthy. Teachers must see in him a person willing to stand on principle and willing to bear the brunt of the attack. The lack of such leadership—the philosophy of "loyal-up-loyal-down," which simply means the administrator backs only persons who mindlessly follow him—is the antithesis of trustworthiness. At the present time the typical administrator communicates to teachers that "You can do anything you want, as long as you do not get in trouble, and, if you do get in trouble, don't look for much help from me." A trustworthy administrator would make clear how far he would go in the defense of his staff, the extent and nature of activities he is going to defend, and the behaviors he will not tolerate. He will use educational goals as guidelines for these discussions.

The administrator must defend his right to lead. He, like teachers, can justify his position only if he has something valuable to share. An incompetent educational hack who has risen to his station according to Peter's Principle of Incompetence makes a mockery of educational leadership. An administrator who attempts to placate all educational factions by being all things to all people makes a mockery of educational leadership. An administrator who uses "lack of unity" as an excuse for indecisiveness makes a mockery of educational leadership. A lot of people are drawing substantial salaries making a mockery of educational leadership.

To justify his existence as an educational leader the administrator must convince those he leads (primarily teachers) that what he has to offer is valuable. Then he must demonstrate that he has it. He must be able to assist teachers to gain competence. He must demonstrate the ability to keep the school on the path to its defined goals. He must have the leadership capacity to keep a diverse group functioning as a unit while, at the same time, he encourages pluralism (and that is no mean trick). He must be able to stand firmly against anti-intellectual attacks both in and outside the industry. He must mobilize a constituency of support. He must demonstrate, either personally or by delegation, teaching that is relevant. He must generate a relationship between himself and his staff that serves as a model for teacher-student relationships.

The administrator, in addition to defending his right to his position, must also communicate what he has to offer in a language that is readily understood. Imprecise expression that obfuscates intent destroys the relationship between administrator and staff exactly as teacher-student communication is hampered. An administrator complained to me recently that he just couldn't understand why his staff doesn't understand his motives or his directions. He trotted out dozens of possible explanations for the phenomenon, all of which he analyzed, but he rejected without even cursory examination the most obvious explanation—that he was misunderstood because he had done a miserable job of explaining his position.

And finally, the educational leader-administrator must be "hip." He must be aware that even if he did all that he contracted to do he would still have some staff holding back. Even the most competent educational leader will not be able to inspire everyone. There are those who, with every assistance offered, will still be unable to derive competence, belonging, and usefulness from his endeavors. There will be others who are affronted by the administrator's style or his relationship with other staff. If he is truly "hip," he can smooth over the estrangement by making appropriate adjustments.

A smattering of administrators are educational leaders. They demonstrate that effective administration is possible! More real educational leaders will emerge as leadership is linked to educational activity and solution is based on precisely delineated attributes rather than on seniority, formal degrees, and demonstrated harmlessness. If educational goals are kept salient, far more administrators who are educational leaders will be selected than is currently the case.

Aimlessness of education has led to perversion of leadership, but the structure has also impeded responsible leadership. There is no need for huge, impersonal educational bureaucracies. No educational unit need be larger than a staff of twenty, serving no more than 200 students. One building complex could have a dozen autonomous "schools" that shared the library, the theater, the computer, the gymnasium, and the electronic equipment. The central-office coordination ought never be "over" the school administration. To the contrary, such staff, whose legitimate role is only to provide technical assistance and consultation, should be subordinate to the staff in the school. School organizations have grown to their elephantine proportions because there has been no rationale for school organization. The absence of goals leads ineluctably to gargantuan bureaucracy and to the emulation of business bureaucracy. All of these gross distortions preclude the possibility of educational leadership in any metropolis—so none now exists there. Big-city problems will not be solved by supertalented administrators, but will be found in decentralization of authority; this is possible if there is unanimity about the goals of education.

School organization into small, manageable units eliminates any need for school board control. Once the units are small, the community as a whole can be the responsive decision-making authority. Crucial matters can be referred to community meetings and referendums. That this doesn't become a repressive anti-intellectual intrusion depends on the education that the community receives— and since this is one of the many places we entered, it seems like a good place to end.

Mini Epilogue

The battle is joined between those who would reform education and those who stand pat. I am with the reformers, whereas Max Rafferty is representative of the stay-putters. He will insist that education must be tradition and ritual. He will be persuasive. He will be deceptive and sometimes he may even say something that is supportable. I found that I can agree with Max Rafferty on one point. He identified, as two of the leaders of twentieth century education, Walt Disney and Al Capp.[9] I can't go along with Rafferty on Walt Disney. To me, Disney typified an adulteration of education. He substituted technical skill for intellectual depth. He reduced his efforts to an absolute of educational irrelevance—devoid of any reference to work, politics, culture, or personal growth. But when Max Rafferty, in his praise of Al Capp, argued that if Aristophanes were alive today he would be authoring Li'l Abner—I found myself in total agreement. If Aristophanes were alive today

---

[9] *Rafferty on Education, op. cit.*

he would be over twenty-four hundred years old and probably too senile for anything better.

There is no good way to end a book. Neither bangs nor whimpers help much. And contrary to Rupert Brooke, this *is* the appointed end—and nowhere beyond space or time is there wetter water and slimier slime. Sure, there is much left to be said and some things said could have been embroidered, and some other things explicitly promised were probably only inferred, and with still other things the reader was provided with more than he wanted to know. So be it. Amen. Shalom.

Index